D1598510

PRESIDENTS AND

THE AMERICAN

ENVIRONMENT

Presidents and the American Environment

Otis L. Graham, Jr.

UNIVERSITY PRESS OF KANSAS

Published by the
University Press of
Kansas (Lawrence,
Kansas 66045), which
was organized by the
Kansas Board of Regents
and is operated and
funded by Emporia State
University, Fort Hays
State University, Kansas
State University,
Pittsburg State
University, the University
of Kansas, and Wichita
State University

© 2015 by the University Press of Kansas

Library of Congress Cataloging-in-Publication Data

Graham, Otis L.
Presidents and the American environment /
Otis L. Graham, Jr.
pages cm
Includes bibliographical references and index.
ISBN 978-0-7006-2098-2 (hardback)
ISBN 978-0-7006-2099-9 (ebook)
1. Environmental policy—United States—History.
2. Conservation of natural resources—Government
policy—United States--History. 3. Environmental
management—Political aspects—United States—History.
4. National parks and reserves—United States—History.
5. Presidents—United States. I. Title.
GE180.G734 2015
363.7'05610973—dc23   2015004141

British Library Cataloguing-in-Publication Data is available.

Printed in the United States of America

10 9 8 7 6 5 4 3 2 1

The paper used in this publication is recycled and contains
30 percent postconsumer waste. It is acid free and meets the
minimum requirements of the American National Standard
for Permanence of Paper for Printed Library Materials
Z39.48-1992.

Public opinion is everything. With it, nothing can fail. Without it nothing can succeed. He who molds public opinion goes deeper than he who enacts statutes and pronounces decisions.

—Abraham Lincoln

CONTENTS

ACKNOWLEDGMENTS

I am grateful for research assistance from UNC history graduate students Scott Phillips, Rob Shapard, Carla Hoffman, and Matthew Lubin, and from Kris Smemo and Dustin Walker at the University of California–Santa Barbara (history). Invaluable readings and critical judgment came from James Banner, Sam Wells, Betty Koed, Jane DeHart, and Gareth Davies. At an early stage David Perry, Donald Lamm, Fred Woodward, and Bob Dallek offered astute assessments.

My daughter, Lakin, restored my working environment after surgery. My son, Wade, gave a historian's wise and timely advice.

Carolyn Chapman began by making the words line up right and evolved into an indispensable editorial collaborator. To all my warmest thanks.

PRESIDENTS AND

THE AMERICAN

ENVIRONMENT

The presidency is not merely an administrative office. That is the least of it. It is pre-eminently a place of moral leadership. All of our great Presidents were leaders of thought at times when certain historic ideas in the life of the nation had to be clarified. . . . Without leadership alert and sensitive to change, we . . . lose our way.
—Franklin D. Roosevelt

A century and a half ago a new concern was heard among US intellectuals—that this bounteous "new world" was running out of the abundant resources that had drawn European and (involuntarily) African millions. An early voice was George Perkins Marsh, whose *Man and Nature* (1864) drew a large readership and much influence. "Man is essentially a destructive power. . . . He has felled the forests . . . broken up the mountain reservoirs . . . torn the thin glebe [soil] . . . has ruthlessly warred on all the tribes of animated nature."

Marsh was one of the earliest voices of US conservation, a social reform movement beginning to organize for nature protection as the nineteenth century advanced. In 1890 a small but influential wildlife conservation organization, the Boone and Crockett Club, located in New York City, came to an important resolve at about the same time as a group of professional foresters. Natural resource/nature preservationists could not by their own efforts make a change they fervently wished—the establishment of a system of national forests carved out of public lands in the West and providing protection and management for vital timber resources. Kindred spirits, less well organized, imagined more national parks based on the Yellowstone (1872) model.

The New York–based forest preservationists needed the aid of the citizen serving as the president of the United States. They stirred themselves in 1891 to enlist the intervention of President Benjamin Harrison, who was asked to sign a bill into law and under its authority declare a few national forests. He did so, and at this unlikely place our multifaceted story began.

It goes on today, more than a century later, originally called *conservation*, then *environmentalism*, as social movement and government policy activity expanded beyond national forests, parks, and wildlife refuges to include a vast pollution-control effort at all governmental levels. The first president engaged in this new government commitment to nature protection—Harrison—had to have this new policy area explained to him, which did not take long, as he was only asked to sign some papers preserving federal timber-land. Counting from Harrison, twenty-two successive presidents (including Obama) have with varying degrees of enthusiasm engaged the expanding natural resource protection mission Harrison had accepted for what turned out to be a permanent stay (for environmental policy, not for Harrison) in and around the White House. A slight majority of the twenty-two over the years has aligned with the two energetic Roosevelts and helped make environmental policy a growing enterprise. A substantial minority of presidents resisted nature protective policy expansions over the course of the twentieth century but were only able to delay or weaken it.

Of the many historical accounts of environmentalism, some frame the story as a social movement, which it was and is; others frame it as the ideas of intellectuals such as Marsh, John Muir, John Burroughs, Aldo Leopold, and Rachel Carson, or some combination thereof. This book is built around presidents and federal policy, where there has been a rich environmental engagement ranging from Theodore Roosevelt's establishment of the Pelican Island bird refuge when a lawyer in his office told him the US Constitution did not explicitly prohibit it, to Calvin Coolidge playing hide-and-seek games in the Oval Office while ignoring reports of coastal industrial pollution. Presidents have mattered, a little or a lot, as they used or resisted these new objectives and tools.

I

If we ask when *conservation*—the original name for the broad
concern to protect the US natural environment from damage
and depletion—arrived on the agenda of the federal government, and thus of presidents, we discover a surprise. It took a
century after the founding of the nation. Sustained presidential
engagement came not with George Washington, nor with the
Thomas Jefferson who sent Meriwether Lewis and William
Clark to map the resources of the West, nor with Abraham Lincoln, who mobilized the nation for the Civil War. The environmental protection enterprise in our national life and politics
came to the president's desk in the administration of a much
smaller figure, Benjamin Harrison, elected in 1888. It was still
there, and growing, for all his successors.

It takes only a little knowledge of US history to generate an
immediate objection to this. Although history texts and college
classes are typically built around a narrative constructed out of
the dominating issues posed in our early national life—slavery,
the tariff, a national bank—historians know that few matters
attracted more congressional attention in the republic's first
century than the disposition of one natural resource—the public domain, or public lands. At one time or another 78 percent
of the 2.3 billion acres now constituting the United States was
in federal hands. The original thirteen states, after much quar-
reling, ceded to the federal government 233 million acres in
the decade after the union was formed. The government leaders in Washington, D.C., no matter which political party dominated at the time, pursued the general objective of acquiring

more public lands by war or treaty or purchase, confident that they could figure out later how to pass them on to users, which the federal government was not and did not intend to be. An additional 523 million acres (MA) came with the Louisiana Purchase in 1903. Florida (43 MA) and much of the Pacific Northwest (180 MA) were added by treaty. The nation gained 334 MA from Mexico at the end of the Mexican-American War and 365 million with the purchase of Alaska in 1867.

Thus the fledgling federal government owned a huge part of the US environment, which land-hungry citizens wanted transferred to them as farmers, miners, loggers, livestock herders. Inevitably, then, the public lands acquired by the new federal government as a sort of splendid dowry concerned the Continental Congress and every federal Congress from the first. There was general agreement that the government should transfer—a word that could mean lease, sell, give—to citizens use of this dowry of land mostly west of the first thirteen states. In its highest-minded form the impulse to privatize public lands would turn landless and unskilled laborers into Jefferson's "sturdy yeoman farmers," who were the necessary core, in a broadly held view, of republican democracy. Beyond this, the national government had no long-term goals of its own with respect to the public lands other than to strike some political balance between contending goods, such as fostering development, pleasing constituents, and raising revenue.

Striking that balance was the source of endless partisan and regional political infighting. Congress, as well as state legislatures hoping to influence Capitol Hill, wrangled incessantly about the best ways to transfer the lands to land-hungry citizens and the corporations they were forming. Federal land was used to pay soldiers for their service; to provide a source of revenue from sales; to help found land-grant, state-run universities and other educational institutions; to help the states with a variety of development projects; to aid railroad expansion westward. Conflict came not just from infighting over these competing uses but also from sectional divisions. Some in the East wanted high fees from land sales in order to discourage the drain of coastal labor westward. Others in the East and Midwest, moved by mounting antislavery sentiment, argued for essentially free land for homesteaders, who would carry those sentiments into the new territories and states. Southerners supported land sales priced for maximum revenue so that the tariff, the main source of federal revenue, could be cut.

Public land law was thus in a constant state of dispute and satisfied no one, given especially the fraudulent manipulation of those laws by speculators, corporations, fence-erecting squatters, grazing outfits, and illegal timber cutters. These issues gave many Congresses much to orate about—what was on and under public land and how to give it away or sell it. These were not environmental matters as we use the term, and there was no backdrop of actual or impending scarcity. President John Quincy Adams in 1828 set aside almost 1,500 acres of oaks on Santa Rosa Island in Pensacola Bay for future naval masts and spars and was harshly criticized for it in the next election.

The disposal of public lands would seem an easy assignment but was not. It came in fits and starts, influenced by economic conditions and wars with Indian nations, and it sometimes came in large hunks. Several (mostly southern) states were given millions of acres of what were regarded as useless marshlands in 1850. By the end of the Civil War, the Homestead Act of 1862 had begun its distribution of 288 million acres in 160-acre parcels. Grants to states peeled off 328 million acres; to railroads went 94 million. By 1867, with the purchase of Alaska, almost 1.5 billion acres were still in federal hands, but the acquisition phase was over, and "disposal," the unanimously agreed-upon goal of national land policy, began to relentlessly shrink the nation's immense land dowry.

From time to time presidents became involved with the public land issue through territorial acquisition. Think of Jefferson buying the Louisiana Territory, or James Polk making war on Mexico and annexing much of its northern acreage. This was nation building and was occasionally presidential business. Yet the disposal of public lands was the messy job of the General Land Office in the executive branch, working under an immense tangle of laws annually piled one on the other by Congress. In Paul Gates's magisterial history of public land law, he estimated that Congress had passed 3,500 separate land laws (when he counted them in the 1960s) with no overall coherence, provoking a cascade of disputes.

This arena of national policy was usually beneath presidential notice. One turns to the many biographies of US presidents from Washington to Harrison and finds in the indexes of these books virtually no entries under "public lands." Notable exceptions would be Andrew Jackson's unpopular efforts to keep white settlers from stealing Indian lands and Lincoln's signing of the Homestead Act of 1862, the Republican Party's effort to expand the number of farmers in the West by offering 160 acres to individual settlers upon five years of cultivation of the land. Millard Fillmore in 1851 became one of several pre–Civil War presidents to recommend sale or lease of mining claims, an idea with little traction. Congressional attention to the public land law of mining accelerated contentiously in the 1870s, notably crippled by the almost total absence in US government of either the will or the regulatory capacity for establishing a government-regulated or -owned mining industry.

This mostly forgotten and contentious history of public land disposal can by no stretch be called "natural resource management." It was certainly not environmental protection as we understand it. Presidents—and Congresses—were not in that business yet, in the century between Washington and Harrison.

Thus nature's abundance was still evident. Historian William Cronon tells of New England colonists who saw spawning alewives, smelt, and sturgeon so thick they fancied they might walk across the water on the fishes' backs; waterfowl so dense at migrating time that "some have killed a hundred geese in a week, fifty ducks at a shot, forty teals at another"; and "millions of millions of passenger pigeons so thick that I could see no sun."[1] It was there in inexhaustible bounty to be used, most assumed, and any needed replenishing spoken of in the Book of Genesis would come from the land and the creatures themselves. Any changes made by humans represented progress, as the US wildlands were turned into cities, farms, gardens.

Armed with this basic exploitative outlook, the US population expanded westward. A population of 4 million at the founding grew to 23 million by 1850, then tripled to 76 million by 1900, expanding to the Pacific and settling even the remote, inhospitable sectors of the national territory sufficiently so that the Census Bureau declared in 1890 that the frontier, in the sense of a line of settlement moving westward, could no longer be said to exist. This growing population daily enhanced its technical capabilities to clear land; dam and divert rivers; drain swamps; plow; reap; mine; manufacture goods; build expanding cities. Expansionists, as their bible instructed them, were being fruitful, multiplying, and subduing the continent (and the original inhabitants), while leaving the replenishing to nature itself.

DEFORESTATION IN AMERICA

A billion acres of forest covered the part of the continent that was to become the United States, three-quarters of it east of the Mississippi. The forest cover of New England—vast stands of maple, birch, and hemlock only slightly modified by Indian ground-clearing fires—was the first to give way to plowed fields and the search for timber for home heating and other energy uses, fencing, railroad ties, housing, naval stores, and household products. By the mid-nineteenth century household timber cutting was augmented by mechanized crews in the expanding mobile lumbering industry as it spread into the Ohio Valley and then to the states on the western shores of the Great Lakes—Michigan, Wisconsin, and Minnesota—leveling forests of white pine, maple, oak, hemlock, cedar to feed into the steam-powered circular and band saws of portable mills following the tree-topplers. A growing country demanded more wood products, and industrial lumbering veered southward, responding to boosters such as William H. Harrison of Chicago, whose *How to Get Rich in the South* (1888) promised the "supply of timber is inexhaustible."

It may have seemed so in the 1880s, when the Appalachian forests had been severely thinned by individual settler/farmers and the appetite for naval stores had drawn small timber outfits and sawmills into only the easily reached virgin forests of loblolly pines and hill-country hardwoods of the Carolinas. South and west of that, most of the South's original forest cover was intact. One writer remembers the forests along the Natchez Trace in Mississippi:

> It was the Garden of Eden had the people only known it. The finest hardwood forest that ever grew out of the ground covered . . . this great State of Mississippi and it was fine. . . . The massive yellow poplar . . . the red gum, . . . its texture as fine as mahogany. . . . Then the ash, hickory, beech and white maple. . . . This greatest of all forests was a haven for the deer, wild turkey, wild hog, grey fox.[2]

Historian Tom Clark, in his lyrical *The Greening of the South* (1984), writes of a vast 147 million acres of longleaf pine that "hovered around the Atlantic and Gulf Coasts," stretching from southern Virginia to eastern Texas, and of a larger area of cypress hardwoods in river bottoms and adjacent highlands, "400,000 square miles lying silently and awesomely in virgin woods."[3]

Down from the exhausted virgin forestlands of the Great Lakes region came the "timber carpetbaggers," in Clark's phrase—lumber companies from New York, Michigan, and Illinois—joining the undercapitalized southern outfits, buying private lands or access to them, claiming public lands when possible, cutting illegally as well as legally. There was virtually no reforestation and no forest research. Industrial lumbering companies moved on to the next stand. Clark renders a harsh verdict on the lumbering industry "that seemed destined for oblivion and left more than 150 million acres of forest lands [in the South] an economic shambles."[4]

AWAKENING TO WILDLIFE DEPLETION

To those felling timber in and across seemingly endless forests, destiny commanded those doing the work—westering, nation building, economically developing. Worriers about the permanence of North America's vast forests were eventually heard, but the first doubts about the new nation's conquering and settling style came from the hunters. The deer were deemed "overhunted" in New England, reflected by a closed season in Massachusetts as early as 1696 and intermittently across New England thereafter. Elk were thinning out east of the Appalachians as the nineteenth century began, and the last bison on that side of the range was reported killed in 1801. By midcentury the 60 million beaver estimated in North America when Columbus landed were gone but for patches retreating from the pelt gatherers into the high country of the West.

Most game hunters were subsistence and market hunters, but some were sportsmen, ranging on weekends out from New York and Boston into the Adirondacks or northern Maine, from Philadelphia and Washington, D.C., into the watery edges of the Chesapeake Bay. They were often keenly aware of the dwindling numbers of waterfowl, turkey, deer. As early as 1844 the secretary of the New York Sporting Club informed a local newspaper that "the objects and pursuits of the club . . . are confined solely to the protection and preservation of game." It may have been the first private conservation organization in the United States, but in the 1850s such groups formed in other states.[5]

The sweeping habitat alteration brought by deforestation and expanded farm acreage in the second half of the nineteenth century and into the twentieth combined with aggressive hunting and improved firearms to reduce wildlife numbers. Then the unimagined began to happen. Astonishingly dense and vast flocks of passenger pigeons were commonplace in the early

days of the nation. One ornithologist saw a flock in Kentucky in 1806 he estimated as a mile wide and forty miles long, and John James Audubon reported a flight of the birds in Ohio that blotted out the noonday sun as in a
solar eclipse. The Carolina parakeet seemed equally numerous in the Carolinas and Florida. Without qualm, hunters knocked or netted them out of the
air for meat, decorative feathers, or mere sport. Incas, the last parakeet, and
Martha, the last pigeon, died in zoos in the second decade of the twentieth
century.

Equally sudden and astonishing was the diminishment of the vast herds
of buffalo (bison) stretching from the East Coast to the immense migrating
herds on the Great Plains, perhaps 60–100 million animals. After the Civil
War the railroad carved up their habitat, and there began a great slaughter
for hides or tongues or Indian impoverishment or sport, the annual kill estimated at 5 million in the early 1870s. By the mid-1880s only remnants of buffalo adding up perhaps to one thousand in all remained in pieces of Texas,
Colorado, the Dakotas, and along the Yellowstone River. This storied animal's complete extinction was glumly predicted.

These dramatic modifications of the US environment brought by population growth, dispersion of that population across the continent, and the relentless pace of industrialization generated a slowly building literature
characterized by expressions of alarm. Complaints about wildlife depletion
had been heard for generations, but in the 1870s there was an astounding increase in national and local groups of sportsmen and their national magazines. *American Sportsman, Forest and Stream,* and *Field and Stream* were founded
and gained wide readership in that decade, and historian John Reiger has
counted 308 hunting and 34 fishing groups active not only in comradeship
and storytelling but in pressing local and state governments to enforce game
protection laws (some of which dated back to colonial times), establish
game preserves, plant trees to restore habitat, and establish fish and wildlife
commissions (with little power and low budgets).[6] This little-noticed ferment over wildlife depletion, although it had little impact on the slaughter of
beaver, buffalo, passenger pigeons, Carolina parakeets, and other once-
abundant game, would flow into the public land controversies of the 1890s.

Seen in the centennial year of 1876, just to choose a vantage point, the im-
pressively growing country was racing through its resources of timber, soil,
and wildlife with only scattered complaints from naturalists and nature writers and spasmodic attention by local governments. Presidents and Congress

were occupied with the really important national issues of slavery and seces-
sion, tariffs, the money supply. Then, in the last three decades of the century,
the foremost (and essentially the only) natural resource policy issue facing
the federal government on an ongoing basis—public land disposal—took a
remarkable new turn.

RETHINKING NATURE AND THUS THE PUBLIC LANDS

An essential part of the context for that change of mind about the public domain to the west was the dramatic clear-cutting of US forests by industrial
lumbering companies in the second half of the nineteenth century. The production of lumber increased eightfold from 1850 to 1910, more than double
the rate of population growth, which tripled in that period, Douglas Mac-
Cleery tells us in *American Forests* (1992). At the start of the twentieth century
US timber was being cut much faster than the rate of growth, and forest
cover was shrinking while demand for timber continued to increase. Fire destroyed 20–50 million acres annually, and the lumbering industry was
shockingly wasteful of the timber it did cut from the earth. There was virtually no reforestation or long-term forest management from the private sector. Knowledgeable people began to warn of a "timber famine" ahead.

Against the background of this headlong destruction of forests, two new
streams of thought on natural resource matters gained momentum in the
last decades of the nineteenth century and began to converge. The first was
the growing popularity of the nature appreciation themes pioneered in the
fiction and essays of Washington Irving, James Fenimore Cooper, Henry
David Thoreau, and Ralph Waldo Emerson and other writers who both reflected and legitimized a sharp turn among readers from terror and revul-
sion of wilderness to appreciation of it. Artist George Catlin wrote that the
next step beyond appreciation and capturing (as he did) the landscapes of
the West in portraits, sketches, and essays during an nine-year visit from
1832 to 1841 was to "imagine places like Yellowstone as they *might* in [the]
future be seen (by some great protecting policy of government) preserved in
their pristine beauty and wildness, in a magnificent park, where the world
could see for ages to come."[7] The year Catlin arrived in the West, 1832, Congress set aside the Arkansas Hot Springs area for preservation, with the limited intent of protecting the area's medicinal springs as a tourist attraction.

Catlin seems the first to have articulated a preservationist alternative to public land "disposal"—though a case might be made for Jefferson, who in 1767 on a walk in Virginia came upon what he called "the most sublime of Nature's works." The natural bridge was a 215-foot-high limestone arch that he bought and declared, "I view it in some degree as a public trust and would on no consideration permit the bridge . . . to be masked from public view."[8]

Thoreau, a century later, urged the readers of the *Atlantic Monthly* to see wilderness areas as places of spiritual nourishment and asked, "Why should not we . . . have our national preserves, . . . in which the bear and panther, and some even of the hunter race, may still exist?"[9] These voices for wild terrain preservation to the benefit of people from all corners of the nation reflected the strength of many forms of a broad nationalist impulse, among intellectuals at least. A similar spirit animated the urban park impulse, of which New York's Central Park was the chief expression, as well as the historic preservation movement, its major project the purchase, restoration, and protection for public access of Washington's home at Mount Vernon in the 1850s. The landscape painters and photographers of the Hudson River school and artists such as Albert Bierstadt acquainted a distant public with the stunning beauty of Yosemite and the Rockies.

Another stream of natural resource preservationist thought flourishing in the latter half of the nineteenth century was the rise of professional forestry, a science-based, new discipline that began to fashion a fundamental challenge to the reckless behavior of those, from small-lot tree cutters to the giant lumbering corporations such as Weyerhaeuser Lumber Company, Kirby Lumber Company of Texas, and the Northern Pacific Railroad, which acted as if the free-market lumbering practices stripping away US forest cover could preserve the forest resource base for future generations.[10]

Why the new wilderness fixation? Historians offer a multifaceted explanation: the public optimism and confidence in social progress in the pre–Civil War years were giving way toward the end of the century to worries about the fundamental direction of an economy wracked by severe depressions in the mid-1870s, 1880s, and 1890s—worries about labor unrest, distress in the Farm Belt, the growth of socialist parties. If the Census Bureau was correct that the frontier no longer existed, and if historian Frederick Jackson Turner, writing in 1892, was right that frontier experience accounted for the vigor of US democracy and the optimistic national temperament, was the nation on the wrong course as it raced toward an urbanized future? One last theory has its sponsors—that settlers of this country resented the European sense of cultural superiority when they compared their cathedrals and royal gardens with what the New World had built—until places like Yellowstone were presented in paint, photo, and prose. Historian Donald Worster argues that this growing impulse to "embrace . . . wild nature" had by the end of the nineteenth century "become one of the most popular pursuits in the modern world."[11] He finds it rooted also in a search for religious alternatives to the established Protestant churches.

To a growing number of writers and readers a different, intimate, and respectful engagement with wilderness fulfilled a complex set of modern yearnings. As time went on, Thoreau became less a singular voice and more the literary patron of a growing number of notable, successful followers. John Burroughs, born on a New York dairy farm in 1837, wrote nearly thirty books offering to his large readership accounts of immediate, detailed, and affectionate encounters with birds as well as speculations on the merits of scientific, as contrasting with religious and aesthetic, sensibilities. At the end of the century and until his death in 1921, he was, in the words of his most recent (and best) biographer, "the most famous and widely published nature writer in America."[12] This was quite an achievement, for the field was rich in talent, including female nature writers with large audiences—Olive Thorne Miller, Mabel Osgood Wright, Florence Merriam Bailey (whose "bird books" had immense sales), and novelist Gene Stratton Porter (who made the Linderlost Swamp an appealing destination for her heroines).

If Burroughs had a rival it was John Muir, born one year later in Scotland, then migrating with his parents to a Wisconsin farm in 1849. After attending the University of Wisconsin–Madison and fired with enthusiasm by a class in botany, Muir decided to transfer to the "university of the wilderness" and walked a thousand miles from Indiana to Florida, keeping a journal that he later published. Muir then moved to California in 1868, finding work as a sheepherder and ranch hand. This drew him into the Sierra Nevada Mountains, where he was profoundly moved by the sight of Yosemite Valley, the "grandest of all special temples of Nature." He began to write about the Sierras and was published in prominent magazines in the East as well as in California. Muir's lyrical voice and quasireligious engagement with nature combined with a national "back-to-nature" cultural movement to make him a distinctive and widely read national writer and the strongest voice for wild nature since Thoreau: "The tendency nowadays to wander in wildernesses is delightful to see. Thousands of tired, nerve-shaken, over-civilized people are beginning to find out that going to the mountains is going home; that wilderness is a necessity; and that mountain parks and reservations are useful not only as fountains of timber and irrigating rivers, but as fountains of life."[13]

His was the much-quoted sentence expressing the core of what would in time be called *ecology*: "When we try to pick out anything by itself, we find it hitched to everything else in the universe."[14] His reputation drew several prominent writers to visit and hike with him in the Sierras: Robert Underwood Johnson, Emerson, Gifford Pinchot, and, in 1903, President Theodore Roosevelt.

RETHINKING THE FUTURE OF THE PUBLIC LANDS

With the mention of Roosevelt I get ahead of the main story, which was a rethinking of our floundering national policy on the disposal of the public domain. The nature writers were a part of that rethinking, but they generated no action agenda. That would come from the increasing number of activists appalled by what was happening to the forestlands and wildlife of the United States and especially on that large remainder of the public domain Congress had not yet given away.

The government's stewardship over these lands had been a scandal throughout the nineteenth century. The problems fell into two categories. Most public lands were in the arid Great Plains and Mountain West, vast regions too high and dry for agriculture. The project of transplanting to it farming homesteaders from the East had a high failure rate because they lacked capital, equipment, appropriate local knowledge, and rainfall. The second and larger problem was the lawlessness of land-hungry and impatient western ranchers and miners. The General Land Office, established in 1812 and lodged in the Department of the Interior after 1849, was an incompetent unit run by political hacks who took full advantage of opportunities for fraud and graft as they decided who got which acreage. The government in Washington, D.C., could not protect the land from invasion by poachers—timber cutters, miners, ranchers overgrazing fragile grasslands, and squatters. Archaeological sites were plundered by thieves carrying away Native American artifacts and dispersing, destroying, and desecrating indigenous sites.

This uncontrolled private rip-off of national assets intensified in the post–Civil War era of materialism, which historian Vernon Parrington memorably named the "Great Barbecue." This mostly western story of abuse of natural resources was conveyed to the public in the new mass media magazines and newspapers in the second half of the century, along with another story of reckless exploitation, the harvesting of the eastern and southern virgin forests by lumbering outfits ever on the move and uninterested in reforestation. Congress was intermittently unhappy with the situation on the public lands, concerned with the struggling homesteaders, and oblivious to the environmental damage from lawless timber cutting and range overgrazing. Remedies were in short supply; half-hearted about the issue, Congress often favored just distributing the public lands among the states.

Two streams of thought converged in the mid-nineteenth century to generate a far-reaching reform movement, producing an alternative concept of the future of the public lands. The first, an increase in the appreciation of wilderness that began early in the century, was augmented in the 1870s by a second stream of thought and reformist energy drawing much of its talent from the ranks of a new and mostly eastern fraternity (they were almost all men) of scientifically trained bureaucrats calling themselves professional foresters. They shared with the wilderness defenders the goal of convincing members of the US public that they must make fundamental changes in values as well as personal and political behavior, or this bountiful continent would lose its forests and fertile soils as had ancient empires around the Mediterranean.

One mighty book provided the indispensable history-based vision of a grim future toward which the young republic was headed. George Perkins Marsh, a lawyer and US representative from Vermont, found Washington political life in the 1850s boring and spent most of his time learning foreign languages and helping launch the Smithsonian Institution. He eagerly accepted from President Lincoln a post as minister to Italy in 1862, served also in Turkey, and traveled widely in countries around the Mediterranean, where he noted the link between deforestation and the decline of civilizations. "The earth," Marsh wrote in his remarkable 1864 book *Man and Nature; or, Physical Geography as Modified by Human Nature*, "is fast becoming an unfit home for its noblest inhabitant, and another era of equal human crime and human improvidence . . . would reduce it to such a condition of impover-

ished productiveness . . . as to threaten the depravation, barbarism, and perhaps even extinction of the species." Great civilizations around the Mediterranean, he wrote, had already gone through the destructive cycle of
deforestation, erosion, flooding, weakening of agriculture and commerce.
Several modern societies seemed to him on the same path—Australia, South
Africa, the United States. All this in 1864! The book sold 10,000 copies before the year was out, was reprinted several times and revised, and had a
large and continuing influence.[15]

Marsh proposed no real action program, but others who shared and were
influenced by his warnings soon pushed a modest reform agenda for change
in US public land policy. Carl Schurz was a Wisconsin senator with a reputation for civil service reform when new President Rutherford Hayes in 1877
appointed him secretary of the interior. He welcomed the appointment because he knew the department to be the most corrupt of all federal agencies,
a place where this civil service reformer could make a large difference. He
also carried in his memory from years in his native Germany a model of farsighted and firm timber management he wished to bring to the United
States. He quickly launched an intensive study of timber policy on public
lands, issued a report charging western lumbermen of "not merely stealing
trees, but whole forests," and proposed sweeping changes—selling timber
at market value, sending enforcement teams to crack down on illegal cutting
and milling on public lands, and initiating reforestation. In his first annual
report, in 1877, Schurz offered a bold idea: "All timber lands belonging to
the United States should be withdrawn from the operation of the preemp-
tion and homestead laws."[16]

In his memoirs Schurz complained, "I found myself standing almost soli-
tary and alone. Deaf was Congress, and deaf the people seemed to be."[17] "Almost" alone because he had a small group of allies in the newly formed
American Forestry Association (AFA), and history was quietly moving in his
direction. In 1817, historian Louise Peffer tells us in her indispensable book
The Closing of the Public Domain (1972), Congress gave the president authority to
permanently withdraw certain lands from entry, to allow Schurz to create military posts and lighthouses. Then in 1832 Congress, without much discussion, agreed to set aside for permanent public use the Arkansas Hot Springs
for their medicinal value. Few sensed the extraordinary potential of the precedent, in Peffer's words, that "ground possessing extraordinary natural values" could be "kept from becoming private property on the theory that a

wider public good would be served by retaining title in the government." As we have seen, Catlin, writing in 1832 about the "probable extinction of buffaloes and Indians," advocated a large national park where both indigenous people (not his terminology) and wildlife might be preserved. The idea broke through again when Thoreau, in an influential article in the *Atlantic Monthly* in 1858, asked, "Why should not we . . . have our national preserves . . . and not be 'civilized off the face of the earth'—our forests . . . [used] not for idle sport or food, but for inspiration and our own true recreation?"[18]

A place to apply a version of the idea was soon found—a majestic valley on public land inside the borders of the State of California and in the Sierra Nevada Range. The high, remote Yosemite Valley had been seen by the time of the Civil War by only 600 or so tourists, so stunned by the sight of its overhanging granite cliffs and waterfalls that its fame had spread to eastern magazine audiences. On May 17, 1864, with the Civil War an all-encompassing national preoccupation, California Senator John Conness introduced a bill to set aside the Yosemite Valley and nearby Mariposa Grove of sequoias—sixty square miles of federal land—to California on the condition that it never be sold to private parties but "preserved for public use, resort, and recreation . . . for all time." The acreage to be granted was "for all public purposes worthless but which constitute . . . some of the greatest wonders of the world."[19] Conness admitted the backing of "various gentlemen" of California, "of fortune, of taste, and of refinement." Not much is known about this almost furtive preservationist impulse arising in California. The preliminary work of ideas had been done except for the part about making the gift to a state government. The bill passed without significant objection and was signed by President Lincoln without comment. The federal government had given a large piece of the Yosemite area away to the people of California, though Senator Conness spoke of the "benefit of mankind."

Soon it was obvious that giving the Yosemite Valley floor and the Mariposa Grove to the state government in Sacramento was a flawed solution to the question of what to do with remaining US public lands—especially those of exceptional grandeur. Illegal homesteaders began to construct lodgings and other tourist facilities in Yosemite, moving faster than the government in Sacramento, where the governor of California, with the gift of Yosemite on his desk, appointed a board of commissioners to oversee the new state park. Among them was Frederick Law Olmsted, designer of New York's Central Park. Olmsted prepared a report on management issues that linked public parks to the principles of the Declaration of Independence and stressed the necessity of protecting the asset. The state government went on the cheap, hiring one man, Galen Clark, at $500 a year, to maintain roads and guide and house tourists. Inevitably, individuals abused the park, and a particularly aggressive homesteader named James Hutchins built housing and claimed property rights. But Muir was by now a frequent Yosemite visitor and interpreter as well as a nature writer with a growing audience reaching to the great cities of the East. He drew attention to abuses of the valley floor in Yosemite and denounced sheepherders for bringing "hooved locusts" who devastated the fragile alpine grasses. In September 1890, a national park bill for Yosemite passed both houses of Congress and was signed by President Harrison. Congress had reclaimed the abused asset, clearing the way for Yosemite and other places to evolve toward a national, not state-led, public park system in the United States.

The struggle over what to do with Yellowstone after it was declared a park in 1872 was fought out among eastern politicians, several of whom had visited the high, remote region and told incredulous easterners of its erupting geysers, hot springs, and stunning scenery and wildlife. A nineteen-man party visited the region in 1870 and reported a campfire agreement that the region should not be carved up for individual properties but "set apart as a great National Park." Others, most persistent among them corporate officers of the Northern Pacific Railroad, liked the idea because it conjured up dreams of a tourist economy. The terrain, like that of Yosemite, was said to be fit for little else, certainly not farming by homesteaders. Congress debated several ideas—divide the region up into individual plots or perhaps give it to Wyoming when it became a state. President Ulysses Grant on March 1, 1872, signed a law establishing at Yellowstone the world's first national park—2.2 million acres of spectacular mountains, waterfalls, geysers, and hot springs and an unsurpassed diversity of fauna including buffalo, elk, wolves, more than 300 bird species, 70 mammal species, and 128 butterfly species. Some congressional doubters were won over by the argument that Yellowstone was too high and cold to be suitable for farming and therefore "economically worthless" unless seen and "used" as a tourist attraction because of the natural wonders found there. No one in the Grant administration spoke of the legislation as a far-reaching precedent beneficial to citizens from other, eastern and southern states, not to mention future generations.

Grant's memoir makes it clear that he understood and agreed with the basic argument for a park at Yellowstone, a place of such stunning beauty (he claimed to have visited there with his wife) that it should be reserved for all US citizens, not a few homesteaders. He must, however, have been ignorant of the facts on the ground, because he said nothing then or later of the need for military or other protection against poachers or artifact thieves.[20] Disorder and violence continued—some of it brought by illegal hunters who killed all but a handful of bison and 4,000 of the park's elk herd in one year, some by the US Army's war against the Nez Perce as it drove them from the park. In 1886 General Philip Sheridan sent Cavalry Troop M and eventually three more to police the park—boring duty, most troopers complained, riding horseback over 2 million acres in an effort to curb poaching, vandalism, and careless campfires.

This shift at Yellowstone from disposal of public lands to individuals or corporations toward what was vaguely called a "reservation" alternative was not just a western curiosity. The New York Forest Commission in 1872 halted the sale of state forestland without indicating what would replace "disposal," and in 1885 New York established the Adirondack Forest Preserve, 715,000 acres to remain forever as "wild forest lands." But preservation of wilderness valued for itself was not the primary motive even here. The Adirondack park was the watershed from which New York City took most of its water, and a recent drought bringing low water to the Erie Canal had moved the legislators to prevent development in the watershed.

A SOCIAL MOVEMENT GROWS—FROM THE TOP DOWN

We can now see that a social and political mobilization was taking place— one without a name—that would transform public land policy and mark the national policy debut of one of the longest-running US social movements. The social base of the critique of the nation's reckless squandering of its natural endowment mobilized first among sportsmen, people who greatly enjoyed hunting and fishing and had become alarmed about the depletion of their quarry. The spark came in the 1870s when a sportsmen's magazine counted 34 organizations devoted to fishing and more than 300 to hunting, most of them only recently formed. It is not clear whether the emergence of four major national sportsmen's magazines in that decade—*American Sportsman*, *Forest and Stream*, *Field and Stream*, and *American Angler*—was cause, effect, or both. What is clear is the commitment of these organizations and magazines to go beyond journalism of outdoor exploits to include a sustained editorial complaint about wildlife extinction and the advocacy of actions citizens and governments might take to protect both the wildlife and its nurturing habitat.

Another elite mobilization took place among people increasingly worried over timber depletion. The AFA was founded in 1875 and the American Forestry Congress in 1882, the latter led by Bernhard Fernow, a German-born and trained forester who tirelessly extolled the German model of timber management. These groups, joined by the new (1873–) and prestigious American Association for the Advancement of Science (AAAS), were in agreement that US forests must somehow come under more protective federal management, and they made sure their views were heard in the eastern media and in the halls of Congress.

These two concerns ran on separate tracks throughout the 1870s and 1880s as they gained strength. In at least one influential organization in New York City, they sat down together on a December evening in New York in 1887 at the invitation of a short, nearsighted man named Theodore Roosevelt (TR).

As a child growing up on the family estate at Oyster Bay, Long Island, TR read books about nature and built a "Roosevelt Museum of Natural History" in his bedroom. He studied natural history at Harvard in the hope that he could have a career like that of John James Audubon. He visited the South Dakota Badlands in search of the outdoor hunting and ranching life that might remedy his asthma and wrote several "nature books," such as *Hunting Trips of a Ranchman* (1885) and *The Wilderness Hunter* (1893).

On that 1887 evening in New York TR asked ten amateur riflemen from the city's elite to join him in establishing the Boone and Crockett Club. They did so, and the club, at first limited in membership to male hunters of big game, might well have become only a drinking, eating, and bragging club. But its leaders were TR and his close friend George Bird Grinnell, editor of the influential magazine *Forest and Stream* (1873–), and the club soon became something larger. As Grinnell tells it, "Beginning as a club of riflemen . . . it early discovered that more important work was to be done in the field of protection than in that of destruction," in arousing in the country the feel-

ing club members shared that the "selfishness of individuals was rapidly doing away with all the natural things of this country."[21] At Grinnell's suggestion, the club was opened to those whose outdoor interests lay not only in
big-game hunting but also in birds or fish or both, and the membership
soon came to include many of the most respected men in the Boston-Wash-
ington corridor—Elihu Root, Henry Stimson, Owen Wister, Henry Cabot
Lodge. The club members chose TR as their first president—a brilliant
choice because he had an interesting future ahead of him. He was appointed
New York police commissioner in 1895, became assistant secretary of the US
Navy in 1897, was elected governor of New York in 1899, and became vice
president of the United States in 1901, the year in which an assassin killed
President William McKinley and gave TR his best and last promotion.

Again I have edged ahead of the story, which is the coming together in the
1880s and 1890s of the intellectual and organizational elements of a small,
upper-class, energetic social movement determined to convince the US public and government to think about and treat nature differently. Before the
Boone and Crockett Club organized, Grinnell established the Audubon Club
in New York in 1886, though he was too busy to expand it. Not so the determined and resourceful Augustus (Harriet) Heminway of Boston, who was
outraged at the bird slaughtering that was mostly driven by women's' pur-
chases of plumed hats. She formed the Boston Audubon Club in 1896, and it
quickly spread to other cities and states, becoming the National Audubon
Society in 1905.

On the West Coast, Muir and his close ally Johnson, publishers of New
York magazine *The Century*, convened in 1892 a meeting in San Francisco of
some influential friends such as David Starr Jordan, the president of Stanford University; Warren Olney, an Oakland lawyer soon to be mayor; Muir's
artist friend William Keith; and several professors from the University of
California–Berkeley and Stanford. The principal goal was to form some sort
of group to help push for a change in the management and if possible also
the size of the new Yosemite National Park, so designated in 1890 after California failed to protect the Yosemite Valley floor from harmful intrusions.
The grassland along the river, Muir wrote, "is downtrodden, frowsy, and like
an abandoned backwoods pasture."[22] After Civil War hero Sheridan condemned the squatting, wildlife poaching, and vandalism of the thermal
springs, Congress half-heartedly tried assigning ten "protective assistants"
to protect the part of Yosemite that was still a national park. When vandal-

ism continued, the US Cavalry patrolled the four new national parks from 1886 to 1916—Yellowstone, General Grant and Sequoia National Parks, and, in California, the parts of Yosemite not given to that state—without clear goals or much enthusiasm for duty in these remote outposts. It seemed time to form a lobbying group, which they called the Sierra Club. Muir hoped "we would be able to do something for wilderness and make the mountains glad," whatever that might be. Yosemite was foremost in their minds, though they were fully aware of growth pressures on all West Coast natural places. The club quickly enrolled 300 members—prominent Bay Area educators, scientists, politicians, and business leaders—and pledged itself to "explore, enjoy, and render accessible the mountain regions of the Pacific Coast" and "to enlist the support . . . of the people and the government in preserving the forests and other natural features of the Sierra Nevada Mountains."[23]

ORGANIZING FOR CONSERVATION

These three mostly male, Caucasian, East Coast, upper-class organizations were the most visible of many lobbying groups arguing for different federal (and state) land policies. Yet the demand for better governmental protection of natural resources was broader, deeper, and growing. The National Audubon Society had chapters in sixteen states by the end of the century, and its members were beginning to talk about habitat protection along with discouraging the "buying and wearing . . . of the feathers of any wild birds." The ranks of Audubon chapters were chiefly female, reflecting an expansion of women's civic clubs after the Civil War. By the 1880s women's clubs could be found in every sizable city and every state, many of them taking up environmental issues broadly defined as including tree planting and protection of nearby natural and archaeological sites. They were brought together when the General Federation of Women's Clubs organized nationally in 1890, the world's largest women's organization, with considerable clout in city, state, and national politics.

We can see in all of this the beginnings of what would be called the conservation movement, a term apparently invented in 1907 by the most prominent and influential forester of that generation, Pinchot, trained at Yale University and in Germany. We now recognize conservation as part of the larger progressive reform movement, a middle-class mobilization of social criticism and reform ideas that played a large role in the social and political life of the United States from the 1890s to the end of World War I and onward.

What did these newly organized conservationist reformers want? They would have answered in broad terms, quoting Emerson, Marsh, Burroughs, Muir: the end-of-century United States needed changed public attitudes and behavior regarding the land and its creatures. Their tools for such changes were the educational effect of lectures, books, tracts, illustrated articles in the new magazines with national circulation. Then came the formation of voluntary citizens' associations. Then governmental action, usually starting with governments close to home. Several states in and after the 1870s had established forest study commissions, offered tax incentives, and declared Arbor Day for tree planting as well as enacted forest and hunting regulations (poorly enforced).

As with the campaigns for abolition and women's suffrage, against child labor and alcohol, and other reforms of the Progressive Era, the natural resource protectors found state governments usually slow, irresolute, poorly staffed for regulatory assignments, overmatched by national corporations as well as local poachers. Those concerned with wilderness/wildlife protection and those focused on forestry/public lands soon realized the importance of gaining command of the federal government. As the 1890s arrived, their national policy goals were just becoming clear to them—more national parks and national forests and better protection for those already established, especially the crown jewel, Yellowstone. Beyond this, the nation's public land law and administration must make a historic shift from privatization to preservation (and management) of permanently public space. The road to this shift was not yet clear—which translates as "leadership wanted."

I am aware there is a parallel story cluster churning through the nineteenth century of park building in the heart of US metropolitan areas, including Central Park in New York and smaller green spaces in virtually every large city. The best account of this story is my son Wade Graham's *American Eden* (2011). Read these books together.

BENJAMIN HARRISON, GROVER CLEVELAND, AND WILLIAM MCKINLEY THE IDEA OF PRESERVING THE PUBLIC LANDS FINDS CAUTIOUS PRESIDENTIAL SPONSORS, 1891–1901

2

Man is everywhere a disturbing agent. Wherever he plants his foot, the harmonies of nature are turned to discords. . . . Man alone is to be regarded as essentially a destructive power.
—George Perkins Marsh, 1864

It was the threat of commercialization within Yellowstone that forced the reformers forward. George Bird Grinnell, editor of *Forest and Stream*, who had used the 1880s to wage a long campaign to educate the magazine's sportsmen readers on the importance of forests as habitat for the wildlife they hunted, soon realized that the act establishing the first park at Yellowstone allowed the secretary of the interior to grant leases giving broad latitude to private persons or corporations to build roads and tourist facilities, cut timber, and kill wildlife with no regulation.

An opportunity opened in 1891. Congress through the 1870s and 1880s had been made acutely aware that public land "disposal" law and policy were an angry tangle of disagreements and criticism of the government's unhappy stewardship. Applicants for homesteads were having difficulty establishing viable farms in their 160–320-acre plots in the arid West, frequently selling out to speculators who channeled land to mining and lumbering corporations. The General Land Office was acknowledged to be a swamp of political appointees facilitating deals through "dummy entrymen" fronting for land speculators. President Grover Cleveland (1885–1889) had appointed as land commissioner one William A. J. Sparks, unaware that he would become a relentless enemy of the administration and exposer of the pattern of fraudulent practices in public land "disposal." Sparks's caustic annual reports and demands for a troop of cavalry to protect Yellowstone from poachers, illegal fencing, and vandalizing of the mineral deposits around geysers got him fired in 1887. But public land law and practice as the 1890s began was a scandal Congress found increasingly embarrassing, especially given the volley of stories and editorials about the vandalism in Yellowstone published by Grinnell in *Forest and Stream*. Sparks had also recommended in his first annual report that public lands in the watershed of the Mississippi River be permanently withdrawn from sale or commercial entry, an idea that drew no attention then but had legs for the future.

In early 1891, Theodore Roosevelt (TR) took the occasion of the Boone and Crockett Club's annual dinner to invite Washington's political elite, none of whom seem to have turned down the invitation. TR and Grinnell made rousing speeches, then TR read a club resolution urging passage of a bill "for protection and maintenance of the Yellowstone National Park" and declaring the club "emphatically opposed to the granting of a right of way to the Montana Mineral Railroad or any other railroad." In the audience were President Benjamin Harrison's newly appointed secretary of the interior, John W. Noble, as well as the secretary of the Department of War, the speaker of the House, and several members of both houses of Congress, along with the secretary of the Smithsonian Institution. Noble was the key person in that elite group because the Interior Department housed the General Land Office, where the public domain was surveyed and given away or sold at bargain prices.

Noble, a Missouri lawyer, was not known to have ever hunted or fished or to have any particular interest in the outdoors. Yet he responded positively when TR, Grinnell, and their ally William Hallett Phillips, a Washington lawyer, lobbied him on park and public land protection and invited him to Boone and Crockett events (he became an associate member). All were aware that public land policy had recently moved up on the list of public concerns. Both major party platforms in 1888 denounced land policies that gave away the public domain to railroads and "syndicates" instead of honest homesteaders.

President Harrison's Inaugural Address contained one opaque sentence urging fairness to "settlers in the territories," in that "their titles should be speedily adjusted and . . . confirmed." That affirmation of the traditional idea that public lands should be shifted to private users was apparently as far as Harrison intended to go on the public land tangle. But pressures from a fledgling social movement exerted influence. The newly formed American Association for the Advancement of Science (AAAS) wrote to Harrison in 1890 urging his support for public forest reserves. Some two hundred bills designed to end the fraud carried out under the timber culture and desert land laws moved around in the 51st Congress, and pieces of them were joined and passed by both houses of Congress as Section 24 of the General Revision Act of 1891. Few people understood this blizzard of legislative tinkering, and no historian thinks this act a remedy for the very real failings of the chaotic public land puzzle, but a handful of people realized that the bills moving forward could be a vehicle for something far-reaching. Noble intervened as the legislation reached the conference committee and declared that he would not allow Harrison to sign it unless they added a clause authorizing the president to set aside timberlands as "forest reservations." So Section 24 (later called the Forest Reserve Act), not previously discussed in either house, was added at the eleventh hour, stating that the president of the United States "may, from time to time, set apart and reserve . . . any part of the public lands wholly or in part covered with timber . . . as public reservations."[1]

So the public reservation option was authorized in the legislation, and the government's public land mission of disposal was now augmented with permanent federal custody to protect forests. Congress sent the Sundry Civil Service Act of 1891 with the forest reserve clause embedded in it to President Harrison on March 3. "It is highly doubtful if the Congress knew what it had done," observed Marion Clawson and Burnell Held in their classic history, The Federal Lands (1957).[2] The legislation stated no overall purpose or means of achieving such.

BENJAMIN HARRISON

Now we have a president as a player in this new environmental protection story. Why had this role not descended upon Presidents Polk, Taylor, or Fillmore, each of whom had been briefly drawn into congressional disputes over illegal mining on public lands, where federal law was entirely unclear?

Because the only policy ideas swirling around pre-Harrison presidents were limited to giving public lands to states, railroads, or potential farmers. A positive, permanent, federal protective and possibly management role on the public lands was if not an unthinkable at least an undiscovered idea to US citizens of that era. By Harrison's time, a social movement including energetic and professionally ambitious foresters had put a new federal role on a president's desk to be signed into law. Harrison now had an opportunity for some sort of leadership—veto the legislation with a vigorous message of disapproval; sign the legislation with its last-minute and possibly little-understood modification, without a word of explanation; or sign with a resounding endorsement and act upon the new authority it conferred on him. Or let it languish. Presidents sometimes matter.

Harrison, grandson of a president, short and bearded and polite, an Indiana lawyer who became the "dignified, quiet little Senator from Indiana" in the words of journalist William Allen White, had been narrowly elected president in 1888 after a campaign in which he, like his opponent, rarely left home and offered no new themes or proposals. Harrison became one of those unmemorable presidents in the Gilded Age (Mark Twain's phrase) about which novelist Thomas Wolfe said: "Garfield, Arthur, Harrison, and Hayes . . . for me they were the lost Americans: their gravely vacant and be-whiskered faces mixed, melted, swam together in the sea-depths of a past intangible, immeasurable, and unknowable as the buried city of Persepolis."[3]

Wolfe had the order of these figures wrong but did well to remember four of them. One of Harrison's biographers, straining to render a favorable assessment, pointed out that "he had no major scandals and no major war during his term in office."[4] Perhaps no major scandals, but Harrison quickly attracted the reputation of "king of spoils" for hiring friends and political allies in place of civil-service workers. TR had a mixture of pungent views of this president. He called Harrison a "genial little runt," the "little gray man in the White House," an "absolute mediocrity." On a more generous day he called Harrison a "very able man" who was flawed by "repellent manners" not described.[5] However, in this one instance Harrison stepped out of that undistinguished crowd and unwittingly lined himself up with historical change.

He had been visited in the White House and lobbied—apparently on several sides—on public land forestry issues in 1890–1891 by representatives of the American Forestry Congress (AFC), the AAAS, and the formidable and antireserves John Wesley Powell of the US Geological Survey.[6] Harrison proved ready to play his part in a different approach to federal forests. He left no hint of why he was receptive to the reserve policy pushed by Noble and the Boone and Crockett Club. Was it because he liked to hunt ducks, and to do that you had to be a sort of outdoorsman, and the ducks needed wetlands nourished by forested watersheds? The record is unclear on his thinking. He had served on the Senate Committee on the Territories, but with no known effect. Harrison signed what was later known as the Forest Reserve Act of 1891 in March, two weeks after he received it, as urged by Noble. He did not stop there. Members of the Boone and Crockett Club wanted action on enlarging Yellowstone, and with the new law as a basis, Noble drafted for Harrison an executive order setting aside as the nation's first such reserve the Yellowstone Park Timberland Reserve, effectively expanding the park by 1.2 million acres to the east and south into Wyoming.

In retrospect we can see that the national forest system, today more than 190 million acres, was born then. Harrison went on to establish at Noble's request fifteen additional forest reserves totaling 16.3 million acres, including the Afognak Island Reserve in Alaska.

Gifford Pinchot called Section 24 the "most important legislation in the history of forestry in America," and to historian Charles A. Beard it was "one of the most noteworthy measures ever passed in the history of the nation."[7] Yet the 1891 presidential authority was a very puny infant. Congress had specified no management principles or procedures and appropriated no money. In the West, rebellion was brewing after initial quiet.

Now Harrison moves off our stage. He barely won renomination by an unenthusiastic Republican Party in 1892, lost the election to the man he had beaten in 1888, Grover Cleveland, and retired to Indiana. He wrote two books composed mostly of his speeches. *Views of an Ex-President* (1901) offered bland essays on the Declaration of Independence, Benjamin Franklin, and such topics. *This Country of Ours* (1897) declared, "This volume does not deal at all with the material resources of our country." It was about government. In the chapter on the Departments of Interior and Agriculture, Harrison called it a "curious fact" that prospectors "aflame with the lust of gold . . . roamed over the public lands . . . and took out a fabulous store of the precious metals. . . . They were in a strict sense trespassers" who essentially wrote their own laws, showing the "Anglo-Saxon's instinct for organizing civil institutions."[8] This from the first president to set aside land so that prospectors aflame with lust of gold might still take the risk of poaching but were at least on paper forever barred from owning the public lands where gold might hide. A president who accepted a small role in moving away from a federal land stewardship role amounting to near anarchy, he understood his role so poorly (judging by this one published comment on public lands) that he reflected on that episode only once and appeared to be in sympathy with the trespassers.

But we should assess presidents on their achievements in their particular circumstances, not on what they say in their memoirs or after-office musings. These achievements or lack of them must be judged in terms of the urgency of the problem(s) and the contours of the existing political setting. Harrison, under urging from insiders he trusted, had lined up with a major, history-making environmental-protection statute and policy redirection, encouraging with his signature the new conservation movement as it built its agenda for the future. He did not, however, explain this to the public. This is followership rather than leadership, a president aligning himself with the wisest counsel he heard and only on one piece of legislation. It goes on the record that he appointed to the top administrative post affecting vast public lands, secretary of the interior, a man in sympathy with the only environmental-protection issue on the national government's agenda, listened to him and his reform network, signed the legislation they urged, and then exercised the authority it gave him. The environmental-protection forces of the day, a small but influential minority, did not ask more of him.

The law of 1891, with its radical assertion of presidential land-reservation authority, was on shaky political ground when affected interests in the West—grazers, miners, poachers in pursuit of minerals, wildlife, or timber—learned of the new reservation authority unaccompanied by clear administrative rules. "The West was now teeming with people," wrote historians Dennis Lynch and Stephen Larrabee, "who had come to regard the public lands as virtually theirs for the taking."[9] One thing seemed at least temporarily clear when Interior Secretary Noble issued regulations prohibiting any use at all of the new forest reserves. This apparent lockup of resources was a shaky ruling and probably had not been the intention of most of the plotters and the drafters of Section 24, who understood that some compromise with potential users of these resources was necessary for the survival of forest reserves. Noble left office without clarifying the status of the new reserves,

asking Congress to provide administrative guidelines and also to appropriate money for their enforcement. The Harrison team was finished. Into the
White House in early 1893 came Grover Cleveland again, for his second
term, and his secretary of the interior, Hoke Smith of Georgia.

GROVER CLEVELAND

The new president would have an opportunity for leadership on this newly
forming issue, and he was reasonably well acquainted with the fraud-ridden
system of public land disposal because of the one-man crusades of Sparks in
Cleveland's first administration. Cleveland, former mayor of Buffalo and
governor of New York, had no education beyond small-town schools and
law office apprenticeship. He had never seen the United States west of
Chicago. His political career before his first presidential term was an education in a small range of urban problems, particularly corruption in the civil
service, which he was fiercely against and which he made one of his two
presidential interests, the other being lowering the tariff.

He was a Democrat. The differences between the two parties in those
days were nearly opposite those of today. The Democrats did not believe that
the federal government could or should foster great national enterprises and
held that its limited powers were and should be restricted to certain commercial fundamentals (tariffs, the money supply) and defending the nation
against meddling foreign powers. That Cleveland hailed from that party was
not an encouraging sign for those who wanted the government to take on a
new and more active role in public land management. As for his conception
of the presidency, it was the same as those who had preceded him, back to
Andrew Johnson. Congress made the laws, and the president executed
them. Cleveland wrote a friend when he entered the White House the first
time that "if a botch is made at the other end of the avenue, I don't mean to
be a party to it. . . . I did not come here to legislate."[10]

Like Harrison, Cleveland campaigned for the White House (both times)
without any hint of a new program to meet some national need, unsurpris-
ing for a probusiness Democrat who believed in minimal government from
Washington. Public land reformers could possibly take heart from his support, as governor, of the establishment of the Adirondack State Park and another park at Niagara Falls. Perhaps some of them knew that, in the words of

one of his biographers, Allan Nevins, "No early problem of his [first] administration worried Cleveland so much as . . . [the] wholesale spoliation of the West" (Cleveland's word for what happens on the frontier when it is in the custody of Washington clerks). This was described in lurid detail in the yearly reports of his interior secretary in the record of the General Land Office—rampant fraud by railroads, cattle barons, and lumber companies.[11]

If Cleveland, as Nevins and other biographers claimed, "worried" about the scandalous "spoliation" of the West, he at first took very limited action, issuing a proclamation in 1885 denouncing illegal enclosures. The "spoliators" President Cleveland denounced in his first term were railroads and poachers who broke existing public land law, which he staunchly defended at its philosophical core—all public lands should be transferred to homesteading farmers who would make Wyoming look like Ohio. In 1891, with Cleveland at home in Buffalo, Harrison signed the bill establishing this new thing called forest reserves—apparently permanent ones. Would reelected President Cleveland repudiate an innovation enacted by the man who ousted him?

Neither man had campaigned on the matter. Was it good news for public land reformers that President Cleveland was known to be fond of fishing and waterfowl hunting, apparently at least as much for the eating and drinking in camp with his male friends as for the allures of stream and forest? Secretary of the Interior Smith seemed to be in favor of the forest reserve idea as he understood it, but neither he nor the president had any thoughts of where to go next. Cleveland's habit in this and other matters was to continue Harrison's practice of asking Congress to provide more statutory guidance and money to enforce the law in the new reserves. Neither was forthcoming. Leadership had to come from elsewhere, from the same cadre of energetic reformers who had nurtured the forest reserve concept in the first place. The AFC stepped in, convincing the interior secretary to ask the National Academy of Sciences (NAS) for a study of the issues involved.

In the meantime, the first years of the new forest reserves were not happy ones, as seen from Washington, D.C. Reports came in describing widespread timber cutting by "tree poachers," sheepherders trespassing on grazing lands, and fires started by all the illegal harvesters of public resources. The US Army was asked to patrol the reserves but ruled this activity beyond its constitutional duties. Cleveland, on the advice of the Department of the Interior and without consulting Congress, in 1897 set aside the 19-million-

acre Ashland and Cascade Forest Reserves in Oregon, after which his administration decided to stop the expansion process until it could warn western
citizens that trespass would be sternly punished. Sheepherders contemptu-
ously tore down such posted notices, and western politicians expressed defi-
ance.

The Forest Commission of the NAS went into the field but could not complete its work there before Cleveland left office. It was divided between those
who wanted the reserves simply as reserves—"locked up" was the indignant
term of enemies of the very idea of reservation—and those, led by Pinchot,
who wanted to concede some controlled resource exploitation under the
guidance of expert foresters in order to shield the whole new forest reserve
idea from mounting western political opposition. In late October the report,
straddling the central question, went to Cleveland, with a unanimous commission request that the president designate thirteen new forest reserves.
Plunge in, they advised, and define the new policy later. A cautious Cleveland
delayed, and then on February 22, 1897, just days away from leaving office
and without consulting western governors or anyone else, set aside thirteen
new reserves covering 21.3 million acres, doubling their size and including
what became Olympic and Mt. Rainier Forests. An agitated Congress sent
forward confused legislation that appeared to some to end the president's
reservation authority. Cleveland vetoed it (without a statement, hence a
pocket veto) just hours before he rode with William McKinley to the new
president's inauguration.

The hot potato was tossed to the new administration but turned out to be
not so hot. An uneasy truce had somehow been reached on Capitol Hill, and
the Act for the Administration of the Forest Reserves was made law in early
1897, granting the secretary of the interior the power "to regulate the occu-
pancy and use" of the forest reserves. The key words were: "No public forest
reservation shall be established, except to improve and protect the forests
within the reservation, or for the purposes of securing favorable conditions
of water flows, and to furnish a continuous supply of timber for the use and
necessities of the citizens of the United States."[12]

Use and necessities, Pinchot's conciliatory approach between forest managers and western users, had prevailed for now. Forest reserves were now
apparently an acceptable idea to the majority in Congress, and public use of
them was stipulated. The 1897 law, years later called the Organic Act, was
not repealed despite some grumbling, and it opened the door for a new

management role for the federal government if it could build the administrative capacity and a continuing base of public support.

HOW MUCH PROGRESS?

Did the United States now have the beginnings of a new system of national forests that struck a compromise between preservation and management for use, one well-founded on public understanding and support? Far, far from it. A handful of forests had been set aside by two presidents, but the management and public purposes of these places had been fuzzily codified and were still hedged about by critics. A sort of foundational law had been passed—actually, two, both so complex that the newspapers of the day could not explain them but that historians interpret as a bipartisan compromise to move from "spoliation" to no one knows what. History books tell us that Harrison and Cleveland, a Republican and a Democrat, both broke new ground, at the request of others, by setting aside public lands in what would become a new national forest system.

The next president in that little queue was noncommittal and uncertain. Without comment on the forest reserves one way or another, McKinley was soon embedded in war with Spain. Neither of the first two had initiated the idea of permanent forest reserves. Neither contributed at all to the vital tasks of public education about and administrative innovation with respect to what turned out to be a historic shift away from privatization to a new governmental and public role in caring for the nation's lands. Both lacked particular gifts in a vital part of their historic opportunity, perhaps especially Cleveland. A "colorless man of few words," in the assessment of biographer Henry Graff, Cleveland left us in the few paragraphs devoted to public lands in his State of the Union Addresses numbing examples of his leaden prose, his inability to see and convey the larger picture, his ingrained habit of appealing to Congress to somehow fix the mounting disorders in the government's stewardship over the nation's lands instead of proposing something himself—that is, acting as a leader.[13] Then came the third barely-a-leader— McKinley, the third president who acted as advised by his interior secretary. One president away from TR's dazzling performance, Cleveland's leadership seems reactive and uncommunicative. To his credit, he let the experiment inch forward and passed up an opportunity to declare that the

Democratic Party, which he led, was ideologically opposed to activist government in the public lands.

WILLIAM MCKINLEY

A new president was inaugurated in March 1897—a Republican, another bearded midwesterner, the last of the Civil War veterans to reach the White House. After the war, this poorly educated man made a career out of politics, rising from the Ohio House to congressional delegation to governor. He ran for president in 1896 without a hint of any program for a nation caught in a third year of the most severe economic depression ever experienced, a nation wracked by high unemployment along with labor and populist rebellions. A man without curiosity, McKinley's core instinct was caution. His commitments, after caution, were to a tariff protecting US industry and a sound currency. "McKinley keeps his ear to the ground so close," commented Speaker of the House Joseph Cannon, "that he gets it full of grasshoppers much of the time."[14] A poor speaker and dull writer, he was ill suited to shaping public opinion, which in any event was not his conception of what politicians do. In his five years in the White House he set aside no national parks and only 7 million acres of forest reserves on the advice of the Interior Department—one-third of Cleveland's total, one-half of Harrison's. He had nothing to say on this largest, really only, federal environmental policy issue of his time.

But what of McKinley's Pinchot connection? On the advice of his secretary of the interior, wealthy New York businessman Cornelius Bliss, and because McKinley himself "was impressed" by the tall, confident forester, the president in 1898 appointed Pinchot head of the Division of Forestry in the Department of Agriculture. Whether Bliss or McKinley expected this or not, Pinchot, whose research position gave him no forests to manage, used his position in the administration to travel widely and advocate public forest management as part of the government's responsibility. Beyond this appointment, none of McKinley's biographers record any other contact between this president and the swirl of innovation that had just begun to reshape US forest- and public land policy, except that he signed the 1897 law Bliss, Pinchot, and others had sponsored. The indexes of the three best (in my view) McKinley biographies, authored by Margaret Leech, H. Wayne Morgan, and Lewis Gould, do not contain entries for forest reserves, public lands, conservation, or Pinchot—let alone the near extinction of the buffalo and other wounds an expanding nation was inflicting upon the lands wrested from indigenous nations. McKinley lived his life through decades of human assaults on the environment that awakened increasing numbers of citizens but drew no comment from him.

What of his appointment of Pinchot to a position promoting federal forestry? Pinchot accomplished little in the McKinley administration beyond broadening his circle of contacts and making speeches about federal forestry—in contrast to his achievements after 1901, when he began work under another, far more engaged president, and we see what a difference a president can make. Educated citizens had been awakening to the heavy environmental costs of expansion and expressing growing concern over the future resource situation of the nation for their descendants. Custodial maintenance by the federal government of what was left of the public domain in parks, forest reserves, and wildlife refuges was an idea churning upward for decades among nature writers, foresters, hunters, women's club members, birders. McKinley, apparently, heard none of this. With his death and replacement by TR, it became clear how much a president could have been doing that McKinley felt no impulse to do.

THE EMERGING MODEL OF CONSERVATION LIEUTENANTS

With the passage of the 1897 act, the "stage was thus set," wrote Stewart Udall in The Quiet Crisis (1963), "for Gifford Pinchot, who strode on the Washington scene in 1898 with a plan and a program for the systematic management of American forests."

Pinchot was then 38 years old, well born and well educated, a man who combined the perspectives of nineteenth-century science, a naturalist's emotional connection to the outdoors, keen political instincts, and a vision backed by moral fervor that allowed him to mobilize young professional foresters for government careers that had never before existed. His job in the Agriculture Department made him a forester in charge of research but no actual forests, and he became a master countrywide networker, lecturer, and author promoting the idea of a permanent national forest system managed by professionals toward the twin and, in his view, compatible goals of permanence as well as "use"—access to the timber, minerals, and grazing re-sources for those westerners who had to be won over to this new conception of government's role in national development. A million copies of his pam-phlet, A Primer of Forestry (1898), would be distributed or sold.

Pinchot's vision had administrative and political components. He felt strongly that the remaining public lands should essentially be withdrawn from disposal and held in perpetuity as forest reserves and parks, the former managed by the new profession of foresters, of which he was one of the first. He very soon became convinced that the General Land Office in the Interior Department could never manage the forests. It was staffed by second-rate lawyers and political appointees with no knowledge of forestry and little ex-perience out in the field. He insisted on a new agency staffed by trained foresters, and the Department of Agriculture seemed the right place for it.

The political aspect of his vision was more important. The purpose of the national forests, as Pinchot and others saw it, was to guarantee timber re-sources in the interest of posterity while some resources would be used in the present under expert supervision. Pinchot was convinced that citizens in the West, living on and around public lands, would never support perma-nent government ownership solely for "sentimental" appreciation of scenic or wilderness places. The users—lumberers, miners, grazers, homestead-ers—had legitimate claims and the ear of Congress. Pinchot tirelessly talked to lumber, mining, and irrigation corporate and trade association audiences in an effort to bring them into a political coalition that would support sus-tainable public forests under the control of experts in the public service. He had considerable success with the larger lumber companies in the West, who saw the advantages of federal fire prevention, scientific research, refor-estation—as long as there was access for the harvesters.

THE DIVIDE WITHIN CONSERVATIONISM

Pinchot—tall, energetic, and fervent in his sense of mission about public forests—did not win over every listener among conservationists. John Muir seemed for a time in agreement with the forester. In 1895 Muir had written, "The forests must be, and will be, not only preserved, but used . . . like perennial fountains . . . to yield a sure harvest of timber." When he and Pin-chot met in 1896 during work on the NAS Forest Commission, both men expressed delight at the other's talents. But Muir had not been listening closely to Pinchot, who had said to the Society of American Foresters, "The object of our forest policy is not to preserve the forests because they are beautiful . . . or because they are refuges for the wild creatures of the wilderness . . . but the making of prosperous homes. . . . Every other consideration comes as secondary."[15] When the 1897 Forest Management Act made it clear the reserves would contain no wilderness areas, and when Pinchot told Muir in a Seattle hotel he was in favor of permitting grazing in the reserves, Muir denounced the intrusion of "hooved locusts" and told Pinchot, "I don't want anything more to do with you." Looking back, it seemed to some historians a fundamental rift had opened between the preservationist and the management-for-use wings of the fledgling conservation movement (a name it did not acquire until 1907). Without question, an important divide within conservationism had been opened. This division should not be exaggerated. Pinchot's most recent biographer, Char Miller, speaks for many historians who question whether the Seattle confrontation between Muir and Pinchot actually took place and notes that these two seminal figures continued to correspond despite having discovered how differently they saw the forests.[16] But the preservationist versus pro-use division was real and would widen.

As the century closed, what would soon be called the conservationist movement lacked national political leadership. President McKinley, preoccupied with the conflict with Spain, had no interest in public land policy. Boone and Crocket Club founder TR commanded an 1898 charge to take control of San Juan Heights overlooking the town of Santiago, Cuba, riding the fame earned there to run successfully for governor of New York and then for vice president on the McKinley ticket in 1900, where Republican Party bosses hoped he would be safely marginalized.

Pinchot had the opportunity to write, think, travel, and attempt to build alliances of foresters and forest users. In retrospect we can see that Pinchot, a minor and marginalized administrator of a tiny federal office in a corner of McKinley's Interior Department, was on a path to serve as the foremost of lieutenants so indispensable to any aspiring president intending to sponsor social change and make a large mark on the nation's history.

3

Leave it as it is. You cannot improve on it, not a bit. Men can only mar it.
What you can do is keep it for the children.
— Theodore Roosevelt, upon seeing the Grand Canyon for the first
   time

On September 6, 1901, while visiting the Pan American Exposi-
tion in Buffalo, New York, President William McKinley was
shot by an anarchist drifter, Leon Czolgosz, and died eight
days later. Theodore Roosevelt (TR) was sworn in as president.
At 42, he was the youngest on record.

He headed the government of the most rapidly industrializing nation on the planet, with a population of 76 million that
was growing 20 percent per decade because of a combination
of a fertility rate of 3.5 children per woman (this rate had been
slowly dropping for decades) and a widening stream of immigrants from Europe. In wringing their livelihoods from the earth
and pursuing the pleasures of game hunting, denizens of the
United States at the start of the twentieth century were generating major environmental harms—ravaged forests, soil erosion,
wildlife extinction, pollution from burgeoning cities pouring
sewage and wood and coal exhaust into nearby waterways and
directly into the air. Only one of these and other assaults on the
natural environment had come to the attention of the federal
government—the shrinkage, and misuse, of the publicly owned
land dowry dating back to the nation's founding. Taking all timberlands together, the country cut and consumed far more trees
annually than it grew. As a response, the US government at the

end of the nineteenth century had hesitantly designated a few forest reserves—some 50 million acres—it could not protect and had no idea how to manage. In 1900, less than half of the public domain land from the original 1.442 million acres, or 557.6 million, remained.

Those who despaired at this puny response to the only environmental problem recognized by the government at the end of the nineteenth century had little to say about the possibilities of presidential leadership on anything, because they had seen none of it since Abraham Lincoln. They had certainly never seen it on matters having to do with damage to the natural environment. TR was to be very, very different, and after him natural resource policy as well as the presidency itself would never be the same.

THEODORE ROOSEVELT

Born in 1858 into a wealthy New York family, the slightly built and asthmatic "Teddy" (he disliked the nickname but could not curb its use) was an avid reader of books on wildlife and frontier adventure. Encouraged by the natural history interests of his father and his "Uncle Rob" (Robert B. Roosevelt, a fish commissioner for the State of New York), young TR relished holiday and summer rambles in the Hudson highlands or the Adirondacks. He took notes on sightings of birds and other creatures; started his own "Roosevelt Museum" of animal, bird, and plant life at home; and resolved to study natural history at Harvard in order to become a naturalist like the admired John James Audubon. Finding at Harvard that what people then called the science of natural history had mostly shifted from fieldwork to the lab, young TR, who had no taste for labs and did not need to work for a living, decided instead to "help the cause of better government in New York." He attended Columbia Law School and was elected in 1882 to the New York Assembly.

The outdoors itch pulled him westward, and in 1883 he began a series of visits to the South Dakota Badlands, a canyon-land region in western North Dakota geologically formed by the 500-mile canyon of the Little Missouri River. Here he experienced a strenuous life of big-game hunting, cattle-punching, prodigious horseback exploration of mountains and canyons, and eventually ownership and personal management of a ranch. Frail TR became a barrel-chested, thick-necked cowboy with remarkable stamina. By 1894 he had authored three books on hunting and ranching in the Dakotas and the

THEODORE ROOSEVELT | 39

mountains to the west. In autumn 1887, while hunting alone for weeks, he realized that he was seeing an increasingly abused landscape, encountering fewer animals, and noticing that certain migratory birds seemed to have vanished. "For the first time," wrote biographer Edmund Morris, "he realized the true plight of the native American quadrupeds, fleeing ever westward in ever smaller numbers."[1]

Upon returning to New York, TR felt the need for some sort of political action on the wildlife issue and started the Boone and Crockett Club with explorer, hunter, birdwatcher, and editor of *Forest and Stream* George Bird Grinnell, who knew the entire West better than TR and broadened the latter's knowledge, along with reinforcing his sense of alarm at the rapid disappearance of the frontier. TR had acquired an impressive and invaluable lieutenant.

Gifford Pinchot had concluded at the end of the century that reaching the potential of the new forest reserves required major administrative changes, which meant a sustained promotional campaign. He and TR met sometime between 1889 and 1895 and formed a strong friendship. TR invited Pinchot to the New York governor's mansion in 1898 to consult on the state's forest reserves, and they boxed a few rounds in the gym, where Pinchot years later claimed to have knocked the governor "off his very solid pins." It was a rare moment of conflict, for they were instantly friends and allies. Pinchot and Frederick Newall, a former aide of John Wesley Powell, wrote portions of the governor's second annual message. Surely no governor in the United States in 1900, or before, had given a major address devoting such space to forest preservation, watersheds, flooding, soil erosion, forest fires, illegal hunting, and wildlife generally. He urged the establishment of more "great parks kept in perpetuity for the benefit and enjoyment of our people," extolled the "necessity of preserving both the trees and the game," and denounced "timber thefts on the State land [as] . . . a grave offense against the whole public." In words Pinchot and John Muir might have agreed upon, he proclaimed, "A primeval forest is a great sponge," performing many vital functions humans could not do without. It was pure Pinchot when the governor opened, "The forest and water problems are perhaps the most vital internal questions of the United States."[2]

In October 1901, because of the act of an assassin, Pinchot, the chief forester, now worked for President Roosevelt—the first activist president on forest issues Pinchot or anyone else had ever seen. TR soon made it clear to the public that a Roosevelt government meant progressivism had finally come to

Washington after two decades of battles in the cities and states against political corruption, corporate monopoly, urban slums, child labor, alcoholic beverages. His own reform agenda was full: mastery of the corporate "robber barons," especially those who ran the railroads; government regulation of food and drugs; and vigorous enforcement of the 1890 Sherman Act, aimed at breaking apart monopoly power. Yet in his first State of the Union Address, written in part by Pinchot, TR left no doubt as to what led the list by repeating the line, "The forest and water problems are perhaps the most vital internal problems of the United States."

TR's environmental engagement began with Pinchot's forest-protection agenda and then expanded. The president endorsed the forester's conception of how the federal forests should be managed, starting with moving their administration out of the Department of the Interior. The political struggle to achieve this lasted until 1905, with Pinchot using that time to hire new foresters, survey sites for future reserves, and produce educational materials for the public. In 1905 the Forest Transfer Act moved the forest reserves—henceforth to be called national forests—to the Department of Agriculture, whose secretary directed Pinchot to manage the forests "for the most productive use for the permanent good of the whole people, not the temporary benefit of individuals or companies."

TR, exercising his broad conception of inherent executive powers, quickly gave Pinchot more forests to manage, adding in his first year of office thirteen new national forests encompassing 15.5 million acres to the existing 46.4 million acres. In 1907, just hours before Congress revoked the president's authority to set aside reserves in six western states, with the help of Pinchot and a platoon of foresters who knew the terrain, the president added 75 million more acres constituting twenty-one new forests in the six states.

Most of this was land in the far West, though TR also established national forests and refuges in Arkansas, Florida, and Minnesota. Deforested hillsides in the watersheds of the Monongahela and Allegheny Rivers in Pennsylvania were the acknowledged cause of a disastrous 1907 flood inflicting $100 million in damages statewide and $8 million in property losses in Pittsburgh alone. This spurred discussion of national forests in the East, where the acreage would have to be purchased rather than carved out of public lands. TR in 1905 had urged a program to establish forests in the East, and by 1911 Congress, pressured by the Appalachian National Parks Association, created a mechanism under the Weeks Act for selecting and purchasing private forestlands. There are fifty national forests east of the 100th meridian today, the first of them Mount Pisgah National Forest in North Carolina, named in 1916.

To this expansion of national forests (to a total of 150 attributed to TR), historian Douglas Brinkley calculates in *The Wilderness Warrior* (2009), TR added 6 national parks, 51 bird sanctuaries, 4 national game preserves, and 18 national monuments (4 to become national parks). To list his federal land set-asides (180 million acres) is stunning, yet it risks making TR appear the singular actor-hero and misses the dynamics at work. They can be seen especially well in the struggle over the Grand Canyon. TR's first visit to that magnificent landform came in 1903, and when he saw it, "his jaw dropped in disbelief," Brinkley wrote. "I hope you won't let a building of any kind mar the grandeur and sublimity of the canyon. You cannot improve upon it." This canyon of the Colorado River simply must be saved for future generations, he quickly concluded, and time was short. TR had warned against a "building of any kind," but the site was already marred. Forester and game manager Aldo Leopold toured the Grand Canyon rim in 1915 and told of signs jutting out over the rim, garbage without receptacles, peddlers, raw sewage.[3] The national park designation process seemed almost always a tedious and unpredictable battle with the political representatives to Washington from the western states, where mining, ranching, and tourist industries always had a strong hand and sometimes fought park designation. TR was determined to enfold the canyon in a national park as soon as the 1904 election strengthened his hand. Then his allies in Congress changed the game and gave all presidents an indispensable public land preservationist tool in passing the Antiquities Act of 1906. TR's reliable ally, Congressman John Lacey, chair of the House Committee on Public Lands, and his allies in the small social movement working to preserve the prehistoric cliff dwellings in the public lands of the Southwest were slowly mobilizing support for legislation that would become the act "for the preservation of American Antiquities." Antiquities were defined as "historical landmarks" and "other objects of scientific interest," such as the prehistoric cliff ruins of the Anasazi communities in Colorado and other dwellings of displaced peoples of the Southwest. Sharing in drafting the law were anthropologists from the Smithsonian Institution and other centers for study of prehistoric peoples. Helping to build a grassroots movement for preservation was the "John Muir of the Southwest," trail guide John Wetherill of the Four Corners region, a well-known critic of the thou-

sands of poachers of wood fossils, shards, and petrified logs from Arizona's
Petrified Forest.

TR welcomed, to say the least, the Antiquities Act, which gave him a new
weapon—the national monument, loosely defined—for the president to use
when he found the congressional process for designating national parks too
lengthy and obstructive. In Brinkley's richly detailed biography of TR, he tells
the story of the new president's impatience when he was ready in 1903 to set
aside a bird refuge, and the Antiquities Act was only an idea. A friend and lieutenant (someone who knew more even than TR about some part of nature,
such as birds in this case), Frank Chapman, curator at the American Museum
of Natural History, became essentially a subordinate officer and scout, guiding
TR to a crucial point he was not reaching on his own. Chapman, an Audubon
activist who understood that saving birds meant saving their habitats, along
with other bird lieutenants Grinnell, William Hornaday, and William Dutcher,
urged TR to read some wading-bird books, in particular one about a 5.5-acre,
federally owned brown pelican rookery near Vero Beach, Florida. TR quickly
saw what was familiar to Florida Audubon members—the assault on Florida's
wading birds by itinerant plume hunters who killed up to 5 million birds a season just to satisfy the New York and larger eastern urban market for feathers
and other plumage. TR loved wading birds and was easily outraged. Chapman
gathered allies and met with the president to explore options, including an executive order. "Is there any law that will prevent me from declaring Pelican Island a Federal Bird Reservation?" No, the lawyers in the group answered. "Very
well then, I so declare it," he said, by executive order.[4]

It was a classic TR moment, expressing his view that if an action was not
prohibited in the Constitution, it was permitted by order of the chief executive.
This was a conflict-producing view, though he and successive presidents successfully invoked the Antiquities Act. For TR this act, of which some readers
thought the language confined national monuments to small areas where
"scientific treasurers" must be protected, could be stretched. He converted
the Antiquities Act into a "blanket authority" (Brinkley's phrase) to set aside
for protection areas too small or otherwise unsuited for national park designation. Roosevelt pushed the boundaries of the act's language defining a
monument as "historical landmarks . . . and other objects of scientific interest . . . confined to the smallest area compatible with . . . proper care and management." This language did not confine TR on size or much of anything else.
Frustrated by gridlock on national park status for the Grand Canyon and

alarmed by local plans for urbanization near the canyon and a railroad along the rim, TR in January 1908 decided that 818,650 acres was not too large and proclaimed it a national monument. It was declared a national park in 1919. In his time in office TR created his awesome list of more than 200 reserves, from Florida to Oregon, Hawaii to Alaska. Acting under the Antiquities Act, he created 18 national monuments to protect places not only of scenic grandeur but also of archaeological value.

If President Benjamin Harrison took the first small steps toward the establishment of permanently public landscape, TR essentially nationalized a huge portion of US land (234 million acres, or 1 out of 10 acres of the United States, including Alaska) that had seemed destined to be eventually given or sold cheaply to individuals and corporations. Imagine Donald Trump buying Yosemite as home for several lit-up resort hotels and casinos with their sprawling parking lots, the Marriott chain checking you into an expensive night in Yellowstone, the Mormon Church buying and closing Bryce Canyon to all but its members, and my family but not yours (because my great-grandfather, not yours, obtained it by fraud during the great land giveaway of the nineteenth century) enjoying a splendid, gated summer camp in one of the remaining groves of great sequoias not felled to provide building materials for expanding US cities and suburbs.

As we have seen, the TR-Pinchot expansion of national forests was matched by the set-asides of national parks, game reserves, and national monuments urged on a willing president by many other lieutenants, such as Muir, Audubon activists Chapman and Dutcher, tireless lobbyist for preserving Crater Lake William G. Steel, and many others who helped the first president who shared their preservationist passions. "Setting these places aside" against fierce opposition must be judged an immense achievement for posterity.

However, presidential declaration of protection and permanent public ownership for national forests and parks was only half, at most, of the job. Who, and how, was to protect these magnificent natural endowments from the "skinners of the land," in TR's words, the mostly western lumberers, grazers, miners, and game poachers who scorned the claim of "national ownership"? This question had not been squarely faced. Yellowstone National Park was set aside in 1872, but poachers had free rein there until (and even after) a small contingent of US Army cavalry was posted to patrol this immense place in the 1890s. The idea of the National Park Service (NPS) struggled into life in 1916, the shaky beginning of an experiment in federal management of an expanding string of special national places. The new bird and wildlife refuges TR designated had sporadic and minimal protection from Audubon volunteer wardens, some of whom were killed by poachers.

Pinchot had thought more deeply than others about what must follow presidential set-asides of public lands. He fervently believed the solution was augmentation of the growth of the administrative state. National forests, where he concentrated his attention, required a US Forest Service (USFS) staffed by trained, green-coated foresters, civil servants with eastern training and a lifetime of western experience. TR gave him his management agency in 1905 (inside the Department of Agriculture), but Congress starved and ignored the new service. Rooseveltian state-building in the natural resource management arena was a strong new idea with formidable political opponents. How would Pinchot and his successors find a secure foothold in the federal bureaucracy?

A recent book by Timothy Egan tells of the "Big Burn" fires of August 1910 in the drought-parched national forests of the northern Rocky Mountains of Idaho and Montana. As it turned out, these provided the catastrophe Pinchot needed. The horrendous fires scorched 3 million acres and killed more than 100 people, including several rangers, despite the heroic and futile firefighting efforts of a thin string of forest rangers along with the 25th Infantry Regiment belatedly sent in by President Taft. The blame should fall upon Congress, Pinchot thundered in national magazines and in nationwide speeches. Firefighting should be a foremost mission of the USFS, Pinchot and TR had agreed from the beginning. "Forest fires can be controlled," TR had written to Pinchot after the fledgling agency's first two years, claiming that only one-tenth of 1 percent of USFS lands had burned since their designation. Pinchot and others spun the catastrophe of 1910 as a lesson in the need to provide the USFS more men and equipment. Somehow Pinchot won that struggle for public opinion, and in one year the USFS budget was doubled and the firefighting mission entrenched despite Pinchot's growing suspicion, shared by a few other foresters, that fire should be seen as a permanent part of the nature they meant to protect.[5]

What else would conservation look like, after national parks and forests and state and federal protection for bison and wildfowl? A further agenda ran with the wild rivers, those flowing on the surface and the aquifers below. The serial droughts of the 1880s in the arid regions of the Southwest and Great Plains spurred the formation of small private irrigation companies, whose lack of experience and capital created a history of failure, impeding the western growth much thought about and talked about east of the Mississippi. Water in most of the nation ran to the sea in rivers, attracting private capital to dam building for water supply and storage. Failure here was less frequent than in irrigation ventures but spectacular when poorly engineered private dams such as the thirty-seven-year-old earthen dam built on the South Fork of the Conemaugh River, a tributary of the Allegheny River, was swollen to the top by constant spring rains. On May 31, 1889, the dam gave a shudder and dissolved, releasing 16 billion gallons of water that formed a thirty-foot wave, virtually erasing the town of Johnstown, Pennsylvania, and killing 2,200 people.

Should the government, rather than overconfident, underfunded, and inexperienced private companies, make and manage irrigation systems and dams? TR and many other conservationists were sure of it, and in his first State of the Union Address, drawing on the thoughts of Pinchot and his engineer partner Newall, the president urged a program of "great [water] storage works" built by the government—dams, irrigation systems, canals. Congress responded with legislation—the 1902 Newlands Act—permitting the establishment of what became the US Bureau of Reclamation, an irrigation and dam-building federal agency that over time, in conjunction with the Tennessee Valley Authority (TVA) and the US Army Corps of Engineers (just to begin the tally), put 60 dams on the Missouri River and its tributaries, 25 on the Tennessee, 14 on the short Stanislaus River in California, and 1,200 "major dams" in that state alone. Before the 1902 vote on the Reclamation Act, no committee of Congress asked the hard questions about the costs when wild rivers are dammed or aquifers are pumped so that soils are turned into filters trapping salts and minerals. TR's enthusiasm for the Bureau of Reclamation was at its usual high volume. He had many reasons for his zeal. As a conservationist, he was appalled by the "wastefulness" of allowing all that water to run to the sea. Thinking of himself as an adopted man of the West, he knew water was the key to spurring a population growth doubling that of his day and permitting the Pacific regional domination that had long been his dream for the United States.

US WATERWAYS—PRIVATE OR PUBLIC?

Washington, D.C., in TR's era was full of people who had thought a lot about the federal role in the orderly and rational development of the nation's waterways—that is, what they believed the federal role *should be*. As things stood at the end of the nineteenth century, congressional committees decided where to spend the limited federal funds for water projects, and they had no guiding national goals. The Rivers and Harbors Act of 1824 had given the US Army Corps of Engineers authority to undertake construction projects facilitating navigation. That meant there was no national water policy but only the pork-barrel decisions of congressional committees responding to local boosters from congressional districts and to large power companies eager to secure a fee-free license to build power sites. The words *pork barrel* convey the charge that benefits have been exaggerated and costs underestimated. This was not the sort of nationally planned waterway policy imagined by TR's lieutenants, although they were not agreed upon how to move in a new direction.

To western growth boosters, the government was now in the irrigation business along with a few private irrigation entrepreneurs, which should be a good thing for homesteading farmers and western economic development generally. The subsequent history of federal irrigation efforts was less than happy, but to conservationists such as Pinchot and W. J. McGee, who could not see that future, there was already a large piece of unfinished business. What was lacking was an overall national water plan to merge "local projects and uses of inland waters in a comprehensive plan designed for the benefit of the entire country" rather than a few hustlers in a few congressional districts. TR quoted these words, written by McGee, as he appointed the Inland Waterways Commission in 1907. That body's short report, no longer than a dozen pages, led to no new programs but forcefully expressed the conservationist conviction that the country's waterways needed stronger national management. US rivers annually drained 1 billion tons of fertile topsoil out of the fields, and their power-generating sites were being sold or given away to monopolistic corporations. Decisions on where to build dams, power plants, and irrigation systems and invest in water transportation should not be made by localist-dominated congressional committees not guided by a larger national plan. These ideas would strongly resurface after the Great Flood of 1927 devastated the entire Mississippi River Basin and notified a complacent public that the nation's waterways were an abused and sometimes dangerous resource, an inviting target for private-power monopolists.

TR's time was short because he had unwisely pledged that he would not seek another term in 1908. The climactic moments of his seven years of public education and exhortation on conservation were the two 1908 Conferences of National Governors. The theme of the first conference in May was set by TR in an opening speech some thought the best he ever made: "The enormous consumption of . . . resources and the threat of imminent exhaustion of some of them" must be seen as a "problem of national efficiency, the patriotic duty of insuring the safety and continuance of the Nation."[6] TR's speech, and indeed the speeches and papers of governors and various experts, is almost an embarrassment today. "Stores of . . . oil and gas are largely gone," the president said without evidence or rebuttal, and one governor predicted the end of coal in 200 years. But if the main point was to have an apex US leaders' meeting to look ahead to resource supply and rates of depletion, the event earned the satisfaction of its organizers. The nationalist tone was vintage TR and resonated well with citizens in his era, whose basic confidence had been shaken by tumultuous change—the rise of monopoly capital, laborer and farmer unrest, mass immigration from the different societies of the European perimeter, the end of the frontier.

The conference, a gathering of about one thousand national figures including almost all state governors, was a huge success given the goals of organizers TR and Pinchot, in that the press coverage was wide and favorable, and all the governors seemed sympathetic and unanimously voted support for a declaration for conservation of natural resources. They also recommended that the president appoint the National Conservation Commission (NCC)— instantly done—to undertake a natural resources inventory. No intellectual resistance had raised its head. A carefully selected list of invitees helped guarantee this. Pinchot refused to invite Muir lest he raise his usual preservationist complaints. The governors went back to their states, and thirty-six of them formed state conservation commissions to study local resource problems and needs. The NCC quickly completed its three-volume report, which offered a rushed inventory of natural resources emphasizing depletion of timber, petroleum, and coal. Two new items surfaced. The first was an appeal for "conserving our chief source of strength by the prevention of disease and the prolongation of life," a bold expansion of the accepted range of conservation concerns to public health that did not catch on. The second was a chapter on population-growth trends that failed to make a connection to the report's catalog of looming resource shortages. A second conference of governors was held in December, and, in his last month in office, TR set in motion a North

American Conservation Conference bringing together Mexico, Canada, and the United States in February 1909. The international meeting did not take place because President Taft canceled it.

Aside from these large events in 1908, TR surpassed even himself on July 1 when, in what he called his "crowded hour," he created an unprecedented number of forest reserves recommended earlier by Pinchot and his USFS colleagues. Forty-five new national forests located in eleven western states were signed into existence by a president who scarcely left his desk all day. All told, in one day, ninety-three federal forest sites were created, many with well-known Indian names such as Nez Perce National Forest in Idaho and Sioux National Forest in South Dakota, or wee places TR had visited more than once, such as Bighorn in Montana and Teton in Wyoming. It was a day of culmination for Pinchot, who must have set a record for Oval Office visits in one day.

In his waning days in office TR had fully seized the moment, repeatedly climbing behind what he called the "bully pulpit" of the presidency to educate and promote. To him that pulpit was not just the president making a speech, but when Congress was resisting or ignoring public opinion and some great national need, a presidential or national commission could give an issue sustained and respected attention, providing a sort of national planning bureaucracy the Constitution had not provided.

Some members of Congress did not think TR's commissions harmless. Aware that presidential commissions were an old idea—Washington in 1794 sent a commission to report on the Whiskey Rebellion; Andrew Jackson asked one to study the Navy Department—some on the Hill disliked TR's free-wheeling commissions promoting his agenda, and Congress refused to fund several of the seven he appointed (Pinchot paid for both governors' conferences). TR was blunt about his working assumption that, in pursuit of the plain public interest, he was authorized to do what the Constitution did not explicitly prohibit. In these and other ways, our first conservationist president strengthened the presidency vis-à-vis the Congress, raising for some people important constitutional questions about the balance between states' rights and federal authority as well as about the executive versus legislative balance of powers. With respect to the issues he cared deeply about, TR (correctly) believed the legislative branch in his era to be parochial, shortsighted, and dominated by moneyed interests. The conservation crusade, like much of the progressive reform agenda, was altering not only the role and functions of the national government but the balance of power among the three branches.

ASSESSING TR

TR's activist, reform-oriented presidency was over in early 1909, and to some historians (and to TR himself) the attention he gave to environmental concerns and his achievements there overshadow even the substantial changes he made in governmental regulation of business and in strengthening the presidency as an institution.

Contemporary scholars of our nation's environmental history may challenge this perspective. Conservation in TR's day will seem to us remarkably limited. The activists' agenda, while bold and important in the stream of history, did not include environmental problems historians know to have been present at the time and acute in some parts of the country—primarily urban air and water pollution from human and industrial wastes. The severe air and water pollution found in the nation's fast-growing eastern and midwestern industrial cities, like other specifically urban problems, generated some local reform efforts, such as the antismoke movement that grew up in New York, Chicago, Pittsburgh. But these were not yet national problems. The South and West had few large industrial cities experiencing severe pollution, and urban pollution was seen as a local problem. It never broke through into national politics in the nineteenth and early twentieth centuries. Such nuisances were left to city and state public health officials and a scattering of urban reformers.

With fine hindsight, we are almost embarrassed at TR and Pinchot's confidence in government, in trained and professional civil servants working always for the public good within the new administrative state. Still, those of us who take pleasure in the majestic parks and forests and wildlife refuges must applaud a cohort of reformers who, a century ago, reserved for us some part of the public landscape even though we were not voters because we were not yet born.

THE LEADERSHIP OF WORDS AND IDEAS

The conservation of our natural resources and their proper use constitute the fundamental problem which underlies almost every other problem of our national life. . . . There must be the look ahead, a realization of the fact that to waste, and destroy, our natural resources, to skin and exhaust the land . . . will result in the undermining in the days of our children the very prosperity which we ought by right to hand down to them amplified and developed.[7]
— Theodore Roosevelt

In his last State of the Union Address, in December 1908, TR described, with slide illustrations attached to the document and supplied by Pinchot, the denuded mountain slopes and gullied hillsides of China, where forests had been recklessly cut down, and told the audience in front of his pulpit that he had seen such deforestation also in Palestine, around the Mediterranean, and in Africa, where powerful civilizations had withered away.

LIEUTENANTS AND IDEAS

In view of these remarkable Rooseveltian contributions from the "bully pulpit," it is important to emphasize again the essential roles of the president's allies, most of whom he never saw—the radical amateurs and professionals at the center of the social movement, the sympathetic legislators who moved the lawmaking conveyor belt, and the Washington-based supporting intellectuals and bureaucratic entrepreneurs especially prominent and influential within the male camaraderie of the TR White House.

One example underscores how TR's leadership was augmented by his inner circle of lieutenants. After one term his presidency was being seen as an assemblage of a few of his chosen progressive reform causes—antitrust; food, drug, and railroad regulation; and a lot of set-asides of parks and forests. There was no real coherence to all this beyond the "progressive" label, which was good enough for him. Then one February morning in 1907 Pinchot, riding his horse in Rock Creek Park in Washington, had a sort of vision. Preservation and management of forests, waterways, wildlife, minerals, and petroleum all may have been scattered across the expanding governmental bureaucracy but were unified and given authority when seen as parts of the "one great single problem of the use of the earth for the good of man," he later wrote. Coping with this "is the key to the future." Uncertain of the implications of this thought, Pinchot discussed it with several friends, especially the sagacious McGee, who linked these various resource-protection efforts to progressivism by seeing in each a battlefront in the elemental fight against monopoly generally. Somebody, recalling that government forestlands in British India were called conservancies, suggested the unifying label *conservation* for the TR administration's central idea and impulse now fragmented into policies for forests, parks, wildlife, and river development. It was certainly (Pinchot later recalled) McGee who pointed out that the conservation cause should extend British philosopher Jeremy Bentham's famous principle that the wisest policies are those that produce the "greatest good for the greatest number" and extended it by adding the phrase "for the longest time." Pinchot carried these thoughts to TR, who at once embraced the term *conservation* and realized its political potential. He would later write, "When we say, 'for the people,' we must always include the unborn as well as the people now alive, or the democratic ideal is not realized."[8] "Our duty to the whole," TR wrote in *A Book-lover's Holidays in the Open* (1916), "including the unborn generations, bids us restrain an unprincipled present-day minority from wasting the heritage of these unborn generations." Pinchot himself had the language perfected in his 1910 book, *The Fight for Conservation*, in which he gave McGee full credit for borrowing from Bentham and put their new term in wide circulation: "Conservation means the greatest good to the greatest number for the longest time."[9]

TR and his close collaborator rarely differed or at least rarely exposed a disagreement in public. Here was a fundamental one, worth an argument it never got. The unborn are stakeholders (to borrow a modern term) who are not to be forgotten and left out, but do they have an equal claim against all others?

TR seemed to assume so, although Pinchot vigorously stated a different view in *The Fight for Conservation*: "There has been a fundamental misconception that conservation means nothing but the husbanding of resources for future generations. There could be no more serious mistake. Conservation does mean provision for the future, but it means also and first of all the recognition of the right of the present generation to the fullest necessary use of all the resources. . . . Conservation demands the welfare of this generation first, and afterward the welfare of the generations to follow." Here was an argument never had (in public) among these two founders, undoubtedly because both were skilled politicians who sensed the power (for good, they were sure) of their new brand name.

"So the child was named," Pinchot wrote in his *Breaking New Ground*. "In 1907 few knew what conservation meant. Now it has become a household word."[10] He was not far off the mark. The word *conservation* did not appear a single time in *Poole's Index to Periodical Literature* from 1802 to 1881 but was wedged in between "conscience" and "conservatism" once in the 1890s to call attention to an article about conservation of energy. The more popular *Readers' Guide to Periodical Literature* began publication in 1900, noting only one article on conservation of energy for the period 1900–1904. Then, in a burst, came this new "household word." Thirty-one articles on "conservation of natural resources" were listed in the pages of the index for 1905–1909, eighty from 1910–1914. TR's lieutenants had given the cause a label and definition and had provided birdwatchers, foresters, and the president himself a unifying vision and a constituency far larger than the current voters, for it included all future children. It was a priceless invention.

With the presidency of TR, our story gains an engine. Presidents before him came into office expecting to confront a familiar, even shopworn agenda of sectional, tariff, and monetary-policy issues. Harrison, Grover Cleveland, and McKinley navigated these old issues as best they could (McKinley also managed a war), and each in turn was surprised to be obliged to react also to something new in national policy disputes—a growing concern over the environmental consequences of the privatization of public lands, a topic none of them fully understood or welcomed. In TR's White House years the presidential agenda was permanently altered to make room for this new cluster of issues called *conservation*—understood to have to do with setting aside and protecting national parks, national forests, national monuments, wildlife refuges. This would probably have happened in a less dramatic way had McKinley picked a different vice president in 1900, for the expansion of the US economy and population was wounding its landscape at so many points that nature preservation issues were relentlessly pressing forward. TR's leadership was a decisive turning point. A social movement had been given a name, description, and the core of an ideology in the phrase "greatest good for the greatest number over the longest time." It could claim a central place in the progressive reform enterprise energizing the nation's public life and reaching the national level with TR.

CONSERVATIONISM'S INTERNAL DIVISIONS

TR's successors in the office would encounter complexities in this new nature-preservation policy arena that his moralistic cast of mind and rhetoric had obscured and that he did not deal with in his voluminous writings. He and his allies presented conservation as a simple though morally compelling cause—natural-resource protection from "land skinners" and monopolies, in the interest of all the people, including future generations. Yet it was obvious even in the 1890s, before his presidency, that the movement was already divided into two camps, symbolized by the personalities and ideas of Muir and the wilderness-protection persuasion as against Pinchot and the "wise use" or utilitarian emphasis. As we have seen, Muir and Pinchot, originally warm friends, had personally clashed over sheep grazing in the reserves and distrusted each other thereafter. They spoke different versions of the conservationist language. As Muir put it in *A Thousand-Mile Walk to the Gulf*: "The world we are told was made for man—a presumption that is totally unsupported by facts. . . . Why ought man to value himself as more than an infinitely small composing unit of one great unit of creation?"[11] Pinchot countered in words written for TR's first State of the Union Address: "The fundamental idea of forestry is the perpetuation of the forests by use. Forest protection is not an end in itself; it is a means to increase and sustain the resources of our country and the industries which depend upon them."[12]

The two persuasions came most visibly into conflict, as TR left office, over the proposal of the City of San Francisco to dam for water supplies the Tuolumne River running through the Hetch Hetchy Valley, twenty miles northwest of Yosemite Valley and within the boundaries of the park. Some called Hetch Hetchy even more beautiful than Yosemite, though photographs of Hetch Hetchy before flooding do not quite convince me. It was beautiful enough to deeply stir the passions of preservationists, especially Muir and his new Sierra Club, and many influential easterners, including the thousands of members of the General Federation of Women's Clubs (GFWC) who conducted an impressive publicity campaign against the dam. "These temple destroyers!" wrote Muir in his last and most passionate battle: "These temple destroyers, devotees of ravaging commercialism, seem to have a perfect contempt for Nature, and, instead of lifting their eyes to the God of the mountains, lift them to the Almighty Dollar. Dam Hetch Hetchy! As well dam for water-tanks the peoples' cathedrals and churches, for no holier temple has ever been consecrated by the heart of man."[13] Yet on the side of building the dam was Pinchot (and a few other California conservationists), who argued that the public need for water should not be blocked by the "intermittent esthetic enjoyment of less than one percent."

This important internal division between use and preservation should not be exaggerated, for it could sometimes be fudged. The battle over Hetch Hetchy was not resolved until TR had left office, and he avoided a clean break with Muir and the Sierra Club by expressing regret that the voters in San Francisco seemed too formidable a political force to resist, by making frequent statements such as, "Lying out at night under those giant Sequoias was like lying in a temple built by no hand of man," and by vigorously taking steps to "preserve from destruction beautiful and wonderful wild creatures" on game and bird refuges, including buffalo on reservations at Yellowstone and in Montana. Although TR and many other conservationists sometimes leaned one way and sometimes another, and although the conflict between preservation and immediate human use was sometimes muted by shared hostility to resource exploitation and waste by large corporations, or TR's "land skinners," there had clearly emerged in the founding years of conservationism a real fault line running through the movement, one that persists today, as does another division within the conservationist army. TR and (most of) his lieutenants instructed the country to see conservation as an invigoration of US democracy. Like the other parts of the progressive movement, conservation was framed as an effort to use government to defend the "people versus the powerful interests," mostly big corporations. Yet the politics of conservation were, unsurprisingly, not so simple. Historian Samuel P. Hays was one of the first to point out that the conservationists allied with TR were an elite group of highly educated white males, almost all technically, scientifically, or legally trained. Their commitment to efficiency, ending waste, and planning for the future often made them more comfortable with large corporations in the extractive industries than with the common citizens, who from time to time were also poachers on public land or violators of hunting laws (sometimes for subsistence reasons). An example: "The objective of this organization," said Dutcher, president of Audubon in 1905, "is to be a barrier between wild birds and animals and a very large unthinking class, and a larger but more harmful class of selfish people." The first we shall "educate out of their ignorance," he went on. The others "we shall control through the enforcement of wise laws, reservations or bird refuges, and the warden system."[14]

Conservation, for the Rooseveltian lieutenants, was a great public cause. Of course, their public service passion was muddied by the fact that this crusade also built professional careers for themselves in the expanding public sector. This recognition of conservationism's elitist professional, male social profile and governmental job machine is part of the nonstatist upsurge of grassroots citizen organization around natural resource issues represented in the emergence and activities of the far-flung chapters of the National Audubon Society, the Izaak Walton League, the Daughters of the American Revolution, and especially the GFWC. The latter organization, active in conservation from the

1890s on, was present in almost all the states, where local chapters often had conservation committees. The national office of the GFWC had a Conservation Department and delivered 1.5 million petitions to Congress in 1909 urging protection of the Mariposa Grove of sequoias. Conservation from TR's day forward has been a nationwide grassroots eruption as well as a sort of public-spirited elite plot, and this should surprise no one. Stephen Fox, in *The American Conservation Movement* (1981), has made a distinction between the "professional conservationists" and the "radical amateurs," who often cooperated yet frequently pulled in different directions. The ranks of the "amateurs" did not yet include racial minorities, an expansion of the conservationist impulse that has only recently begun, but it certainly included many activist women who provided additional energy and, often, fresh perspectives. Successful citizens for the most part, they were also rebels and troublemakers, their enemies endlessly said, including the "short-haired women and long-haired men" complained of by San Francisco's city engineer as they blocked his dream of designing a dam backing up the Merced River in order to make a lake out of Hetch Hetchy Valley.[15] The conservation movement gathering force in the United States at the hinge of the centuries was indeed a reinvigoration of democracy even if it was, like most or perhaps all social reform movements, no cross section of society. It counts for a lot in considering conservationism's democratic credentials that no other social movement made such frequent reference to the intergenerational obligations current citizens owe to the vast public yet to be born.

Roy Robbins, in his classic *Our Landed Heritage* (1962), tells us, "As he approached the end of his administration, Roosevelt was convinced that as yet no really satisfactory national conservation program had been established."[16]

Pinchot had good reason to argue that TR's central achievement was his lead role in the definition and promotion of what several of his cohort almost simultaneously termed *conservation*. (They soon dropped the words "gospel of.") In the twentieth century a different view gained ascendancy among historians and other scholars of our governmental system. In this view the constitutional architects had designed a system in which "checks and balances" too often prevented corrective governmental action when an expanding society developed maladies. TR (and Lincoln) looked at government in this activist way, as did Woodrow Wilson, who revised his book on the presidency in light of TR's exploration of presidential activism. In sharp contrast to the agendaless presidents who paraded sluggishly through the late nineteenth century proposing no remedies for the economic dislocations and growth strains of that era, TR offered a seven-year tutorial on the president as activist, enhancing the federal government's capacity for timely innovation and adjustment.

The two presidents just before TR might have registered a mild complaint to this account. Historian Lewis Gould has effectively reminded us that the modernness of twentieth-century presidents could be seen before TR. If you called the White House by telephone to speak to President Cleveland, he would have answered the phone, as would have Harrison, the first president to have the gadget in the Oval Office. This was not because they were snoopers but because the president in those days had only six staff in and around his office. McKinley gets credit for hiring George B. Cortelyou as his office manager, who set up for the first time a system of managing and logging in presidential papers and mail and boosted the staff to thirty. TR kept him on and appointed a commission under a senior career public servant (Charles Keep, hence the Keep Commission) to recommend administrative streamlining of the executive branch.

More important by far, in his seven years TR added a key element of the modern presidency—his view that because presidents were elected by the whole people, they were empowered by the Constitution to do what was required in safeguarding the general welfare—the Supreme Court concurring or standing aside.

As TR approached the close of his presidency, he remained active at the bully pulpit, writing a series of articles for *Outlook* and *Scribner's Magazine*, and in the last six weeks in office, aided by a team of US ornithologists, designated bird refuges in Hawaii, elsewhere in the Pacific, and in the marshlands along the Pacific flyway. "I have been full president right up to the end," he justifiably boasted. When TR left the White House in the ninth year of a young century, Pinchot was often heard claiming that his presidential friend's chief accomplishment had been his central role in encouraging and shaping conservation. It was indeed a remarkable achievement, the mobilization of a social reform movement gathering in meetings of the Boone and Crocket Club in New York, the Sierra Club on the other coast, and the Audubon and GFWC in hundreds of cities and towns. What they had achieved in advance of TR's oath of office was major steps toward the preservation of the national landscape in national parks, national forests, bird refuges, and national monuments. These building blocks of a new national public land policy had by the arrival of the twentieth century begun to replace the inherited, directionless policy of "disposal" of the public land dowry.

Conservationism was launched with a potent core idea with which to combat those TR called the "land skinners and land grabbers": the "greatest good for the greatest number for the longest time," along with Thoreau and Muir and others' linkage of wilderness exposure to emotional and religious health. The land grabbers and the politicians who spoke for them were surprisingly thin on intellectual foundation and argument. They had not (and have not yet) devised a compelling label for themselves. "Not one cent for scenery," was the mantra of Speaker of the House Joe Cannon.

Conservationists had their own limited horizons. Muir, TR, and Pinchot did not write or speak about the universal habit of urban and industrial sewage disposal into local air and waterways. They were eloquent critics of forest and wildlife devastation but took decades to notice a fast-moving and deadly fungus brought from Japan at the first of the century that killed off 4 billion chestnut trees in forty years. No one in TR's lifetime reached the public with a good argument that the nation's "swamps" (wetlands) were either beautiful or valuable in their undrained form or objected when builder Henry Flagler pursued his plans for draining most of the Florida Everglades. Henry Ford brought out his fast-selling Model A automobile in 1904, other companies followed in their fashion, and no one seems to have warned that the one auto for every 1,078 Americans in 1905 and for every 13 million in 1920 had any implications for the future of the national parks.

An imagined conversation will remind us that they were improvising.

TR: "President Harrison, what a pleasure to see you here in the Afterlife!"

BH: "Why Theodore, I should be calling you president, also. Before we go our separate ways, a question: Just what did you and those Boone and Crockett fellows have in mind when Secretary Noble persuaded me to create that handful of 'Forest Reserves'?"

TR: "Truly, some of us were not clear about our goals. Pinchot and I were consciously aiming at setting aside national forest reserves rather than giving the acreage to railroads or homesteaders or states. We hoped for several national forests, even some in the East, and a federal agency to practice scientific forestry on them in order to protect watersheds and the nation's remaining forests. Some of my friends also dreamed of a few more national parks to supplement Yellowstone and Yosemite."

BH: "I trust you have followed those hopes from your perch on Mount Rushmore in your beloved Dakotas. How did the plans work out?"

TR: "I'm glad you asked. At the end of the twentieth century, four federal agencies managed 653 million acres of land still owned by the American people. Eighty-four million acres are set aside in 51 national parks and 190 million acres as 156 national forests. Pinchot would be proud, indeed, that his National Forest Service is an agency deploying 40,000 employees and managing 190 million acres of public lands that would presumably otherwise have been sold or given away to rapacious strippers of the land. After you left the White House to return to Indiana, proud of your early role, I trust, yours truly and successive presidents, sometimes with congressional cooperation and sometimes without, set aside some 362 units—50 of them the "crown jewels," as we call the national parks—as well as 91 million acres in 91 national wildlife refuges. Other public sites are national monuments, historic sites, scenic parkways, and seashores. It would be false to claim that my fellow presidents followed a detailed grand plan in shaping this magnificent public land heritage. The ranks of preservationists helping these presidents were deep, loyal, and dedicated. It is a splendid legacy."

WILLIAM TAFT, WOODROW WILSON, WARREN HARDING, CALVIN COOLIDGE, AND HERBERT HOOVER THE CONSERVATION AGENDA, 1910s–1920s

4

Thousands of tired, nerve-shaken, over-civilized people are beginning to find out that going to the mountains is home, that wilderness is a necessity.
— John Muir

The US government was in motion in the early decades of the twentieth century, making a controversial journey from the "weak state" model of the nineteenth century toward the more activist, socially engaged "regulatory state" (some began to call it) of the twentieth. Often at the center of this transformation was the presidency, taking on new powers and functions from an expanding agenda of which conservation was now a significant part. Another activist Roosevelt, Theodore Roosevelt's distant cousin Franklin, rode a promising political career in New York. But in between the Roosevelts there were three presidents who had no enthusiasm for or knowledge about the many campaigns for conservation (William Howard Taft, Warren Harding, Calvin Coolidge) and two whose commitment was modest (Woodrow Wilson, Herbert Hoover). TR recognized that he had made a serious mistake in 1904 when he promised not to run for reelection the next time around. Because of TR's ill-advised blunder, his secretary of war, Taft, became president (1909–1913), all 300 pounds of him disapproving of the activist tendencies in the White House, especially conservationism cranked up full throttle, as TR and Gifford Pinchot discovered too late.

Taft in the White House was to disappoint conservationists. TR did not live long enough to see the performances of Harding, Coolidge, and Hoover, "brown" presidents with no time for the remaining conservationist agenda. The conservation crusade was one of the parts of the progressive movement's organized social base, but it rested upon a narrow organizational foundation of upper-class hunters/hikers in the Boone and Crockett and Sierra Clubs anchored on both coasts, professional foresters, the perhaps 50,000 dedicated birders in the National Audubon Society, and the formidable branches of the General Federation of Women's Clubs (GFWC). The political base of conservationism did not change much in the 1920s, though here and there a gifted mobilizer, such as Will H. Dilg, fired up a new group, in his case the Izaac Walton League. This organizational base of conservationism was essentially stable throughout the 1930s, when most of the energies and ideas came from the White House and other federal agencies.

To the retreating wildlife, the establishment of national forests and national parks in the TR era did little to slow the devastation produced by the reality behind two revered words, *national growth*. The human population, in 1900 at 76 million, was then roughly ten times the size of the indigenous population when the European invasion began and vastly more technologically advanced. It grew to 123 million by 1930, migrating from rural to urban settings and spreading westward into the Great Plains and southward toward the tropical allure of a watery Florida seen as begging for improvement—which meant drainage and development. None of the perils TR and his lieutenants warned about—deforestation, soil erosion, flooding, wildlife extinction—had been arrested during this era of growth, let alone reversed.

Environmental problems were also growing in new places. Expanding industrial cities were shifting to highly polluting soft coal for heat and power, dumping poisonous fumes into the air as dwellings, workshops, and factories used both air and nearby water as dumps for their often toxic wastes. The petroleum industry, from extraction to refining, was rapidly expanding to meet the demand from a fast-growing automobile fleet and the industrial needs for lubricating oil. Its spills and waste dumping fouled more waterways and beaches each year. The petroleum extraction industry pulled 60 million barrels of oil from the ground in 1900 and 600 million in 1910. All major US cities in the early twentieth century lacked sewage-treatment facilities, as did the rural areas, channeling human, animal, and other wastes into nearby waterways or fields.

WILLIAM HOWARD TAFT

In the winter of 1909 TR was a former president, making plans for a hunting trip to Africa, confident in the promise of his handpicked successor, Taft, of whom he had said: "I do not believe there can be found in the whole country a man so well fitted to be president."[1]

But TR had made an uncharacteristic and costly misjudgment of a colleague. Taft, born in Cincinnati, educated at Yale, a lawyer and judge by trade and temperament, had no burning desire for the presidency because he had no conception that the nation needed to be led toward some sort of deep moral and practical change. His wife passionately wanted him to be president, but she shared his lack of a good reason. Genial, intelligent, somewhat passive, banal and stiff at speaking, seriously overweight, and on the lazy side, Taft (when asked) gave the impression of endorsing the entire TR conservation program, though he had almost nothing to do with it apart from sitting in on cabinet meetings. It was a rare occasion, such as his July 1908 acceptance speech at the Republican, or Good Old Party (GOP), National Convention, when he aligned himself with it: "The preservation of our soil, and of our forests . . . will properly claim from the next administration earnest attention and appropriate legislation." The fire was not in Taft's ample belly.

Secretly, Taft harbored serious doubts about TR's conception of the presidency itself. Article II of the Constitution set out the functions of the chief executive, and to Taft, if a presidential power was not explicitly conferred there or by act of Congress, a president acted unconstitutionally in exercising it. This belief was in sharp contrast with that of TR, who boldly stated that if the power were not explicitly prohibited, he had a warrant from the people to exercise it.

"Taft is going to be with us in this work," Pinchot wrote to a friend in February 1909. Soon enough it was evident that he was not "with us," or if so, only in a general and limited way. Doubtful of their legality, Taft terminated TR's National Conservation Commission (NCC) and plans for a world conservation congress. More ominous to the TR-Pinchot camp, he passed over Secretary of the Interior James R. Garfield and appointed to replace him Richard A. Ballinger, whose frequent disagreements with TR's land policies were well known from his service as head of the General Land Office prior to his huffy resignation in 1907. Beneath the disagreements lay Ballinger's anticonservationist views, which he sometimes expressed when out of Washington and earshot of the press corps: "You chaps who are in favor of this conservation program are all wrong. You are hindering the development of the West. In my opinion, the proper course to take with regard to this [public lands] is to divide it up among the big corporations and the people who know how to make money out of it."² Or, in a 1910 speech in St. Paul, Minnesota: "It seems to me that we should not try to impose the whole burden of conservation on the federal government but leave it to the states and the municipalities to work out."

Having appointed a man with such views to head the chief federal agency supervising natural resources, Taft had no grounds for surprise when the much-publicized trouble called the "Ballinger-Pinchot affair" broke out in 1909 and mobilized the conservationist forces against his administration. The intricate details of this episode have been explored in several books. We need to know only the broad outlines, ending, and impact. Secretary Ballinger pursued irrigation and waterpower-site policies that struck Chief Forester Pinchot (and other TR followers) as fundamental policy mistakes and reversals. Ballinger resented and impeded Pinchot's freewheeling interference in public land issues across the span of involved federal bureaus and complained about Pinchot to a sympathetic Taft. Ballinger was attacking a basic part of the enduring TR conservation apparatus. "By jamming the machinery of interdepartmental cooperation and denying Pinchot his role as coordinating agent," writes historian James Penick, "Ballinger threatened the ad hoc system of unified planning which made the conservation movement a 'movement.'"³

Pinchot was of course putting on full battle gear. He was indignant and suspicious upon hearing Ballinger had authorized legally questionable leases of Alaska coal land to corporations that had consulted (i.e., paid) the interior secretary when he was a Seattle lawyer. He attacked Ballinger in a series of speeches across the West that reached the national media and used stronger language against Taft in private and in his memoir, *Breaking New Ground*, in which he wrote, "Taft sided with every predatory interest seeking to gobble up natural resources or otherwise oppress the people" and was an "accomplice to land grabbers and water-power grabbers."⁴

At first this was a policy power struggle of which the public knew little and did not understand. Taft's underlying constitutional scruples about the TR-Pinchot program were simplistic and without merit as well as clearly stated only later. Is the president "to play the part of a universal Providence and set all things right?" Taft wrote in 1925, and added, "anything that in his judgment will help the people he ought to do. . . . The wide field of action that this would give to the executive, one can hardly limit."[5]

The political classes in 1910 could not be unaware, however, of one visible source of conflict: Ballinger and the president were aware of and not unsympathetic to fierce western resistance within the Republican Party to the Pinchot-Roosevelt stance on public lands. They had heard a thousand times that the conservation movement "interferes with the development of the West" and had heard westerners such as Representative Frank Johnson of the State of Washington complain that his constituents were "literally being conserved out of existence." Some southern politicians and chambers of commerce talked this way, but Republicans naturally did not see them as part of their base. Taft faced a reelection battle in 1912 and for both political and ideological reasons worried far more about anticonservationist feeling than had the hugely popular TR.

By autumn 1909 stories in *Collier's Weekly, McClure's Magazine,* and other mass media focused on Ballinger's links to large corporations receiving Alaska coal leases, and the dispute rose to an indictment of the integrity of one of Taft's cabinet members, with rumors of a sharp break between TR and his chosen successor. Taft reviewed the report of a special agent from the General Land Office along with Ballinger's defense and sided with Ballinger. A well-publicized congressional investigation exonerated Ballinger and exposed his differences with TR-era policies. In a few months Ballinger resigned, but not before Taft had fired Pinchot in January 1910 for insubordination and for being, Taft said privately, a "radical and a crank." He certainly was on the border of insubordination by attacking the head of another cabinet-level department. But the larger context was the Taft administration's conservative policy drift away from the progressive wing of the Republican Party over tariffs and Taft's refusal to join TR's reform-oriented GOP fight against the bullying tactics of House Speaker Joseph "Boss" Cannon. In allowing matters to get to the point at which TR's close friend Pinchot had to be fired, Taft had very publicly aligned his administration against the reform-oriented wing of the party, a fatal political mistake. TR broke with Taft and entered the Republican presidential primaries in 1911–1912, then formed the Progressive Party when Taft narrowly held the Republican nomination. Democrat Woodrow Wilson was narrowly elected president in 1912 against a split GOP and Socialist Party candidate Eugene Debs.

Taft's one-term presidency was over, and with respect to the environment it was without leadership, guided entirely by negative instincts and void of any affection for or intimate knowledge of any part of nature. He put in office and staunchly backed Interior Secretary Ballinger, who broke the momentum of TR and Pinchot toward resource protection and planning with regard to public lands. It counts for only a little that Taft signed the popular Weeks Forest Purchase Act in March 1911, authorizing US Forest Service (USFS) purchase and management of private land in the East and South for watershed and wilderness protection, because the idea and the pressure came from eastern conservation and preservation groups. Taft made no presidential statement on signing the act but took the occasion of a large 1911 public land convention to say that the "fetish stage" of the conservation movement was over and the nation could now "settle down to a calm consideration of what ought to be done."[6]

Perhaps he is owed some credit because his second interior secretary, Walter Fisher (successor to Ballinger), convened in September 1911 at Yellowstone the first national parks conference at which railroad representatives and other industrial leaders expressed strong support for the expansion of the national park idea. Similarly, he agreed to support (with a message to Congress) Secretary Ballinger's proposal (urged on him by liberal Republicans in the American Civic Association) to establish in the Department of the Interior a new bureau of "national parks and resorts" to bring protective management to the growing number of parks. This timely and necessary idea eventually became the National Park Service Organic Act of 1916, signed by Woodrow Wilson, directing that the parks be left "unimpaired for the enjoyment of future generations." Credit is owed. Absent these two presidential endorsements and Wilson's signature, no NPS would have existed, with the frequently enlightened leadership it has supplied since 1916.

In his last annual message to Congress, just weeks before he would leave the White House, Taft wrote revealingly of a recently growing "demand for conservation of the public domain" that had been "excellent in the intention which prompted it" but "has had some bad effects." Taft argued that we need to "attain the golden mean," which by implication was where he would be found, not over on the "erring" conservationist side. "The present administration has done what it could in this regard, but the necessity for reform and change remains, and I submit to Congress the wisdom of a full examination of this subject."[7]

This is failed leadership on the issues at hand, in the very shadow of another model. One looks in vain for any instance when Taft put himself at the head rather than joining up at the rear of a column of conservationists already formed. His final hours in office are a last example of his ineptitude. TR had established fifty-three bird refuges by the time he handed the office to Taft, but this was only a small beginning on wildfowl protection. Congress had appropriated no money for management, and the National Audubon Society was attempting to hire a few wardens whose legal basis for policing the refuges was cloudy. Citizen bird-protection groups, led by Audubon, pressed for a federal law protecting migratory waterfowl in whatever state they happened to be. The fervor of these groups, and novel techniques such as showing a film of bird slaughter to Congress (historian Ann Vileisis called this "likely the first conservation film ever") brought passage of the Migratory Bird Act of 1913.[8] Taft opposed the legislation without clear explanation. In the rush of his final hours in office on March 4, 1913, he accidentally signed it into law when it came to him buried in a twenty-eight-page statute covering several topics.

Thus Taft made more disruptive than helpful contributions to the newly shouldered environmental preservation work of the federal government, for his heart was not in the preservation-of-nature project. Even if he had seen any of this as high-priority presidential business, he lacked the ability or impulse to serve as educator to the public. One can envision him in the final hours of his term, unaware that he was signing into law the Migratory Bird or Weeks Acts, silent while others spoke up for federal action to end the slaughter of birds and animals for hat decorations and trophies. It was below-average leadership in an office where even average environmental attention has never been good enough.

THOMAS WOODROW WILSON

Taft rode down Pennsylvania Avenue in March 1913 to the inauguration of Thomas Woodrow Wilson, the first Democrat elected president since 1892, a winner only because TR put a third party in the field and split the Republican majority.

Who was Wilson, and what was his leadership potential in general and for matters environmental in particular?

The evidence as he took the oath was oddly mixed. The son of a Presbyterian minister and his college-educated wife, raised in several southern states, Wilson studied law, then earned a Ph.D. in political science at Johns Hopkins University and was promoted from professor to the presidency of Princeton University. In 1910 he was handily elected governor of New Jersey, where he emerged as an articulate and forceful progressive reformer. On the surface, he appeared to be the best-educated president since James Madison. Wilson's influential first book (which went through twenty-nine editions), *Congressional Government* (1885), described the presidency as the weakest of the three branches, dominated by Congress, in which real leadership potential was located, especially if the legislature could be reformed to more resemble the British cabinet system. Events, however, led Wilson to call for a much stronger presidency. After the war with Spain during William McKinley's presidency, he revised his book, writing that in foreign policy the "President of the United States is . . . at the front of affairs." Then, observing the presidency of TR, Wilson wrote approvingly in 1908, "We have grown more inclined to look to the president as the unifying force in our complex system. . . . His is the vital place of action."[9] All of Wilson's adult life he had been drawn to the record of statesmen who moved the public through the power of oratory, and his own successes came far more from his skill with words than any administrative genius.

Thus it appeared that the US political process had selected, in an unusual election in the center of a reform era, strong, articulate presidential leadership. Yet at the time of his nomination, one element was lacking. Wilson was an aspiring leader who had not figured out the direction in which to persuade the country to go. "In the summer of 1912," wrote historian Arthur S. Link, the campaign already under way, Wilson was a "candidate in search of a program."[10] In August, fatefully, he met the brilliant Boston attorney Louis D. Brandeis, who convinced him to build his campaign around the "trust issue," that generation's label for corporate monopoly. Wilson's campaign quickly took on the spiritual overtones of a crusade for a "new dawn of liberty" for a middle class "being crushed between the upper and nether millstones" of monopoly power and proletarian radicalism.

That Wilson meant to be a leader in such a cause was soon obvious. He resurrected a practice not followed since President John Adams, presenting his December 2, 1913, State of the Union Address to Congress in person and addressing that body four times in his first year. Impressed by TR's presidential activism, Wilson knew that his personal addresses to Congress would be given front-page coverage in newspapers and that he was speaking across Congress to the public. He thus set the agenda and pushed through a reform program including an antitrust law, lower tariffs, a federal reserve bank, child labor laws, an income tax, and the Federal Trade Commission (FCC) to regulate business. He frequently and effectively appealed over the heads of Congress to the public for support in enacting his programs. Conservationists who noticed the new president's style of leadership must have taken heart.

What to expect of Wilson on the topic of the human relationship to nature? Wilson's life had been devoid of any interest in the outdoors. Raised in Presbyterian manses in a series of southern towns, he grew up as a bookish boy often in poor health, dominated by the theological intensity of his clergyman father, who filled the youth of "Tommy Wilson" with biblical and classical readings, discussions, and writing exercises. Thoroughly educated in British, European, and US history, Wilson appears to have been utterly ignorant of natural history and devoid of interest in the nonhuman life outside the manse, the church, and the college. In reading his campaign speeches in 1912, one turns with curiosity and hope to the only phrase remotely touching upon the environment, "Life Comes from the Soil." This was the title he gave to a speech about how the "natural growth of a great tree" reminds us that "nations are renewed from the bottom, not from the top." So, we should have faith in the "common man." So much for trees or soil. He had nothing to say on them as agenda items. If this 56-year-old professor brought to the White House a single environment-related commitment or interest, his biographers have not found it.

THE CONSERVATION AGENDA AFTER TR

A conservation agenda already existed in Washington when Wilson arrived, formulated by the conservation social movement and TR's followers, resisted by public domain resource users and western chambers of commerce. This reality offered Wilson (and his successors) the choice either to give some degree of support and even leadership to the "conservation crusade" already in progress, avoid it as much as possible as a marginal issue, or lead a resistance and rollback. He blended the first and second options. In fairness, we cannot forget the unique context in which Wilson operated. World War I issues from 1914 to 1920 inevitably crowded out the time and attention Wilson initially had given to his progressive reform interests.

To the reader who samples Wilson biographies and histories, it might seem he chose not to engage environmental topics at all. Turn, for example, to the influential one-volume synthesis of his presidency written by Wilson's magisterial biographer, Arthur S. Link (also of Princeton), *Woodrow Wilson and the Progressive Era* (1954). In this detailed narrative of Wilson's impressive domestic reform record, followed by the momentous events leading to US entry into World War I and the postwar settlement, there is one paragraph about his interior secretary, Franklin K. Lane, who we know to have been embroiled in controversies over natural resources—and it tells us only that Lane was the cabinet gossip and the main reason Wilson held few cabinet meetings and rarely made important decisions there. Historian Kendrick Clements, in *The Presidency of Woodrow Wilson* (1992), found little room for any issue related to public lands, natural resources, or wildlife preservation, with one exception. In 1913, just before his inauguration, he delivered a brief speech in which he offered his opinion that a "policy of reservation is not a policy of conservation" but is a locking up of resources rather than wise use. Plainly enough, he saw himself at this early point as a Pinchot conservationist and had yet to learn that astute public figures—such as Pinchot—always tried to have it both ways.

Historians have tended to skip over the Wilson administration's substantial involvement with resource policy issues inherited from the TR days, and for good reason. US entanglement in the European war from 1914 forward tends to overshadow even Wilson's substantial domestic reform agenda, where conservation issues would be encountered. Another reason seems to have been that much of his administration's record was made off center stage by Interior Secretary Lane dealing with matters inherited from TR and Taft.

Three old contests ground their way in the early Wilson years to a sort of cloudy resolution: the emotional Hetch Hetchy issue, the institutionalization of the management of the national parks, and the numbing complexities of policies for mineral leasing and for water-power projects, which I will try to narrate without the numbing.

Wilson signed the grant of permission to build Hetch Hetchy Dam in December 1913, acknowledging the opposition of "many public-spirited men" whose views he "scrutinized" and found "not well founded." TR would probably have swallowed hard and done the same. Wilson, an unknown quantity on natural-resource issues, was apparently not conflicted by John Muirish preservationism.

TR and Taft had left an administrative mess in the expanding list of national parks, monuments, and historic sites haphazardly housed for administrative purposes within the Departments of the Interior, Agriculture, and War. The US Army had been "managing" Yellowstone since 1886, which meant cavalry patrolling to scold or arrest poachers. Congress had created essentially no management plan for the people's parks, and a vigorous campaign began in 1910 to create a central bureau to oversee these public places. The influential lieutenants in this campaign had stepped forward without any presidential encouragement and mobilized the substantial national sentiment in favor of the national parks—among them urban planner J. Horace McFarland, landscape architect Frederick Law Olmsted, Chicago self-made millionaire and avid mountain climber Stephen T. Mather, and Muir. Historian Roderick Nash correctly argues that these energetic individuals were the most visible parts of a social movement Nash and other historians call wilderness preservation and Pinchot and TR had taught many Americans to call conservation. Their numbers, energy levels, and organizational and promotional talents were impressive. Ready for another fight after the disappointment of Hetch Hetchy, they convinced President Taft and Secretary Ballinger to back the idea forming on Capitol Hill for "complete and comprehensive plans" to end the disarray and vulnerability of these public reservations. These lieutenants mobilized public opinion through feature stories on the threatened parks in major national magazines and annual conferences well attended by railroad and automobile industry lobbyists eager for well-managed national parks as tourist destinations.

Enter Wilson, to conservationists as well as anticonservationists an unknown quantity. In his Inaugural Address he had called vaguely for action on a long list of national problems, concluding by noting "watercourses undeveloped, waste places unreclaimed, forests untended, fast disappearing without plan or prospect of renewal, unregarded waste heaps at every mine." Poetic, but only faintly suggestive of his views. He confirmed this in the few words on the "problem of conservation" in his first State of the Union Address when he told the nation, "We must use the resources of the country, not lock them up."[11] A stronger clue to his outlook on natural-resource matters perhaps came when, in composing his cabinet, Wilson passed over the nominees urged by conservationists and western developers and instead appointed Californian Lane to lead the Department of the Interior. He did this in order, writes Link, "to steer a middle course between the extreme conservationists and an anti-conservationist coalition of Westerners and spokesmen of private interests." Link's description of Wilson's rationale suggests Wilson saw himself not as a conservationist but as something better—a moderate between extremes.

The Hetch Hetchy decision had been almost inevitable. The idea of creating a new bureau to manage the national parks, housed in the Department of the Interior, had Secretary Lane's support, of course, and he convinced Chicago conservationist Mather to come to Washington to lead the lobbying effort, which he did brilliantly, hiring a publicist who helped place more than 1,000 articles about the parks in national magazines as the legislation came to a vote. In August 1916, the National Park Service Organic Act was signed by Wilson without a statement. The new National Park Service (NPS) had been created within the Interior Department and "the fundamental purpose" of the national parks defined to be:

> To create a Service to be called the National Park Service (which) . . . shall promote and regulate the use of federal areas known as national parks, monuments, and reservations, whose fundamental purpose [is to] conserve the scenery and the natural and historic objects and the wildlife therein and to provide for the enjoyment of the same in such manner and by such means as will leave them unimpaired for the enjoyment of future generations.[12]

TR would have approved, except that by 1916 he approved of nothing Wilson did. But in this measure Wilson was doing his part to continue the TR project. It was good to create parks, but not enough. They needed firm management and appropriate goals, and now these were written into a law. Was the primary emphasis in the National Park Service Organic Act and its legislative history on the words "conserve the scenery . . . and wildlife . . . unimpaired for the enjoyment of future generations," or the words "use and enjoyment" and promoting "public recreation and public health"? Historians debate this, but there was language justifying a "preservation" tilt as well as a "use" tilt, and now that would be decided by the NPS managers (Mather was made first director) and future directors, along with Congress. Having the NPS in charge of all parks was a necessary step, though time would reveal that it only moved environmental problems on the public lands into a new phase. Automaker Henry Ford began to turn out his inexpensive (at $300) Model-T car in 1913 and sold 500,000 in the first year. People were coming to the parks, and the "enjoyment" goal would begin a long conflict in the national parks, forests, and monuments with the other promise to "conserve the scenery . . . and wildlife unimpaired." When Wilson signed the act in 1916, the Department of the Interior oversaw fourteen national parks, twenty-one national monuments, and the Arkansas Hot Springs and Casa Grande Ruin Reservations. Only Acadia National Park in Maine lay east of the Mississippi River.

Wilson had shown little interest in either Hetch Hetchy or the effort to give the national parks a clear mission and bureaucratic headquarters, but he had lined up with, if not offered leadership to, these battles inherited from the days of TR. Tougher fights were ahead because the conservationist impulse to manage rather than give away the public lands forced the government—and therefore whoever was president next after Taft—to take a position on two contentious fronts: mineral and water-power policy on the remaining public lands. On both issues the stakes were high and started with the possibility of monopoly control of minerals and hydroelectric power, a major theme of concern among conservationists and progressive politicians. Perhaps more important, anticonservationists—who had not come up with a name for themselves and still have not—remained unreconciled to the core idea of the conservation crusade: the public lands and their resources must not be given away or cheaply sold anymore but should be retained for the entire public and exposed to human uses only under close protective management. By the end of the Taft administration western politicians and writers were with increasing zeal challenging the very concept of federal natural resource management, an issue by no means settled. "States' rights" sentiment, often expressed by southerners, seemed to be strengthening also in the West, and a recurring coalition of "Southern reactionaries and . . . [Western] turkey buzzards," in the words of prominent conservationist William Kent, was expected to mount a campaign when Wilson took office not only to write probusiness language into new mineral and water-power legislation but to turn over all decision making and perhaps the public lands themselves to the states. Wilson, the first southern president since Andrew Johnson, ran in 1912 on a Democratic platform that promised "respect" for "states' rights." To anticonservationists it seemed a good time to repeal all the radical preservationist changes in public land law made since Benjamin Harrison, all the while discrediting the ideas and values behind it.

The record Wilson (and Lane) made on these inherited issues is complex and stretched over both his presidential terms. Mineral (especially oil and coal) leasing decisions were a familiar though tangled topic inviting bitter and legalistic struggle, as Ballinger and Taft had learned. Conservationists desired leasing policies that did not allow monopoly control by one or a handful of big extractors, were for limited periods and revocable, and brought the public a good price. Their instinct was to conserve the underground mineral deposits for the future because plenty of oil remained under private property in the United States. They condemned industry's wasteful methods without much idea of how to curb them. Pollution from mining and drilling was not yet a concern. Extractive industries wanted maximum freedom to exploit these "locked-up" resources, which meant sale at cheap prices, leases without ending dates or recapture provisions, and no fees.

Nobody liked the existing mineral-resource laws, and Taft had unsuccessfully urged Congress more than once to write new and clearer laws on the use of the public lands. Wilson and Lane faced a similar situation, and the two Wilson terms were legislative and lobbying battlegrounds without decisive victory. The general public was hard put to follow the details or grasp the larger picture despite commendable coverage by national magazines, such as Colliers Weekly, Harpers, and Outlook. The general public, even most conservationists, then as now, was more easily aroused by the abuse of animals, such as the Yellowstone buffalo and the birds in forest and flyway, than coal and phosphate mines in the public domain. Two conservationist organizations, however, closely followed these controversies—the National Conservation Congress, based in Seattle, and the Pinchot-founded National Conservation Association, ably led by Harry Slattery as secretary and listing as board members former Harvard president Charles W. Eliot and an array of reform celebrities such as Jane Addams, Samuel Gompers, Carrie Chapman Catt, and Ben Lindsey, a judge.

Secretary Lane pledged in his first annual report to work for a conservationist mineral-leasing policy, and US House legislation embodying these views was blocked by the US Senate. A long stalemate ensued. Wilson, who on at least one occasion (in summer 1914) summoned all parties to a White House conference (that produced no resolution), seemed soon after this to have given up on a new, conservationist-tilted mineral-leasing law. His December 1914 State of the Union Address briefly complained about this deadlock without explaining it, or the stakes involved, to the public: "We should have acted; and they [the ores, forests, and water power] are still locked up." These words may have been written by Lane, for they spoke of resources "locked up" beyond the reach of "thousands of vigorous men, full of initiative, [who] knock clamorously for admittance." Wilson in that message indicated (without details) his support for two House measures he hoped the Senate would accept and spoke vigorously about the benefits of resource unlocking so that "vigorous men" from "great industries" could make "economical and profitable use" of them, the "rights of the public being adequately guarded the while, and monopoly in the use prevented." This was Wilson's most visible effort to explain what was at stake in the complex dispute over the regulation of access to minerals on the public lands. He seems to have felt no personal interest in all this, and his mind moved to other matters. When he finally signed a mineral-leasing law in 1920, the declaration of conservationist victory by Lane claimed too much for this cloudy and flawed statute.

The other arena of protracted conflict was the disposition of water-power sites on public lands, soon broadening to sites on all major rivers. Hydroelectric power companies wanted leasing authority given to the states, where they knew they had a political advantage. They also demanded the longest and most lenient terms, that is, no regulation of their rates and no charge for the lease. Conservationists began by wanting clear federal regulation on sites within the public domain but in the Wilson years began to insist on controlling access to sites on all navigable waterways in the nation. Federal authorities, they argued, should be empowered to prevent monopoly pricing of electricity rates on power generated at these sites, issue revocable permits, and charge fees reflecting the real value of sites the public was releasing for a specified (and not too long) period of use.

Assumed to be speaking for Wilson, Lane staked out his guiding principles in his first annual report and in a series of magazine interviews, planting one leg on facilitating electric power development by private company lessees and another leg on federal regulation of interstate rates and prohibition of monopoly. To this he mixed in some Wilsonian music, intoning, "We must keep the individual free." Over the next seven years of wearying conflict on the Hill and his own policy positions as interior secretary about water-power sites, Lane veered back and forth between extractive corporate "users" and conservationists, but the middle ground was always shifting. The House and Senate were stalemated for years, and in 1916 Wilson seemed to have lost interest in the issue.

In April 1917 the United States went to war, and Wilson took a renewed interest in hydroelectric power, essential to defense production. He called a White House conference of legislators over the Christmas holidays in 1917, and soon an "administration bill" emerged with three bold innovations—federal jurisdiction over power sites on all navigable waterways, the new federal Water Power Commission to oversee leasing and regulation, and—the seeds of the Tennessee Valley Authority (TVA)—authority for the government to develop electric power on its own initiative. This proposal attracted considerable congressional support in wartime that would have been unthinkable earlier. Yet legislative maneuvering went on until spring 1920, when a bill finally went to Wilson's desk. Should he sign? "He had both lost and won," wrote conservationist Judson King. The proposed Water Power Commission was a poorly staffed and part-time body, the fees charged to private companies a pittance. However, "the door was left open for public development," and federal jurisdiction of all navigable rivers was affirmed. Louise Peffer in The Closing of the Public Domain goes a bit further. The mineral-leasing and water-power laws represented the end of a struggle over fundamentals and "acceptance of a major part of Roosevelt's conservation program."[13] Wilson signed the Federal Water Power Act of 1920 in June, joining other conservationists in steering water-power policy past the threat of capitulation to control by the states.

WILSON'S CONSERVATIONIST PERFORMANCE?

How to assess Wilson's performance on these leading public-lands and other natural-resource issues? Link, who usually finds his man on the righteous side of most issues, wrote that "both Wilson and Lane stood firm in support of the principle of national ownership and control" on mineral and water-power leasing. Lane, he concluded, made "important contributions toward the maturing of progressive policies for Alaska, water power, and western resources in general" (whatever "maturing" means).[14] A leading historian of US oil policy, John Ise, comes to a different conclusion: "A fair argument might be built up to show that he [Lane] was one of the most dangerous men that have ever held the office of Secretary of the Interior, because, while he was working persistently to promote the end of exploiting interests, he was writing articles on conservation."[15] Lane biographer Keith W. Olson depicts the secretary as a patient, honest broker but one with a decidedly "utilitarian bent." The implication is that we should enthusiastically permit somebody to use the resources while making nice about vigilance against monopoly power. In an address at Brown University in 1916, Lane was uncharacteristically blunt about his conception of nature, whether on private or public land: "Every tree is a challenge to us, and every pool of water and every foot of soil. The mountains are our enemies. We must pierce them and make them serve. The sinful rivers we must curb."[16]

However one judges Lane's seven-year conduct of Wilsonian public land policies and legislative lobbying, it is hard to defend a blunder the president made all by himself. The federal government had edged into a role in the development of inland waterways as early as 1824, when the Army Corps of Engineers was assigned to keep the rivers and bays navigable. TR and his friends loathed the fragmented, shortsighted, pork-barrel system for making federal decisions about things as interconnected as river systems from ridgetops to ocean, and they dreamed of an agency that might plan for multipurpose waterways development—navigation, flood control, power-plant siting, reforestation. Their Inland Waterways Commission, established to brainstorm this concept and perhaps evolve into such a planning unit, was killed by Congress in 1905, which preferred pork-barrel decision making in legislative committees. Conservationists persisted and surprised even themselves by creating a new Inland Waterways Commission in 1917, owing to the leadership of Senator Francis G. Newlands. This had not been on Wilson's mind or daily calendar and, when it came to his desk, pressed by wartime duties, he neglected to appoint the commissioners and the legislation expired. The Water Power Act of 1920 abolished the unstaffed commission, Congress at the end of the Wilson years confirming, in the words of a foremost historian of natural resources policy in those years, Donald Swain, the "haphazard, disorganized program" of inland waterway development in place when Wilson arrived in Washington, D.C.[17]

There is a pattern here in which for eight years Wilson, a superb public educator eager to lead, accepted without much comment the established environmental agenda formed by his progressive predecessor, TR. He appointed an interior secretary who talked like a conservationist and a developer at the same time but whose actions and unpublicized comments sided with extractive corporations. Wilson signed the natural-resource policy acts that came to him. Two he had little to do with—the 1916 act establishing the national park management regime and important waterfowl protection measures.

The latter were driven forward by a coalition led by Audubon and the American Game Protection and Propagation Association and had overwhelming public support. A migratory bird protection law signed by Taft as he left office was acknowledged to be of doubtful constitutionality, leading to the 1916 Migratory Bird Treaty between the United States and Great Britain (so Canada could be covered) and the 1918 Migratory Bird Treaty Act ending spring hunting and prohibiting all hunting of a list of endangered birds. Wilson signed it but played no role in bringing it forward.

We notice that Wilson's role was primarily to sign the legislative results of battles in Congress between conservation-minded forces and what might be called the "use it now" crowd. He did almost no persuading of the public or of legislators on environmental issues with the exception of his brief engagement with congressional leaders in the water-power-site issue. Remarkably, seven of his eight State of the Union Addresses had nothing at all to say on any conservation topic. We have already commented on the indecisive three paragraphs in his 1914 message on mineral policy on public lands.

Could it be said that this somewhat passive but in the end cautiously cooperative positioning on conservation matters of the two-term Wilson administration was dictated and justified by the weakness of conservationists in the national political arena? The argument would run like this: Wilson did the best he could do under the political circumstances and considering how many other important matters, including national security, crowded his schedule.

There can be no questioning of the issue-intensity of the Wilson presidency, beginning with a progressive reform program and ending with involvement in a world war. Whatever your cause and your complaint about Wilson's handling of it, all must acknowledge that history gave him more to do, and more of grave import, than any president since Lincoln. But was the conservation cause, after Taft's fumbling and with TR in ill health, so weakened that Wilson's performance seems the best that could have been managed under the circumstances? Historian Samuel Hays, in his influential book on conservation in its early decades, voiced the opinion that conservation as a movement "disintegrated" when TR handed power to Taft and left town.[18]

This is quite the wrong term because much evidence points the other way. Birder societies, led by Audubon, were growing and politically active. The preservationist forces showed remarkable staying power and innovative lobbying techniques in staving off the decision to dam Hetch Hetchy from 1903 to 1913. Pinchot, Slattery, and their colleagues in the National Conservation Association were aggressively engaged in the mineral and water-power fights. Link seems closer to the mark when he concludes that, in the Wilson years, "the conservationists were one of the most vocal and powerful minorities in the country."[19] There is support for this view in the party platforms of these years. Four parties contested the 1912 election, and all their platforms affirmed their own version of the Democrats' statement that "we believe in the conservation and the development, for the use of all the people, of the natural resources of the country." All party platforms through the Wilson years and into the 1920s lined themselves up with conservation understood as development without waste and vigilance against monopoly. All parties declared in brief sections on conservation that they heartily favored it. This language was an every-four-year brief nod to the popularity of conservation in US society.

Wilson, like the other presidents we have discussed, did not face a well-organized and intellectually coherent anticonservationist argument or faction. From the West, and to some degree the South, came angry complaints that development was being stifled and states' rights infringed. These ran deep emotionally but were not yet intellectually formidable. No anticonservationist text or tract or theorist emerged. Conservationists were denounced as "socialists," grumbling that came from Taft (and many others) more than once—hardly an effective counterattack. Conservation in these years was both intellectually and politically a formidable movement, even if a somewhat internally at odds bundle of ideas and sentiments. Anticonservationism was not only intellectually immature, it lacked an organizing label. Of course, all presidents in that era had to reckon with vigorous opposition to forest and park reserves and wildlife refuges mounted by influential users of forests, minerals, grasslands, but the anticonservationist lobbies were not

yet intellectually formidable. They were merely angry and fairly well organized around their traditional access to the unappropriated lands to the west
of the Mississippi (and everywhere else), which for some individuals meant
traditional and deeply cherished hunting rights and to others in corporations dreams of wealth ripped out of the earth by their workers.

WILSON IN PERSPECTIVE: LUCKY IN HIS SUCCESSORS

Historians who rank presidents on overall performance routinely give Wilson high marks. This is based on his progressive reform activism capped by
his internationalist educational efforts, which his parochial country much
needed in a time of the first global war. Also to Wilson's credit, historians
say, was his vigorous seconding of TR's demonstration that the modern
president, with his unique position as the only leader elected by the whole
people, adds to the US political system an element named by Michael
Uhlmann "proactive government's innovator in chief." Had Wilson followed
TR the contrast of the two would, for many citizens and president rankers,
have made Wilson seem the less energetic and history making of the two.
However, he followed the lethargic Taft and was himself followed by two
men of almost peculiar and certainly memorable inarticulation and incurios-
ity. Wilson, in that company, stands out for his verbal gifts and a leadership
instinct that led him to a positive role in the mainstream progressive causes:
monopoly power, income distribution, banking reform, and—very late—
women's suffrage. His strong oral performance earned him an image far
more positive than the presidents by whom he was bookended, but when we
lift the environmental performance out of his admittedly busy eight years,
we find his handling of green issues cautious and reactive. He consistently
expressed, though on infrequent occasions, his support for various pieces of
the conservationist agenda he had inherited and signed major laws on the
NPS, migratory bird protection, mineral leasing, and water power shaped by
others. Although the conservation movement showed signs of intellectual or
policy leadership in the Wilson years, its members were not to be found in
the administration but in organizations such as Pinchot's National Conservation Congress, the National Audubon Society and other birder groups, or
in the senate offices of midwestern progressives such as George Norris of
Nebraska and Robert LaFollette of Wisconsin.

There are grounds for a sense of disappointment here that one does not feel when acknowledging the modest and limited leadership performance, say, of Harrison. The presidency in the two decades after Harrison had become a more active element within federal governance, mostly because of TR's performance. Wilson, too, was eager to lead his country and had enviable rhetorical and intellectual gifts. The conservation movement was diverse and active, though admittedly anchored in the populous East with little mobilization in the South and a largely hostile West. Wilson usually lined up with the conservationists in the end, for conservation was a progressive cause and he was a progressive. Yet his heart was not in it, nor in any sustained way was his mind, and as a result he did not in conservation matters go beyond cooperating to innovating. He corresponded with some conservationists, such as William Kent of California and his own secretary of the navy, Josephus Daniels, but he never gave his ear or opened his counsel to any conservationist as TR had done in tennis matches or late evenings at the White House or in his hike into the Sierras with Muir. Wilson remained a cooperator, not an innovator, within the conservationist project. He had signed on and was ready to sign the legislation when others created the moment.

What might have carried Wilson to higher achievement? Public education from the bully pulpit and some role in pushing the agenda ahead could have been his legacy. Wilson was an educator by instinct and training, but this gifted verbalist was no teacher on matters of natural-resource protection. Teaching and policy innovation in matters of natural resources come from lieutenants brought into the policy circle of the president and from the staff professionals and radical amateurs below. Here Wilson chose to be isolated. TR, a man full of fresh ideas, was open to being tutored and guided by Pinchot, George Bird Grinnell, Frederick Newall, W. J. McGee. When Wilson's turn came he seemed closed off to policy intellectuals and especially to the influence of a growing component of conservationism, women, who were beginning to rise to positions of prominence in the conservationist social movement.

TR was, all of his life, a "male chauvinist," in the language of the 1960s—a conventional male of that day, who adored his two wives and liked women in general in their traditional place. Wilson was the same, except more so, for he was a southern male. Conservationist lieutenants in TR's day had seemed to be all male, but by the year Wilson took office, the conservationist movement had some remarkably talented and assertive females, and some of them brought not just their individual talents but also a broader conception of conservation. One thinks of Marjory Stoneman Douglas, a 1912 Wellesley graduate who moved to Miami in 1915 after a divorce and, as society editor of her father's *Miami Herald*, quickly turned her columns and stories into a grassroots crusade against politicians, farmers, and developers bringing a habitat-killing "growth and development" to her beloved Everglades. Or Mary Austin, Illinois college graduate and class poet who moved to the Owens Valley in California, became fascinated with the land and people of the arid Southwest, and wrote widely noted science-based nature essays and an influential 1903 book, *A Land of Little Rain*. Or recall Alice Hamilton, a resident and volunteer at Jane Addams's Hull House in Chicago who, after attending medical school, began to investigate and write about the occupational hazards to which workers were exposed in certain industries. Appointed a special investigator in the US Department of Labor in 1911, her published research on the risks of illness and death faced by workers in lead mines, mills, and smelters gained her respect as an informed crusader for public health. She became the first female faculty member at Harvard Medical School in 1919, where she wrote her classic textbook, *Industrial Poisons in the United States* (1925). Historian Robert Gottlieb rightly called Hamilton the "first great urban/industrial environmentalist" in the nation because she was at the head of a growing number of reformers for whom the hazards of the urban and workplace environment deserved at least as much attention as forests and wildlife.[20]

Hamilton was a scientist, and Douglas evolved into a self-taught ecologist. They were female conservationist rising lieutenants, opening up new agendas for conservation. Wilson looked elsewhere for the new leaders he hoped to mobilize in order to revitalize the country. Link tells us that, while teaching at Bryn Mawr, Wilson wrote friends that he disliked teaching women because they threatened to relax his "mental muscles." He welcomed a move to Wesleyan University in 1888 because he was "hungry for a class of men."[21] Clements tells us that when the future president spoke of calling people to national service, he explicitly meant "college-bred men," "liberally trained college graduates" with the vision necessary to guide a modern democracy. In Wilson's defense, his male-only selection of lieutenants and idea sources was inherited from all the presidents before him, but times were changing, even in Wilson's Washington. The only other president after TR to offer memorable leadership on the environment was an assistant secretary of the US Navy in 1917 when Hamilton came to his office and appealed for permission to make trouble for the government by inspecting the production site and internal records of some navy munitions plants. Franklin D. Roosevelt (FDR) heard her out and then ordered a very reluctant admiral to escort Hamilton to the site and give her the necessary access. FDR's presidency (1933–1945) would later demonstrate, among other things, that political leaders who hope to put together above-average performances on the environment (or anything else) raise their odds by enlisting female as well as male lieutenants.[22]

THE 1920S: A BAD TIME FOR SOCIAL REFORM, INCLUDING CONSERVATION?

Involvement in the Great War (it was not called World War I until later) briefly energized the social introspection and reform energies awakened during the Progressive Era in the United States. Yet in the long term war mobilization depleted and fragmented those energies. A new cycle of US politics began as a physically impaired Wilson was replaced in the White House in March 1921 by the handpicked, safe, likable, presidential-looking but otherwise unimpressive Republican senator from Ohio, Warren G. Harding. The pendulum of politics and social sentiment was swinging to the right, toward a renewed confidence in the nineteenth-century faith that "leaving capitalism alone" was the best formula for social progress. In the Progressive Era reformers had increasingly looked to governments, at all levels, as a force to remedy the social problems of a rapidly industrializing society. The 1920s would be shaped by a tilt in attitude back toward trust in the material advances "big business" could bring when turned loose from recent and ill-advised governmental scrutiny and regulation.

In such a time, with no sense of a mobilizing national crisis, we should not expect much exceptionable achievement from political leadership from any quarter, certainly not from any president the US political system would nominate and the electorate select. Leadership would come from the captains of industry, banking, mass marketing, entertainment. The decade after the war was a political time congenial to nineteenth-century, premodern, passive presidents.

So the political system brought forward Harding and Calvin Coolidge, men of inactive and self-limiting conceptions of the presidency. They expressed no pleasure or sense of challenge at finding in the workload of the White House and a handful of other agencies around Washington a cluster of problems and remedies called conservation, that new thing Collier's Weekly in 1909 had called "an unwieldy phrase but a live wire."[23]

TR died in 1919, and when the political machinery elevated Harding and Coolidge, we might have expected conservation's many impulses to wither for lack of leadership. Not so. Conservation was a multifaceted reform movement that did not wait for presidents but internally generated leadership of many kinds while hoping, always, for clarifying, direction-pointing people at the helm. Given the reality that TR was gone and the White House in the 1920s was occupied by the twentieth-century equivalents of James A. Garfield and Harrison's grandfather, conservationists moved ahead on one of TR's favorite causes—wildlife protection.

SAVING WILDLIFE

When the conservation movement came together in the 1880s and 1890s it was, simply put, an unplanned convergence of the forestry elites Pinchot had led for so long and the larger US public uprising against the killing off of wildlife. The latter had been stirred by the near disappearance of the eastern deer, beaver, and otter and the western elk, antelope, and bighorn sheep, whose declining numbers stunned TR on visits to his Dakota ranch. Most dismaying of all was the mindless slaughter of bison. The buffalo herd in Yellowstone shrank to a pathetic twenty-five animals at the opening of the twentieth century.

Yet as time went by, the emotional center of the conservationist rebellion against wildlife slaughter and extermination shifted to the birders, the National Audubon Society forming up for battle late in the nineteenth century in order to combat the killing of birds for plumage or meat or fun. The bird protectors were more numerous than the foresters and were organized all across the nation. They were therefore more politically formidable, especially when lobbying for state hunting regulations. When state bird-protection laws proved too weak or poorly enforced to curb the appetite of plume hunters, restaurants, and recreational hunters, the bird conservationists pushed through Congress the Lacey Act in 1900, prohibiting interstate traffic in birds killed in violation of state laws. This landmark statute owed most to two men, not to any president. US representative and birder John F. Lacey from Iowa rallied a congressional majority, New York ornithologist William Dutcher mobilized birder citizens, Governor Theodore Roosevelt cheered from the sidelines, and President McKinley signed the bill into law.

When enforcement was woefully underfunded the Audubon chapters offered volunteer wardens. Bird protectors were the most active political force within conservationism through the 1910s and 1920s, successfully banning the importation of the plumage of all wild birds, then in the Migratory Bird Act giving the US Biological Survey jurisdiction over all migratory birds, resulting in a prohibition on spring shooting and season bag limits (though generous) on ducks and geese. Despite such measures of protection the plight of the country's game birds seemed to get worse because of a combination of habitat destruction, lack of enforcement of state and federal regulation of hunting, and the sheer increase in hunters, whose numbers (those purchasing a license) doubled to 6 million from 1910 to 1920. By the third decade of the century the trumpeter swan population was counted at thirty-three birds, the whooping crane twenty-seven birds, and the California condor down to fewer than a hundred. Martha, the last passenger pigeon, died in the Cincinnati Zoo in 1914, followed soon by Incas, the last Carolina parakeet.

For good reason, then, the birder conservationists entered the 1920s more angry, more numerous, and better organized than ever, and apparently nobody had told them that the 1920s would not be a decade for reform causes. Although Audubon's leadership was increasingly criticized by some of its younger members for too much emphasis on bird-count outings and a willingness to accept large donations from ammunition-maker Remington Arms Company, a surge of bird-protection energy came into the movement in the 1920s. The formidable and combative zoologist William Hornaday, director of the New York Zoological Society, wrote his best-selling *Our Vanishing Wildlife* in 1913; then, disgusted with the lack of a sense of urgency from the Audubon leadership, raised funds from Ford, Mrs. Russell Sage, Andrew Carnegie, and others for his own organization, the Wildlife Protection Fund. From this base Hornaday tirelessly criticized the Biological Survey as a bureaucracy administering an unwise tolerance of hunting in all wildlife refuges as a result of lobbying by organized ammunition and gun manufacturers.

Hornaday's passion and sense of urgency were matched elsewhere in the 1920s. Out of the Midwest came Chicago outdoor sportswriter Will H. Dilg, an ardent fisherman who sensed and organized an unsuspected public concern about wildlife. "I am weary of civilization's madness," he wrote, "and I yearn for the harmonious gladness of the woods and the streams. . . . I feel jailed in your greatest cities, and I long for the unharnessed freedom of the big outside."[24] He launched the Izaak Walton League in 1922 to lobby Congress for the stupendous sum of $1.5 million to buy private bottomland on both banks of 260 miles of the upper Mississippi River to prevent further levying and drainage and establish a fish and wildlife refuge, the first on the Mississippi flyway. In just three years the league mushroomed to 3,000 chapters in forty-three states; its journal, *Outdoor America*, reached more than 100,000 members at a time when the Sierra Club claimed 7,000. The league not only quickly became the largest conservation organization but gained a reputation for intense member involvement and a remarkable sense of urgency about wildlife protection.

Thus the conservationist social movement if anything gained vigor in the 1920s and thrust several other of its themes and concerns into national discussion in the years following the war. The two newly formed forest and park federal regulatory bureaucracies and their missions flourished, though there were turf battles and internal disputes behind the scenes. The NPS, under the entrepreneurial director and former Chicago businessman Mather, vigorously promoted the national parks with free publicity-gaining park "safaris" for leading politicians and media editors and writers and pressed Congress for rapid expansion of tourist facilities and roads. Park visitation surged from less than 1 million in 1916 to 3.7 million by 1933. This popularity was a success that brought with it a related set of problems. Automobile owners constituted 1 in 265 US citizens in 1910 but 1 in 5 by 1929, and their mobility brought trampling, polluting crowds to the parks, sanitation problems, and both accidental and arsonist fire. Robert Sterling Yard and his National Parks Association launched a campaign for fewer roads and some sort of restraint on access to the more pristine and remote park regions, reminiscent of Muir and the Hetch Hetchy battle, again. The NFS, under pressure from railroads, concessionaires, and the fast-growing outdoor recreation industry, also expanded roads and tourist facilities and experienced internal criticism from those—such as the still-engaged Pinchot—who thought the service was drifting from its original mission of forest protection, restoration, and research.

Here was an emerging pattern of bureaucratic evolution unforeseen by

TR and Pinchot and the founders of the idea of permanently reserved and protected public lands. The lead resource-management agencies, NPS and USFS, increasingly had the look of little subgovernments closely linked to and heavily influenced by their own organized constituencies—recreation-oriented industries along with, in the case of the USFS, the timber and wood-product industries. Ranchers in the West successfully lobbied Congress to fund expansion of predator- and pest-control programs. In 1915 the Biological Survey took over the small USFS programs, and there was no immediate controversy when the agency undertook to eradicate "bad" wildlife, such as the coyote. Bounties for killing predators went back to the colonial era and persisted in some states. Conservationists raised no objections to this federal activity at first, sharing the public view that there were "bad" as well as "good" species—"varmints" such as the wolf, coyote, mountain lion, and prairie dog, who threatened livestock. So the Biological Survey's predator-control programs using traps, poison, and hunting expanded, enthusiastically promoted by farmers, sheepherders, cattle raisers, and others, mostly in the West. They came to think of the Biological Survey and to a lesser extent the NFS as free, taxpayer-funded extermination services. In the 1920s, a handful of scientists inside both agencies began to question the scientific and moral basis for predator control.

This growing influence over the new conservation bureaucracies wielded by aggressive special interest groups with their own strongly negative attitudes toward certain wildlife did not have a name in the 1920s. Fifty years later some student of public administration in the United States called it "clientele capture" and correctly ranked it as a huge, foundational problem the early conservationists (and many others) had not anticipated. How could the common good in public land and wildlife management come out of the behind-the-scenes lobbying of resource-management agencies by today's resource users, who had no thought of the next generation? TR would surely have responded that the president speaks for the whole public and must lead government agencies to pursue the common good. Pinchot would have responded that trained experts in professional agencies would always aim at the common good. Neither of these conservationist founders nor their allies had given much thought to the problems of clientele capture of the infant regulatory agencies they had just established. Sufficient unto the day is the evil thereof.

Thus the 1920s brought not only a worsening of familiar environmental problems along with new ones but also new questions about the functioning of the young conservation administrative apparatus, perhaps constructed with naive zeal.

WARREN G. HARDING

Who was Warren Harding? He was born, and raised for a time, on a midwestern farm, though his father was a country doctor who moved the family to a small Ohio town and bought a local newspaper. Harding learned enough of the newspaper trade to publish his own for a time, after a brief stint at a small local college and a short period studying law. He was elected to the Ohio Senate in 1899, became lieutenant governor from 1903 to 1905, then was elected to the US Senate in 1915, where he missed two-thirds of the roll-call votes. Climbing this political ladder, he proved at every stage to be handsome and likable, with no strong views on anything in particular. He impressed Republican Party managers when he gave the nominating speech for Taft in 1912. They broke a stalemate between three contenders for the GOP nomination in 1920 by picking Harding in the proverbial smoke-filled room in a Washington hotel, sensing that he would spring on them no surprises. In other words, he would not lead.

Harding campaigned mostly from the front porch of his Marion, Ohio, home, where 600,000 Americans traveled to meet his passive self and hear him repeat his main campaign theme, the need "for a return to normalcy." Harding prided himself on his speechmaking, but his assets in this role seem to have been mostly his bearing and appearance. The words that came from him were another matter. Take for example a sentence from his acceptance speech at the Republican National Convention: "I would like the government to do all it can to mitigate, then, in understanding, in mutuality of interest, in concern for the common good, our tasks will be solved." It did not take much of such tortured language to turn many contemporaries into disdainful critics. His speeches, commented former treasury secretary William Gibbs McAdoo, were "an army of pompous phrases moving over the landscape in search of an idea." Writer H. L. Mencken said of Harding's speeches that they "remind me of a string of wet sponges," to which he attached the label "Gamalielese." These scornful contemporaries could not have read Harding's love letters to Carrie Phillips, released in 2014 with little potential to elevate his reputation: "I love to suck / your breath away / I love to cling / there long to stay."[25] The *New York Times* pronounced Harding a "very respectable Ohio politician of the second class"; the *New Republic* called him a "party hack . . . without strength of character." He was elected president by a landslide with 60 percent of the vote. Women had voted nationwide for the first time. The US political system has rarely functioned with less energy and civic vision.

What might conservationists expect of him, based on the record? There were no grounds for hope. Harding had no interest in the outdoors and was poorly and narrowly educated. He and his wife visited Yellowstone on their honeymoon, but biographer Francis Russell reports that "at heart he preferred the even, unspectacular Ohio landscape to this jagged region of bubbling hot springs, foaming waterfalls, and erupting geysers set against the aloof background of the mountains."

The Republican platform in 1920 was hardly distinguishable from the Democratic one with respect to conservation matters in that both contained the brief and meaningless "we are for wise use of our resources" formulaic language on conservation that both major parties had been inserting in their platforms for a decade. The 1920 campaign shed no light on conservationist issues because Harding never addressed any part of that agenda, nor did his opponent, James Cox, also of Ohio. Harding said he was for protective tariffs, a big navy, lower taxes, and immigration restriction. In other words, he was a mainstream Republican. On Wilson's idea of the League of Nations it was impossible to tell where Harding stood. There was one surprise in his campaign self-presentation, a courageous one. He urged a federal antilynching law, better protection of the constitutional rights of "Negroes," and the appointment of more of them to federal posts. After being elected, he addressed Congress in April 1921 and asked for all of these things. He included a short paragraph endorsing the "wise use" of our natural resources.

It seemed Harding was fated to spend four (or eight) years ignoring the conservation agenda, which was at this point, at least in Washington, D.C., a series of running battles over wildfowl protection and grazing rights on the public domain in which presidential support would have been welcomed. He made a good start of ignoring conservation except when he got it wrong, saying in his first State of the Union Address in 1921 that reclamation by irrigation was bringing the government attractive royalties when the program had for some time been attacked for being underfunded and mismanaged.

In his second State of the Union Address he ignored conservation issues entirely, educating the public with the presidential judgment, "I know of no problem exceeding in importance this one of transportation."[26]

However, ignoring the natural-resource-protection agenda was not to be the memorable contribution of Harding's administration, negative as that would have been. On Harding's watch, however, worse was coming. For he appointed Senator Albert B. Fall as secretary of the Department of the Interior, and a fuse started burning on one of the larger public land scandals in US history. Fall, a New Mexico rancher who dressed the part from boots through thin cigar to broad-brimmed Stetson hat, was a capable and interesting character but an astonishingly stupid choice for interior secretary. His views on conservation were entirely negative and well known. In 1912, and perhaps on other occasions, he was quoted as being convinced that the best place for public lands was in private hands. He was also in debt, in arrears on taxes, and hard-pressed to keep up his ranch at Three Rivers, New Mexico. Wheels were in motion to take care of that, because the secretary of the interior had valuable public goods to sell or give away.

The oil beneath western public lands was increasingly valuable as the auto age began and the US Navy converted from using coal to oil. Wilson's secretary of the navy, Daniels, conducted a steady campaign to minimize and delay leases to private corporations wanting to drill into navy-controlled oil reserves. He won from Congress the authority to administer the naval reserves in Elk Hill and Buena Vista in California and the Teapot Dome reserves in Wyoming solely for the benefit of the navy and national security. In a sharp reversal unannounced to the public, Harding's navy secretary, Edwin Denby, joined with Secretary Fall in asking the president to give the Interior Department control of all oil leasing from public lands. Harding agreed in writing, and Fall promptly granted leases to private corporations, without public bidding, in the three naval reserves. The leases went to Fall's friends Edward Doheny of Pan-American Petroleum and Harry Sinclair of Mammoth Petroleum Company. For months there was no coverage in the press of this apparently legal transaction, but rumors that Fall's ranch was undergoing expensive improvements and that he was buying adjacent property (on his salary of $12,000 as secretary) alarmed suspicious conservationists. "The smell of money was in the air" wrote Harding biographer Robert K. Murray.

A congressional inquiry ground on for more than two years, revealing that Doheny and Sinclair had given Fall approximately $400,000 and a herd of blooded cattle. Fall was eventually convicted (on one count—cleared on others) and served nine months in prison, the first cabinet officer to so distinguish himself. Sinclair also did prison time. Concurrently, evidence of scandals seeped out from the offices and drinking haunts on K Street of Attorney General Harry Daugherty—whose pals in the "Ohio Gang" sold immunity from prosecution, pardons, and paroles—and from the Veterans Bureau, where the director was found to have accepted bribes.

Harding proved to have no personal involvement in any of this cascading corruption other than appointing the people involved, but months of media broadcasts on scandal stories from inside his administration burdened his spirits and increased his sense that the presidency was too much for him. "I have no trouble with my enemies," he told a journalist friend, "but my damned friends, my God-damned friends, White, they're the ones that keep me walking the floor nights."[27] "I am not fit for this office and never should have been here," he told Nicholas Murray Butler, president of Columbia University.[28] Exhausted and not in good health though only 59, Harding set out on a rail tour of the Pacific Northwest with a brief detour to Alaska, became ill as his train left Seattle for San Francisco, and died on August 2, 1923, probably of heart failure.

HARDING AND THE US ENVIRONMENT

One is tempted to say because Harding offered no detectable leadership on conservation, he should be put down as "Abs" for Absent. But even the hands-off presidents of the 1920s could no longer avoid some sort of mixture of inaction and action on the small but persistent list of conservation issues that broke into the national media and congressional discussions— among them mineral management on the public lands and wildlife and especially migratory bird protection, over which vigorous policy debates churned throughout the 1920s. Inaction and amiable ignorance rank his leadership performance as an F for failure.

Are there degrees of "F," with Harding an F+? He (or his wife, always his most vigorous defender) might point out from the afterlife that one published bibliography on his presidency contains almost two pages of articles on natural-resource issues. Yet all of them have to do with activities of his commerce secretary, Herbert Hoover, none of them significant (as we shall see when reviewing the Hoover presidency) or urged by Harding. Was there a flicker of green awakening in Harding, at the end? On his western swing in the last weeks of his life, he allowed Hoover to write the speech he gave (his last) in Seattle, and it contained more than the president had ever said on conservation. His delivery was halting, and at one point he dropped the pages to the floor, where Hoover recovered them. Harding was within hours of collapse, using his last hours to finally express some interest in resources on the public lands, in words written by his commerce secretary.

With this end-of-life exception, Harding essentially failed to participate in the natural-resource policy discussions of the 1920s. His two State of the Union Addresses contained brief boilerplate language written, doubtlessly, by the Interior Department; lifelessly reported on royalties to the government from mineral leasing (1921); and announced (1922) that reclamation projects "are worthy of your favorable consideration." There is only one thing to say of his performance on matters of environmental stewardship—he was the president who appointed, in inexcusable ignorance of what was at stake, the worst interior secretary in our history and left no offsetting record of awareness of the environmental harms piling up within the nation he headed.

Historians have pushed Harding (and to a somewhat lesser degree Coolidge and Hoover) toward the bottom of the presidential rankings for not perceiving and addressing the nation's social and especially economic flaws, which the Great Depression of the 1930s exposed. Fewer than a handful have given them poor marks, also, for environmental neglect. As one who does, I acknowledge that the foundation of criticism must address the question: What conservation wounds were known at the time to require attention and remedy? Such awareness is the necessary grounds for the assessments given to all in positions of power. Our brief account finds an expanding social mobilization toward conservation even in the Roaring Twenties, especially in wildlife protection. There was considerable elite awareness of soil-erosion problems in the South and Great Plains and widespread awareness of industrial and urban wastes, along with almost annual public education brought by painful river-valley flooding, especially in the Mississippi and Tennessee River Basins. Any president of the 1920s could read Loomis Havemeyer's *Conservation of Our Natural Resources*, published in 1920, revised in 1930. It seems fair to expect that presidents who ignore environmental degradation should not make things worse. Harding in 1921 wrote to Mr. and Mrs. Domenico Zaccahea of New York, praising them for having their sixteenth child, as reported in the hometown paper.[29]

CALVIN COOLIDGE

Could a quickening of the conservation effort be plausibly hoped for by turning to Harding's designated successor? Harding was buried in Ohio, and his vice president, Calvin Coolidge, was sworn in on August 3, 1923, by his father (a justice of the peace) on their Vermont farm. Informed people would have agreed there was little prospect of significant change in any government policy area and certainly not in the handling of natural resources, for the probusiness, small-government Republican Party was in firm control of all three branches, and an economic boom was delivering to most of the public slowly improving incomes from which to buy innovative consumer goods and the entertainments of movies and professional sports. Remnants of the prewar progressive reform movement could be found here and there and would come together in a third-party presidential run by Senator LaFollette of Wisconsin in 1924, with disappointing results that confirmed Republican domination of politics and of public priorities.

The new president, Calvin Coolidge, was very different from Harding in superficial ways, very much the same in ignorance of any of the environmental scars that mobilized conservationists and in a shared commitment to a passive presidential style and noninterfering federal government.

Coolidge was born in 1872 in a rural community in Vermont, where his father was a dairy farmer, a schoolteacher, and a dabbler in local politics. Young Cal did the farm chores and liked a few of the books in the family's sparse library—especially patriotic biographies and Milton's *Paradise Lost*. He developed little interest in nature beyond domestic pets and had no hobbies. He attended a small academy and then Amherst College, where with mediocre grades he studied the usual curriculum of dead languages, rhetoric, logic, history, and no science.

Admitted to the Massachusetts bar in 1897, he was drawn to politics for reasons he never explained and worked his way quietly (losing only twice) through thirty city and state elective posts to governor of Massachusetts. Coolidge was an obscure and unremarkable New England professional politician until 1918, a year filled with labor unrest in industry, including a

handful of police walkouts in some cities. The Boston police, dismally un-
derpaid and underfunded, formed a union with the intention of affiliating
with the American Federation of Labor (AFL) and walked off the job (after
being ordered by the police commissioner not to strike), leaving the city
without law enforcement. Governor Coolidge vacillated for a time, then
called in 5,000 state guardsmen and backed the commissioner's decision to
fire the strike leaders. Criticized by AFL head Gompers, Coolidge responded
with a statement picked up across the nation: "There is no right to strike
against the public safety by anybody, anywhere, any time."[30] For this he received 70,000 admiring letters and telegrams, including a congratulatory
telegram from President Wilson. Nominated to run for vice president on
Harding's ticket, at age 51 he became the thirtieth US president.

Some contemporaries and historians have had many negative things to
say about Coolidge's qualifications for the highest office. Harding had at
least looked like a president and was genial and hard to dislike. Coolidge, by
contrast, was described as a "small, hatchet-faced, colorless man, with a
tight-shut, thin-lipped mouth" (Harvard professor Barrett Wendell) or as a
"runty, aloof, little man who quacks through his nose when he speaks"
(journalist William Allen White).[31] Coolidge had not been in the White
House very long before he developed a reputation for less-than-cordial
bluntness and taciturnity, for long naps in the afternoon bringing his sleeping time to eleven hours daily, for long and frequent vacations, and for a
strange sense of humor that included ringing the bell for staff assistance
and then hiding under the desk.

Over the years, however, most historians have moved to a somewhat
more mixed picture of Coolidge by adding some other facts to these. He was
a farm-raised Vermonter, and, as president, he came to embody older rural
values slowly losing ground in a rapidly urbanizing nation. The sleazy political tone of the Harding years and the cultural loosening of the Jazz Age worried many of conventional outlook and standards. They perhaps needed and
in any event came to appreciate and vote for this conventional farm boy of
strong character and commitment to frugality. He did not drink, dance, play
cards, or even drive an automobile (other people drove for him). His attractive and intelligent wife, Grace, was also much admired. Coolidge was a
canny politician, easily reelected in 1924 carrying thirty-five states, and he
would surely have won again had he chosen to accept the nomination in
1928. He seemed what most of the people wanted.

As the years have gone by, Harding still seems mentally slow and his language ornate and muddled. But Coolidge, given a closer look, emerges as no dummy at any level. Commerce Secretary Herbert Hoover, who had worked with Harding, reported that "when you tell a thing to Coolidge he listens carefully and understands it promptly," unlike Harding, who had not liked details. Coolidge's state papers and addresses were clearly written, though preachy and full of commonplace homilies with which everyone was in agreement. It is true that at times in social settings he said very little or nothing at all—or delivered a curt put-down. This reflected his personal uneasiness and lack of social graces, not his inability to use words.[32]

A handful of Coolidge-admiring journalist-historians (Schlaes, Silver, Johnson) have lately depicted him as a Republican statesman and have drenched us in the empty homilies in his state papers and the three hundred or so articles he churned out for pay after he left office. Coolidge liked words—in print. He did not like facts, especially news about troubles anywhere in US capitalism. The Vermonter was indeed a much smarter man than Harding, but the two presented the same leadership vacuum at the apex of government. Both presidents were entirely ignorant of the environmental and resource degradation that aroused the conservationists. Both were probusiness Republicans routinely opposed to government interference in economic matters unless it was to confer a subsidy or impose a protective tariff. This almost shuts the door on conservation, in which part of the core idea is modifying and restraining resource exploitation through governmental intervention (the other part is modifying and restraining resource exploitation through education and changed values).

Indeed, Coolidge was worse than Harding in this respect, for he was a didactic ideologue with his own simplistic philosophy of minimal government, on which he gave sermons at every occasion. He identified himself with Thomas Jefferson, who said, "That government is best that governs least." In Coolidge's state papers and postpresidential essays he endlessly repeated his themes that governments should get out of the entrepreneurial individual's way, that all progress comes from strivings of "free" individuals, and that all was well in the nation as long as business was unimpeded. "The business of America is business" was his only memorable sentence. As for the presidency, in his *Autobiography* (1929) he summarized his first principle of administration as "never doing anything that someone else can do for you." He saw the role of the president within US government as appointing good underlings to carry out the laws written by the people at the other end of Pennsylvania Avenue, where the real decisions were made.

Unsurprisingly, then, there was to be no distinctive or coherent Coolidge administration program, unless repeated calls for "economy" and lower taxes amounts to a program. His first State of the Union Address in December 1923 was very much like all those to follow. He talked first on foreign affairs, where he had little to recommend, then rambled on through an unorganized collection of domestic matters, reporting a few facts about such routine issues as transportation, the national debt, the need to restrict immigration because "America must be kept American," the need for farmers to solve their own problems without an expensive governmental subsidy. He repeated Harding's commendable advocacy of a federal law against racial lynchings. Then came one sentence declaring that "reforestation has an importance far above the attention it usually secures," and this was never mentioned again. Another sentiment he expressed only once was to recognize a growing problem of coastal pollution by "oil and refuse" dumped by ballast spills from tankers and wastes from petrochemical plants. "Laws . . . would be most helpful against this menace."[33]

Although Coolidge never returned to either of these topics in his presidential messages or press conferences, a sort of minimalist Coolidgean conception of what might in some quarters pass as the TR conservation legacy persisted through his annual messages. All contained a brief endorsement of western reclamation projects and flood control and navigation improvements in major waterways. Commending these well-established functions of the federal government was merely a nod to the Republican Party's long record of favoring national support for "internal improvements" and probably came up the bureaucratic ladder to land in his State of the Union Addresses. In any event, favorable mention of these two established programs was far from adding a new idea to the conservation agenda. For Coolidge these were words about programs he did not understand. Vermonters have no experience with large rivers, so it could have been no surprise that Coolidge's response to the 1927 Mississippi River flood (after sending Hoover to manage federal relief) was to recommend raising the levees.

On one part of the conservation legacy he declared unrelenting war. One wing of the conservation movement yearned for public power-producing dams on appropriate river sites as a way to cut down the size and reduce the market power of the "electric power trust" (the conservationist-progressive term for big power corporations and their lobbying armies). The two nitrate plants built by the government at Muscle Shoals, Alabama, along with the Wilson Dam to provide electric power at that site, were to many conservationists in the 1920s, especially influential Senator Norris, a model for the future. The Harding administration stopped work on the Wilson Dam and urged sale of the entire facility to private enterprise, ending this war-borne experiment in public power. Coolidge was an even more staunch opponent—strongly recommending the sale of Muscle Shoals (at bargain basement prices) in every annual message and vetoing a 1928 bill Senator Norris managed to push through Congress for expanding Muscle Shoals to a series of government-owned and -operated dams and power plants.

Coolidge had the misfortune of uttering in his last State of the Union Address (December 4, 1928) perhaps the most lyrical and optimistic assessment of the US economy ever written, just months ahead of a vast collapse of the New York Stock Exchange and the onset of the Great Depression:

> No Congress of the United States ever assembled, on surveying the state of the Union, has met with a more pleasing prospect than that which appears at the present time. In the domestic field there is tranquility and contentment . . . the highest record of years of prosperity. . . . The great wealth created by our enterprise and industry, and saved by our economy, has had the widest distribution among our own people. . . . The country can regard the present with satisfaction and anticipate the future with optimism.[34]

This painfully ill-timed assessment has been quoted many times, usually to reinforce an interpretation of President Coolidge as a colossal ignoramus on the real state of the Union. That reputation clings to him. Yet note a paragraph later in that sixth annual message in which Coolidge tells the nation: "We have been coming into a period which may be fairly characterized as a conservation of our national resources. Wastefulness in public business and private enterprise has been displaced by constructive economy. This has been accomplished by bringing our domestic and foreign relations more and more under a reign of law."[35]

This makes little sense, and if I quoted subsequent sentences the situation would only get darker. Conservation as waste elimination in "public business"? Through what "reign of law"? Yet if we turn to a set of speeches

Coolidge published in 1926, he brags about the "elimination of waste" promoted by his administration and tells us, "This represents a movement as
important as that of twenty years ago for the . . . conservation of our natural
resources." It is an "effort for conservation of use of materials and conservation of energy," claimed by Coolidge as a new direction credited to his own
administration.[36]

There is a cloudy idea struggling to surface here, a 1920s Republican re-
definition of conservation as waste elimination, which resonates with everybody. Coolidge was never the source of new ideas, so we must look
elsewhere. Judging by this opaque passage, he had been listening to someone else within his administration—cabinet member Hoover, the hero of
famine relief in wartime Belgium and postwar Europe, food administrator
for Wilson, acknowledged to be the brightest light in two dim Republican
administrations. The language Coolidge used was Hooverian.

Are we detouring from presidents to cabinet members as the center of
our story? Only briefly, forced there by passive presidents making room for
political entrepreneurs operating blocks away from the White House. It was
very "1920s" and post-TR when a president at the end of his run attempted to
take credit for the conservationist-sounding talk of the member of his cabinet just elected to succeed him. We know that prominent Republicans had
been urging Coolidge to find some way to identify his administration positively with conservation in order to separate the party from the Teapot Dome
scandal. Coolidge lacked the ability to pick up that agenda, so he borrowed
some of Hoover's language at the end. We feel some sympathy for Coolidge
as we see him borrowing the elusive thought and language of his chosen
lieutenant, the former commerce secretary and as of March 1929, the president.

HERBERT HOOVER

Conservationists, whatever their particular focus, from the days of Harrison
to Coolidge only had one president who came out of their cause—TR, of
course. The other presidents found this unfamiliar cause on their desk when
they entered the White House and then fumbled away the momentum, cautiously collaborated, or ignored conservation policy issues when not ob-
structing them. The need for decisive and informed leadership had only

once been met. Hoover was somewhere in between. He was an outdoorsman and avid fisherman but encountered the conservation agenda only in midcareer, without any period as an amateur activist.

Born in West Branch, Iowa, in 1874, into a working-class Quaker family, Hoover was raised by an uncle in Oregon after the death of both parents in 1885. Oregon's rivers carried the fish whose pursuit brought him frequently into natural settings and established a lifelong devotion to fishing. Despite uneven academic preparation in a rural academy, he was admitted to the newly opened Leland Stanford Junior University in Palo Alto, California. He excelled in his studies toward an engineering degree and was elected class treasurer. After graduation and some months of hard labor in mining camps in the Sierra Nevada, Hoover's reputation for meticulous detail and reliability led him to a connection with a mining company operating abroad. He became a globe-circling success and a millionaire as a mining engineer and investor operating in several countries, including Australia, China, Japan, and Russia. Eager for public service after his financial success and living in London, Hoover in 1914 volunteered to organize food relief in Belgium and other parts of occupied Europe during the Great War, when the British blockade of the Continent threatened to bring widespread famine. His impressive performance led to an invitation from President Wilson to coordinate food supplies for the wartime administration. The role was unclear, but Hoover accepted the job and became known in the United States as the "food czar," intervening to increase production, dictating prices of "essential commodities," rallying housewives in an effort to curb US consumption.

In just two years, Hoover had vaulted to the forefront of public figures in the Allied war effort, and the publicity was all positive. Surely he had a promising political future to cap his engineering successes.

Hoover had been out of the country from his 20s to his 40s, and his political affiliation was unclear. He had never voted in a presidential election until 1912, when he supported (with a $1,000 check) TR, identifying himself as an "independent progressive" (small "p"). By 1920 he had decided that he was a progressive Republican, and in 1921 chose to accept from Harding the Department of Commerce portfolio instead of that of the Interior Department. One of his predecessors in this post predicted that Hoover would have nothing to do but "put the fish to bed at night," an understandable but colossal misjudgment. Hoover was no man to be sidelined. He energetically pushed his small, mission-less eight-year-old department into an unprecedented expansion of functions designed to modernize the economy—standardizing measurements and tools, encouraging uniform building codes and zoning requirements, aiding in business penetration of overseas markets, promoting highway safety and the new aviation and radio industries.

Secretary Hoover was also busy as a speaker and writer, attempting to communicate to the public an emerging Hooverian conception of the role of US government. He pulled his thoughts together in a slim volume published in 1922, *American Individualism*, in which he tried to establish a middle ground between the "laissez-faire" dogmas of the late nineteenth century and a positive but limited role for government. Government would "intervene" not to dictate but to "induce active cooperation in the private sector." This synthesis was blurry because Hoover was no writer. One biographer called the book "a screed, a pamphlet," and a contemporary likened it to the "wooden verbiage of Grover Cleveland." A briefer statement of Hoover's views came in the preface to the second volume of his memoirs, published thirty years later. "I returned in 1919 from several years abroad . . . steeped with two ideas," he began. First, "through 300 years America had developed something new in the life of a people," moving to the forefront of world spiritual and material progress. Second, "out of the boiling social and economic caldron of Europe" at the end of the Great War had come totalitarian "miasmic infections," in the unsettled postwar days finding some support even in the United States. He went into public life, he explained, in order to "ward off the evils" gaining power in Europe by addressing the "marginal faults" while preserving the core principles of what he called the "American System," the first of which was freedom.[37] He would be a reformer from positions in the federal government not by delivering legislative and regulatory commands from Washington but by fostering collaborative, cooperative relations between the federal government, state and local governments, and the private sector.

From his post in the Commerce Department, Hoover proved to be a master organizer of commissions, committees, and conferences (he organized sixty-two fact-finding commissions while secretary), bringing together business and governmental officials as well as technical experts in order to fashion cooperative solutions to problems the market was not resolving. This vision of the federal government's role, called the "associative state" by historians later trying to describe it, was put forward as a middle ground between the discredited and chaotic laissez-faire policies of the past and the "miasmic" doctrines of socialism and statist planning gaining adherents in Europe and on the left edges of US political life.[38]

His agenda as commerce secretary from 1921 to 1928 made room for several conservationist topics and initiatives. He launched a committee on the reduction of industrial wastes, took a lead role in negotiation and ratification of a 1922 six-state Colorado River Compact resulting in the building of a high dam at Boulder Canyon on the river, established national committees to find solutions to the problems of overproduction and waste in the timber and oil industries, organized a campaign to prevent oil spills along three US coasts from tanker ballast and petrochemical plants, worked to remedy the depletion of fish stock off the Atlantic and Alaskan coasts; and pressured President Coolidge to launch a series of meetings (1924–1927) of a National Recreation Conference attended at the outset by 128 nature and conservation organizations.

This was a moderately full natural-resource agenda recognizable to any conservationist, in which the effort by the secretary appeared at first substantial and sustained. Yet the results were disappointing across the board, amounting mostly to many conferences of business leaders and experts followed by unmeasurable improvements. Aware of dismaying declines in the fisheries off Alaska, Hoover convinced President Harding to set aside protective reserves by executive orders until Congress enacted a weak regulatory law widely ignored by local trawlers. He turned also to the problem of collapsing fisheries of shad, sturgeon, and salmon off the East Coast but decided that only the states could bring regulation to bear and little could be done beyond public education. Tenacious lobbying by large oil companies working through the American Petroleum Institute resulted in a 1924 oil-pollution-control law that was pathetically weak. A 1926 international conference to explore binding rules for tanker ballast discharges beyond the three-mile limit was neutered by Japan, Germany, and Italy's refusal to sign the protocol. Hoover was angry and disappointed at the legislative setbacks that took "my pollution bill" and pulled all its teeth before sending it up for Coolidge's signature. "Official Washington has no knowledge that the American people give a damn about pollution," Hoover wrote complainingly to an ally, Dilg at the Izaac Walton League, which had tried, along with another new group, the National Coast Antipollution League, to tell Congress citizens did very much give a damn.[39] If the energetic commerce secretary displayed little talent for mobilizing public opinion, his sentiments seemed in the right place, and he gave clear signals that he should be counted as a conservationist when he accepted the honorary presidency of the Izaac Walton League and operating presidency of the National Parks Association.

Any US conservationist frustrated after 1920 by weak-government, probusiness Republicans in the White House could be excused for seeing in the commerce secretary's busy and varied schedule and interests a sort of second coming of TR. Nominated for president on the first ballot by the Republican Party in 1928, Hoover said virtually nothing about any conservation issue in the campaign (the same could be said of the Republican Platform), which meant that his election carried no mandate for natural-resource protections. His Inaugural Address did assert a mandate to do wise things in an odd and shapeless assemblage of other areas—education, the "integrity of the Constitution," advancement of knowledge, tolerance, the home. Hoover's vision for the nation was shrouded in the fog of his clumsy rhetoric.

Yet President Hoover soon moved in some conservationist directions, all carrying over from his years at the Commerce Department. His first State of the Union Address included the sentence: "Conservation of natural resources is a fixed policy of the government" and was followed by proposals to increase spending for waterway dredging and flood control, new measures to deal with oil- and gas-drilling abuses on public lands, attention to the problem of overgrazing on some of those lands, and the appointment of the Commission on Conservation of the Public Domain. The speech carrying those proposals came on December 3, 1929, just weeks after the terrible stock-market crash of late October. Hoover's administration was then inexorably drawn into efforts to cope with the deepening depression, and he did not mention conservation again in his remaining three State of the Union Addresses. However, as president he continued to spend some time on parts of the natural-resource front. He supported and in 1929 signed legislation authorizing the construction of the Boulder Dam for water storage, flood control, and generation of electric power to be sold to municipal utilities. The dam seemed to Hoover and other conservationists a major step forward in public river development based on a "grand plan for the Colorado."

He appointed the Timber Conservation Board and Oil Conservation Board to continue his efforts as commerce secretary to find some legal and acceptable way to get those two industries to accept a compact for curbing production to match demand. Hoover associated these ventures with "conservation" because less oil would be pumped and timber cut if a framework could be agreed upon to replace the current fierce economic competition and wasteful overproduction in these two depressed industries. This was "conservation" mostly as camouflage because the overriding goal was to create a government-sanctioned, production-controlling cartel in both cases, which proved politically impossible and potentially illegal under antitrust laws.

Some conservationists, especially those hundreds of thousands of amateurs working on migratory bird protection in the 1920s, had reason to be uncertain just what to make of Hoover's conservationism. He sought but received little publicity for several of his high-priority efforts, such as the complex, behind-the-scenes, and in the end futile negotiations in pursuit of production controls as waste reducers in the oil and lumber industries. His efforts in these areas were unsuccessful in any event.

Occasionally Hoover seemed to be retreating from TR's conservationist positions. A supporter of the government-built and -operated high dam at Boulder, Hoover decided Senator Norris's dreams of giving permanent status to a multipurpose power- and fertilizer-producing (and -selling) government facility at Muscle Shoals on the Tennessee River was "socialism" and "degeneration." In early 1931 he lined up with Harding and Coolidge by vetoing, in his turn, the most recent Muscle Shoals plan Congress sent him. A strong wing of TR's conservationist army had long believed there was a "power trust" in the United States building private dams and charging consumers excessive prices while the Water Power Commission lacked the power or the will to protect the public. Hoover's veto of Muscle Shoals, and his explanation, confirmed that he had none of the ecological doubts about dams that surfaced after World War II but preferred the dams and hydroelectric facilities to be privately owned.

On the problem of overgrazing on the unregulated 200 million acres of mostly desert lands in federal hands but not in national forests, Hoover appointed the Commission on Conservation and Administration of the Public Domain, which gave the president the recommendation he had come to favor, giving these lands to the states. Inexplicably, Hoover and his interior secretary, Ray Lyman Wilbur, thought the states would be better stewards of this fragile, high country, and at one point both suggested all reclamation projects should also be passed over to the states. Wilbur even broached the possibility of dividing USFS reserves among the states. Hoover and Wilbur seemed entirely ignorant of the general incapacity of state governments, especially in regulating large and well-financed businesses and industries. The proposal to shift the grazing lands to state control brought out a storm of opposition led, surprisingly enough, by many western ranchers who preferred the system they knew. It also brought into the fray many conservationists, including an outraged Pinchot, who encouraged an ally, Ward Shepard, to write an article in *Harper's Magazine* denouncing Hoover's "Handout Magnificent."

In only one area of conservation did Hoover walk a short distance in TR's footsteps. He increased the budgets of both the USFS and NPS and signed legislation adding acreage to sixteen parks and creating ten new ones—including the Great Smoky Mountains, Shenandoah, Death Valley, and the Colonial National Monument at Williamsburg, Virginia. This was a 40 percent expansion in four years. He proposed to reorganize the government to bring all eight conservation-focused agencies scattered across five different departments into a conservation division in the Department of the Interior. This interesting and controversial idea was blocked but appealed to some conservationists as a way to give the larger cause greater visibility. It would surface again the next time a president took conservationism seriously.

Then Hoover's four years were over, his administration's failure to end or ameliorate the Great Depression leading to an overwhelming rejection at the polls in November 1932. Hoover lived to be 90, and he, his friends, and his political enemies, along with many historians, engaged over these years in an unusually intense debate over the meaning of his presidency. The debate was intense because it had large implications for our political future.

Hoover led the way in relentlessly arguing that the Great Depression came from war-torn Europe and that his administration's courageous refusal to launch vast spending programs urged by Democrats in Congress had prepared the way for an economic recovery in mid-1932. Then came the campaign of Democratic presidential nominee FDR, Hoover's argument went, whose thinly veiled talk of a regulatory-welfare-deficit-spending state shook the confidence of the business community and plunged the country into the worst depression in its history.[40] This opened the way for the New Deal, which Hoover bitterly fought as a prelude to socialism.

The debate between his interpretation and the more generally accepted view among historians that Hoover failed because his ideological limits prevented him from sponsoring the bolder and necessary governmental economic and social reforms put in place by FDR has dominated all discussion of the great engineer's politically failed presidency and place in history. Only a handful of historians have endorsed Hoover's view. Most, and apparently most of the public, remember Hoover as ideologically rigid, in demeanor if not in his inner impulses a cold and inarticulate figure who could not rise to the admittedly difficult occasion. In the 2008 presidential campaign, Senator Hillary Clinton was reported as saying that GOP presidential candidate John McCain's reluctance to use taxpayers' money to bail out overextended homeowners "sounded remarkably like Herbert Hoover"—who had left office eighty years earlier.[41]

ASSESSING HOOVER

Why did this trout-fishing, "independent progressive," reformist president, who told the public "conservation is the fixed policy of the government," fall so far short of TR's memorable environmental leadership? What is to be learned?

Hoover's image was that of a technician oriented toward facts and realities, undeterred by philosophy or theory. Yet he proved to be an odd combination of a temperamental activist anchored to and constrained by deep-seated and inflexible views on the economic and moral dangers of expanding federal power and the unfailing wisdom of "free markets" and local governments. There was a significant place in his ideology for federal intervention but only as the organizer of private-sector stakeholder consultation and voluntary efforts. His hardened commitments to voluntarism and localism amounted, in Clements's words, to a "radical departure from the prewar practices of the Roosevelt-Pinchot school, who were entirely comfortable with the exercise of national, especially presidential power when the nation's future seemed to them threatened."[42] TR's view of history was that the nation was headed toward a calamitous squandering of its natural endowment, and the remedies began with leadership from the top. Hoover's view, as he expressed it most clearly in his memoirs, was that US history had shaped a uniquely successful society only in need of a few improvements in efficiency, and the most important task of political leadership was to stay well within the established boundaries around federal power.

Hoover's constrained conservationism led him to many points of engagement with natural-resource questions, but there was a limiting pattern evident in virtually all of his conservation policy engagements. He was basically all Pinchot and almost no Muir. In every natural-resource arena he saw only the opportunity for human use. His goal was always to raise the material standards of living for humans, which went as far as to include facilitating outdoor recreation for the masses who could not go fly-fishing. Although he was a modest friend of the existing national park system, he seemed to have no impulse to preserve something in its natural state.

What, then, are we to make of one particularly rhapsodic passage he wrote about the majestic Sierras as he rode among mining camps in the summers of 1894 and 1895? In a letter to his sister written from the shores of Lake Tahoe in August 1895: "No prosaic description can portray the grandeur of forty miles of rugged mountains rising beyond a placid lake in which each shadowy precipice and each purple gorge is reflected with a vividness that rivals the original. . . . Gaunt peaks . . . stand out like buttresses and turrets from a great wall, their sides splashed with snow."[43]

This was an unusual, almost singular outburst of emotion. Hoover in his letters and his memoirs did not release his feelings in Muirish praise of nature. Later in life he did publish writings about fishing, the places he had found the fish, and how he had solved the technical problems of ending their lives by ripping them out of their habitat. A Stanford admirer of Hoover, Hal E. Wert, wrote in *Hoover, the Fishing President* that "fishing . . . was a spiritual experience for Hoover," whom Wert clearly wished to present as an appealing human being who was not all work and grim self-discipline. When Hoover said in a speech to the Izaac Walton League, "The joyous rush of the brook, the contemplation of the eternal flow of the stream . . . all reduce our egotism, soothe our troubles, and shame our wickedness," it was for him a rare touch of Muir.[44]

There was, however, another side of Hoover's outdoor self. After the summers in the Sierras, Hoover's future outings were almost always fishing jaunts in which his interest was entirely the technical challenge (catching fish), and his attire was formal and formulaic—double-breasted suit, a vest depending on the weather, tie, white shirt with stiff collar. When the fishing was over Hoover often led his party back to the water, where he directed the building of dams out of stones and logs, deflecting the river from the path it had naturally chosen. Clements recounts the story of a fishing jaunt on the Thames River in England when Hoover proposed to dump the picnic trash over the side. When some in the party objected, he filled two bottles with water and sank the garbage to the bottom. Out of sight, out of mind—problem solved. Reminded that if everyone did that there would be no river, Hoover only laughed. To him, natural resources and nature itself exist solely for the benefit of human wants. In Clements's apt phrase, "Hoover held a man-centered view of the natural world" and "saw the environment in recreational terms."[45] Recreation—but only after wringing from the earth the materials and power sources needed for economic development into a modern lifestyle requiring outdoor recreation for emotional health. The future president told a reporter in 1924:

Some waterfalls are in the wrong place, where few people can see them. Moreover, in many waterfalls the same effect could be secured by a smaller expenditure of water. Waterfalls could be constructed with a view to their better public availability as scenery; and the sheet of water used to produce the scenic effect could be much thinner. We could save water and we could also have waterfalls in better locations if we handled the subject of waterfalls with the aid of human intelligence . . . through the civilizing of our rivers.[46]

Hoover's prepresidential and presidential engagements with conservationism had been substantial in time and energy yet mostly confined to conventional problems. His efforts across three Republican administrations left no natural-resource problem noticeably improved—not the depleting fisheries off Alaska and the northeastern coast, not shrinking forests, not the mineral reserves on public lands, not the puzzle of coherent waterway development. Only Hoover's modest expansion of the acreage within the national parks and addition of ten new ones conjured up memories of the burly New Yorker for whom Hoover had voted in 1912.

Sympathetic historians have suggested there must have been some immeasurable dividend in the form of public education in conservation matters from the Hoover administration's frequent use of the "c" word. Hoover made it clear there was room for a modest form of conservationism within the Republican Party after the inhospitable regimes of Harding and Coolidge. He called meetings to address significant natural-resource problems yet always found limits to the federal role.

Why did this fishing president not go beyond these modest contributions to provide leadership that made more of a mark on the conservationist enterprise? Apart from the self-imposed restraints of his oversized suspicion of federal activism, his limited contribution to conservationism is explained in part by his profession. Engineers see the world as a thing to reshape. Of all the professions, the natural sciences seem the most nurturing for environmental commitments and understandings. Biology gave us TR; engineering gave us Hoover.

Then there is the communicative chemistry dimension of presidential leadership in any direction, in which Hoover was glaringly deficient. He was a "cold fish," one interviewer reported. "He stares at his shoes." He failed "because of awkwardness of speech and lack of mass magnetism," wrote *New York Times* columnist Arthur Krock. His problem was his "sour, puckered face," commented a British journalist, "his dreary, nasal monotone."[47] One can easily imagine a 1932 meeting of conservationists who had seen TR in action discussing what had been learned over the years about the sort of president conservationists needed to forward their work on a broad front. An interest in nature, we learned from Hoover's presidency, was not enough, even combined with high intelligence and stamina. The pulpit only became a bully one when a leader with a *passion* for nature had the ability, and the calling, to educate and rally the public. Conservationists were about to see another one.

CONSERVATION AT THE END OF THE 1920S

Where, at the end of this reform-weary "prosperity decade," stood the natural endowment and the protective social movement called conservation that the new nation's resource-squandering had so recently called into life?

Although individuals may have asked themselves that question after the word *conservation* had entered the national vocabulary, it had not emerged as a staple in the vocabulary of US public life until TR's second term. He created the National Conservation Commission in 1908 and asked it to produce the first national inventory of natural resources as a basis for remedial action. The commission's 1909 report became the model for a widely read 1910 book by University of Wisconsin president Charles Van Hise. At the end of the 1920s, Havemeyer edited an updated version of that inventory, *Conservation of Our Natural Resources* (1930), published five presidents downstream from TR. The book's conclusion was that we have been losing ground despite our efforts, though some important gains have been made. We may use this as a benchmark for a brief assessment of the conservation enterprise at the end of the 1920s.

The forest cover in place when Europeans sailed to what would be the United States had been reduced by one-third, and cutting in 1930 still exceeded reforestation. Forest fires were annually ravaging what remained, including the 185 million acres of forest reserves. Soil erosion afflicted 40–50 percent of land in tilled crops, and 15 million acres had been totally destroyed by loss of soil cover; 870 million tons of soil moved as silt down US rivers to the sea. Destructive floods were the result, underscored on an unprecedented scale in the great Mississippi flood of 1927. The magnificent wildlife endowment was still receding—the once-great herds of bison, elk, and moose, the flocks of waterfowl, the now-extinct passenger pigeons, sage hen, Carolina parakeet, ivory-billed woodpecker. Yet there were in 1930 twenty-one national parks, many national monuments and game refuges, and eighty-three federal and some state and private bird refuges or regulated shooting grounds.

Hoping to build upon these and other gains reported in the 1930 summation was a slowly growing conservation social movement. Its elite origins had not changed much as the twentieth century unfolded, and college-educated women were increasingly prominent. The Sierra Club's (1892–) membership was stable at 7,000; the National Audubon Society (1905–) was troubled by internal divisions and had declined to 5,000 members; the American Game Protective Association (1911–) maintained its small but influential membership; Pinchot's once-influential National Conservation Association dissolved in the 1920s. Yet new groups were being formed—the National Parks Association in 1919, the National Coastal Anti-Pollution League in 1922, and the tiny but influential Emergency Conservation Committee formed in 1930 in New York by Rosalie Edge, the formidable critic of the stodgy and visionless directors of the National Audubon Society.

These small beachheads added up to modest social reform, in places explosively growing. In mid-decade came the astonishing surge of 100,000 members in 3,000 local chapters in forty-three states of the Izaak Walton League (1922–). The organization was founded and energized by Chicago sportsman and magazine writer Will H. Dilg. Called by William Hornaday "the conservation John the Baptist, preaching in the wilderness" and "an en-

tirely new force in wildlife conservation," Dilg built the league around a
"clubhouse atmosphere of masculine fellowship" among fishermen.⁴⁸ One
key to his success was a brilliant new magazine, *Outdoor America*. The league
focused such a nationwide passion for protection of fish habitat that sometime angler Coolidge and a majority in the US Congress were persuaded in
1926 to appropriate $1.5 million to establish the Upper Mississippi Wildlife
Refuge, the first on that flyway.

Conservation had also established a growing bureaucratic beachhead in
state governments. Although state conservation commissions nurtured by
TR had mostly withered away, in the 1920s every state had a fish-and-game
commission, though state (and local) government wildlife protection es-
caped journalistic or scholarly attention and was woefully underfunded and
ineffective. The largest change in governmental engagement with natural resource issues across the four decades from Harrison to Hoover had been at
the federal level, where the NPS and USFS (and to a lesser degree the Biological Survey) established reputations for high levels of competence and
morale and began to build respectable scientific expertise. For better or
worse (it was both), these agencies also developed a strong constituent
base—the NPS building close ties with tourist-related industries, the USFS
cooperating closely with large firms in the timber industry, the Biological
Survey gaining a support base among ranchers who appreciated the agency's
free and expanding predator-control programs aimed at thinning the numbers of coyotes, mountain lions, bears, wolves, and small rodents. The
phrase "clientele capture" of government agencies had not yet been invented
by political scientists, but the beginnings of it could be seen as conservation's two new Washington bureaucracies established close ties with organized economic interest groups in society at large.

Another important political beachhead had been slowly occupied—
repeated endorsement of conservation by the political parties in their platforms. From the 1890s forward the party platforms of the two major parties
had contained brief commitments to an uncontroversial and little-changing
basket of conservationist-sounding natural-resource politics—reclamation,
flood control, river development. By 1912 the GOP was praising something
larger, the "distinctive Republican Party policy of conservation," claiming it
as its own. The Democrats that year countered by saying, "We believe in conservation and development of natural resources," and both parties with
regularity were endorsing at presidential election time a short list of re-

source-policy commitments ranging from reforestation to water development to even the Water Powers Act (Democrats, in 1928). President Hoover
conceded this bipartisan consensus in his first year when he acknowledged
the "acceptance of conservation as a fixed policy of the government."

There was also within the conservation movement in the early decades of
the twentieth century the ferment of new concerns and ideas. In Hornaday's
influential book *Our Vanishing Wildlife* (1913), a chapter was devoted to a problem that had received little attention—"Introduced Species That Have Become Pests." He had much to say about the gypsy moth, accidentally
imported to Boston in 1868 and soon a scourge of local trees. Hornaday could
not know that a cherished and favorite urban canopy, an estimated 100 million elm trees, would for the rest of the century be decimated by a fungus arriving in 1928 in a shipment of wood from the Netherlands to the Ohio
furniture industry. The wood carried beetles infected with Dutch elm disease.
Another blight, fatal to millions of chestnut trees, was discovered in the
Bronx Zoo in 1904, and a search for a blight-resistant variety still goes on.

In a major sector of conservationist campaigns the 1920s brought another unanticipated problem. Henry David Thoreau, John Burroughs, Muir,
and others who pressed for setting aside national parks and forests did not
foresee that Ford would make the automobile affordable, with one result the
increasing millions of visitors flocking to these attractive recreational landscapes. There were 240,000 visitors to the national parks in 1914, 3.5 million
by 1931. This human visitation wave seemed a very good thing to many US
citizens—the visitors themselves, the managers of the parks and forests, the
nearby locals pleased by the expansion of the tourist trade.

Not everyone, however, thought the auto-borne swarms of outdoor recre-
ators brought all benefits and no costs. Journalist Irving Brant drove his
family across the continent in 1926 to visit Yosemite, then down to the Grand
Canyon by a route that took them to the Petrified Forest National Monument. Here he was shocked to see the "scene of vandalized desolation,"
which he described in a 1930 *Saturday Evening Post* article as a "Petrified Forest . . . looted and smashed to pieces by the motoring public," which carried
away, by the estimate of the tiny monument staff, a ton of petrified wood a
day.[49]

Inside the USFS especially, doubts about this auto-spurred invasion were
developing. Aldo Leopold was born in Iowa, raised in a house on a bluff
overlooking the Mississippi River, and spent his boyhood exploring nearby

marshes and forests, where he closely observed migratory and local birds. He studied ornithology and forestry at Yale and joined the USFS in 1909 as a wildlife manager in the Southwest region. In 1915 he toured the Grand Canyon and complained of the electric signs hung out over the canyon rims, the peddlers hawking wares, the garbage and sewage soiling the sites above and along the river.[50] In the early 1920s he began to express in articles and conferences a growing concern over wilderness lands in the national forests. He began to discuss with like-minded colleagues why the "highest use" of parts of the forests should not be preservation in a wild condition, which he defined in a widely circulated article in 1921 as a "continuous stretch of country preserved in its natural state, open to lawful hunting and fishing, big enough to absorb a two-weeks pack trip, and kept devoid of roads, artificial trails, cottages, and other works of man."[51] In 1924 he persuaded his superiors to designate the Gila Wilderness Area in New Mexico, the first public land ever to be so designated.

Reassigned in 1924 to Madison, Wisconsin, to a job that gave him time to think and write, Leopold became a leading voice in a small but influential "wilderness movement" working within the National Conference on Outdoor Recreation. One outcome was a new "L-20"designation applied to the Gila National Forest as the first to be maintained entirely in the original "primitive" condition. This idea was young and only half-baked. Leopold would continue to be a major intellectual explorer of the wilderness idea within the conservation movement.

Let us return to that 1930 book assessing progress made and not made— Havemeyer and others, *Conservation of Our Natural Resources*. Expanding upon a not entirely new idea, the authors, in "The Conservation of Man Himself," asked why the lengthening of human life through scientific medicine did not belong inside the conservation tent of ideas. The suggestion provoked no response at the time, probably because there was another social and professional movement down the street called public health, organized around just that issue. Yet conservation was on the threshold of expanding to include the well-being of human animals, even in their increasingly industrial and urban habitats.

One new perspective emerging in *Conservation and Our Natural Resources* deserved a wide audience and impact but did not get it: "How much population must we provide for in the future. . . . [What are] the limits of population for the United States" established by our resource base? The population of the

United States had grown, the authors noted, from 76,000,000 in 1900 to 122,700,000 in 1930, making the conservationist task that much more difficult. Fortunately, they concluded, in 1930 our population growth appeared to be slowing both because of declining fertility rates and the restriction of immigration in the laws of 1921 and 1924. The (alarming) demographic estimates of 1910, of a population of 204 million by 1950, were then seen as off the mark. From the vantage point of 1930 this number would not be reached until 2000, after which we could expect a "stationary condition." Our land supply, thankfully, should be ample to produce food for that number, the Havemeyer authors concluded.[52]

This brief and optimistic demographic look ahead was pioneering but wrong. In 2000 our population would not be 204 million and stabilizing, as they projected, but almost 100 million more than that (296 million). The causes were an unforeseen 1940s–1960s "baby boom" (surge in domestic fertility), followed by a large expansion of immigration numbers legislated in 1965. As the population numbers mounted in the second half of the century, so did the environmental impacts conservationists were trying to curb and mitigate. Of course, the social scientists assessing conservation in 1930 could not foresee that their optimistic demographic projections would prove far off the mark, and they deserve great credit for trying to connect population growth's causes and costs with the conservation cause and its prospects.

At least one conservationist in the 1920s thought more deeply about that connection. Sociologist Edward A. Ross, in his little-noticed book of 1927, Standing Room Only?, was gloomy about demographic trends. "Population pressure [is] a foe of the conservation of natural resources," Ross declared, and the limits on immigration imposed from 1921 to 1924 would be difficult to enforce. As for the fertility of the nation's denizens, he did not think birth-rates were coming down fast enough. Ross denounced President Harding for writing a congratulatory letter to "Mrs. Z" of New York City for being the mother (with Mr. Z's participation) of sixteen children.[53] The sociologist seemed alone in his demographic worries.

Conservationism in 1930 was a mostly optimistic enterprise attempting to persuade a growth-oriented and resource-careless society to change its deepest habits. The audacity of this mission, however, produced in some conservationists a deep sense of an unfolding tragedy and of the urgency of their educational mission. Is the conservation movement "merely a temporary flood which will subside?" asked the Havemeyer volume. No, the "tide is just beginning to run" and cannot be stilled. Yet the "outlook is not any too bright," for the lost soil fertility cannot be restored and the burned coal is "gone forever." We will need the "widest applications of science" to secure the greatest good for the greatest number for the longest time.[54]

FROM CONSERVATION TO ECOLOGY

"The widest applications of science"? Is it odd that a book on conservation's prospects at the end of the 1920s ends in an appeal to science? Why not an appeal to presidential leadership? Yet in the interwar years conservationist innovation was coming mainly from a fusion of a new science and some associated social values.

The new science was ecology, which the presidents of that day knew nothing about. A senior Biological Survey civil servant was asked to accompany President Hoover to Camp David in the Poconos, where trout fishing was the attraction. He said to the president as he entered the stream, "Mr. President, you must love books, having written one. May I recommend to you a book I am reading, by the British ecologist, *Animal Ecology*, which is introducing American fish and game managers like myself to the new field of ecology?" President Hoover liked to fish when weekending. He did not like to talk, or listen, while fishing. There is no record of any response.

Actually, I made up this encounter. Half of it, anyway. The part about the ferment generated by ecology among fish and game professionals and academic biologists in the interwar years (and after) is certainly true even if not spoken to Hoover, who had apparently never heard of ecology. The NPS (and somewhat later, the USFS) had recently commenced the scientific study of wildlife, spurred by the need for both a rationale and foundation for providing the public an "outdoor zoo" that would not pose a physical threat. What to do about grizzlies and wolves? Keeping them wild in the parks seemed the only science-based answer, but what of the unlovely coyotes or any predator on federal land who wandered across lines to kill ranchers' stock? The public proved to be interested in such issues, and both houses of Congress created new wildlife committees. Ecology seemed to bring with it a very different view of wildlife and a blurring of the application of "humane" behavior and beliefs. All species, ecologists seemed to agree, deserved life and protection. The National Audubon Society reversed its opposition to vermin and predator control of refuges in 1935. Rachel Carson's first book, the best seller *Under the Sea Wind* (1941), "dispenses with time, place, and human lives," wrote historian Thomas Dunlap. "There is no human point of view, no lessons of life, no person living in Nature. Only the life of the sea.[55] Predators were increasingly seen as a part of the "web of life." Leopold's essay "Thinking Like a Mountain" became a classic account of a hunter's remorse at watching the "fierce green fire" of death enter the eyes of a wolf he had just shot. "Humane societies" and antitrapping groups sprang up in the 1930s and afterward, as did groups organized around a single species, such as Ducks Unlimited, the Bison Society, and groups advocating for wolves, birds of prey, desert tortoises. Conservation as a movement was changing between the wars, its energies flowing to wildlife preservation even as FDR led in reforestation, soil protection, and river-control programs nourished in his own Hudson River upbringing.

5

Conservation is not enough.
— Joseph Wood Krutch

Herbert Hoover's presidency, so promising at the outset, was fatally burdened by the arrival in the autumn of 1929 of a massive stock market crash followed by an economic depression that cut the US economy almost in half by the time he sought reelection in 1932. It was widely expected that whoever the Democrats nominated would replace the engineer in the White House in early 1933 and inherit this immense and bewildering national—indeed, international—economic crisis unless Hoover reinvented himself as a brilliant politician.

Could the Democrats, in the minority since the 1890s, whose core belief was suspicion of federal power, somehow select the strong and well-aimed presidential leadership the Great Depression obviously demanded?

That is how it turned out, though almost not. The Democratic Party's 1932 nominating convention was tied up for three long ballots as front-runner Franklin D. Roosevelt (FDR), governor of New York, was unable to attract the needed two-thirds majority. Apparently deadlocked, the convention almost turned to several mediocre men who would not have provided fresh ideas or keen political instincts. Roosevelt's nomination was brokered just before his support splintered.

The presidential campaign understandably focused on how to end the economic crisis and restore growth, job creation, and business profits. Hoover promised that his probusiness policies would finally achieve recovery, though in three years they had not. In his speech accepting the GOP nomination on August 11, Hoover briefly praised his natural resource policies and "scarcely mentioned conservation again."[1] Hoover apparently saw conservation as a desirable cluster of commitments not directly relevant to economic recovery. Roosevelt tied it to jobs and investment and converted natural resource protection into a political asset.

Hoover projected no convincing recovery plan, while FDR touted a slogan implying remedial change, a "New Deal for the American people," and won by an electoral vote of 472 to 59, carrying all but six states. In his inaugural address in March 1933, he used the term leadership five times, promising an activist presidency with details coming later.

The presidency and the conservation of natural resources were not in 1932 a linkage historically at the center of US presidential politics, and neither major party candidate gave it a major place in 1932. The campaigning before the election came in the third year of the Great Depression, with national economic output cut in half and unemployment idling 25 percent of the workforce. The candidates talked mostly of economic matters: the tariff, sound money, recovery in agriculture and industry, reform of the financial system. They were also asked their views on continuing Prohibition and joining the World Court. The Democratic Party platform in 1932 contained a spare sentence affirming that "conservation and development and use of the nation's water power in the public interest" were a party commitment, and the Republican platform carried two skimpy paragraphs generally endorsing resource conservation. FDR in his acceptance speech at the Democratic Convention rambled through a series of platitudes that must have made his audience sleepy. At one point he spoke of a "wide plan of converting many millions of acres of marginal and unused land into timberland through reforestation," and a "very definite program" offering employment possibilities for a "million men" in the reforestation of "marginal and unused land [as well as] . . . abandoned farms" on "tens of millions of acres" where soil erosion sapped productivity.[2] Media and public reaction quickly appeared to make this undetailed reforestation job program a political asset.

What followed the 1932 election was the promised but only vaguely sketched New Deal of FDR—a five-year burst of liberal reform programs that dramatically enlarged the role of the federal government in economic regulation, social welfare programs, unemployment relief, labor-management relations, and much else. The Depression did not completely release its grip on the economy until war mobilization spending came in 1940, but the New Deal was an overwhelming political success. Roosevelt's programs extended aid to sectors of society long ignored by the government in Washington, D.C., and his ebullient persona and superb gifts as a communicator made him and his New Deal broadly popular (and in the business community, deeply unpopular). Roosevelt was reelected three times, the New Deal and FDR's wartime leadership bringing about an era of Democratic Party domination of US politics that lasted until the 1970s. Probably you knew all that.

Our subject, conservation, is one theme inside this national political story—a much larger theme than anyone anticipated.

THE NEW DEAL AND CONSERVATION

From FDR's inauguration in 1933 to the 1940s when World War II engulfed the nation, conservationist ideas and energies gained a prominence among government programs never before matched in Washington—even in the days of Theodore Roosevelt (TR). Most historians have regarded FDR's many tree-planting, flood control, and public power projects as the accidents of this particular president's hobbies—reflections of his youthful zest for birds and nature as well as his intense engagement in planting trees on the family's Hyde Park estate. This is part of the truth but entirely misses the centrality of the "conservation crusade" to FDR's political philosophy, reform agenda, and leadership potential.

The Second Roosevelt

FDR was born in 1882 in Hyde Park, New York, the only child of a wealthy couple who raised him on their 1,250-acre estate on the east bank of the Hudson River. His father took him on frequent hikes and horseback rides on the estate, and young Franklin was given a gun at age 11 and rambled the grounds building his stuffed bird collection, which he eventually donated, in part, to a natural history museum. He was homeschooled before attending Groton, Harvard, and Columbia Law School, and he was much impressed by the career of his distant cousin (whom he called uncle), Theodore (though FDR's branch of Roosevelts were Democrats) and visited "Uncle Ted" several times at the White House.

Bored by the practice of law in New York, FDR was elected at age 30 to the New York State Senate, then served as assistant secretary of the US Navy in Woodrow Wilson's administration. He was nominated for the US vice presidency by the Democrats in their losing 1920 campaign, then was forced to the edges of public life when a crippling attack of polio came in 1921. FDR never walked again without canes and leg braces, often with the assistance of a son or aide strong enough to offer a supporting arm to the 6'1'', 190-pound FDR. Yet he maintained a vigorous image with the help of an unwritten pact among the news media not to photograph him in a wheelchair but behind a desk or when driving an open-top, specially equipped Ford Phaeton around his Hyde Park home or his Warm Springs, Georgia, estate.

In 1928 he was elected by a wide margin to the first of two terms as governor of New York. The Roosevelt name and this political record gained him his party's presidential nomination in 1932, but some who knew FDR thought him not remotely in the same league as his Rough Rider cousin. "Featherduster Roosevelt," some Harvard classmates called FDR. Noted journalist Walter Lippmann, who served with FDR on a wartime military wage commission in the Wilson government, described presidential candidate Roosevelt in 1932 as a "kind of amiable Boy Scout." (Roosevelt was deeply involved with scouting, among other posts, as president of the Boy Scout Foundation of New York from 1922 to 1937.) In another much-quoted comment, Lippmann said: "Franklin D. Roosevelt is a highly impressionable person without a firm grasp of public affairs and without very strong convictions. . . . He is an amiable man with many philanthropic impulses, but he is not the dangerous enemy of anything . . . a pleasant man who, without any important qualifications for the office, would very much like to be President."[3]

It is best to concede that FDR, like most of his classmates, had no very strong convictions about government or social policy when at Harvard, but he was a work in progress during the years between college and his presidential run, even if Lippmann and others did not detect it. Early in his marriage he attempted to write two novels, and after polio limited (for a time) his political activities he attempted biographies of Alexander Hamilton and John Paul Jones. He discovered that he was no historian but still believed that our nation's history contained guidance for statesmen. "I thought all our histories lacked movement and a sense of direction. The nation was clearly going somewhere right from the first."[4] "FDR never did write books," wrote historian Geoffrey Ward, overlooking *Looking Forward* (1933), a collection of speeches, "and only rarely read anything more demanding than newspapers."[5]

Elected a New York state senator in 1910, he was appointed to the Forest, Fish, and Game Committee because of his expansive reforestation efforts on the Hyde Park estate (where he began to plant trees in 1912 and had planted almost one-half million by the time of his death) and his listing of himself as a "tree farmer," and on other occasions a "forester," in *Who's Who*. He invited TR's top lieutenant, Gifford Pinchot, to speak to that committee in 1912. Pinchot displayed two slide photos of a Chinese valley, the first a picture of a tapestry depicting the valley two centuries earlier. It was a lush scene of fertile croplands, a clear stream descending from the forested heights, a prosperous walled town nearby, bustling with commerce. The second photo had been taken by Pinchot himself on a recent trip to the same valley two centuries later—the forests cut down, the fields ravaged by floods and boulders, the village near deserted, "a region which is now a desert," Roosevelt recalled in a speech in 1934. Pinchot that day told a powerful story of remorseless civilizational deterioration as a result of deforestation, subsequent floods, and loss of farmland.

FDR was deeply affected, and he told this "Chinese valley" story many times over the years. Pinchot's slides and lecture "started me on the conservation road," he told a group at Yale in 1934.[6] His boyish engagement with nature had steadily matured into a larger if slightly fuzzy social reform vision. The editor of FDR's conservationist record, Edgar B. Nixon, noted that references to conservation in his correspondence prior to 1911 were "rare" but became a major theme as he worked regularly on forestry and rural lands problems in New York. He had internalized the core idea of conservation as presented through the Chinese valley slides by TR's top lieutenant. It was a history lesson—that the United States, by squandering its resources, was moving toward a fundamental environmental crisis following the foolish path of the ancient Mayan, Mediterranean, Chinese, and other civilizations by destroying the forests that wre the soil-protecting basis of environmental sustainability, the forests.

Just a few months after the session with Pinchot, the thirty-three-year-old FDR made a speech at the People's Forum in Troy, New York, revealing that he had already begun to think beyond the familiar conservationist formula for correcting the nation's course—that is, establish national forests, parks, and wildlife preserves. Americans, he said, had been largely successful in their struggle for freedom but were now engaged in a new effort to achieve what he called the "liberty of the community." He cited the Chinese valley and called it the "best example I know of the liberty of the individual without anything further." Competition among individuals is useful up to a point, but "cooperation must begin where competition leaves off." FDR really meant regulation of private farmland and forests by state governments, he later confessed, but "cooperation" was less controversial wording. He concluded: "There are many thinking people in the state who believe . . . that the government of the state will rightly and of necessity compel every cultivator of land to pay back to that land some quid pro quo."[7] No contemporary seems to have noticed that FDR had in at least one respect gone quite beyond the TR agenda, in what might (and would) be called a leftward direction.

Compel cooperation? Hardly the words of a moderately progressive "amiable Boy Scout." No one paid close attention to the evolution of FDR's political ideas through the 1920s, because no one (but himself, Eleanor, and his close political associate Louis Howe) imagined that he would be president. Yet his speeches as vice-presidential nominee in 1920 and his public statements and policies as governor of New York from 1929 to 1933 are frequently laced with expressions of a growing interventionist impulse rooted in the conservationist view of history. FDR was, like his cousin, a social reformer with a conviction that the nation's future was threatened by internal strains as well as natural resource squandering. Government must therefore play a larger role in society than in the past. It was novel to hear calls for active government from this Wilsonian Democrat rather than from a Republican, but not for long. Among other things, FDR fundamentally realigned the major parties' views of the role of government in the modern United States.

As FDR became governor in 1929 he was regarded as a progressive Democrat in the Wilsonian tradition of reform efforts bringing lower tariffs, antitrust measures, and banking regulation, and a political style often at odds with the New York City bosses. He was known to be sympathetic to if not particularly active in the urban social work commitments of his wife, Eleanor. What was not much noticed by contemporaries in the 1920s and in FDR's terms as governor were the convictions he held about farming and how his interest in trees, soil, and rural livelihoods pointed toward a new policy role for governments. As governor of New York he became an active participant in an emerging discussion of a body of policy ideas in the 1920s that recent historians are calling either the "new rural conservation" or the "permanent agriculture" movement.[8]

The foundations of this scattered movement reach back to worries about soil erosion generated by the stupendous expansion of increasingly mechanized agriculture across the US continent. Land under cultivation in the United States tripled from 1850 to 1930, from 239 million to 987 million acres, and the costs in deforestation, watershed holding capacity, and soil erosion were major issues driving the conservation movement. For the second Roosevelt, soil erosion topped the worry list, and in the 1920s he can now be seen as on a parallel track with a growing crowd of policy intellectuals passionately sharing a concern for the underpinnings of agriculture. TR's National Conservation Commission called erosion "wasteful" and "evil," and fears of "soil famine" led Warren Harding's secretary of agriculture, Henry Wallace, to appoint a commission on land use. Soil loss was the organizing theme of the Department of Agriculture's 1923 *Yearbook of Agriculture*, and Hoover convened a National Conference on Land Utilization in 1931 that called for taking exhausted land out of cultivation and urged farmers to control erosion. These alarms about the eroding foundations of the nation's agriculture spilled over into the mass media, gained strength in the 1920s, and made their mark in the GOP platform in 1932 and in FDR's major speech on agriculture in Topeka, Kansas.

Two things were new in the early 1930s with regard to these warnings about the eroding foundations of the nation's agriculture. One was their fusion with another TR-era conservation impulse now gaining momentum— public development of hydroelectric power and its transmission, by governments if necessary, into rural regions. The other was the argument that a healthier commercial agriculture sector was a prerequisite for a more balanced national economy. When the Depression came, the rural reform agenda gained many converts.

The policy tools urged by these new rural conservationists included the government purchasing and reforesting tracts of exhausted soil while generating new livelihoods for relocated farmers by spurring the growth in rural areas of small industrial facilities through government-developed and -transported hydroelectric power. FDR embraced this new policy thrust. In 1931, as governor of New York, he gave a talk before the National Governor's Conference in Indiana. In his address, "Acres Fit and Unfit," he enlarged, as he often did, on the "Chinese valley" theme. He lamented the "dislocation of a proper balance between urban and rural life" and noted how many farmers in New York were hanging on to or abandoning unproductive, soil-depleted farms and were thus mired in poverty. He immodestly bragged about his sponsorship of state programs to classify lands, purchase exhausted (judged "unfit" by the state) private lands, and hire unemployed men to reforest them as part of the public domain. In New York, he claimed, they were aiming at a "permanent agriculture," a phrase put into the air by either Morris L. Cooke, a lieutenant of Pinchot, or perhaps he borrowed it from Liberty Hyde Bailey, chair of TR's Country Life Commission (1910), who for all we know may have borrowed it from Thomas Jefferson, who had a gift for memorable phrases.[9]

This second nationally prominent Roosevelt, in short, came out of Harvard with no particular political philosophy or social vision. Yet by the time he plunged into two terms as governor he had fashioned out of elements of Pinchot/TR conservationism a rationale for wide-ranging social intervention that went far beyond a custodial role on public lands. I know of no evidence that he was familiar with John Muir's comment that "when we pick up one part of the universe we find everything else hitched to it," but the tree farmer from the Hudson River Valley readily translated the lesson of the Pinchot slide show into social terms that provided broad guidance for dealing with the Depression. He laced his public and private statements with the words "interdependence" and "balance," proclaiming in 1932, "Our economic life today is a seamless web. We cannot have independence . . . unless we take full account of our interdependence." No part of the nation could prosper over the long term while other parts languished. Historian Kenneth Davis attempted to describe the conservation-based origin of FDR's core outlook: "He had a vision of America that can be described in terms of the organismic watershed concept. . . . There was in Roosevelt's mind a vivid, though vaguely defined, sense of water, flowing water, as means and organizing principle of Union. The watershed became metaphor."[10]

Roosevelt also encountered some difficulty in making clear the link between his conservationist education and the agenda for government-led social reform he brought to the White House. Yet his New Deal social-reformist inclinations grew naturally out of the heritage of the TR-Pinchot nature-protecting interventions and the urgent conviction that the United States was on the path toward resource depletion that had devastated the empires of the Mediterranean, the Yucatan, and China.

Historians, with only a few exceptions, have not described FDR's political assets in this way—as gifts of the intellect, a body of coherent ideas. His ideas, biographers and historians generally agree, were usually superficially expressed, elastic, and shifted over time as circumstances changed. He liked policy and political puzzles, respecting and enjoying conversations with the experts who mastered them. In the spring of 1932 he gave better focus to his sprawling congregation of "advisers" by gathering for frequent meetings with a small cadre of lieutenants from Columbia University that came to be called his "Brains Trust"—professor of government Raymond Moley, economist with agricultural interests Tugwell, and professor of corporate law Adolph Berle. He drew ideas and phrases from everywhere, but these advisers especially were instrumental in helping FDR navigate the issues and problems of the 1932 presidential campaign, in particular drafting parts of speeches.[11] All of his policy advisers, perhaps especially the academics, found FDR elusive, though an enthusiastic listener. His leadership gifts were not to be found in any Rooseveltian "philosophy" fashioned by himself or borrowed from others but were grounded in the realm of temperament and the gifts of communication. "A second-rate intellect, but a first-rate temperament," was the famous assessment of FDR by Justice Oliver Wendell Holmes.

Even if this judgment is far better than if it were formulated the other way around, in my view too many historians and biographers have concluded that FDR's leadership skills were entirely grounded in his communicative gifts and optimistic temperament, not in "ideas." Closer to the mark is the astute assessment of Pulitzer Prize–winning historian David M. Kennedy, who describes the "mind" of FDR as a mixture of "an expansive, generous, restless temperament" married to "an unapologetic embrace of the state" with special commitments to regulating Wall Street and rescuing agriculture. Kennedy acknowledges also FDR's "passionate, even romantic interest in conservation."[12] This "interest" was more than that, more than an inclination to put people to work planting trees or building dams. It was a view of history privileging not only resource protection but also a planning role for government in correcting both social and environmental imbalances as part of the same urgent societal reform project. The New Deal had many roots, but a taproot ran from the mind of FDR back to the Pinchot slide show and TR's gospel of conservation. Both Roosevelts were moved by a strong sense that the nation was on the path to resource exhaustion and decline.

New York governor FDR was elected president in 1932 not because he offered a clear picture of just what he intended to do when power came. His central promise as a candidate did not go much beyond "bold, persistent experimentation." He did not know how to banish the Depression, and his advisers differed. So he campaigned evasively, offering a few hints of a large public works commitment, avoiding hard details about his "New Deal." Years later, when Moley, the convener of the Brains Trust, wrote a memoir of his years with FDR, we learned that the advisers who began to meet with him in April 1932 found that "there was no Roosevelt program," only "near-policies and mere leanings." One strong leaning was public electric power, then "rural rehabilitation, reforestation, land utilization . . . long-term agricultural prosperity . . . linked to the use and availability of land and water resources." FDR "saw the central problem of agriculture . . . as a problem of conservation." So the Brains Trust listed "conservation . . . as the campaign's top priority," with "agriculture" heading the list of items underneath.[13]

One contemporary observer of US politics, however, sensed the outlines of a statist reform "revolution" in FDR's vague and lofty campaign language. The worrier was Hoover, for whom Roosevelt's frequent use of the words "planning" and "interdependence" and "restoration of balance" were ominous signs of a radical inclination toward social engineering. Hoover told the public that the election was not a choice between two men but between two philosophies of government.

He was right about that, but, a moderate conservationist himself, he never imagined that the fundamental source and rationale for FDR's interventionist impulse came not from European collectivist theories but from homegrown ideas at the heart of the social movement his cousin TR, and lieutenant Pinchot, had led.

FDR's inauguration came on March 4, a cold Saturday. A rolling wave of bank closures had by that weekend virtually shut down the nation's banking system. There were no banking services in thirty-eight states and restricted withdrawals in the rest. His first act was to declare a "bank holiday" for a week and then demand that Congress immediately pass emergency bank legislation voted upon and signed the next Friday. The New Deal had begun by putting a large federal finger in the banking dike, not where Roosevelt had intended to start.

He wanted to start with planting trees—for the sake of the trees and soil as well as the economic well-being of the humans who would be organized and paid to plant them, and he did so immediately after the banking crisis seemed on the way to resolution. His first message to Congress carried the remarkable assertion that "forest and water problems" were "perhaps the most vital internal problems of the United States," and in broad terms he promised to launch a program of conservation and reclamation of immense proportions. He had no detailed plans as yet but knew how he wanted to take the first step. In the campaign he had frequently promised an expansion of federal public works in order to create jobs and stimulate broader economic activity, and in his July speech in Chicago accepting the nomination he had spoken of "one million jobs" that could immediately be created in reforestation and erosion control. There was of course nothing new about federal public works projects. Hoover had reluctantly authorized a small increase in infrastructure spending, a slow (and budget-deficit increasing) way to employ some engineers and construction firms. Congress was in session, expecting to adjourn, but FDR, sensing that the public expected something new and decisive from the new administration, demanded that the legislators stay in Washington and pass some laws launching remedial action.

He was able to send a legislative proposal to the Hill before March was out, having already decided on his first public works initiative. The president proposed sending some of the nation's unemployed young men into the forests for the benefits of outdoor work, income, and conservation projects on both public and private lands. Congress authorized the Civilian Conservation Corps (CCC) by the end of the month. By June, 250,000 unmarried men between the ages of 18 and 25 were working in 1,300 camps near or on public lands and run by the War Department—planting trees (2 billion by the end of the project) and building erosion-control dams, fire towers, roads, and facilities in recreational sites. When the CCC was ended in 1942, more than 2.5 million boys (and some "SheSheShe" females according to FDR) had passed through the camps, earning $30 monthly ($25 of it sent home to their parents) and benefiting from physical work and camp discipline. It quickly became the New Deal's most popular single program. In CCC camps, both forested places and humans were rehabilitated. The meaning and appeal of conservation were thereby expanded.

The rest of the early New Deal followed. In the first 100 days, a special session of the 73rd Congress lasting from March to mid-June, fifteen major laws were passed and signed. The New Deal was explosively emerging, a cascade of programs aimed to launch national planning in industry and agriculture in order to bring recovery in those core sectors, along with unprecedented large "relief" and public works programs to expand employment and buying power. It was president-driven in unprecedented ways, though every major program had congressional sponsors who had been pressing for and shaping reforms through the 1920s. The Depression finally opened the reform gates, and the central catalyst was a president who surprised almost everyone by emerging as a master of opinion-shaping through his "Fireside Chats," frequent press conferences, and ten major speeches.

The economy slowly turned upward in 1934–1935, but the Depression hung on, and although FDR remained popular, radical sentiment gathered force on the political right as well as left. Responding to rising political radicalism, FDR moved to the left in 1935 to launch a "second New Deal," combining stiffer taxes on the rich with encouragement for the formation of strong labor unions, a social security pension system, public housing, and even, early in his next term, an effort to enlarge the Supreme Court so that the president could make appointments of liberal judges in order to weaken one of the roadblocks his reforms had faced. By 1938 the first and the second New Deals added up to all the New Deal that FDR could push through. Social and political reforms gave way to a focus upon the rise of fascism and threats of world war.

After the 1930s, US politics would never be the same. Nor would the presidency.

New Deal "liberalism"—the word FDR preferred over the earlier label "progressivism" attached to the reform endeavors of the generation of TR and Wilson—had provided the intellectual foundations of a new regulatory-welfare state and articulated the dominant political philosophy in the United States for three decades.

Our topic, conservation, now swam in the turbulent currents of liberal reform in the FDR era, for he vigorously inserted natural resource preservation programs and ideas where they had never much thrived—in the expanding agenda of the Democratic Party.

Conservation, some five decades old as FDR took the oath of presidential office, represented at that point in US history a social movement organized around a multifaceted commitment to natural resource protection. It was given support by several small, elite citizens' organizations who had developed an impressive library of articles and books and received generally sympathetic coverage in the press. Conservationist ranks had provided many talented presidential lieutenants with clear and passionate convictions about what the government should do (if only they could get the government's—especially the president's—attention).

For them, Hoover, though an outdoorsman and trout fisherman, had been a disappointment. He had been willing to modestly expand the number and acreage of national parks and forests, acknowledged the problem of ocean fisheries depletion and held inconclusive meetings on the issue, rebuffed the advocates of public hydroelectric power, and showed little interest in wildlife protection.

Conservationists hoped for more than this from the tree farmer from New York, even though he was not aligned with the party of TR, where conservation had previously found its chief support. They did not have long to wait. In FDR's first month in office and without much technical or political help, he launched the CCC—not exactly at the center of TR's range of activities but a reminder that tree planting was a good idea anywhere and always. Only weeks later, in that first spring, two other New Deal innovations with conservationist underpinnings quickly followed—the larger one a vast regional planning enterprise anchored in a series of hydroelectric facilities built along the Tennessee River Valley's seven-state meander through the south, the other a series of unprecedented if small steps toward federal regulation of private-land use in agriculture.

In both cases FDR gave decisive support and some shape to projects that had been nurtured through the 1920s by others. Through that decade Nebraska senator George Norris led a mostly southern coalition determined to prevent three successive Republican presidents from selling the hydroelectric facility the government had built at Muscle Shoals, Alabama, on the Tennessee River in the later stages of World War I. The government after the war was no longer in urgent need of the synthetic nitrates produced by the power generated by the Wilson Dam, but Norris and his southern congressional allies fought to keep Muscle Shoals in public hands, providing cheap electricity to keep regional private power rates down and to provide a new supply of nitrate-based fertilizer. Although the Tennessee River Valley was a new focus of attention for the small but growing number of public hydroelectric-power enthusiasts, the generation of electric power by government-owned and -run sites was a long-standing conservationist interest.

FDR, who had often visited Warm Springs, Georgia, was well aware of

the South's stifling poverty and the distressing gullies on the landscape testifying to decades of soil abuse. He knew the source of the Tennessee River's
destructive floods was not rains alone but deforested watersheds—products
of human land-use habits. While touring Muscle Shoals and the surrounding region with Norris in the interregnum, FDR not only adopted the senator's idea of public power at Muscle Shoals but dramatically expanded it. He
imagined a series of dams along the 650-mile river providing cheap electricity, flood control, and a reliable navigation channel. FDR as a governor had
fought the expansion plans of the Niagara-Hudson Utility Company, pushing for a New York State–owned company to offer a "yardstick" low electricity price to undermine monopolies that would otherwise become rich and
powerful selling power generated by dams on the people's rivers. The Tennessee Valley Authority (TVA) idea offered him a far larger river drainage on
which to pursue and link several of his central passions. There should be
promotion of soil conservation through reforestation, improved farming
practices, and the retirement of marginal land. All of this would be entrusted
to a new federal agency operating as a seven-state regional entity, the TVA. It
would bring "national planning for a complete river watershed involving
many states and the future lives and welfare of millions," he said in a message to Congress. "It touches and gives life to all forms of human concern."
In a press conference months later, he said: "Power is really a secondary
matter. What we are doing there is taking a watershed with about three and a
half people in it . . . and we are trying to make a different type of citizen out
of them."[14]

So was born the TVA, a regional multipurpose planning authority that
would build sixteen dams on the Tennessee River by 1940 (there are twenty-
nine today) providing flood control and a nine-foot shipping channel from
Knoxville to the Ohio River, attracting international attention as a vast experiment in planning to transform a nation's lagging region. The TVA quickly
acquired a reputation as one of the New Deal's most innovative ventures,
given major credit for the South "catching up" to the nation's other regions
in economic development.

As the years went by, the TVA evolved into a corporation whose "conservationist" commitments were overshadowed by its function as a supplier of
relatively inexpensive electricity generated more by environmentally unfriendly coal and nuclear plants than water cascading down from artificial
lakes. But in FDR's day and for a bit longer, the TVA seemed a brilliant re-

gional combination of the public water–power-development ambitions of TR's generation of conservationists with a range of planned interventions to transform southern rural life in beneficial ways.

US farmers were too numerous, politically influential, and economically desperate not to gain the new administration's early attention, even if FDR had not placed agricultural recovery at the top of his list—which he had. The New Deal's main framework for responding to agriculture's troubles, the Agricultural Adjustment Act of April 1933 (amended many times) launched federal intervention to aid and subsidize the nation's farmers in complicated ways. It established a policy framework that persists, much modified, to this day.

What might subsidizing farmers have to do with conservation? Nothing, one could conclude from the design of the first nationwide federal program to bail farmers out of the overproduction crisis—the Agricultural Marketing Act of 1929, signed by Hoover, which encouraged cooperatives and voluntary production controls. US commercial farmers and their huge lobby, the American Farm Bureau Federation (AFBF), were not satisfied with the Hoover plan and pressed the next administration to pursue higher prices for farmers using other tools—higher tariffs against foreign grain and other food products, or sending money directly to farmers, or both.

The New Deal's farm program did indeed send farmers money and other services and attempted to help them get higher prices by cutting output. But the New Deal would turn out also to have FDR's strong ideas about changing US agriculture—ideas incubated in neighborhoods of the conservation impulse. The new president, though thinking of himself as a friend of farmers and a tree farmer himself, had a long record of concern for what some farmers were doing wrong as they cleared the land and carelessly plowed and exhausted the soil, sending it downstream or downwind and undermining their resource base. He had been loosely aligned through the 1920s, as we have seen, with a constellation of agricultural reformers who went beyond the public land preservation focus of the generation of Muir-Pinchot-TR to propose policies affecting the use of private agricultural lands. FDR's first sustained policy discussions with one of these reformers of rural regions apparently came in lengthy conversations at Hyde Park in the prenomination summer of 1932, and again in the interval between FDR's election and inauguration, with a member of his Brains Trust, Tugwell. They discovered that they both shared an outlook that opened new vistas in agricultural policy.

For Tugwell's part, he learned in one-on-one talks over the summer that FDR "had an old concern for conservation" that went beyond his passion for tree planting. Trees for FDR had a larger purpose than habitat for wildlife, aesthetic appeal, and practical use for humans. Trees made, and held, soil. He took over management of Hyde Park at age 28, looked at estate records, and found that his ancestors had grown prize-winning corn at Springwood in 1840. In just seventy years the yield on corn was down by half, with a similar decline for vegetables and grain. Huge gullies had developed, feeding mud into the creeks. "I can lime it, cross-plough it, manure it and treat it with every art known to science," FDR had complained, "but it has just plain run out."[15] In 1912 FDR asked Syracuse University's College of Forestry for a reforestation plan and by 1945 had planted a half million trees at the Hyde Park estate.

FDR, Tugwell learned, also had concerns for tenant farmers and talked of somehow breaking the link between poor land and poor people. Here emerged a potential new dimension to federal public policy—moving millions of farmers off the land they had ruined and preparing at least some of them for other ways of livelihood. Tugwell was surprised and pleased to hear of the new president-elect's "proprietary interest in the nation's estate" and to learn that FDR was a "devoted conservationist" who as governor of New York had sponsored a small program of state purchase of submarginal land.

In Tugwell the New York governor/presidential candidate had found an expert adviser whose main interest was a land-use intervention agenda compatible with the new rural conservation so congenial to FDR. With an activist administration about to take power, the Columbia professor would be asked to continue his conversations about rural-related public works and other programs with the president-elect. In the long interval between election and inauguration, Tugwell visited Hyde Park more than once and noticed that the small band of newspaper reporters who had followed FDR during his years in Albany were also sometimes the governor's social companions. But they were city men who could not talk with him about his rural interests. "With conservation they easily became bored" because "it had very little news value," Tugwell noted in his account of his early talks with FDR. The president-elect "was determined that somehow he would change this," finding a way to put conservation on the leading edge of the news.

How many Americans could be engaged in a national program of resettlement off gullied, exhausted lands, he asked Tugwell? Four million families, the professor unhesitatingly estimated. Now "*there* was a program" waiting to happen, they agreed. "We talked about it in some length," Tugwell remembered. Where were those families? In the South, the economist suggested, reminding FDR of the gullied southern landscapes he knew, making his point by citing the memorably scarred terrain around Ducktown, Tennessee. Another region ripe for a resettlement program was in the "dust-blown plains of the short grass country," which "ought to go back to grass." "There was no end to the possibilities," they agreed.[16] They had as yet no clear idea how to relocate farmers off "submarginal" lands, not to mention how these farmers were to find livelihoods elsewhere.

The story of conservation in the thirteen-year presidency of FDR began with early policy innovations derived from his own rural reform passions—the protection and wise use of trees, water, soil—given focus in the CCC and the TVA. The third programmatic thrust, equally innovative, took a bit longer to emerge—the attack on the mistreatment by US citizens of their own and their descendants' soil, most of the abuse taking place on private land Washington had ignored for more than 140 years and through twenty-six presidents.

Again FDR discovered and enlisted as one of his key lieutenants another of the new rural conservationists who had been actively exploring rural interventions during the 1920s. Reformers from that movement naturally gravitated to the New Deal when FDR showed an interest in steering US farmers toward a "permanent agriculture" rather than just higher prices for growing cotton, corn, and wheat in the same old ways with the same old damage to the soil.

The person who would become the lead New Deal lieutenant for soil protection was already a national figure in agricultural circles. Hugh Hammond Bennett, a North Carolina–born soil surveyor for the Department of Agriculture beginning in 1909, had become a passionate prophet of the dangers he described in many articles and speeches, including a widely circulated essay of 1928, *Soil Erosion: A National Menace*. "For Bennett, soil conservation was almost a religion," historian Arthur Schlesinger, Jr., wrote, "and he preached the consequences of 'geological suicide' with 'Old Testament wrath.'"[17] In 1930 Bennett, reporting that 50 million acres of the nation's 600 million acres of arable land were ruined and an additional 150 million were so eroded as to be unprofitable, persuaded Congress to establish (it was understood that it would be under his leadership) a small Bureau of

Soils to set up a few experiment stations to measure erosion and test various remedies.

Bennett's tiny beachhead for erosion studies in the federal government was well timed. That year, 1930, turned out to be the first of the hot, dry years of a severe weather cycle that would give Bennett's soil-destruction prophecies an unexpected urgency. A wet weather cycle in the 1920s, combined with the lure of the enormous European market for wheat that US farmers had gladly captured during the war years, invited expansion of acreage westward. Borrowing to buy acreage in the inviting prairie grasslands west of the corn belt, along with the steam- and gas-powered tractors allowing plows to cut the deepest sod, farmers pushed beyond the 100th Meridian, where rich soils lay under a cover of native grasses. The "great plowup" had begun on the Great Plains.

And something else changed. A drought that began in 1930 worsened each year, and as much of the South and some of the Midwest experienced drought in the early and mid-1930s, on the arid Great Plains the winter snows were especially light, the rain sparse, and the summers uncommonly hot. The year 1934 brought no rain at all to the southern plains—affecting a tier of states from the Texas and Oklahoma panhandles northward through western Kansas and Nebraska and eastern Colorado, and as far north as the Dakotas. In May great clouds of brown and yellow dust, once soil beneath thick grasses but now exposed to the winds, were carried aloft around the region and to the East, "black blizzards" rising within but not confined to the newly named Dust Bowl region. To Americans in the Midwest, South, and East these towering dark storms, often a mile high, were a gritty, lung-irritating, unwelcome nuisance. To the farmers and rural populations of the Great Plains the periodic "dusters" were a choking intruder into homes and barns and lungs, a demoralizing, life-threatening replacement for the rain clouds of the 1920s. In one storm in the spring of 1935, weather researchers in Wichita, Kansas, reported zero visibility and estimated that the winds over the city carried 5 million tons of dirt. Timothy Egan in *The Worst Hard Time* (2008) reports contemporary estimates by government meteorologists that 850 million tons of topsoil blew away from the 100-million-acre Dust Bowl, eight tons for every American.

Agricultural officials in Washington sent emergency aid in the form of seed and feed for livestock, some of them increasingly aware that the Dust Bowl demanded a more fundamental response.

In the early months of the New Deal, Bennett found himself and his soil erosion mission urgently embraced by the new administration. FDR called him to the White House, where Bennett again insisted that the "dusters" blowing eastward across the plains were only the most visible evidence of wrongheaded, soil-destroying farm habits. They were not the acts of God but of humans. It was time to accept appropriate blame, to alter human behavior harmful both to nature and to the people, who thought their domination came at no price. FDR found Bennett "his intellectual soul mate." The same was true of two of FDR's leading conservationist cabinet officers who wanted Bennett to work for them—Secretary of the Interior Harold Ickes, who was concerned about soil erosion in the parts of the arid West under his jurisdiction, and Secretary of Agriculture Henry Wallace, a longtime erosion worrier who wrote in 1934, "I doubt that even China can match our destruction of soil."[18]

Bennett was testifying before Congress in April 1935 on legislation that would establish a federal agency charged not only with research but also demonstration projects to confront erosion on the farm. Members of Congress, asked to appropriate money to teach farmers how to farm, were apathetic or skeptical. But Bennett, informed that a major dust storm from the Plains states would arrive in Washington that afternoon, asked the legislators to move to the windows and look to the West. A dark cloud of brown dust from Kansas and Nebraska drifted across the capital city, coating roadways and auto windshields. Dirt was for the first time a forceful airborne lobbyist in Washington, D.C. That day it educated reluctant US representatives, who wrote legislation announcing that "the wastage of soil and moisture resources on farm, grazing and forest lands . . . is a menace to the national welfare." A new Soil Conservation Service was authorized, launching a small-scale but unprecedented federal effort to persuade US farmers across the entire country to form local soil-conservation districts in which they might experiment in crop rotation, contour plowing, stubble-retention, and other ways to alter old habits, preserving rather than mining and stripping bare the soil.

And the Dust Bowl—was it not a unique disaster requiring more than just contour plowing? The administration was divided. Wallace, Ickes, Tugwell, and others thought there were too many farmers in rural regions in the first place, especially undercapitalized farmers on submarginal land, especially those who had unwisely moved West to plow up the arid Great Plains region on the assumption that the rains of the 1920s would "follow their plows" out onto the rich soil beneath the prairie sod. They should be resettled, their "worn-out" land purchased and converted to parks or other public but nonagricultural uses—or, in the Great Plains, to grass and cattle-raising. Tugwell was remarkably candid, not always in private and in memoirs, about his dislike for soil abusers, reminding us of TR's scourging of "skinners of the land." "Those of us who were concerned with the land," Tugwell wrote of his time during the New Deal, "did not love the plowers of the plains, not very much the cattlemen, and not at all the sheep and goat runners," who he considered "plunderers."[19] Some of them should move elsewhere, with government help of course, and all would benefit from Bennett's lessons about how to farm without erosion.

This sort of language might be taken to suggest that New Dealers "concerned with the land" harbored some animosity toward farmers generally, just as the language of "wastrels and exploiters," "economic bandits," and "land butchers" was aimed at the waves of cut-and-run loggers by Pinchot's aroused generation of professional foresters. This accusative language was heartfelt and misleading. The "rural reformers" such as FDR, Wallace, Tugwell, Bennett, and Lewis Gray repeatedly insisted poor land made poor people as well as the other way around, and their mission was to break that link through a combination of relocation, education in care of the soil, and rising incomes permitting longer time horizons for the users of the resources. Our narrative leads through the erosion-prevention efforts, but we should not fail to note that there was within New Deal agricultural policy an unprecedented concern for the humans who worked but did not own the land—for example the tenant farmers, roughly half the farmers in the South and one-third of those farming US land. Were these tenant farmers, the poorest of the poor, also "skinners of the land" in TR's words or the "plowers of the plains" Tugwell and others "did not love"? The New Deal rural reformers of the 1930s did not address this question, unless it was in launching both a range of soil-erosion-prevention programs as well as, in 1937–1946, an unprecedented governmental effort (pursued by the Farm Security Administration) to break the poor land–poor people linkage out of concern for both.

Tugwell called the mission "to purchase exhausted lands and to resettle the people . . . the higher levels of conservation." Some old-line agricultural bureaucrats, however, were horrified by the relocationists. "Boys with their hair ablaze," Agricultural Aadjustment Administration (AAA) head George Peek called the Tugwellians, those liberal lawyers and professors with sometimes little background in agriculture who had come to Washington to help the New Deal change the country. Bennett's soil-conservation districts, with their demonstration projects, were acceptable to both groups because they might be a part of the solution.

And FDR? There can be no doubt he had long thought it part of modern government's assignment to improve rural life; this included programs (that he sponsored in New York and within the New Deal) to "resettle" some rural families either on more promising farmland or into planned suburban communities, and "resettle" often included educational social work toward behavior modification as well as the sort of agricultural research and demonstration the Department of Agriculture had long pursued. Part of the government's assignment, FDR had long believed, was the purchase and transformation of the "worn-out," submarginal lands into some higher use—public parks and forests, recreational areas, wildlife refuges. He had said as much in that "liberty of the community" talk he gave in Troy, New York, in 1912, in the "Acres Fit and Unfit" speech in 1931, and in other public statements as governor of New York and as president. Historians can add more evidence from his private correspondence: "If a farmer in up-State New York or Georgia . . . through bad use of his land, allows his land to erode," FDR wrote to Wallace in 1937, "does he have the inalienable right as owner to do this, or has the community, i.e., some form of governmental agency, the right to stop him?"[20]

The right to stop him? The principle of government regulation of commerce had been energetically expanded in the Progressive Era, including the birth at local levels of city-government regulation of land use through zoning. But rural zoning could not get out of the starting gate, though the ethical foundations had been explored. "No man really owns his acres," Cornell agronomist Liberty Hyde Bailey said at TR's Second National Conservation Congress in 1910. "In a higher sense," said FDR to the National Soil Fertility League in 1912, "the man in whose name the title stands is not the real owner of the land. The fertile fields were placed here by God Almighty for the use of humanity for all time." "All men are transients." said three-time Democratic nominee for the presidency William Jennings Bryan. "What right has the tenant of today to impoverish the estate upon which generations to come must live?"[21] When President Roosevelt expressed similar thoughts to Wallace in 1937, he had followed the soil-erosion worry to the edge of an experiment in some form of national rural zoning.

But FDR was a politician and moved cautiously on the Dust Bowl problem. First, plant trees. This was not an entirely new idea on the vast plains of Russia and also the United States, where farmers had long experimented with trees as windbreaks. The president authorized the US Forest Service (USFS), using CCC labor, to plant a "shelterbelt" of trees stretching from the Canadian border to the Texas panhandle. A variety of trees with the promise to survive in the plains were planted at right angles to the prevailing winds, mostly in ten- to twenty-row strips 100 feet wide and a mile or so apart, with some larger clumps around buildings. The hope was to break the wind, conserve moisture, and provide wildlife habitat. Twenty years later a survey showed a 42 percent survival rate, along with some evidence of local wind reduction and wildlife revival.

This could be called a harmless diversion, albeit popular with ordinary people. A larger plan, and vision, was needed to deal with the soil erosion in the air over the Great Plains and in other less visibly dramatic parts of the US landscape. No one knew this better than FDR, who remarked to a journalist: "Many million acres of such land must be returned to grass or trees if we are to prevent a new and man-made Sahara."[22] He asked his new National Resources Board for an inventory of the nation's land and water resources, along with recommendations, especially grappling "with the problem . . . of worn-out and eroded lands." The report came in November, and the section dealing with land found soil erosion the "most acute resource problem," requiring a combination of educational efforts, public assistance, and "government controls," such as government purchase of 76 million acres of submarginal land. Underpinning these policy recommendations was the larger idea that this moment in our national history marked a transition from a tradition of soil exploitation to a time of public stewardship of all national lands, public and private. Another distinguishing feature of the report was the board's look ahead to population projections, as was appropriate for the nation's first national planning agency as FDR had intended it. The board's projections were to be proven wrong, its estimate of stabilization of population at 140 million in 1960 failing to foresee the unexpected "baby boom" after the war, but its estimates were accepted among most demographers in the 1930s.

FDR sent the report to Congress with a stirring plea for a permanent planning board to continue such important analysis of national problems and the likely shape of the future. Congress refused to authorize a national planning agency, though the president tried several times.

And the Dust Bowl? The 1936 election was approaching, and FDR seems to have sensed that when he campaigned in the states of the arid West he must have a more compelling statement of his administration's vision. In September he asked Morris L. Cooke, chairman of the Great Plains Drought Area Committee and a man of exceptional communication skills, to give him a committee report setting forth a "long-term program . . . for the Great Plains area." This request quickly produced The Future of the Great Plains, one the most penetrating analyses of the problems of US settlement in the arid West, issues addressed fifty years before by John Wesley Powell. The difficulties of agricultural development in the Dust Bowl region, the report argued, were not to be resolved by some new crop or farming technology or even a new government program: "The basic cause of the present Great Plains situation is an attempt to impose upon the region a system of agriculture to which the Plains are not adapted and to bring into semi-arid and arid regions methods which . . . are suitable only for a humid region."[23]

Too many people, the report went on, were trying to live in the arid regions of the West, farming in the wrong way. The government must "consider how great a population, and in what areas, the Great Plains can support." The homesteading distribution of public lands had, in the arid West, "been mistaken." A new economy based on conservation and effective use of all water available was necessary. Intelligent adjustment to the ways of nature must take the place of attempts to "conquer her." Aldo Leopold was not one of the drafters of the Great Plains report, but he often expressed ideas that became a part of New Deal environmentalism. "What, concretely, is our ambition as a city?" he said in the late 1920s to the Chamber of Commerce of Albuquerque, New Mexico. "100,000 by 1930? Shouldn't our efforts be diverted to betterment instead of bigness?"[24]

The Future of the Great Plains was delivered to FDR on a campaign visit to Bismarck, North Dakota. He endorsed the report nationally in a Fireside Chat and sent it to Congress, where it seems to have had little impact.

Fittingly, conservationists' core goal was undramatically realized in 1934 when the second Roosevelt president signed a law few understood. Quietly, in 1934, Congress enacted the Taylor Grazing Act, intended to "prevent overgrazing and soil deterioration" on the more than 60 million acres of arid grazing lands in the formal ownership but never under the effective management of the Department of the Interior. We can bypass the interesting details of this sobering case of what would later be called "clientele capture" of the apparatus of the state for private ends (underpriced grazing on fragile grasslands). The Taylor Act was a hinge of history. It allowed the president by executive order to close the rest of the public domain from further entry, which FDR did. It was the formal end of a long era of disposal of our landed inheritance to homesteaders and corporations.

FDR had once said, "I want to be a preaching president like my cousin." All presidents, it may be said, seek maximum favorable publicity for their winning or promising ventures, but FDR's intention to be a "preaching president" committed him to a certain amount of "lecturing" about why the people had gotten themselves into trouble and how they must change their ways. Not many presidents have held a press conference as FDR did in 1936 when he raised a fundamental question about the wisdom of the grains export/soil erosion economy of so much of the US heartland. "We must avoid any national agricultural policy," he said in a press conference in January 1936, "which will result in shipping our soil fertility to foreign nations. You can put that in quotes." This was a rare scolding tone for a politician, but for FDR it was a part of the job description, though less important than lifting the spirits of a people enduring mass unemployment. In a 1939 letter to governors he wrote, "The nation that destroys its soil destroys itself," and everyone knew he was scolding farmers—who vote. This was a preaching president in full voice, and alert listeners of the second President Roosevelt would not be surprised.[25] A national audience listening to his second inaugural heard: "The presidency is not merely an administrative office. That is the least of it. It is pre-eminently a place of moral leadership. All of our great Presidents were leaders of thought at times when certain historic ideas in the life of the nation had to be clarified." Most historians recognize his intellectual gifts as primarily those of communication rather than cognition— choice of vocabulary and phrase, emotional warmth, selecting or inventing appropriate settings (Fireside Chats). FDR was elected every time he ran for president (four), and his daily mail, averaging 5,000–8,000 letters a day, ten times that of Hoover. FDR's tree/soil/watershed interests gave the broad conservationist agenda a prominence not matched since the presidency of his cousin. His administrations made much use of the new media of the day. The Dust Bowl was a spectacular event making its own publicity as it sent black clouds of dust eastward, but millions of Americans gained something of an ecological understanding from the Works Progress Administration (WPA) documentary *The Plow That Broke the Plains* ("Our heroine is the grass," Director Pare Lorenz declared) with dramatic music by Virgil Thompson.

Our story of conservation in the FDR years has led through early job-creating innovations—the mobilization in the CCC of a new forestry work-force, soil-protection programs on private land, and building in the Tennessee River Valley an agency for hydroelectric power and other purposes. Conservation and a president-led economic recovery and political reform movement were exploring a symbiotic partnership with exhilarating policy implications.

What of the established core of the conservation agenda that had pushed itself onto the desk of every president from Benjamin Harrison through Hoover—national parks, forests, wildlife protection? FDR and his New Deal engaged these on a broad front, spurred by ranks of lieutenants eager for employment, influence, and a place to put a shoulder to the wheel of conservation's established agenda. FDR's New Deal was a magnet for talent, and as much as he needed lieutenants he expressed a measure of realism when he once described some of them—probably including Ickes of the Interior Department and A. E. Morgan of the TVA—as "prima donnas."[26]

The national parks enjoyed a positive public image and an expanding public visitation coming into the 1930s, and the trend continued. In 1933 the parks were visited by 3.4 million tourists, rising to 16.7 million by 1940. FDR was a frequent visitor and booster, and on the expansion of the National Park System, Congress agreed. The twenty-two national parks and forty national monuments of March 1933 were increased by FDR to twenty-six parks and eighty-two monuments by 1940—along with the Civil War battlefields, national memorials, national cemeteries, and national capital sites FDR consolidated under National Park Service (NPS) control. There were also three national parkways and a farsighted commitment to the preservation of historic sites and buildings launched in the Historic Preservation Act of 1935. Although majorities in Congress agreed to fund all of this and individual representatives often exerted decisive pressure in support of parks/monuments/forests in their districts, FDR was the lead expansionist (with Secretary Ickes a close second). FDR used the Antiquities Act to protect cultural resources on twenty-nine occasions to TR's fourteen (admittedly, FDR had thirteen years to accomplish this; TR had seven).

Appropriations rose throughout the 1930s, but park facilities were under-staffed and undermaintained. Here FDR acted in his first month in office, with an infusion of CCC labor seen as a bonanza by NPS (and USFS) man-agement but criticized by "purist conservationists," in the words of Phoebe Cutler, historian of changes in the US landscape during the 1930s. These "purists . . . viewed the Corps arriving in national woods as a farmer might welcome a herd of elephants to a lettuce field," as she phrased it.[27]

Good metaphor, but "purists"? Wrong word. The conservationist critics of the CCC's work in parks and forests were from the Muir-preservationist part of the nature-protection movement, and they did not like the tourist-promotion policies of either national bureaucracy, the NPS or the USFS. When the New Deal came, they were critical of the CCC's energetic building of roads, recreation areas, and firebreaks in the parks and forests and com-plained of the bragging by CCC publicists that they were "opening up the wilderness." These were not new complaints. Throughout the 1920s both the NPS and the USFS had drawn criticism from inside and outside the agen-cies for excessive road building and pandering to tourists.

FDR handled this unending "preservation versus use" quarrel inside con-servationism, when he was forced to deal with it, much as had his cousin TR, who managed to stay on good terms with both Muir and Pinchot. Probably FDR knew of the contradictory or at least paradoxical language of the 1916 Organic Act of the Park Service requiring the agency to preserve the parks "in absolutely unimpaired form" while also making them available for the "use, observation, health and pleasure of the people." This language asked the new agency to square a circle. When the issue could not be dodged, FDR adroitly expressed sympathy with both goals, minimized the necessity of choice, and thus frustrated both sides. He enforced no policy consistency, nor made any extended commentary, on this stubborn and irrepressible issue. In a meeting late in 1933, for example, FDR gave Secretary Ickes either permission or a command to use Works Progress Administration money and NPS resources to help build the popular but environmentally and socially intrusive Blue Ridge Parkway and name it a national park (boosters came up with "an elon-gated park"). He quietly tolerated Ickes's full-throated conversion to the preservationist side on national park issues generally. In talks with reporters as well as in private the secretary increasingly used words such as "Coney Is-land" and "hordes of tourists" as he complained of overcrowding in the parks. This top conservationist lieutenant joined those who condemned the pernicious influence of the automobile inside the parks he administered, and his boss did not chide him for breaking ranks.

The other of the two largest conservationist management assignments of all post-TR presidents, after the national parks, was the national forests. The government owned 25–30 percent of remaining US forests when the second Roosevelt took office. They were managed by a widely respected agency, the USFS, and it surely seemed to most conservationists that all Hoover's successor need do on this front was expand the acreage and number of national forests under the agency's management. This happened under FDR, 11.4 million acres being added to bring the total in 1940 to 175 million acres of national forest across forty states, mostly in the West. The shape of the expansion owed much to FDR. In his first summer in office he directed Secretary Wallace to acquire land for forests in the "yellow pine belt," from Florida to Louisiana, and also in the Carolinas—in other words, expand the national forests in a southeasterly direction.

The really urgent problems were outside the government-managed forests, FDR was informed in a letter from Pinchot (who addressed him as Franklin) received in January 1933, just weeks before his inauguration. Of 500 million acres of remaining US forests, 20 percent were in private woodlots and 55 percent under "private industrial ownership," Pinchot wrote. On these private lands clear-cutting without reforestation was rampant, followed by erosion and floods. Fire, reasonably well controlled in the national forests (here Pinchot expressed the unjustified optimism about fire suppression in national forests widely shared in the 1920s and 1930s), was also another cause of the denuding of private lands. The result was that the nation "is being deforested with appalling rapidity." Pinchot went on: "Voluntary private forestry has failed the world over. . . . Private forestry in America as a solution to the problem is no longer even a hope. The solution of the private forest problem lies chiefly in large-scale public acquisition of private forestlands."[28]

The irresponsibility of private owners and harvesters of most US timberlands was one of the themes of the noted 1932 report *A National Plan for American Forests*, sponsored by New York Senator Royal Copeland and compiled by the USFS. The United States was consuming twice as much wood as it was growing, a path to "serious depletion" of forest reserves. Federal regulation of cutting on private lands was part of the solution. The guiding intelligence behind that report was a remarkable young forester stationed in (but because of inherited wealth and boundless energy, never confined to) the Bureau of Indian Affairs, Robert Marshall. He published *The People's Forests* in 1933, essentially calling for the nationalization of the remaining large tracts of private forestlands. He converted the sixty-eight-year-old Pinchot to his view and drafted Pinchot's letter to FDR, who praised the letter. FDR quietly agreed about private forestry, but all he could squeeze out of the machinery of government was a goal of buying 76 million acres of worn-out farmland and cut-over timberland. He had to settle for 11.6 million when the war essentially ended the land "retirement" program.

FDR doubtless expected the USFS to require little of his attention, continuing its meritorious and uncontroversial course, while, with his occasional help, expanding the number and size of the forest reserves. He was chagrined to encounter unexpected disputes over the public forests from within his own cabinet. Interior Secretary Ickes coveted the USFS and passionately advocated a transfer from the Department of Agriculture to the Department of the Interior as part of his larger plan to consolidate all natural resource management agencies (under his authority) in a Department of Conservation. The ensuing feud between Ickes and Wallace and their affiliated lobbies and congressional allies created distracting battles among friends. Was the proposed reorganization a good thing for conservation? Conservationist leaders recognized the possibility that public attention to conservation would be heightened if all the government action was in one department, but several made public statements opposing the reorganization, mostly out of distrust of the Interior Department, always captive to western ranchers and miners. FDR seemed to lean toward the change, but he came to resent the drain on his time of this internal warfare and in the end sided with the stronger political forces behind Wallace. No Department of Conservation.

This noisy squabble looks trivial today, though it received media attention because powerful personalities were involved. Almost no media attention was drawn to a growing ferment among forestry-trained conservationists that gained momentum on FDR's watch, though he appears not to have been aware of it. As we have seen, critical voices inside and around the USFS began in the 1920s and carried into the 1930s an intragovernmental debate over the loss of "wildness" on the public lands and over how the land management agencies should respond. Their intellectual leader was Leopold, whose stream of articles on wildlife management and other conservation issues throughout the 1920s was increasingly anchored in the new science of ecology. But Leopold, by temperament no activist, was in faraway Wisconsin when FDR came to office. Marshall was in Washington working within the New Deal, maintained a wide correspondence, and took the lead in giving the wilderness idea an organizational focus.

Marshall first thought there should be a Wilderness Planning Board within the government. After many conversations with like-minded friends, the idea of a Wilderness Society emerged. Marshall joined with imaginer of the Appalachian Trail Benton MacKaye and others interested in preserving wilderness who took a break from a meeting in Knoxville, Tennessee, to drive to a nearby CCC camp. They pulled to the side of the road and drafted a manifesto for a Wilderness Society. Marshall contributed $1,000, an office was opened in Washington, Leopold was asked to be president (he joined the board), and a magazine, the Living Wilderness, was launched in 1935, promising to nurture a "new attitude . . . an intelligent humility toward man's place in nature." "There is a particular need for a Society now," Leopold wrote in the September 1935 issue, "because of the pressure of public spending for work relief" projects on public lands. What he meant was, US citizens in expanding numbers were buying automobiles and heading for scenic public vacationlands, and the New Deal was making a mistake by being both cheerleader and facilitator with little regard for wilderness invasion. Articles in the Living Wilderness were intended to educate the public about the real source of threats to still unspoiled public lands, not simply rapacious lumber companies but trends in the US public standard of living and mobility—1 million registered autos in 1913, 10 million in 1922, 23 million by 1929, or one for every five Americans.

Most of the leadership of this new conservation organization had professional ties to FDR's government's conservation activities and meant to offer an informed, critical, albeit sympathetic voice raising questions about matters such as the CCC's role on public lands or the three recreational parkways luring auto traffic into forest reserves. Mostly, they would advocate wilderness protection.

FDR's administration did not see the new organization, formed inside its ranks, as a problem or an antagonist—simply "antiroad." Then so was Secretary Ickes, who permitted the society's magazine to reprint one of his speeches critical of "more roads in the National Parks than we have to build."[29] Conservation had a new voice, sometimes critical of the New Deal's makers' unqualified enthusiasm for automobile tourism.

One founding member of the Wilderness Society, especially, was to express a critique of New Deal conservation that would grow into a substantial reorientation of conservation itself. Leopold, in an article written for the small audience of foresters ("The Conservation Ethic," *Journal of Forestry*, 1934), wrote that "public ownership . . . while highly desirable and good as far as it goes, can never go far enough." What was needed was a new ethic based on the emerging science of ecology. It was time in human history for land policy and treatment no longer to be based on human self-interest calculated strictly by economic criteria but by a new conservation ethic that embraced the entire "land community" of soils, plants, and animals. A few pioneering thinkers had asserted that the despoliation of land was a moral wrong, he wrote, "and I regard the present conservation movement as the embryo of such an affirmation."[30]

Leopold's readership was small though influential, his message fuzzy in places, and few had heard of or thought about this new science he was exploring in vivid prose. FDR invited Leopold to the White House to offer him a place on a committee reporting on wildlife policy revision (which he accepted), and Leopold told his son that FDR "was the most impressive man he had ever talked to." But Leopold had at best a mixed view of New Deal conservation activities and in a 1934 article warned that public ownership "won't work" as a main strategy to counter land abuse. He argued that we must "induce the private land owner to conserve on his own land." He declined an offer to head the Biological Survey and continued the intellectual work leading to the publication in 1948 of *Sand County Almanac*, a book that would move conservation toward a new orienting perspective and help give it a new name.

If TR had taken better care of himself, he would have been seventy-eight in 1936 when the electorate passed first judgment on cousin FDR's performance of his duties. TR would have been especially interested in the core of the conservation front—forests, soil, national parks, wildlife.

The second Roosevelt shot some birds when a small boy, but neither before nor after his polio attack had he hunted big game or confessed the sort of worries about the grim prospects for the large plains animals we find in TR's books on the West. Early in the New Deal, Secretary Ickes reported to FDR that a water project in the Santee and Cooper Drainage in South Carolina would threaten migratory ducks, and the president airily dismissed the issue. He was oriented toward human needs, in this case flood control and electric power. He did not take the lead on wildlife issues, but, as it turned out, responded well if and when lieutenants, and circumstances, brought them forward with a tolerable political and fiscal price tag.

One such lieutenant started as a stinging critic and never did get over his doubts about FDR. J. N. "Ding" Darling was an influential cartoonist for the Des Moines *Register*, nationally syndicated in 300 newspapers, an avid outdoorsman and duck hunter, and a Republican not friendly to the New Deal in general. The blistering drought that settled in over the Plains states in 1930 decimated the wildfowl populations using the Mississippi flyway, duck numbers by one estimate declining from 100 million to 20 million by mid-decade. Darling was appointed a member of the President's Committee on Wildlife Restoration, which issued a February 1934 report urging that $50–75 million be spent to buy 12 million acres for refuges. The White House disliked the high price tag and would not respond to the report. Darling, though complaining about FDR's foot-dragging, agreed to an invitation from Secretary Wallace, a fellow Iowan, to head the Biological Survey. There he formed a Migratory Wildlife Division, wheedled more money from Congress for refuges, and helped shape the Duck Stamp Act of 1934, which levied a fee on hunting licenses to pay for refuge maintenance. When possible he lectured FDR about wildlife issues. Darling resigned in late 1935 and put his reservations about FDR as a conservationist into speeches and cartoons. But pondering his experience inside the government led him to conclude that FDR would have taken stronger stands on waterfowl protection if the conservationist lobby were large and potent enough to match that of the gun and ammunition companies and give the president some political room. Accordingly, Darling joined with others to unite the thousands of small wildfowl protection organizations into the National Wildlife Federation (NWF), becoming its first president. He was an example of a conservationist who spent more time as critic than lieutenant, one who came to understand that a president can do more for the cause if his allies are organized. By 1940 the government had added 159 new bird refuges covering 7.5 million acres, a doubling since FDR took office.

Organizing Americans around bird appreciation and protection had long been the easiest part of the wildlife issue. The threat of extermination of wading birds and the bison had drawn enormous public sympathy and outrage at the beginning of the conservation cause. These protective impulses extended to the "beautiful" animals the public could see in the national parks—bison, elk, deer, bear, antelope, eagles. State game-protection laws and federal game refuges were the conservationist answer for the threats facing "game," the good animals that humans liked to hunt. Then there were the "varmints"—coyotes, wolves, poisonous snakes, crop eaters such as gophers. Two federal agencies associated with conservation, the Biological Survey and the USFS, after 1905 began the study and practice of poisoning rodents, pest birds, wolves, coyotes, and other predators. Predator control programs were welcomed by ranchers and farmers and built strong constituencies for these agencies, especially in the West. Only in the 1920s did a few zoologists begin to challenge federal and state policies aimed to "exterminate" certain "bad" species.

When the New Deal arrived, the NPS saw its mission as preserving all wildlife within its jurisdiction, and the agency expressed opposition to poisoning and trapping. The USFS still carried on predator programs, though attacked passionately by small conservation groups such as the Anti-Steel Trap League and the influential if miniscule Emergency Conservation Committee led by the formidable Rosalie Edge, and, toward the end of the 1930s, the rejuvenated (not rejuvenated enough for Rosalie) Audubon Society. In the 1920s and 1930s, parts of the conservation movement were responding to a new set of values. Well, not so new. Muir had told Pinchot, on one of their overnights in the Sierras in the 1890s, not to crush the scorpion they came upon, as he had as much right to life as Pinchot. This new conception of the relative value of human and animal life was gathering scientific support during the interwar years from the new study of ecology as well as from changing social values.

World events then pushed domestic issues and reforms to the wings of the stage. Fascist expansionism took hold in Japan, which seized Manchuria in 1931 and invaded China in 1937. Italy invaded Ethiopia in 1935, Germany rearmed under Adolf Hitler, allied with Italy and Japan, and launched World War II by attacking Czechoslovakia and Poland in 1938. Japan plunged the United States into that war with the Pearl Harbor attack in 1941, and the conservation campaigns went to the outer margins of the US government's attention. FDR found time in the war years to act on only a small handful of natural resource issues, such as support for Kings Canyon National Park and his veto of a bill to abolish Jackson Hole National Monument.

With the commander in chief's leadership energies necessarily directed disproportionately to military matters, wartime damage to nature had to be accepted in the emergency. The US environment and resources were badly scarred and depleted during wartime—accelerated fossil fuel combustion, more industrial toxic wastes, more modification of landscapes on a vast scale, the invention of a toxic new energy source from the atom. Much of the damage had to be permitted even on the most cherished public lands, the national parks. The NPS was moved to Chicago to make room in Washington for war-related agencies, and its staff was cut from 4,500 in 1942 to 1,500 in 1945 as the budget shrank by half. The NPS reluctantly granted more than 400 permits for army and navy use of 16 million acres of park lands for artillery and bombing ranges and temporary camps, along with the mining of salt in Death Valley, tungsten inside Yosemite, and the logging of Sitka spruce in Olympic National Park. The War Production Board removed as scrap metal statues as well as cannon and other weapons from historic sites. Public lands and historic sites preserved during half a century of conservation efforts were required to absorb their own losses in a war that claimed more than 400,000 American lives.

Most historians assess FDR's conservation leadership as the equal of TR's, and a few place it one notch higher. His knowledgeable passions about land and forests provided the vision and focus for several of the New Deal's public works programs. There seemed no part of the government's conservation portfolio he did not engage, usually expand, and encourage. Leopold described the New Deal's arrival as "a mighty force, consisting of the pent-up desires and frustrated dreams of two generations of conservationists, passed near the national money-bags while opened wide for post-depression relief. Something large and heavy was lifted off and hurled into the galaxy of the alphabets. It is still moving too fast for us to be sure how big it is."[31]

Of the earlier presidents who had given timely support to some conservation challenge, not even TR matched FDR's gifts of communication and persuasion. Presidents can lead with many tools of the office, and the main one may be using their bully pulpit to gain public attention and shape public perception and therefore the agenda. In this FDR had no peers. No president in the radio age, from Harding to Dwight Eisenhower, used that medium with FDR's gifts of warmth of voice, confidence, clarity on complex public issues. His invention of the Fireside Chat reached a radio audience of half of US households by 1935, augmenting presidential speeches and press conferences, engaging the public informally, and mobilizing the electorate. He was undeniably justified in claiming to have educated the public on the importance of natural resource preservation, though it is a difficult thing to measure. There is much evidence on his side. A lengthy essay in the *Saturday Evening Post* in September 1936, for example, observed, "Just now, the potent and all-pervading word is Conservation . . . the chosen synonym for practically everything the New Deal is doing . . . a word which public imagination seizes upon."[32]

Certainly FDR's presidency steered conservation toward a different place on the US political landscape. After the New Deal, the Democratic Party, entering a generation in which it would be dominant, became the home of most conservationists, especially the younger ones, whereas the Republican Party gradually began to lose its tie to TR.

The word "planning" is not in the Constitution, but FDR insisted that the federal government start doing a lot of it. Planning entered US public life in the early twentieth century as a tool of city growth controls, but FDR was converted to it through his contact with rural and river valley problems, and he made repeated efforts to graft some form of national planning into the executive branch. Congress disliked the prospect of policy coordination from the White House (as well as looking far ahead) and never gave funding or legal status to any version of FDR's evolving planning committees.

He fared only slightly better with a related reform, reorganization of the executive branch. He appointed a committee of three noted experts on public administration, the (Louis) Brownlow Commission, whose 1937 report began with the words, "The President needs help." The group recommended that the White House staff be expanded and that the executive branch be overhauled, all 100 independent agencies situated within one of the cabinet departments, where the president could better manage them. It also called for a permanent planning board. FDR might earlier have gained these reforms, but his 1937–1938 effort to "reform" (enlarge) the Supreme Court caused a political storm, strengthening his opponents. In 1938 he got a watered-down reorganization of the executive branch that fell far short of the "help" presidents needed. And no planning board. He left on the record his sermonizing about why national planning was needed for natural resource management and much else.

Within two decades of FDR's death the conservation movement had significantly changed, absorbing the findings of the new science of ecology, reacting to the disappointments that so often came from relying on bureaucracies in Washington, even calling itself by a new name, environmentalism. To the new generation of nature protectors emerging in the ferment of the 1960s and 1970s, Progressive Era and New Deal conservationism would begin to exhibit serious flaws. Perhaps the most striking change was the challenge to the romance of dams. No one book called into question all the prodam pieties so passionately expressed in TVA Director David Lilienthal's *Democracy on the March* (1946), first implied by FDR when he attended in 1935 the opening of the Hoover Dam's stunning concrete curves and impounded waters: "I came, I saw, and I was conquered," the president said when he saw the largest of the 5,459 flood-controlling, electricity-generating, high dams built in the first half of the century in the United States. By the 1970s the cost of such dams was beginning to enter and even dominate the discussion—the destruction of downstream riverine habitat, water loss from reservoir evaporation and leakage, inundation of river valley human settlements. In my research on FDR, especially in examining the conservation-focused work of Anna Lou Riesch Owen and Edgar Nixon, there is no evidence FDR lived long enough to hear or read the ecology-based critique of dams. The Hoover Dam "conquered" Roosevelt when he visited in 1935, and every TVA dam and the lake behind it was precious to him. But the heresy of dismantling dams to liberate rivers may have reached FDR without spurring a response for the record. Darling, the Republican convert and lieutenant who served on a New Deal wildlife committee, was an outspoken critic of the "great power dams" that "have been pretty hard on nature's protective blanket of ground vegetation and of the wild creatures who have their homes there" and "strangle the biological resources of our waterways and convert them into aquatic deserts." If FDR heard such thoughts, his response is not on the record.[33]

It is true that FDR made only a few comments about the need to accord nature a fundamental respect. "It is an error to say we have 'conquered Nature,'" he wrote in a message to Congress in 1935. "We must, rather, start to shape our lives in a more harmonious relationship with Nature."[34] But looking back from the 1960s, what caught the attention of many environmentalists was the technological hubris expressed in the New Deal's romance with dam building, stream channelization, and irrigation projects moving water vast distances from where it fell. After the CCC, the TVA drew FDR's largest enthusiasm, and in 1937 he asked Congress for seven other "little TVAs" in major watersheds. "You dream of a physical America controlled, plowing of the land controlled, river flow control, floods controlled at the flood source?" asked dramatist Sherwood Anderson in his epic poem *Puzzled America*.[35] He knew the answer, for it was New Deal conservation's dominant melody: the US government should harness flowing waters, all of them. Two decades later, by the 1960s, federal dam building was seen by a small but growing number of interested parties as part of the problem, its rationale under siege.

The Boone and Crockett Club conservationists who asked Harrison to sign a bill on forest reserves requested a relatively small act of leadership, forthcoming also from Grover Cleveland and William McKinley. Soon all of them were astonished to see TR—and after him, Wilson—provide a tutorial on something the founders feared and nineteenth-century Americans only saw a handful of times—a strong president leading the country. There was robust argument about this emerging activist model of the presidency. Its origins were broader and deeper than the temperaments and ambitions of TR and Wilson but were fueled by Progressive Era reform currents and US emergence as a global giant. The presidents of the 1920s appeared to repudiate and abandon the "modern" or strong president model, but FDR then offered strong, "progressive" leadership of the executive branch for thirteen years, pursuing and advancing several causes, conservation prominent among them—the "higher conservation," some of his lieutenants unsuccessfully tried to dub it as the 1940s arrived. It offered him and many of those allied with him not only crucial policy ideas but also a reform vision built on what he and some lieutenants began to call a "permanent country." Without conservation, FDR would likely have remained the "feather duster" of his undergraduate days at Harvard.

Taken as a whole, FDR's New Deal and strong presidency changed, some said, the constitutional order. Strong feelings ran in both directions about the Roosevelt-Wilson-Roosevelt presidencies—the liberal policies, the activist executive. After FDR's death, independent and university-based scholars began to produce streams of research and argument on these two evidently connected topics, the regulatory-welfare state and the expanding presidency. Many were drawn to study the historical role of the second Roosevelt, for his leadership had indeed been strong, long, and voter-affirmed, toward both a liberal polity and a new, strong, presidential "balance" of powers. Clinton Rossiter's best-selling *The American Presidency* gave much credit to FDR for Rossiter's own "feelings of veneration, if not exactly reverence, for the authority and dignity of the presidency," which had become to the public, Rossiter acknowledged, "a combination of scoutmaster, Delphic oracle, hero of the silver screen and father of the multitudes."[36] Roosevelt's conservation-based policy ideas and sense of vision were one foundation of this governmental transformation.

How fared conservation as an organized movement, a cluster of pressure groups, during the FDR years? The established organizations from the 1920s—Audubon, Izaak Walton League, Sierra Club (headquartered in San Francisco)—soldiered through the 1930s with stagnant memberships made up of elite, white, well-educated folk. Thousands of small groups were scattered about the country, protecting local birds and landscapes, protesting iron traps for predator control. There was also intellectual ferment leading to the formation of two new national organizations—the Wilderness Society, as we have seen, and then in 1940 a gathering in a DC hotel under the urging of Morris Cooke and Hugh Bennett of some sixty people who founded Friends of the Land to pursue a "wider outlook" involving many concerns—"soil, grass, trees, songbirds, game, flowers, livestock, landscape, outdoor recreation." The meeting and the group's magazine, The Land, foreshadowed a 1960s tone, calling for a move away from the dominant utilitarian and anthropocentric emphasis on human economic ends. The organization, which reached a membership of 10,000 before declining, disbanded in 1954.

Calculating a social movement's strength is difficult work, especially for periods when public opinion polling was nonexistent or, as in the 1930s, in its infancy. But if one looks to organizational memberships and political activism, conservation at the end of the FDR presidency seems no larger (or smaller) than in the 1920s, still an enterprise based upon upper-income elites. There was intellectual ferment within those ranks, stirrings of an ecological sensibility. But as a social movement conservation entered and left the depression years about the same in size and social composition. Regionally, conservation was anchored in New England, the Midwest, and the West Coast, conspicuously weaker in the South.

FDR occasionally asked to be judged by what he achieved given the organization of political forces around him, but he also lauded, and promised, presidential leadership. He set a high bar in the ability to arouse, educate, and motivate a social movement at crucial moments and was plotting a new way to do this as he entered his third term and final year. Prodded by Pinchot—no mean leader himself—FDR acknowledged the need for an apex institution to gather, perhaps annually, in the nation's capital to ask, How are we doing? Where next should we go? Cousin TR had created in 1908 a National Conservation Commission to prepare a resource assessment and agenda for a National Governor's Conference that year, bringing 1,000 people to the White House to hear a call for action from the president.

Could this or something like it have been usefully repeated by FDR? Perhaps as late as 1938 such an apex convocation might have been convened. After that year his presidency was captured by national security urgencies. In late 1944 conservation was far from what TR had justifiably called it in 1908, the "weightiest problem now before the Nation." Pinchot wrote to FDR in December 1944 urging an International Conference on Conservation as the Basis of World Peace. The second Roosevelt encouraged the idea and pressed a foot-dragging State Department to move forward. Then his time ran out.

One now-forgotten contribution to the conservation enterprise at the end of the 1930s should not remain forgotten, though it came not from FDR directly but from the network of his land-use-reform lieutenants. Beginning in the 1920s, Bennett, Tugwell, Cooke, Wallace, and others talked of the urgent need for changes in land use in the United States that would bring a "permanent agriculture," a phrase often heard among the rural-oriented conservationists.

But what was conservation's larger goal? Cooke, then head of the Rural Electrification Administration (REA), wrote the 1938 essay "A Permanent Country," in which he speculated on what might be required for conservation to succeed: "We have to arouse something akin to a war psychology if we are really to make this a permanent country." The borrowing from philosopher John Dewey was obvious, conservation as the moral equivalent of war. The idea was not well developed, but the phrase had great promise: a "permanent country" was Roosevelt-think, and the president responded positively when Cooke sent him the essay, although he never put that exact phrase to work. He moved a few steps in that direction in a press conference in March 1936 when he said that it should be our hope "to hand back to the next generation a country with better productive power and a greater permanency for land use than the one we inherited."[37]

Cooke's "permanent country" did not quite capture FDR's ear and become the accepted nomenclature for a needed vision of where conservation was meant to take the nation. Many environmentalists would be drawn to the word "sustainability" sixty years later.

On his return from the Yalta Conference in mid-January 1945, FDR, weary and two months from his death, rode in a plane across part of Saudi Arabia with King Ibn Saud, who appealed to the president to look out the window at his poor, suffering country. "What should I do?" FDR gazed down on the sandy desolation, then answered: "Plant trees."[38]

The two Roosevelts believed in and taught the necessity of presidential initiative in the US system—and never expressed any concerns that our constitutional balance might be upset by a steady diet of that doctrine. Born to wealth, both saw themselves as counterweights to corporate economic and political power and—FDR especially—as the friend and sponsor of the working and middle classes. "In the years to come," he said to a Cleveland crowd at the end of his third electoral campaign, "that word, President, will be a word to cheer the hearts of common men and women everywhere."[39] His remark expresses an assumption gaining strength within society as a whole as well as within conservation as it evolved from the first Roosevelt to the second—that the presidency alone of the three branches tended to speak for the majority of citizens.

6

We have met the enemy, and he is us.
— Cartoon character Pogo

For the first time in the history of the world, every human being is now subjected to contact with dangerous chemicals.
— Rachel Carson, 1962

Not a single US citizen is on record as having wanted the Great Depression to continue. All, we can assume, wished for the full employment of World War II to be followed in peacetime by a new economic boom somewhat like the 1920s, this time without Prohibition. After the war the boom indeed came, a cascade of consumer goods and economic growth with occasional brief slumps, extending from the 1940s into the late 1970s. The gross national product (GNP) of the United States doubled from 1940 to 1950 after wartime production spurred the extraction of minerals, the logging of forests, civilian as well as military consumption, and the production of wastes. The petrochemical industry expanded the production of the new materials and their toxic wastes—nylon, rayon, solvents, plastics of all kinds, and an array of pesticides, such as DDT, which exterminated malaria mosquitoes threatening the health of Allied troops in the South Pacific and the Mediterranean as well as people in the southern United States. At the apex of US achievement in science and technology was harnessing atomic energy, promising enticing civilian uses beginning with nuclear reactors for electric power production, with three in operation by 1957, seven by 1962, fifty-five by 1975.

One force behind the boom was unexpected acceleration of the nation's population growth. The total fertility rate (TFR, or number of children per family) had been declining since the mid-nineteenth century and had reached 2.3 by the mid-1930s, headed (apparently) toward or below 2.1, the rate that would eventually produce population stabilization (if immigration were negligible). Then in the late 1940s the fertility rate unexpectedly surged upward, reaching 3.7 by 1957 and remaining above 3.0 for eighteen consecutive years. This produced a baby boom generation 72 million strong, driving national population from 131.6 million in 1940 to 150.6 million in 1950 to 179.3 million in 1960, rising to more than 200 million by 1970. Because population growth had been a constant throughout our national history there was little discussion of the accelerated pace that came with the 1940s or of the global history of population of which it was a part—the human population reaching 1 billion in 1804 (demographers' best guess), 2 billion by 1927, 3 billion by 1960, rising to 4 billion by 1975, 5 billion by 1988, 6 billion by 1999.

At the end of World War II, the cause of conservationism had enjoyed the presence of a Roosevelt in the White House for nearly half of the years of the unfolding twentieth century. As much or more than any constituency of Franklin Delano Roosevelt's, conservationists were both stunned and uncertain about the future when a brain aneurysm ended the president's life on April 12, 1945, in his cottage at Warm Springs, Georgia.

HARRY S. TRUMAN

Who was this vice president, now President Harry Truman, and what could his record tell conservationists to expect or hope he would do?

The basic facts were not encouraging. First, Truman was no FDR. The vice president, to the few US citizens who knew much about him, had until 1944 been a little-known US senator from Missouri whose flat, midwestern voice came without rhetorical flair, his unimposing physical appearance apparently matched to his very ordinary political gifts. His every election to a higher position had seemed a surprise. He loved politics, but, like most office-holders in the United States, he did not have the pulpit gifts or any particular cause that could serve as, in Henry Adams's words about presidential leadership, "a course to steer, a port to seek."

Born on a farm in southern Missouri in 1884, Truman was mostly raised in small-town Independence before a family economic setback sent him back to eleven years of labor on his father's farm. Truman had little to say about those years pulling a livelihood from the soil. His memoirs began with the presidency, and the few pages in his autobiography devoted to his youth are mostly about his family and relatives. "Vivian [his brother] and I used to play in the south pasture" was about all he told us about the natural environment of his childhood. Later, at his father's urgent request, "I went to the farm in 1906 and stayed there, contrary to all the prophecies, until April 1917. . . . It was a great experience." Apparently not, as he gave those years of labor on his father's farm only two pages, describing unrelenting hard work behind the plow and the binder.[1] Biographer David McCullough tells us that the days began with his father's call at 5 a.m., he "disliked milking cows," raking hay was "a cussin' job," "every day was work, never-ending work."[2] In Truman's rural world there was little leisure apart from an occasional county fair, no nearby woods with wild animals or birds to be hunted or observed, no river or commanding bluff, no fish to be caught, not even any seasons memorable enough to be described before he took his life story where he preferred to live it, into urban Missouri.

Young Truman did well in the public schools and was something of a bookworm, confining his voracious reading mostly to the biographies of great men, particularly successful generals. He apparently read nothing on science or biology and had no higher education unless one counts courses in bookkeeping, shorthand, and typing at Spalding's Commercial College in Kansas City and, in the early 1920s, a few courses at Kansas City Law School. He held a series of jobs, mostly clerical stints for banks or the railroad. When World War I came to the United States in 1917 Truman joined the Missouri National Guard unit with which he had briefly trained, and he served in France as battery commander of an artillery regiment until armistice. He returned to Kansas City, married Elizabeth (Bess) Wallace, and started a haberdashery that failed in the 1921–1922 recession. Army ties gained him the backing of the Pendergast political machine, which dominated Kansas City, and he was elected Jackson County judge, an administrative position. By the time of his 1934 election to the US Senate, Harry Truman's only notably successful mark in life had come as a competent, well-liked, and, on one occasion, battle-tested captain of artillery.

Now, in the spring of 1945, Harry Truman was president. The conservation movement got precious little attention, let alone leadership, from FDR during the war. Truman inherited exactly the same overwhelming workload of commander in chief and commander on the home front. He, too, could be expected to devote little or essentially no time to nature preservation, at least until wartime issues retreated a bit.

And when the war ended? National security threats to the United States after the Japanese surrendered did not subside to prewar levels. Truman found himself commander in chief during an escalating conflict with the Union of Soviet Socialist Republics (USSR) and then also with China, leading to a cold war that became hot with the eruption of military conflict in Korea in 1950. He had made the decision to drop the atomic bomb ending the Pacific war and began to steer policies for future development of nuclear weaponry and technology. Postwar economic adjustments were difficult, the president vexed with strikes in the steel industry and railroads. Early in his presidency (September 1945) he proposed another New Deal he called a "Fair Deal" and was entangled in fierce partisan battles over this liberal agenda up to, through, and after his reelection campaign. Still, conservationism of a particular sort received attention as a minor theme running intermittently throughout the foreign policy–dominated Truman presidency.

This should not be surprising. No one would call prepresidential Truman, in his suits, bow ties, fedoras, and no record of having slept under the stars, a conservationist. However, he was a staunch New Dealer of the moderate sort and promised in his first cabinet meeting to "carry on Roosevelt's policies." Four months after assuming office he adopted what he thought was the conservationist part of FDR's program along with the rest, out of some mixture of loyalty to the FDR agenda and the hope of attracting voters who liked the sound of federal spending on water projects in their areas. In September 1945 he sent a message to Congress calling for his Fair Deal, a twenty-one-point program amounting to an extension of the New Deal—enlarged Social Security, national health insurance, full-employment planning. One of the twenty-one points—the seventeenth—was titled "Public Works and National Resources."

To be allocated half of one point out of twenty-one is to be squeezed almost off the table—a reminder that this president was managing, among other things, postwar economic adjustment, labor disputes, cold war challenges, and the demands of new social movements with civil rights agendas. What he saw as the conservationist to-do list coming out of the war was surprisingly narrow. He began by expressing alarm at the wartime depletion of "our natural resources"—naming copper, petroleum, iron ore, and tungsten. Also worrisome to FDR's successor was the wartime interruption of public works projects for flood control, electricity, and irrigation. We should resume investment in these, the new president told Congress, and he particularly recommended continuation of the dam building the Tennessee Valley Authority (TVA) had made the core of an attractive regional political package of inexpensive electricity, flood control, navigation, and recreation, all spurring economic development in impoverished regions. These became an unwavering part of Truman's basic program—though he seemed to have no grasp of or enthusiasm for the regional experimentation for which FDR and TVA Director Arthur Morgan had hoped.

Truman's plea for more dams and electricity and fewer floods ignored criticisms being raised here and there within the conservationist community about unanticipated costs of high dams on large rivers—silt piling up behind the dams, disruption of river ecologies (a word Truman apparently never used) and wildlife habitat, along with flooding of human communities. It was not clear what launching more TVAs had to do with his promise of "discovery of new deposits of minerals," but the thrust of the seventeenth point was clear enough. Truman knew that the dams at Boulder, Bonneville, and Grand Coulee had supplied crucial electrical power to the aluminum and aircraft industries on the West Coast. Dams in Missouri and the West had many friends, just as the TVA was popular in the South. Truman was glad that FDR in 1943 had asked the Bureau of Reclamation to plan for postwar water projects in the West as a way to offer jobs to returning veterans (the bureau quickly came up with 236 water projects after the war), and he surely remembered FDR's message to Congress on January 13, 1944, in which the president repeated his conviction that water projects in the West, including TVA-type regional river authorities, were crucial to the nation's economy.[3]

Truman, like FDR before him, understood the deal. Dams were stunning structures making energy from water headed for the sea, and neither president had to intellectually confront the environmental cost. Dams were also wonderful public works projects controlling floods, producing electricity, and paying many workers who then voted for their members of Congress and probably also the guy in the White House. The New Deal enthusiasm for dams, in this era when the romance of dams was only beginning to be challenged, was justifiably called by historian Kevin Powers the liberal dream of "pork-barrel dams" on every major US river.[4] A high-powered set of government institutions of conservationist origins—led by the Bureau of Reclamation and the Army Corps of Engineers—was ready to prepare more dam plans in which costs came in lower than benefits. Truman wanted more rivers dammed and more water moved to where it would do the most good for an expanding nation for some of the same reasons FDR had. However, FDR, especially with the TVA, had many other goals in mind. He died before he taught his successors the full agenda for US watersheds. Truman and many other New Dealers (and conservationists) were at midcentury still in the thrall of the romance of dams.

This was conventional, mainstream conservationist thinking and leadership from Truman, whose career was closed off to new ideas by his nonreading habits and general lack of curiosity about the outdoors. His friends after hours were poker players, including White House staffers and former journalists Charley Ross and Harry Vaughan. In Truman's career he had collected not one green lieutenant—another word might be tutor—who was not far away and could drop in to tell him something new and pressing. Some conservationists knew it was time to consider taking some of the older dams out rather than unquestioningly building more.

Removing dams rather than building more never came into Truman's thinking, which included projects in which water was moved somewhere nature was not taking it, as when the Army Corps of Engineers joined with state, local, and private public works entities to drain wetlands, in particular a very big one called the Everglades. Much benefit might have come if the president had read one of the best-selling books of 1947, The Everglades: River of Grass, by Marjory Stoneman Douglas. The book, called by reviewer John Hersey a "remarkable almost poem," transformed public perception of this (and all other) "worthless swamps." When the book came out Douglas was leading a campaign that succeeded in the designation of a southern portion of the Everglades as a national park. Truman traveled there in 1947 to dedicate the park. He should have invited Douglas to lunch so they could talk about many things ecological. She might have advanced his education by repeating something she had written, that the Everglades would be the "only National Park in which the wildlife, the crocodiles, the trees, the orchids, would be more important than the sheer geology of the country."[5]

It would not have been a dull lunch between Truman and this writer-activist. Douglas sat in a back row as Truman made a few remarks. There is no evidence that they spoke. As the years went by the Army Corps of Engineers' flood-control project continued to take the lead in digging more than 1,000 miles of canals and levees to channel and drain the glades on the north and east edges. The park was too small for ecological integrity even as Truman dedicated it, and Douglas had become alienated from all "developers," including the government. The term, for her and her Floridian allies, included government engineers whose project was to push the glades southward out of Florida, making room for suburbs. "Conservation is now a dead word," she said in 1982. "You can't conserve what you haven't got. That's why we [Friends of the Everglades] are for restoration." Conservation leaders keep informed of movement sentiment and impending battles.[6]

Had Truman conversed with a conservationist skeptical of more dam-building plans in the West, the president would surely have pointed out that his (and FDR's) water policies had in the past and could in the future continue to have a beneficial payoff politically. Truman was a conservationist because FDR had been one and because it was a political foundation of liberalism. Congress gave FDR and Truman (and the West) many dams—the Army Corps of Engineers building 400 dams and 3,400 flood-control projects between 1936 and the 1970s, the TVA completing 4 dams on the Tennessee River or its tributaries, the Bureau of Reclamation building 41 multipurpose dams on the Columbia River and elsewhere. But Congress would not agree to more TVA-like river valley authorities, including Truman's favorite, the Columbia Valley Administration (CVA). Truman never made a clear statement to the public on what, if anything, was lost with abandonment of the TVA model, about which he seemed to have doubts, and his administration went ahead with dams without a TVA/CVA framework because this seemed to translate into western votes for Democrats.

To make sure the westerners knew what he had done for them, Truman devoted major speeches (examples are the State of the Union Addresses, the economic report in 1948, and a special message to Congress in July 1947 and again in April 1949) on the benefits of what he was calling "conservation." From the State of the Union Address of January 5, 1949: "In our present dynamic economy the task of conservation is not to lock up our resources but to develop and improve them."[7] He traveled frequently to flood-damaged regions in the Mississippi and Columbia watersheds to remind the locals that President Harry Truman was for dams and against floods—take your choice. In the 1948 election he carried ten of eleven western states and won the race the pollsters and media assumed he would lose.

When the 1950 congressional elections approached, the president, eager to strengthen his party just two years away from his chance to run for another full term, went on a western swing to make four major speeches in Idaho, Oregon, and Washington, hoping to rally the victorious coalition he had put together in 1948 with hydroelectric power and irrigation as the core. Dam-based economic development played a major role in winning the war, he told western audiences. In Baker, Oregon: "There must be continued development of the natural resources of the Northwest" if the region was to "keep right on growing." Hydroelectric power development "will keep us the most powerful nation in the world."[8]

Truman did not anticipate resistance coming from two sides. Grumblings of dissent about spending on more dams and water-diversion projects had begun as early as wartime from parts of the conservation enterprise itself. In the summer of 1945, Democrat A. Willis Robertson of Virginia, chair of the House Select Committee on Wildlife Conservation, launched yearlong hearings intended to shift resources from water projects to wildlife protection. Wildlife managers and biologists from within and outside federal agencies testified on the damages to US ecosystems effected by war and economic growth. The committee reprinted an editorial from *Sports Afield*, one of the nation's top outdoor recreation magazines, arguing that current water development plans by the government posed a serious threat to wildlife. The director of the Izaak Walton League called the Army Corps of Engineers and the Bureau of Reclamation in 1946 a "swarm of locusts scouring the country trying to find every possible site for a dam. . . . All over the country, the destruction is going to be terrific." In late 1946 the Oregon Fish Commission concluded that the proposed dams on the Columbia River "would literally destroy the . . . salmon fishery."

Such comments reflected a looming collision between the water-diverting western conservationists to whom Truman was trying to appeal and the growing part of the movement increasingly oriented toward wildlife and wilderness values Truman did not understand or share. The open warfare within conservationism broke out in a particular, spectacular, irreplaceable place in a remote part of the Colorado River drainage.

As Bureau of Reclamation engineers were finalizing their plans in 1947 for a dam (initially two) on the Green River at Echo Park in the southeast corner of Utah as part of the ten-dam Colorado River Storage Project, they had no idea this would become the Hetch Hetchy of their day, if indeed they recalled that epic dam-builders' battle against John Muir–led preservationists half a century earlier. The proposed Echo Park Dam would submerge under 500 feet of water the remaining fossils the Dinosaur National Monument was intended to protect from theft and vandalism and flood a network of spectacular canyons rich in animal and plant life. The engineers and planners at the bureau had not anticipated the impact of mounting alarm and political mobilization among preservationists over a surge of postwar encroachments into public lands—a proliferation of resorts and roads deep in the Quetico-Superior National Forest in Minnesota, proposals to harvest Douglas fir in Olympic National Park, proposed water projects in King's Canyon Park to supply thirsty Los Angeles. Interior Secretary Oscar Chapman had said, at his confirmation hearings, that conservation "does not mean . . . the locking up of some resource in order to keep people from touching or using it. It means to develop the resource in a wise way."[9] He held a hearing on the Echo Park Dam in April 1950 at which leaders of several preservationist organizations expressed opposition. Chapman in June approved the dam, apparently under orders from the president, who had come under pressure from several western members of Congress. He spoke for those who believed in conservation defined as "wise use." Writer and unbending preservationist Irving Brant wrote the secretary to be sure he understood the passionate commitments on the preservationist side: the Dinosaur National Monument issue was "one more move in the incessant drive to break down the national park system by subordinating all values not measurable in dollars." It was time for the Muir conservationists to fight.

A monumental battle had begun over the proposed dam at Echo Park in defense of the monument and all the other national parks that might be invaded by dam builders with dubious cost-benefit calculations. David Brower, executive director of the Sierra Club, and Howard Zahniser, director of the Wilderness Society, led a large and resourceful coalition of conservationists—78 national groups and 236 state organizations formed 3 separate lobbying groups, Brower told historian Rod Nash in a 1962 interview, noting that Muir had been able to call on only 7 national and 2 state organizations.[10] A joint emergency committee was formed to lead the coalition of groups, and it produced and distributed nationally a wide range of communications—illustrated pamphlets, a documentary film, a collection of essays and photographs called *This Is Dinosaur: Echo Park Country and Its Magic Rivers* (1955) edited by noted historian and novelist Wallace Stegner, and a burst of articles in national magazines such as *Life*, *Readers Digest*, and *Newsweek*. Stegner also drew a wide readership for his 1960 "Wilderness Letter": "Something will have gone out of us as a people if we ever let the remaining wilderness be destroyed . . . if we drive the few remaining members of the wild species into zoos or to extinction."[11]

The message of the campaign was pro-park rather than anti-dam. Brower proved brilliant at publicity, especially speaking to crowds or testifying before governmental panels. He brought down the house at an presentation in Denver when he said he didn't object to dams on the Colorado River as long as the Bureau of Reclamation would build a "comparable canyon somewhere else."[12] Few enemies of the dam had access to Truman, but Brant drew upon his relationship with FDR to reach Truman with the view that the Echo Park Dam proposal brought "needless trouble" to the administration. Truman answered that he found it all an "interesting subject for discussion," but in fact he had already made up his mind. "It has always been my opinion that food for coming generations is much more important than bones of the Mesozoic period." In writing about this battle to save the Colorado River from another dam, historian Donald Worster artfully summarized the passionate attachment of the preservationists to the river the dams would harness and transform:

Once the West had been a land of canyons . . . where tamarisk and cottonwoods rustled in a slight breeze. . . . A region of broad flatlands where sandhill cranes aligned . . . to spear at frogs and crayfish . . . deer came out . . . to browse in the bottomlands, wrens singing a bright, bubbling melody had echoed from the canyon walls . . . swallows wheeling and dipping over a stream for mayflies. Salmon came fighting their way upstream from the ocean, seeking their birthing place . . . and everywhere the water purled on, free and uninhibited, racing and slackening, curling back on itself . . . meandering under empty skies, a thing always alive.[13]

Many wise-use conservationists as well as preservationists did not enjoy this internecine warfare over the dam that threatened harm to the monument and were relieved when Chapman, in November 1951, announced that he supported a search for an alternate site. The ball was on the way to the next president's court. When Truman left office in early 1953 Congress had not acted to authorize the dam. No one in Washington, D.C., had ever seen the conservation movement so politically formidable and skilled at drawing US citizens into one of their preservationist campaigns.

The organized conservation movement had been quiescent during the war, when the nation had win-the-war priorities. In early 1946, Bernard DeVoto, a historian and essayist of the West born in Utah but for years located in the East, decided to take advantage of the end of gasoline rationing and with his family took a three-month auto trip across the West to see as much as possible of the region he wrote about. He cultivated contacts with officials in major national parks and national forests, and when he visited was stunned to hear that a drama of theft of public lands was under way in the West.

The Taylor Grazing Act of 1934 had been touted as a solution to the damage inflicted on more than 200 million acres of the high, arid grasslands in federal custody in the West. But it was in fact only a vague formula for federal regulation, which meant there would be a war conducted by the ranching interests either to repeal the law and get another more to their liking or to capture the federal regulatory apparatus. Conservationists were not yet adequately aware that every federal law entrusting a governmental agency to protect natural resources was only the beginning of an unending war between client capture and conservationist counterlobbying and exposure of agency maladministration. DeVoto discovered in his travels in 1946 that the war over who would use grazing lands and how to use them was, without fanfare or public notice, being lost. The chief lobbies of the ranchers, the American Livestock Association and the National Woolgrowers Association, had a firm grip on western congressional delegations. Led by the formidable Senator Pat McCarran of Nevada, they had already neutered the grazing service and reorganized it into passivity. Now the big ranchers' plan, DeVoto learned, was more ambitious: cession of all the grazing lands to the states, who would convey property rights in perpetuity to them. Conservationists had as yet put no soldiers on the field.

DeVoto "went west in 1946 as historian and tourist," wrote his biographer Stegner: "He came back an embattled conservationist."[14] He had learned of an enormous, outrageous land grab, and he had the journalistic gifts and passion required to awaken a large national audience. In a series of articles and essays and in his column "The Easy Chair," published in the influential *Harper's Magazine*, DeVoto told the history of western ranchers' abuse of the high grazing lands the faraway federal government failed to protect from overgrazing, illegal forest cutting, and resulting erosion. Unsatisfied with unregulated access to public grazing lands, the ranchers now planned "one of the biggest land grabs in American history. The plan is to get rid of public lands altogether, turning them over to the states . . . and eventually to private ownership. This is your land we are talking about."[15] To some admirers he was a literary match for Muir; asked for the justification for national parks, he responded: "First of all, silence. In any park, three minutes walk will permit you to be alone in the primeval."[16] DeVoto published more than forty articles about the West, all but three or four about the ranchers' misuse of the public lands and heavy lobbying for a retreat from the regulatory possibilities envisioned in the Taylor Act. Allies quickly gathered around him, sharing information. Stegner and others turned out articles to mobilize opposition, and the public responded with mail to Capitol Hill. A bill by two Wyoming members of Congress designed to distribute the grazing lands to the states was withdrawn in 1948.

Before his death in 1952, DeVoto remained in full action mode as a protector of the public lands in the West, challenging the dam-building ambitions of the Bureau of Reclamation and the Army Corps of Engineers and exposing the deteriorating conditions of the national parks, underfunded for controlling vandalism and maintaining facilities under pressure from rising numbers of visitors. Apparently DeVoto was never invited to the White House for a debriefing or strategy session. Unlike the president's offices in the time of Teddy Roosevelt (TR) and his cousin, so frequently visited by strategizing conservationist lieutenants, Truman had no such contacts and nearby advisers from the organized world of nature protection.

What to say of Truman and the environment? Forced by international conflicts to build the basic narrative of his presidency around international crises—the atomic bomb decision, the cold war, the Korean War, and other national security clashes—Truman only occasionally engaged in what he called "conservation." By that term he meant damming and diverting the waters in US rivers, with an occasional word for reforestation, in which he had not the slightest interest. The US Forest Service (USFS) continued during his seven years on a path enthusiastically chosen during the war years, all-out production of wood from the national forests, seen by the agency principally as tree farms. Timber sales from the national forests rose from 1.3 to 3.1 billion board feet from 1939 to 1956, an increase of 238 percent. By war's end drain was exceeding growth, and USFS budgets in the Truman years, created jointly by the administration and Congress, continued to push for timber production while cutting back on reforestation as well as watershed and wildlife protection. Critics of the agency from the inside and outside complained, mostly to each other, of the "domesticated forest" outlook of top USFS management as well as of the aerial use of pesticides and the treatment of wildlife as either "pests" or "game." Some ecologists called for a "new forestry" that viewed trees "not as outputs for human consumption," in the words of writer Tim Foss, "but living biological entities deserving respect."[17] This struggle over the basic orientation and goals of Gifford Pinchot's beloved USFS received little public discussion and no attention from the president.

This example makes the larger point that Truman gave only one natural resource issue his attention—flowing water that could be harnessed. He displayed no interest in wildlife, little in the national parks and forests. The intellectual and legislative battles leading up to the Clean Water Act of 1972 began during Truman's presidency, but the creative and dedicated architects were in Congress—Senator Edmund Muskie and US Representative John Dingel. Biographies of Truman almost uniformly have no index entries under "conservation" and only rarely one or two items under "natural resources." Truman's memoirs never touch on these matters. In his Farewell Address, a painstakingly prepared summation of his achievements by a team of writers closely supervised by Truman, not a word was said on protection of natural resources.

His presidency, widely regarded in public opinion polls as he left office as a weak performance, is now regarded highly, even near great by some polls of historians. He decided on the durable foundations of US cold war policy, a conflict that did not break out into nuclear war, in which the United States eventually prevailed. He took decisive, if small, steps toward racial integration in the military.

And on matters environmental? It is a new question for Truman scholars. Historians have paid very little attention to Truman's unimaginative engage-

ment with the river-damming piece of conservation, and his autobiographi-
cal writings confirm that his only interest in the natural world was in rivers,
and what, when modified, they could do to increase the wealth of individuals
and thus strengthen him and his party politically.

His political instincts here were astute and were reinforced by a forty-
three-page memo on strategy for the 1948 presidential race prepared by special counsel Clark Clifford, arguing, among other things, that there would
be a political payoff in the western states if Truman enthusiastically identified with the river-development conception of conservation. Acceptance of
this advice probably helped him carry ten western states in 1948, though
many other factors were at work (the Clifford memo gave most emphasis to
Truman's stance on the cold war and on domestic matters put natural resource development fifth out of six program areas of greatest political importance).[18]

Looking back, Truman's form of technocratic, resource-exploiting conservationism, whatever its political impact, took a turn in the Colorado River
battle that irritated, alarmed, and therefore energized the growing wilderness
commitment within the conservation community. "With the tenacity of a
Missouri mule," wrote essayist Karl Brooks in a searing critique of Truman's
environmental record, "Truman hauled New Deal models for controlling
rivers into the postwar era . . . defining the postwar environmental goals
solely in terms of prosperity." This came at a time when the movement itself
was increasingly uneasy with and moving away from FDR's river-control passions and searching for an agenda including the restraint Muir tried to teach
Pinchot when he spared the scorpion on their camping trip in the Sierras.[19]

One may point out only a handful of minor exceptions to such an assessment of Truman's role as conservation policy maker. He traveled to speak at
the dedication of Everglades National Park in a successful effort to fend off
real-estate developers' efforts to reduce its size and intervened to confirm a
controversial expansion of Olympic National Park. But on neither occasion
did he articulate a compelling rationale for valuing resources that had no immediate economic benefit. There is justification for the conclusion that Truman's basic conservation impulse did not go beyond asking Congress to
allocate money for dam-building, water-diverting, landscape-altering federal agencies that had lengthening reputations as key parts of one of Washington's most formidable "iron triangles," to use a term introduced by
political scientist Theodore Lowi. One corner of such a triangle was a federal

agency—in this case, a water mover. The second was composed of a handful of pork-seeking congressional committees. The third in this case was a coalition of western ranchers/developers/growth boosters, the local constituency providing lobbying pressure. One result of the power of this formidable water-policy iron triangle was the prolific dam building mutilating more rivers in ways not yet widely understood. Some 4,000 dams were built in the United States in the 1930s and again in the 1940s, after which the pace quickened—11,296 in the 1950s and 18,833 in the 1960s. An unexpected by-product was a counterattack by national park/wilderness defenders such as DeVoto and his many readers, a new generation of leadership and followership in the Sierra Club and other organizations beginning to call themselves environmentalists. For seven years after FDR's death, Truman, hard-pressed on many fronts, found a piece of FDR's legacy he could aggressively promote while failing to understand or lead in the transformation of conservation to a larger and more intellectually vibrant movement beginning to explore the policy responses to the problems of endangered species.

The wilderness-protection sentiment that awakened during the 1920s and 1930s had a vague if appealing Muirish rationale, asserting the benefits to the human spirit of wilderness contact. The new science of ecology had been slowly working its way into a commanding intellectual position among wildlife professionals and protectors, leading them first to question predator controls. Ranchers and farmers wanted "varmints" exterminated on public lands, but wildlife managers influenced by ecologists increasingly saw this as reckless and costly mutilation of the interdependent web of nature.

The acknowledged lead writer exploring the implications of ecology for wildlife and public land management and conservation in general had been Aldo Leopold, one of whose influential essays, "The Conservation Ethic" (1934), we have earlier noted. To him and others, ecology taught the interdependence of all living things in an environment and led to the awareness that nature should not be seen simply as a commodity to be exploited and debased but as a community to which we belong. If we did not make that ethical and practical shift, he argued, society's ecological foundations would continue to be tragically eroded. Leopold's thought did not turn first to government. After initial skepticism he found some benefit in the New Deal's infusion of human resources and energy into Civilian Conservation Corps (CCC) wildlife- and soil-protection programs, but he fervently believed the key challenge was to rally the public. We have to "help businesses and consumers become conservation minded" on private lands and in their daily lives, as important as were the public lands and their maintenance. Government reservation and regulation of resource uses were essential but insufficient. Each US citizen must learn to act "with a respect for living things."

Leopold's audience had been small throughout the interwar years until the publication in 1949 (a year after he died fighting a forest fire on a neighbor's property) of A Sand County Almanac, a collection of essays tracing his own voyage from avid hunter to advocate of a "land ethic" fundamentally at odds with the frontier heritage. "The land ethic simply enlarges the boundaries of the community to include soils, waters, plants, and animals, or collectively, the land." According to that ethic, "a thing is right when it tends to preserve the integrity, stability, and beauty of the biotic community. It is wrong when it tends otherwise. . . . A land ethic changes the role of Homo sapiens from conqueror of the land-community to plain member and citizen of it."[20]

A Sand County Almanac cannot be adequately summarized. The book brilliantly explores the ethical meanings of the concept of ecology, drawing upon Leopold's on-the-ground experience as a hunter and game manager in the arid Southwest and later as a restorer of his soil-depleted Wisconsin farm. The book was soon recognized as a classic to be ranked with the writings of Muir, Henry David Thoreau, and John Burroughs. In contrast to the TR-FDR years, in which conservation sometimes seemed a cluster of federal programs, Leopold called for profound changes in citizens' values and behavior. His challenge was to the exclusively human-centered, moral foundation of US society. His book was an influential marker as government-centered conservation began a turn toward a more activist, grassroots configuration.

Other books that altered and expanded the intellectual world of conservationists came forward at the midpoint of the century. The central warning of the influential writers of the first generation of conservation intellectuals—George Perkins Marsh, TR, Pinchot—had been the imminent decline of our civilization, like others before it, as a result of soil and forest misuse and the squandering of mineral resources. One generation and two world wars later, that prophecy was repeated with updated demographics and a global perspective.

William Vogt, ornithologist and former editor of the National Audubon Society's Bird Lore, produced in Road to Survival (1948) a planetary story of human population pressures upon fragile environments. The United States was not spared. He wrote at the time, "We are probably now overpopulated" at 100 million, especially as the coming "petroleum famine overtakes us." Most Latin American countries were already overpopulated, in his bleak Malthusian assessment, and famine was ahead for much of Asia and for the USSR. Only the "control of populations and the restoration of resources" bringing all societies within the "carrying capacity" of their environments will allow a continuation of "civilized life." Vogt's best seller was complemented that year by Fairfield Osborn's shorter polemic, *Our Plundered Planet*, a historical and global tour of civilizations that collapsed when they abused their environments. "The tide of the earth's population is rising," Osborn warned. "The reservoir of the earth's living resources is falling."[21] Both authors vividly warned of a historical global population boom and its environmental damages. They did not probe deeply into its reasons or remedies beyond "birth control" achieved through the global availability of contraceptive information and technologies urged by a social movement launched by New York nurse Margaret Sanger with Planned Parenthood much earlier in the century.

These 1948 books were widely discussed declarations of what would later be termed ecopessimism, calling into question the progress narrative on which western history was based. They met with praise but also stiff resistance, especially from US engineers, scientists, and technocrats, for whom the foremost lesson of World War II was confirmation of the apparently unlimited problem-solving capacity of technology operating within a free economy. "There is almost nothing, however fantastic," declared TVA Director David Lilienthal, "that, given competent organization, a team of engineers, scientists, and administrators cannot do today." Also in 1948, news media reported that the United States had just become, for the first time, a net importer rather than net exporter of petroleum. This sounded like the ominous depletion of a vital resource. Some economists saw no problem here because foreign imports were the free-market solution to resource shortages. The experience of World War II, however, brought sobering lessons. Japan's seizure of much of Southeast Asia at once cut off US access to major rubber plantations, and the just-in-time crash program to create a domestic synthetic rubber industry taught conflicting lessons—soaring confidence in our ingenuity and alarm at the vulnerability of our increasingly mineral-export-dependent industrial economy.

When the Korean War broke out in 1950 these fears were heightened, and Truman, sounding briefly like TR warning of the depletion of the nation's basic energy and mineral supplies, appointed the President's Commission on Materials Policy, chaired by CBS executive William S. Paley. The commission's report, *Resources for Freedom* (1952), found "many causes for concern. In area after area we find soaring demands, shrinking resources. As a Nation, we are threatened, but not alert, always more interested in sawmills than saplings." For we were now a raw-materials *deficit* nation, the world's largest importer of copper, lead, and zinc. By 1952 the United States took out of the earth thirty times the amount of oil it did in 1900. Given the US population growth ahead, the commission found, energy use would double by 1975.

A reader might ask why population growth should be a "given," that is, outside the bounds of policy discussion. "We share the belief of the American people in growth," the commission lamely explained. "Granting that we cannot find any absolute reason for this belief, we admit . . . it seems preferable to any opposite, which implies stagnation and decay."[22] So Truman's commission warned of shortages of basic resources and then flinched away from the very concept of population limitation, ignoring Vogt's suggestion that the United States was already overpopulated as growth rates accelerated at midcentury. The surge of US fertility rates as well as a rise in immigration from virtually zero in the 1930s and war years to 300,000–500,000 immigrants annually in the 1950s further enlarged the nation's population. Rising fertility rates and immigration canceled the expectation in *Recent Social Trends*, the respected 1933 report by the President's Research Committee on Social Trends, that the nation's population would stabilize at 160 million, replacing it with an endless-growth scenario.[23]

Vogt seemed the only prominent conservationist wanting to take up what he called the "carrying capacity" issue—how many people could our land support? The commission assumed a "free world" where trade met some of nation's needs turned this into a global resources inquiry with a US focus. This assumption dodged the fact that the US population consumed half the raw materials, though the report nonetheless deserved attention. One resource shortage deeply worried members of the Paley Commission: "Petroleum is the great enigma of future energy supplies." Looking ahead, as governments rarely do, the Paley Commission correctly prophesied a long energy crisis and crafted advice deserving attention it did not get when it wrote, "The U.S. must now give new and deep consideration to the fundamentals upon which all . . . daily activity eventually rests—the contents of the earth and its physical environment."²⁴

Truman's popularity with voters, never robust, declined sharply after the Korean War reached a costly stalemate. His approval rating in his second term never rose above 32 percent and was often lower. His party turned in 1952 to Illinois governor Adlai Stevenson as its presidential nominee, and Truman (and DeVoto and Interior Secretary Chapman) attempted to tutor Stevenson on the correct position on issues, including conservation. Stevenson seemed receptive. He was a New Deal liberal and assumed conservation was part of his portfolio, though he knew little about it. The Republicans, desperate to break a string of five Democratic possessions of the White House, nominated General Dwight "Ike" Eisenhower, former supreme commander of Allied forces in Europe, who had recently discovered he was a Republican.

There were many issues roiling the waters during the 1952 presidential election, but conservation was not one of them, except in some western states—and there only intermittently and on the far edges. The two major national parties had not in the past sharply differed on the conservation issues, whether one consults party platforms or presidential history. Republicans Benjamin Harrison and William McKinley had been cautiously moderate on the natural-resource issues they could not avoid, as was the Democrat serving between their terms, Grover Cleveland. TR then created conservation as a political and policy issue of large proportions with a Republican brand. William Taft blurred this alignment somewhat; then Woodrow Wilson pursued a moderate conservationist set of policies. Following Wilson, Republican presidents in the 1920s were inconsistent on the same policies and problems. Because of TR, most conservationists were Republicans until the FDR performance, when the second Roosevelt decisively grafted conservation into the Democratic Party's DNA.

Truman, as we have seen, tried to extend this shift in party alliances. In the 1948 run for the White House the Republican Party, at least when it spoke with one voice in order to write a platform, did not cooperate with the Truman Democrats' ownership claims on conservation. The Grand Old Party (GOP) Platform section on conservation in 1948 could hardly be distinguished from its rivals' plank. It urged action not only on waterway development and national forests but also on protection of "soil . . . our basic natural resource." In 1952 the Democratic Platform offered eighteen paragraphs on forests, parks, wildlife, minerals on public lands, and river-basin development. This platform went on at some length endorsing river development, soil conservation, and reforestation.

The Republican Platform in 1952 resembled that of 1948 on "natural resources"—in the opening lines. Yet there was other language in the GOP plank that year opposing "efforts to establish all-powerful Federal socialistic valley authorities," pledging not to "undermine state control over water use," proclaiming "states rights to resources . . . beneath inland and offshore waters," promising "local control" of soil-erosion programs, and expressing sympathy for the "rights and privileges" of western sheep ranchers. Astute readers educated by writers such as DeVoto could hear in this platform language, if they read such mendacious documents, the voices of angry-sounding western politicians inside the GOP tent, along with newspaper editors and chambers of commerce who filled the election season air with denunciation of natural-resource protection on public lands as "socialism" and demanded the "unlocking" of natural resources on public lands by bureaucrats and politicians in the East.

The GOP was in turmoil throughout the 1940s, looking back over five failed consecutive presidential contests. The 1948 Republican Platform on "natural resources," which had straddled an uneasy centrist "we are for this but" position, had veered right by 1952, expressing a conservative suspicion of conservation. By nominating Eisenhower instead of anti–New Deal, probusiness Senator Robert Taft of Ohio, the divided Republican Party had chosen a much-respected military hero who sounded like a moderate without strong partisan instincts (he had never voted for a president, had no personal record on any domestic policy issues, and even for a time seemed uncertain as to his party affiliation).

How should a conservationist vote in 1952, given the two major parties' offerings and assuming the futility and irrelevance of that year's third-party (Progressive Party) candidate, FDR's agricultural secretary, Henry Wallace? Was one political party on the whole proving more reliable and sympathetic to nature protection than the other? On this cluster of issues, did parties matter?

The historical record was mixed, and the situation was in flux. One should have sympathy for the perplexed conservation voter in 1952. Truman campaigned for and gave issue advice to Stevenson in 1952, urging an attack on the GOP conservation record. He insisted that the parties represented a different set of preferences on the only resource question he seemed to understand—federal hydroelectric power. "If the Republicans win this election it will be a long time before you see another new structure of this kind," Truman said as he dedicated Montana's Hungry Horse Dam in October.

Were the Republicans in 1952 no longer the party of TR on resource protection? Their most recent presidency had been twenty-four years ago. In 1952, unless equipped with DeVoto's intimate knowledge of western politics and the "land-grab" fever running among many Republicans in that region, conservationists in other parts of the country had grounds in 1952 for nervous uncertainty. The Republican Roosevelt was farther back in the past than the Democrat from Hyde Park. More important, the Republicans in TR's day had been the statist, strong-government party, the Democrats suspicious of Washington and talking endlessly about "states' rights." That was reversed over the FDR years, fundamentally altering the politics of conservation in ways hard to anticipate.

And the candidates? Stevenson, who as governor of Illinois had zero involvement in any kind of conservation issue, made two speeches in the West conveying his enthusiasm for development of water resources, Truman-style. On a western tour, Eisenhower's speechwriters received much advice and language from Republican governors in the region and produced opaque lines such as this one spoken in Seattle and Sacramento: "We need river-basin development . . . but not at the expense of accepting supergovernment in which the people of the region have no voice."[25] Behind speeches crafted by speechwriters for regional audiences, neither candidate had strong views or personal knowledge on any part of conservationism. On water-power policy, they sensed regional political advantage but had no grasp of the details or the ability to articulate a larger vision. The voters entrusted the White House to Eisenhower, who had only recently affiliated with the party of TR.

DWIGHT D. EISENHOWER

Dwight Eisenhower was born in Denison, Texas, in 1890, one of six sons in a religious (Mennonite, converting to Jehovah's Witness) and economically hard-pressed family whose reading material at home consisted of the Bible. The family moved to Abilene, Kansas, where "Ike" was raised in a modest home and attended public schools. Later he fondly recalled being taught by a friendly neighbor how to fish and set traps for wildlife on the Smoky Hill River. He lived in a state experiencing a wet rainfall cycle, so therefore had no exposure to the educational experience of the Dust Bowl. After high school he worked for two years as a night foreman at a creamery where his father was maintenance engineer, then entered West Point in 1911. He graduated without distinction in the top half of his class, rose slowly in the ranks (was a major for sixteen years), and on paper seemed a quite ordinary officer and person. World War II came, and his impressive leadership gifts along with some influential patrons among senior officers carried him to the post of supreme commander of the Allied forces in Europe.

After the war he adjusted to civilian life with a stint as president of Columbia University and was "drafted" to run for the higher presidency by a party that did not know exactly what he stood for on the large political issues of the day.

What Eisenhower stood for turned out to be steering his party and the government toward what he called "moderate" or sometimes "dynamic" conservatism that would curb New Deal regulatory and spending excesses and preserve a "free economy" while containing the expansion of communism without war. Predictably, his time and energies would be dictated far more by events abroad and both routine and unforeseen developments at home than by his campaign promises, party platform, and mostly unknown priorities within what he called his "mandate for change." Post–World War II presidents not only had a large and complex nation to preside over but also the "leadership of the free world." When we glance at the index to his memoir or any history of his presidency, we see the clamor of "issues" converging upon President Eisenhower—conflicts or dangers in Korea, Indo-China, Cuba, Formosa, Suez, Hungary, Laos, Israel; policy tangles during the recessions of 1953 and 1958; farm policy; Senator Joe McCarthy; foreign trade; public housing; and his personal least favorite, "patronage" for "deserving Republicans." His watch included an unwelcome (to him) almost-new agenda item Truman had confronted in the integration of the armed services that no president since Lincoln had faced—a social movement seeking racial equality and provoking in Eisenhower's first term a crisis in Little Rock, Arkansas, requiring a presidential decision on the use of National Guard troops, then subsequent civil rights legislation.

What and where in all of these claims upon President Eisenhower were the various elements of the conservation "crusade"? Not on his mind when he arrived in the White House. The president's core interests were in the foreign-policy and national-security challenges of the Korean War and cold war. Left to his own preferences, Eisenhower would have ended the run of eleven consecutive presidents who had made a mark on conservation policies, all the way back to James A. Garfield, the last president who had not encountered natural-resource-management conflicts.

It was too late for that, even if it had been Eisenhower's inclination. Herbert Hoover had put it bluntly in 1928: "Conservation is the settled policy of the government." One has to dig to find it as Eisenhower's presidency began, however. Virtually all Eisenhower biographies and presidential histories lack an index entry under conservation, natural resources, national forests, national parks, wildlife, pollution, Dinosaur National Monument/ Echo Park Dam, let alone a word not much in use in his day, environment. Occasionally one learns from the Eisenhower histories that he liked to fish and to hunt quail and wild turkey in Georgia, though his favorite hobbies were golf, bridge, and painting. He had not read Thoreau, Marsh, Muir, Burroughs, or Leopold. Biographer Emmet J. Hughes tells us that his reading habits ran toward occasional "light fiction." His chief of staff, Sherman Adams, reported that in the evening the president sometimes read histories of the Civil War or western novels, but "Eisenhower was not much of a reader."[26] He insisted that all briefing papers come to him condensed to one page.

However, Eisenhower's two-volume presidential memoir, 1,329 pages in all, gives us at least a glimpse of what conservation meant to him. He situates himself in volume 2, *Waging Peace, 1957–1960,* with the sentence: "Those of us who venerated Theodore Roosevelt's example were determined that America's extraordinary natural resources and national beauty would not be 'civilized off the face of the earth.'"[27] What he did to prevent this was summarized in that volume in a few pages calling attention to "significant achievements . . . in quiet corners of government." He bragged, mostly in footnotes, about adding 11 million acres to wildlife refuges to the 17 million he inherited and signing the obscure Fish and Wildlife Act of 1956. In an odd addition to the conservation agenda, he pointed out that he signed a bill authorizing a $10 million investment in plants to convert saltwater into fresh, which he thought a major step toward vastly expanded "converted water" supplies. "Industries will rise on the Gulf Coast," the "Southwest will bloom," and "vast, vacant spaces in Mexico, Brazil, Africa" would be settled, according to him.²⁸

This was a half-hearted, perfunctory, and even bizarre summary. Only in a short chapter in the first volume of his memoir did Eisenhower write with conviction and even some passion of his administration's principal natural-resource preoccupation—dam building and other water projects, under-taken "in cooperation with the states"—and here it got fuzzy—"and local interests," a "partnership." He agreed with Truman that conservation meant one main thing: controlling rivers. The two presidents sharply differed on who would take the lead and how much to spend.

Neither man nor party ever made a clear and compelling argument or par-ticular case for a core water-development policy. Truman tried to repeat FDR's winning argument that multipurpose river-basin development in the hands of federally chartered regional authorities would provide cheap power as a "yardstick" by which to discipline private power monopolies, along with many other subsidiary good things—flood control, navigation, recreation. Electricity came first, spurring economic development in less-developed re-gions of the nation. Eisenhower (and the 1952 Republican Platform Com-mittee) had clearly thought enough about this to be bent on replacing it with a substitute—without repealing any federal role. After all, the president was a self-avowed TR conservationist. The Eisenhower water policy, he said of-ten in his 1952 campaign and repeated in his first State of the Union Ad-dress, would be a "partnership" in which rivers would be dammed for power and other purposes by private enterprise or state/local government, with the federal government "coming in as a cooperating partner where this seems necessary or desirable"—circumstances he could never clearly define, though he discerned them in the Bureau of Reclamation's plans to build sev-eral dams in the Upper Colorado River Basin project, while he preferred a proposal by the privately owned Idaho Power Company to build three high dams on the Snake River.²⁹

The president could not explain the difference to the public. There was clearly no room in his cloudy water-policy views for more TVAs, which he once called "creeping socialism" in a speech on a western tour and of which he said in private, "By God, if ever we could do it, before we leave here, I'd like to see us *sell* the whole thing."³⁰ Because that seemed politically impossi-ble and TVA had already survived a Supreme Court test, the president said several times that he was not seeking to terminate it, though he looked for opportunities to curb any enlargement of TVA: "No one has worked harder than I have to stop the expansion of TVA," he wrote in private correspondence.[31] He was "constantly complaining about TVA to his Cabinet," biographer Steve Ambrose wrote.[32] In the one area in which Eisenhower's views on water policy were clear, there was no opening for policy change.

What do the historians have to say about Eisenhower's conservation views and record? They find the topic marginal to his presidency, his leadership on it spotty and inept as well as out of touch with growing environmental problems.

First, Eisenhower was required to appoint a secretary of the interior who then had to appoint senior resource-management officials, personnel changes that would determine whether the department in charge of public lands would have the policy tilts of Harold Ickes, Albert Fall, or someone in between. To that post the president appointed Oregon car dealer and former governor Douglas McKay, whose appointment was greeted by the *Idaho Statesman* with enthusiasm: "There will be a long-needed cleansing of the Interior Department. The fuzzy-haired boys will be gone." The cabinet appointment of a former car dealer added to the new administration's image as a leadership team of "twelve businessmen and a plumber" (his secretary of labor). Eisenhower hardly concealed his intention to preside over a business-friendly government. McKay proved verbally accident-prone as well as development-minded and made enough key appointments and rulings favorable to public land resource users to earn him (among Democrats, and somewhat unfairly) the title "Giveaway McKay." A ring of White House aides shielded the president from the irritating public land issues out West. Historian Elmo Richardson's meticulous account in *Dams, Parks, and Politics* (1973), a study of public land/river-development politics under Truman and Eisenhower, is forced in the pages on Eisenhower to repeatedly use phrases such as the "men at the White House" or "Eisenhower's men" to describe the Eisenhower White House staff response to some natural-resource squabble his aides deflected from the president and handled on their own, with his apparent agreement.

Some conservation-policy issues, inevitably, required presidential decision making, and an early one seemed to conservationists to give a signal about Eisenhower that TR would have disliked. During the campaign Horace Albright, former National Park Service (NPS) head and president of Resources for the Future, asked both candidates to agree to endorse a

Mid-Century Conference on Natural Resources, the sort of thing TR would have done. Eisenhower's chief of staff and other Republicans suspected a conference dominated by New Dealers, so the president drew back from full participation, agreeing to make a few remarks at a luncheon when the conference was held at the end of 1953. Eleanor Roosevelt expressed a growing (and correct) sentiment when she told the press upon hearing of his decision that Eisenhower did not seem much interested in conservation.

A discouraged DeVoto, suspicious of Republicans—or at least western Republicans—since he began writing on public land issues in the late 1940s, summarized the Eisenhower regime's record in an August 1954 article in *Harper's Magazine*, "Conservation: Down and on the Way Out." "Through many little measures," he began, "most of them scantily reported in the press, the Eisenhower Administration is reversing the nation's seventy-year-old policy for protecting our natural resources." Eisenhower's airy talk of a new "partnership" in waterway development between the federal and state/local governments and private citizens turned out to be an empty phrase, DeVoto concluded. The White House never formulated or clearly articulated such a strategy, allowing influence over water projects and public land policy to shift to the "boys in the backroom"—trade associations, lobbies, special interests keen to convert public lands and resources to private profit. DeVoto described in detail some resource-policy choices the public would not find in the news media—the weakening of the Soil Conservation Service, the changes in the Federal Power Act making it more favorable to private companies, the hints of attacks on the TVA, and bills in Congress that would grant ranchers more rights on grazing lands. He did not mention the administration's cuts in the USFS budgets, except for road building, or the White House opposition to wilderness legislation. "In a year and a half," he concluded, "the businessmen in office have reversed the conservation policy" in place for seventy years. In western regions, "population pressure steadily increases. The rivers fill with silt, the water table drops, the rains run off as floods."

DeVoto could not of course discover Eisenhower's fingerprints on any of this, though it happened on his watch, adding fuel to the image of Eisenhower as a golf-playing, lightly engaged, mediocre president whose administration's conservation policies were set by the likes of Giveaway MacKay. What a "shining issue" all of this presented to Democrats in 1954 and 1956, DeVoto observed at the end of the dreary story he told.[33]

The troublesome Dinosaur National Monument fight that had started under Truman also intruded upon the new administration's time. We have seen the mobilization of preservation resistance to the Truman government's plans for two dams on the Green River in Utah, threatening to submerge the monument and to serve as a wedge to further more water projects in national parks. In November 1952, just weeks after Eisenhower's election, Richard Leonard, new president of the Sierra Club, recommended that the 7,000-member club with an annual budget of $50,000 hire as full-time executive director the editor of the club's *Bulletin*, David Brower, who had demonstrated excellent public relations skills.

It was a brilliant appointment because Brower, handsome, eloquent, and a prodigious hiker in the Sierras, proposed a campaign against the Echo Park Dam and became an impressive witness in congressional hearings: "The river, its surge and its sound," he testified, "the living sculpture of this place, would be silent forever." To bury Dinosaur National Monument in water would constitute the "tragedy of our generation." The Izaak Walton League and other conservation groups joined the effort and produced a movie on the splendor of the areas to be submerged behind the dam and an impressive critique of the water-evaporation estimates of the Bureau of Reclamation that informed Brower's and other conservationists' testimony before a House committee in January 1954.

The conservationist coalition, organized as the Council of Conservationists, coordinated a multifaceted public relations campaign, placing stories in major national magazines such as *Life, Sunset,* and *National Geographic* and organizing a letter-writing barrage of Congress. Brower persuaded respected author Stegner to edit *This Is Dinosaur,* of which every member of Congress received a copy. Mail from the public to House members ran eighty to one in favor of keeping the Echo Park area wild. The message agreed upon by the council was not "no more dams, anywhere" but "no dam in Echo Park, an irreplaceable place of beauty." "Wild country," a National Parks Association official testified, is the "place we rediscover ourselves" when "troubled, confused, or dismayed." Wilderness places such as Dinosaur National Monument were a sanctuary from the "tensions and anxieties of the civilization we have created," said Oregon senator Richard Neuberger.[34]

In March 1956, Secretary McKay agreed to drop the Echo Park Dam proposal. It seemed an enormous victory for conservationists, but in the political bargaining they had essentially agreed to the proposed Glen Canyon Dam on

the Colorado. Eisenhower detonated a dynamite charge beginning construction of the Glen Canyon Dam in October 1956. Dinosaur National Monument
was saved from inundation, but Glen Canyon would be submerged by water
destined for Phoenix, Arizona, swimming pools and toilets.

Still, the preservationists' campaign against the Echo Park Dam impressed river dammers with the public relations skills and energies of the
opposition. The City of Los Angeles withdrew its claims to power sites in
King's Canyon National Park, anticipating attacks from the formidable
preservationist lobby. The city council members were right. Immediately after the Dinosaur National Monument decision, Wilderness Society Director
Zahniser launched a campaign to pass federal legislation to make alterations
of wilderness conditions within the national parks and forests illegal.

Brower, who had floated the Green River through Dinosaur National
Monument but never the Colorado River through Glen Canyon, regretted the
"trade" for the rest of his life. "My own bitter lesson there was that you don't
give away something that you haven't seen."[35]

Eisenhower made no public statement during the battle, leaving that to
MacKay. He had seriously misjudged public sentiment and dismissed the
opposition as zealots, which did not make for a good argument. At the end
of his first term, his administration's position on the dam at Echo Park had
angered and aroused preservationists, and his larger water-power policy was
as poorly stated and understood as was Truman's different but also pro-dam
position. Conservationists were sensing the need to rethink their positions
on damming rivers at all, whether the dams were built by government agencies or corporations. Still, the Eisenhower years confirmed modern Republicanism was not very different from 1920s Republicanism. Public land
resources should be sold or leased to private developers, the Eisenhower administration believed, and the power monopoly issue raised so frequently by
the Democrats was a fraudulent partisan diversion.

Just as he had stubbornly taken the least popular as well as wrong stance
on federal dam building on some spectacular and cherished western sites,
so Eisenhower fumbled another water-related issue, a new one that again
caught him thinking in outdated ways. As the United States urbanized in the
twentieth century, the disposal of human and household waste could no
longer be managed by rural latrines and outhouses or municipal sewers conveying waste into local rivers, lakes, or bays. Crude primary treatment plants
were sometimes constructed by public works departments prodded by pub-

lic health officials, but there was no time in the twentieth century when municipal government sewage-disposal and -treatment facilities kept up with population growth except for the six years when the New Deal's Works Progress Administration (WPA) paid part of the costs (1933–1939). Pressure from municipal officials prodded enactment in 1948 of the Water Pollution Control Act, a feeble package of federal grants for research along with authorization of low-interest loans for sewage plants. Congress failed to fund the loans. If there was a growing presence of raw sewage and/or industrial waste in Lake Michigan, on the lower Hudson River, the Mississippi River, or Atlantic and Pacific beaches, it was a problem for the mayor and city council of Chicago, New York, Memphis, Mobile, Los Angeles. In the 1950s municipal officials increasingly requested federal help, and little-known US Representative John Blatnik, a Minnesota Democrat, found it easy to build a coalition of mayors, environmentalists, and labor unions for a small federal-grant program for sewage-treatment facilities. Eisenhower signed a 1956 water-pollution law authorizing a small grant program. However, he did not like federal intrusion into this aspect of local life and rallied Republicans against Blatnik's continued efforts to strengthen and expand the law from 1956 through 1960. In that election year the Democrats pushed Blatnik's bill through both houses, forcing the president to choose a politically risky veto or accept a new federal role that violated his political principles. The veto message came, describing water pollution as a "uniquely local blight" best handled by local and state government.[36]

Eisenhower's role in resisting nationalization of the regulation of water and air pollution was a consistent record of objections, but it was not treated as a major story in his memoirs or most biographies. There were, however, exceptions—occasions when the conservation story in the Eisenhower years rises up from obscurity or the footnotes to reveal a more complex, or at least inconsistent, president. The detailed account of the Eisenhower presidency found in the second volume of Stephen Ambrose's biography, *Eisenhower*, weighs in at 675 pages and is written almost entirely from the president's personal or official documents. Like his other biographies, this one is backed by an index containing almost none of conservation's familiar topics. Yet there is one exception—three references to "soil conservation" in which one learns Eisenhower expressed concern about soil erosion in private conversations and in at least one cabinet meeting and pledged support for government purchase of worn-out farmland—very New Dealish sentiments. He convinced his reluctant secretary of agriculture, Ezra Benson, to sponsor a conservation reserve, or "soil bank," program in which the government would subsidize the removal from cultivation of up to 12 percent of croplands, returning them to grasslands or national forests.

Biographer Geoffrey Perret also reports that Eisenhower had spoken of his concern about soil erosion on the few occasions that he grappled with farm policy. On one such occasion in 1955, the president told Chief of Staff Adams it was no longer acceptable to allow individuals to ruin the land simply because they owned it. In Rooseveltian language used with an aide, though not in public, Eisenhower asserted that a "nation cannot divest itself of an interest in its own soil and water."[37]

What kindled the president's rare concern for citizens' abuse of their land instead of caring for it as a natural resource belonging in some sense to the nation? Was his attention drawn to media coverage of Dust Bowl–like storms experienced in Kansas (and other prairie states) in 1954–1955? There is no direct evidence of that. Perret does tell us Eisenhower had been reading "one of the earliest works promoting environmentalism," *Big Dam Foolishness* (1954), by Elmer Peterson, an Oklahoma farmer who offered a vigorous indictment of "big-dam" projects for (among other things) having a short life span because of siltation and being "arrogantly totalitarian in procedure," inhospitable to wildlife, expensive, and far less effective at flood control than conservation methods far upstream where grass, trees, furrows, and small reservoirs could "tame" the heavy rains.[38]

Who gave, or recommended, that book to the president? He had no education or interest in matters environmental, but his gifted younger brother, Milton, worked for the Agriculture Department in Washington, D.C., from 1929 to 1942. Nominally a Republican and initially hired by the Hoover administration, in the 1930s Milton Eisenhower became a respected member of the New Deal agricultural policy team, working closely with Rex Tugwell and Secretary Wallace, even developing a personal relationship with FDR. His assignments included soil-erosion controls and land retirement. While he worked on these New Deal initiatives, his brother Major Dwight Eisenhower was in the nation's capital as an aide to General Douglas MacArthur. The Eisenhower brothers were close, and when president-elect Eisenhower entered the White House, his younger brother often spent three-day weekends working out of an office in the Executive Office Building. It is easy to imagine Milton in the 1930s (and after) conveying to his brother enthusiasm for the New Deal's soil-conservation work and years later recommending an iconoclastic 1954 book on big dams, in effect serving as the only conservationist lieutenant President Eisenhower ever had.

Congress paid no attention to the president's suggestion that it fund a federal farmland acquisition and retirement program. The more modest soil-bank initiative was launched toward the end of his first term, and the federal bureaucrats in a Republican administration were outmaneuvered by farmers just as the New Dealers had been. Farmers took federal money and contracted to idle their worst lands while increasing fertilizer and output on the rest, leading to miniscule soil-protection gains and persistent surpluses. The program was ended in 1959, though some contracts continued for ten years.

One last episode on the conservationist backroads the Eisenhower administration traveled should be noted. The historical president we have come to know, a man with no prepresidential interest in or sense of urgency about the preservation of natural resources—except worries about soil erosion—made a decision affecting the National Park System when a lieutenant and prominent Republican made a strong case for an expensive new program he would normally have resisted.

NPS Director Conrad Wirth had become alarmed at the neglect and deterioration of the park facilities following the sharply curtailed appropriations of World War II extending into the cold war. Interviewed in late 1954 by a writer from *Reader's Digest* for "The Shocking Truth about Our National Parks," Wirth warned prospective visitors to the 29 national parks and 150 historical sites and monuments that they would discover "discomfort, disappointment, even danger. . . . It is not possible to provide essential services. . . . Comfort stations can't be kept clean and . . . some of the camps are approaching rural slums." The 17 million park visitors of 1940 had become 56 million by 1955 (80 million by 1964, when Eisenhower wrote his first memoir of his White House years), but appropriations over that period had actually declined. DeVoto a year earlier had written a series of articles in the *New York Times* proposing the federal government close half of the national parks so that the NPS could try to keep the other half clean and open on the puny budget Congress allotted it.

Wirth also worried and then acted. He launched a task force within the agency to draw up Mission 66, a well-designed appeal to Congress to fund a crash program to restore and expand park facilities for the 80 million visitors expected by the fiftieth anniversary of the NPS in 1966 (the estimate was too low by nearly half; 155 million came during that anniversary year).

The president received thousands of letters from readers of the DeVoto articles, and in his memoirs Eisenhower also reported receiving a personal note from John D. Rockefeller lamenting the condition of the parks. This got Eisenhower's attention, opening a door for Wirth to promote Mission 66. When the White House staff learned of the task force and proposal, a briefing was promptly scheduled at a cabinet meeting on January 27, 1956. Eisenhower had commented days earlier to Secretary McKay: "I must admit to a very considerable ignorance in the field [of the national parks and monuments], but if we are actually neglecting them merely to save a relatively inconsequential amount of money, then we should take a second look."

After Wirth and his top assistants presented Mission 66, Eisenhower said: "Why was this request not made back in 1953?"[39] Wirth had feared that the president, per his habit, would first ask the Bureau of the Budget (BOB) if it objected to the expenditure of all that money. Somehow, in 1956, a sympathetic BOB official had been persuaded to state that the bureau had no objection. The president then firmly endorsed this ten-year plan for the maintenance and improvement of the national parks and historic sites: "This is a good project. Let's get on with it." In this case the leadership had come from the natural-resource bureaucracy. Eisenhower endorsed Mission 66 and mentioned it with pride in his State of the Union Address a year later. Congress came forward with a $1 billion appropriation that translated into reconstructed trails, campgrounds, water and sewer systems, service and administration buildings, and more rangers in the national parks.

Wirth and Eisenhower both claimed Mission 66 as a triumph for the conservation cause, and it would be obtuse to favor instead the status quo that brought it about, that is, the degradation of the national parks as a result of congressional parsimony. Still, several conservation groups expressed unhappiness with the program, objecting to the "overdevelopment" and "urbanization" represented by paved roads providing access to (among other things) a new yacht harbor and hotel near Everglades National Park, new motel complexes at Grand Teton and Yellowstone National Parks, and the damage done to surrounding terrain by widening and paving Tioga Pass Road into Yosemite National Park. If a growing population riding in an expanding fleet of automobiles and powerboats was "loving the parks to death," in the language of one NPS communication, was an occasional Mission 66 an adequate long-term answer? Wirth's solution to the deterioration of the parks seemed to some friends of the parks a superficial and temporary response, lending urgency to the efforts of those conservationists pressing for a wilderness act that would permanently protect at least parts of the parks from commercial development and hordes of human visitors.

The parks and their users and admirers were grateful, some of them keenly aware Eisenhower had almost no interest in the conservation agenda. This was his one aggressive intervention. He marshaled little or no attention to other areas where nature was under siege, such as national inattention to sewage and hazardous waste disposal and steady degradation of the Chesapeake Bay, Lake Erie, the lower Mississippi River, and lesser waterways such as the Cuyahoga River near Cleveland. Mission 66 was a small achievement, better than nothing or than Warren Harding's or Calvin Coolidge's inattention. From retirement on his Gettysburg farm, Eisenhower might have reminded us of another "proenvironment" initiative he took, though conservationist organizations had almost ignored it. In 1958 he appointed a committee to report on US military assistance programs and, fatefully, appointed as chair a Wall Street broker, William H. Draper, whose real abiding passion was fighting against global population expansion undermining economic gains in the underdeveloped world. His report convinced Eisenhower US foreign aid ought to include birth control and represented the first step toward anti–population-growth policy within US social intervention. Here Eisenhower was ahead of the conservationists of his day, and three of his successors were to follow his lead in raising the "overpopulation" issue, one of them (Richard M. Nixon) appointing a commission on the benefits to be gained from stabilization of the population of the United States.

No one has made a serious case that Eisenhower paid a political price for his unenthusiastic stewardship of natural resources. Many Republicans further down the political ladder, however, were more vulnerable. Members of the Republican leadership, rattled by the loss of their majorities in both houses of Congress in 1954, went into the 1956 and 1958 elections worried that, among other things, the party's candidates would be hurt by Democrats' assaults regarding the "Giveaway McKay" image of the GOP. To put its best foot forward, the party shortened the tedious, plodding, and Harding-Coolidge-sounding 1952 GOP Platform statement on natural resources and replaced it in 1956 with a statement claiming that this policy area had been for the past four years "one of the brightest areas of achievement and progress." The president in his reelection campaign stirred himself to line up rhetorically with TR on conservation and made public a letter to former NPS head Albright saying, "My boyhood experiences taught me many of the principles of true conservation."[40]

These gestures had little impact. There is evidence several Republican seats in the West were lost in part on this issue, though one White House poll showed voters in Oregon did not know what Eisenhower's "partnership" was, and another found that the electorate in western states had as little information on and ill-formed opinions about natural-resource issues as did voters in Chicago, Atlanta, or Rochester, New York. Eisenhower had not made any vision or battleground of conservation a political winner in any region of the country, and on his watch no part of the public lands received expanded protection—not even soil, his only resource concern. The political price for this deaf ear on conservation issues, if there was a price, was paid lower on the GOP ticket. He was elected and reelected, something no Republican had accomplished since McKinley.

The fifteen years after FDR's death had been a discouraging time for the conservation movement. The membership of national organizations was static, and few new organizations were founded. Two presidents sporadically and without inspiration had offered occasional lead-footed leadership, but only on the question of who should build dams and other water projects and where. They said almost nothing about problems of air and water pollution or agricultural pesticide hazards. Truman signed the weak Water Pollution Act of 1948, and as late as 1960 Eisenhower continued to object to strengthening the federal role in urban sewage treatment.[41] Both presidents, and even to some degree the informed conservationists of the 1940s and 1950s, deserved Leopold's complaint in A Sand County Almanac about a national conservation policy debate fixated on how to build the most economically profitable dams and irrigation systems. Leopold urged a deeper discussion of the noneconomic dimensions of the "ecological conscience" he had labeled the "land ethic." "In our attempt to make conservation easy," he wrote, "we have made it trivial."[42] Leopold wrote this in 1948. Change was on the way, owing much to his writing.

JOHN F. KENNEDY

A new president was elected in November 1960. Had the reforms of the 1960s arrived? Only on people's calendars.

The 1960s! The word brings to mind and heart a time of turbulence brought on by intellectual and social movement challenges to conventional values and institutions, decorating the national story with televised images of civil rights, antiwar, and feminist marches and protests along with college campus rebellions.

But those times had not yet arrived when, on a wintry Saturday in January 1961 the youngest president (forty-three years old) was inaugurated and told the world, "The torch has been passed to a new generation of Americans— born in this century, tempered by war, disciplined by a hard and bitter peace, proud of our ancient heritage." John F. Kennedy's words were intended to evoke a mood of renovative national change, but the 1960 election had not been a mandate for social change. JFK brought to the White House a youthful cohort bristling with confident ambition to steer the nation in a new and better direction, yet in retrospect he can be seen as the last of the three 1950s presidents. Yale University president Bart Giamatti once wisely remarked that the 1960s was that turbulent period between 1963 and 1968. One could make an equally good case that journalist Theodore White had it right when he wrote that the "Storm Decade ran from 1963 to 1974."

In either case, JFK did not live to see or engage the storms of the 1960s, though his presidency and assassination encouraged both the sense of expanding possibilities and dismaying violence that were the main currents contributing to the upheavals ahead. There is evidence that he sensed a difficult era ahead. He told biographer James Macgregor Burns during the 1960 campaign that the "1960s will be a terribly difficult time," an astute intuition that anticipated not only international crises but also the domestic turbulence that lay ahead. His education had been broad enough to include demographic perspectives, and he was able to tell a group at Yale in October 1963 that the population increase, for example, of eighteen-year-olds from 2.6 million in 1960 to 3.8 million in 1965 posed a "tremendous problem for us."[43]

"Jack" Kennedy was born in 1917 in a suburb of Boston, the second son of Rose and Joseph Kennedy, whose growing family size and wealth led to larger homes in prosperous suburbs of New York City. He attended a mix of public and private schools in urban/suburban settings and joined a local Boy

Scout troop for two years, though he left no record of any engagement with nature. He finished his college preparation at the prestigious Choate School, where he spent more time trying out (with only modest success) for athletic teams than in serious study, a pattern he repeated as a "C" student at Harvard, class of 1940. In 1937 FDR appointed Jack's father ambassador to the Court of St. James (Great Britain), and young Jack enjoyed a self-arranged series of European tours that made him familiar with London, the continent, and European politics. He joined the US Navy in 1941 and managed, with the help of family connections, to win assignment as commander of Torpedo Boat PT-109 in the Solomon Island campaigns. In August 1943, a Japanese destroyer rammed and cut his boat in half in the dead of night, and JFK was remembered and decorated not for being at the helm but for his cool heroism in leading, and in one case personally towing, injured crew members to safety.

This heroism in combat and his father's financial backing provided an adequate base from which to vault into politics, and JFK was elected to three congressional terms representing the Eleventh Congressional District of Massachusetts, then two US Senate terms from 1953 to 1960. The presidency was his (and his father's) goal, his youth and Roman Catholicism thought to be serious obstacles. But JFK was handsome, dynamic, verbally gifted, and the author of two books, one of them a Pulitzer Prize–winning study of eight exemplary US senators, *Profiles in Courage* (1956). He won the Democratic presidential nomination in 1960 and very narrowly defeated the GOP candidate, Eisenhower's vice president, Nixon.

Conservation issues made virtually no appearance in the 1960 presidential campaign. JFK occasionally criticized the Eisenhower administration's conservation record for a "no new starts" policy on federal water-power projects and for vetoing a water-pollution-control bill. He seized this political opportunity in an October 1960 speech in Ohio: "I am not a part of an administration which vetoed a bill to clean our rivers from pollution."[44] The candidates debated four times on national television (and radio) before audiences estimated at 60–80 million each time, 80 percent of the adult population viewing at least one debate. The candidates were asked no questions about conservation issues. Except for an eight-word comment by JFK on how Republicans disliked the TVA and a claim by Nixon that his party added more hydroelectric power in two terms than in any previous period, they had nothing to say in these face-to-face debates on engagement with their natural environment. The debates produced tedious, cautious banalities and homilies about whether the "free world" or communism was "ahead" or "behind," what the United States should do about Quemoy and Matsu Islands off of China, who was to blame for labor bosses such as Jimmy Hoffa, how the country could enjoy faster economic growth, who was to blame for farm surpluses, what to do about teachers' salaries or the minimum wage or communist subversives inside the United States. *Life* magazine invited both to write essays in the late summer of 1960 on their visions for the nation, and each matched the other's insipid cliches about how best to lead the free world and sustain US prosperity.

Why was it, then, that I stood with a dozen friends for two hours in the cold November rain on a street corner not far from the Columbia University campus, where I was a history graduate student, in the hope of glimpsing JFK's cavalcade of cars as it moved down Manhattan toward a Times Square campaign event? He had been a junior US representative and senator with a short voting record but no legislative achievement. His votes positioned him somewhere in the moderate, centrist middle of the Democratic Party. When asked early in his US Senate career if he was a liberal, he told a reporter: "I'd be very happy to tell them that I am not a liberal. I'm a realist."[45] My friends and I were in our 20s and were mostly liberals, aligned with the social movements working for racial equality, conservation, and women's rights.

I knew JFK was not closely attuned to any of these causes. Yet my classmates and I stood in the cold rain, hoping for a glimpse and a wave, sensing the emergence into our national political life of a young politician committed to presidential leadership toward national rejuvenation. Our evidence for JFK's promise as a national leader was mostly derived from his rhetoric and style rather than his tangible record. It was rumored he had read Richard Neustadt's seminal *Presidential Power* (1960), a subtle manual on how a president could focus his limited political resources on historic changes the public might not have explicitly authorized. I had also read James M. Burns's campaign biography, *John Kennedy: A Political Profile* and remembered the passage earlier quoted: "The 1960s will be a terribly difficult time . . . all the pigeons coming home to roost": global poverty, population growth, nationalism in underdeveloped societies, new weapon technologies. "The age of consolidation is over and . . . the age of change and challenge has come upon us. The responsibility of the next president . . . will be especially great." He must "serve as a catalyst, an energizer . . . defender of the public interest."[46]

The challenges JFK listed were mostly global. He had little to say (and Nixon nothing to say) in this campaign about the agenda being put forward by the nation's growing social reform movements and social critics. "Let us get America moving again" was Kennedy's foremost, oft-repeated, and empty campaign slogan. We liberals gathered in the rain near the Columbia campus knew this was cheaply evasive, but coming from a national newcomer with a decisive manner and high-sounding style, it seemed the best offer we social movement folks had been made by a politician in recent years.

JFK appointed several task forces to prepare policy recommendations for early action. The first such study groups addressed national security issues, but in time he appointed task forces on smallish domestic issues such as wheat and cotton. One of these was on natural resources. It was formed at the urging of his nominee for secretary of the interior, Stewart Udall, former US representative from Arizona.

JFK's impressive Inaugural Address, devoted exclusively to international matters and addressed almost equally to foreigners as to US citizens, was an early sign of his preferred policy terrain and audiences. "It really is true," he addressed Nixon in an early 1961 conversation, "that foreign affairs is the only important issue for a president to handle, isn't it? I mean who gives a shit if the minimum wage is $1.15 or $1.25?"[47] "I don't want to hear about agriculture from anyone but you, Ken," JFK said to a campaign adviser, Harvard professor John Kenneth Galbraith, "and I don't want to hear about it from you, either."[48]

The new president's anticipation of and preference for a foreign affairs–dominated presidency were prophetic, though not happily so. In April 1961, he authorized an ill-fated invasion of Cuba by Cuban exiles based in Florida and Mexico. Deterioration of relations with the USSR led to a crisis over Berlin in the early summer of 1961 and then to an October 1962 confrontation over Soviet installation of nuclear missiles in Cuba. This unrelieved series of overseas crises distracted from the administration's domestic agenda, which in any event faced not very promising prospects. Although the Democrats controlled both houses of Congress, the GOP had narrowed the gap in the 1960 elections, and a coalition of conservative southern Democrats frequently allied with Republicans stood in the way of liberal change—for which the election had given no mandate. The domestic component of JFK's "new frontier" began with the novel (to liberals) idea of a tax cut for economic stimulation and then unfolded in a series of messages to

Congress in the spring of 1961 recommending changes in health care, federal aid to education, public housing, agriculture, regulatory agencies, civil rights, and other subjects—including natural resources.

Arthur Schlesinger, Jr., the Harvard historian who worked in the JFK White House, wrote that the president approached conservation "with a good deal more initial warmth" (than agriculture, which he did not want to hear about) and "cared deeply about the loveliness of lakes and woods and mountains . . . detested the clutter and blight which increasingly defaced the landscape" and "loved ocean beaches, gulls wheeling in the sky." Schlesinger offers no evidence for this deep caring, and there seems to be none. The historian concedes JFK "remained unregenerately a city man," and "in the pressures of presidential life in the sixties, conservation had a rather low priority." "Intellectually he is fine," Secretary Udall said about the new president. "When the problems are brought to him, his response is excellent. But he doesn't raise them himself."[49] "The trouble is, Jack," commented Supreme Court Justice William O. Douglas, "you've never slept on the ground." "An outdoorsman he was not," said journalist Ben Bradlee.[50] "He didn't hunt, fish, tent, backpack, or slip away alone into the wilderness," observed biographer Michael O'Brien.[51]

At the first cabinet meeting Secretary Udall proposed a conservation agenda "worthy of the two Roosevelts," and the president was receptive. The result was the first serious statement on conservation of JFK's political career, a special message to Congress on February 23, 1961, written by White House staffers Ted Sorenson and Lee White. The message began by conveying JFK's discovery that the government's "widely scattered resource policies . . . have overlapped and often conflicted." He proposed to issue executive orders establishing a focal point for "coordination" of "resource policies" in—of all places—the Council of Economic Advisers. How to coordinate "resource policies" was an important issue going back to Ickes's proposal to turn the Interior Department into the Department of Conservation. JFK had rediscovered the issue of how to organize conservation, but his thinking had not moved very far. He had at least made the correct judgment that a focal point for natural-resource policies should be in the office of the president, not in one of the cabinet departments. He asked for more money for familiar federal activities—forest management, flood control, municipal sewage plants, research on air pollution, nuclear power development, and water desalinization (there it was again). JFK seemed unaware his recommendation of more roads into public forestlands to increase timber harvesting would be unpopular with parts of the conservationist community. His February 1961 message called attention to a public land issue botched in the follow-through after the Taylor Grazing Act (1934), pointing out that the 152 million acres of grazing land in the public domain deserved better protection. That was quite an understatement. In 1963 Secretary Udall followed through on the president's words, infuriating many western US representatives and senators and all the ranchers by raising grazing fees on these severely deteriorating high grasslands, taking an important first step toward restoring the range and ending the government subsidy for grazing livestock.

It was a traditionalist message, dealing with the Pinchot side of things, the consumable resources. The Muir component was brief. The president in a few words urged passage of the wilderness protection bill stalled in Congress and asked legislators to establish more national parks or recreation areas on the coasts, such as the proposed site at Cape Cod (where his family had a summer home).

By November the Cape Cod National Seashore was in place, and Congress appropriated more funds for wetland acquisition. Udall, complaining that the "president is imprisoned by Berlin" and that cabinet meetings were infrequent, wrote JFK again—they almost never had one-on-one meetings—to urge a "national conservation effort more significant . . . than any similar program begun by either of the Roosevelt Presidents."[52] JFK agreed to let Udall's writing team go to work, and a second message on natural resources went to Capitol Hill on March 1, 1962, claiming some progress on issues mentioned the year before and promising to convene a White House Conference on Conservation as TR had done. There was some press attention to his two conservation messages and White House conference, generally favorable. Udall claimed the administration had put the word *conservation* back in the national political discourse.

The language of JFK's two messages to Congress on natural resources was bureaucratic and managerial, the president speaking almost exclusively about incremental improvements on established programs to expand resources for human consumption—more timber, more minerals, energy supplies, clean water, edible fishes in the sea, recreational space for the vacationing masses, and more research and federal money in all areas. The second message did contain some Muir-and-Leopold-ish language: "The concept of wilderness that has been cherished by Americans is the idea of lands where man and his works do not dominate the landscape, where the earth and its whole community of life are untrammeled by man, where man himself is a visitor who does not remain."[53]

His other occasional brief statements on conservation, as when dedicating the National Wildlife Federation Building or speaking to the National Academy of Sciences, were banal and uncontroversial. On conservation, JFK was not a preaching president like the two Roosevelts. His concept of conservation, at least initially, repeated the language of Truman and Eisenhower: national parks and forests are good; so are "developed" rivers dammed for power, flood control, and navigation. Udall lent his own green writers to the White House for the two conservation special messages to Congress, and in these documents JFK's language on the subject improved. His unrehearsed messages remained wooden. When Udall organized the White House Conference on Conservation in May 1962, JFK did not make time to give a prepared welcoming talk, showed up only on the last day, and in his remarks turned quickly to the value to the "people of the world" of US technological skills in water desalination, irrigation, and harvesting more food from the oceans. He also called for more national parks for the growing number of tourists and identified "this administration" with "this cause"—conservation—which he thought should be exported abroad.[54] Addressing the conference as it prepared for its final day, JFK spoke extemporaneously and, as was his habit on this topic, he was not well informed, had not been to the places or program sites he mentioned, and had not verbally assimilated the lyrical phrasing of the two White House speechwriters assigned to natural resource issues—Sorenson and White. Udall complained that JFK in his second year had not yet learned to use the White House as a conservation pulpit.

A coalition of southern Democratic conservatives and Republicans blocked much of the proposed new legislation. JFK signed laws raising the minimum wage and Social Security benefits and providing some development money for poor regions, but legislation was stalled in committees on aid to education, health insurance, a ban on racial discrimination in public accommodations—and the Wilderness Act.

Udall twice convinced JFK, who had carried only four western states in 1960, that a western trip would pay political dividends. "I don't know that I'll enjoy it, but I'll go," was the president's response. On a short trip in 1962 the president dedicated a dam in South Dakota, stopped for speeches in Colorado and California, and visited Yosemite, which he toured by car and heli-copter, Udall in tow. "He lacks the conservation-preservation insights of FDR and TR, and it will take some work to sharpen his thinking and inter-est," the secretary recorded in his journal.[55] But it was a "good trip, a master stroke for us," and should be an annual event, according to Udall.

In the late summer of 1963, with the 1964 reelection contest not far off, Udall and conservationist Senator Gaylord Nelson of Wisconsin convinced JFK to make another tour of the West in October and of course to talk about conservation issues. Udall "was convinced that the President cared nothing about conservation issues," wrote historian Richard Reeves, so "the trip pro-vided a chance to practice." During a five-day, eleven-state trip the president on the early stops delivered speeches beginning with a ritualistic salute to TR and touching on the staple conservationist themes—dam building, reclamation so that water would "never run to the ocean unused," outdoor recreation. In North Dakota on September 25, 1963, he hailed the Garrison Dam, where "man improves what nature has done." If there was a theme, it was the Pinchotian stress on science-driven development for the needs of a population expected to reach 350 million by 2000 and an implied rebuke to preservationists. "A conservationist's first reaction in those days was to pre-serve, to hoard," but "it is not enough to put barbed wire around a forest or a lake . . . or restrictive laws and regulations on the exploitation of resources. That is the old way of doing it." This was obviously Massachusetts urbanite JFK, not Udall. The president went on to argue that US science and technol-ogy should open new resources in the oceans, desalinization of seawater, and new opportunities in coal slurry, oil shale, nuclear energy. An occasional leaden sentence testified to improvisation: "We have to purify our water." Our country "is going to be richer than ever."[56]

These speeches were so ridden with cliches as well as policy ideas that would have irritated most conservationists that JFK must have been ad-libbing from bullet points rather than reading a speech by Udall's writers. However they prepared him, it was toward "matters that bored him," for "he cared nothing about conservation issues," in biographer Reeves's words.[57] Though the audiences were large, the responses were merely polite—whether because of the platitudes uttered by the president or his lack of en-thusiasm, one cannot tell. Then in Great Falls, he thanked Montana senator Mike Mansfield for his help in pushing the Limited Test Ban Treaty through the US Senate the day before, and the crowd gave wave upon wave of applause. His next stop was Salt Lake City, and JFK departed from reclamation and hydroelectric power to talk again about the test-ban treaty and the search for a peaceful and successful end to the cold war. Again a western crowd responded with enthusiasm as JFK asserted that the "tide of history has begun to flow in the direction of freedom."

He realized that he had hit his stride, touching the deepest concerns of the public with his preferred rhetoric about the defense of freedom. Peace through strength and economic growth would be major themes in his re-election campaign, which had already begun. Who could question his political judgment, formed after testing themes on audiences in the East and West? Udall, however, thought the trip a disappointment, with JFK's speeches overemphasizing the utilitarian side of conservation. "I long," he wrote in his journal, "for a flicker of emotion, a response to the out of doors and overwhelming majesty of the land." After an overnight at the Grand Teton Lodge in Jackson Hole, Wyoming, Udall urged JFK to take a morning walk to enjoy the views and wildlife and was turned down. "Imagine a conservation trip where the leader never gets out of his suit or steps off the asphalt," Udall complained, suspecting that the reporters were right that JFK preferred to spend time with the "girls and mattresses" that came on the backup plane.[58]

When JFK's presidential time ran out in Dallas in November 1963, it could be said that his cautious and conventional conservation leadership bore a considerable resemblance to that of his two immediate predecessors, who soldiered on (Eisenhower on occasion quite reluctantly) with the now-traditional parks/forests/water-development part of the Rooseveltian agenda. One exception deserves note. Eisenhower basically rejected any federal role in controlling water pollution beyond the funding of research and spent much of his second term struggling to eliminate the construction grant program attached to the 1956 water-treatment act. JFK from the outset accepted the idea of federal water-treatment grants, a position that by 1961 took little courage, and he was able to sign authorizing legislation after six months in office.

This assessment of JFK's conservation leadership as no real departure from his predecessors (if one subtracts the two messages to Congress by Udall's speechwriters) must be qualified by the reality that he was denied the seven- to eight-year learning curve Truman and Eisenhower had. JFK was a quick study who did have close at hand at least one gifted lieutenant and tutor because he had appointed this century's best (or second-best, admirers of Ickes would say) secretary of the interior, who while in office wrote with the aid of several writer friends and especially Stegner an influential and accessible summary of what he called *The Quiet Crisis* (1963) in conservation. JFK signed his name to an admiring introduction to the book that was probably also Stegner's handiwork. Udall was hurt to learn that JFK glanced only at the book's table of contents. Whoever wrote the presidential introduction, it contained the well-crafted leadership words attributed to JFK and, at the least, claimed by him: "We must do in our own day what Theodore Roosevelt did sixty years ago and Franklin Roosevelt thirty years ago: we must expand the concept of conservation to meet the imperious problems of the new age . . . [and create] new instruments of foresight and protection and nurture."[59]

Thus, although JFK's conservation record bore a basic resemblance to the Truman-Eisenhower pattern of stale policy ideas and inattention to new environmental problems, we cannot forget he was president for only thirty-three months, a time crowded with consuming foreign crises (Bay of Pigs in April 1961, Berlin in June–July 1961, and Cuban missile crisis in October 1962). One can plausibly imagine that, with more time and without the range of ailments and haphazard drug regimens reported in Robert Dallek's biography as with him his entire adult life, JFK might have fashioned a leadership position on environmental matters matching his conversion from extreme caution to a strong civil rights position after the Birmingham interracial violence in June of the year he died. The growing power of the civil rights movement convinced JFK to move more boldly on racial justice issues, and we now know the conservation movement was expanding its numbers and horizons. Politicians tend to go where and when they are pushed. The Truman-Eisenhower-Kennedy years generated an insufficient conservationist push, but that was about to change. The 1960s were a-comin'.

When we look from presidents to the conservation movement in these postwar years, we will be surprised at what we find in a 1952 Stephen Rauschenbusch article, in which he complained conservationists were politically enfeebled because they were "atomized," with no lead organization at the top to give direction. In agreement, respected political scientist Grant McConnell in 1954 found that the "fires of the earlier movement have subsided and still burn only in scattered groups." Once the "most conspicuous cause on the American political scene," he wrote at the time, the "movement is small, divided, and frequently uncertain."[60]

Udall offered a historically grounded explanation in his 1963 book. "The conservation effort was confused and sidetracked by the catastrophic events that began in 1939," he wrote. Decades of war and cold war spurred spectacular innovations in science and technology that appeared to solve or greatly diminish conservationist fears of resource shortages. Atomic physicists tapped unlimited energy from inert elements, and the "alchemies of research" in petrochemical technology created synthetic products from wood-replacing plastics to nylon to new metals. "Preoccupied with the urgent issues of the hot and cold wars," US leaders failed to "expand the conservation concept," to keep it "abreast of the times." An increasingly affluent and expanding economy was piling a new set of problems "on the nation's doorstep"—litter, worn-out autos, overflowing junkyards, pollution, and contamination.[61] "America today stands poised on a pinnacle of wealth and power, yet we live in a land of vanishing beauty, of increasing ugliness, of shrinking open space, an overall environment that is diminished daily by pollution and noise and blight," he continued. He asked if our national-growth trajectory was in need of reexamination. "What is the ideal relationship of the human population to our environment? It is a law of nature . . . that every species in any environment has an optimum population."[62] These unusually bold and farsighted words marked an important intellectual transition, ironically to the credit of the head of the federal agency notorious for giving away the public lands or leasing them to exploiters for a pittance.

Udall's warning about new postwar forms of damage to the US environment was hardly the first. Immediately after the war a pent-up demand for affordable housing for 14 million returning, family-starting veterans was supplied by mass-production home builders pushing housing tracts into rings of suburbs expanding out to surround virtually every metropolis. The most famous of these, featured on the cover of *Time* magazine in July 1950, was Levittown on Long Island, New York, where 10,600 prefabricated houses sheltering 40,000 people were erected within days on a treeless tract. Suburban sprawl was in full swing, the 114,000 new housing starts of 1944 surging to 1.9 million in 1948. Although inexpensive housing, hastily thrown together by developers unconstrained by local zoning or planning, seemed at first an integral part of the US success story, criticism surged through the magazines, books, and other conservation media of the 1940s–1950s to the present day. Anti–suburban-sprawl discourse condemned loss of agricultural land from all the construction, flooding and erosion from bulldozed land contours, runoff from paved surfaces, groundwater pollution from septic tanks, loss of open space for recreation to roads and lawns, destruction of wildlife habitat from bulldozing of open fields, forests, and marshes.[63]

Popular magazines in the 1950s began to carry frequent sprawl critiques, and a few writers tapped large book-buying audiences. Galbraith's *The Affluent Society* (1958) held a place for several months atop the best-seller lists. The book complained that unprecedented mass consumption was lowering the quality of life in unexpected ways. A family in a large, new auto, he wrote, "passes through cities . . . made hideous by litter, blighted buildings, billboards," only to picnic beside an unkempt public park crossed by a polluted stream. Several writers in the 1950s, among them Vance Packard in *The Waste Makers* (1960) and William Whyte in influential essays begun in 1957 and in *The Lost Landscape* (1968), reached a large readership with complaints about the ugliness of the human-made environments in cities and suburbs, where junkyards had to be expanded yearly to contain 80 million tons of paper, 100 million old tires, 60 billion cans, 30 billion bottles, 5 million old cars, countless discarded appliances.

Although overflowing mounds of trash and the spread of landscape-defacing, treeless suburban tracts and commercial strips spurred books and articles in the postwar years complaining of the ugliness of the built environment, a human-health-hazard dimension had larger potential for mobilizing discontent. Few US cities at midcentury diverted their sewage to well-equipped treatment plants but rather directly into nearby waterways, which also absorbed untreated industrial waste. Rural and some suburban housing injected waste into septic tanks, of which the contents, increasingly laced with detergents and other synthetic compounds, seeped into groundwater or were eventually dumped into waterways. Public Health Service studies in the 1950s documented 20,000 "point sources" of municipal or industrial water pollution, leaving aside the general runoff into waterways of chemical fertilizers and pesticides from fields and lawns.

Air pollution, too, was an expanding by-product of US industrial and urban growth. Filthy, even sometimes dangerous, air and water had a long history in US cities or industrial sites, and citizen protest movements had been a minor part of the conservation movement of TR's era, generating many local anti–industrial-smoke and water-purification movements and a national patchwork of ineffective urban regulations along with monitoring by public health agencies with small budgets. Neither of the Roosevelts folded these urban pollution problems into their national resource-protection agendas. By midcentury, the expansion of the world-leading US industrial economy set the stage for an urban air-pollution crisis. Metropolitan areas had long allowed businesses and citizens to dump wastes—industrial smoke, automobile exhaust, and fumes from coal-burning heating systems—into the air. I vividly remember the negative effects as I walked from home to school in Nashville, Tennessee, in the winters from 1949 to 1953. The air was dark gray with soot and fumes from coal furnaces. One could not see clouds or the sun, visibility was less than one city block, the air smelly and irritating to my eyes and throat. The legal term for this sickening air was "nuisance," and we were free to sue our neighbors, or nearby factories, in local courts.

In midcentury the "nuisance" began to get more serious and receive more media attention. On November 28, 1939, a temperature inversion trapped the urban smoke of St. Louis rather than allowing it to drift eastward as was the prevailing pattern, giving residents a "day the sun didn't shine" and a number of deaths from respiratory failure. In October 1948, an atmospheric inversion settled in and stifled air movement over the steel-manufacturing towns in Ohio and western Pennsylvania. A noxious cloud darkened the air over the small factory town of Donora, near Pittsburgh, for five days, sending one-third of the town's 14,000 residents to hospitals and killing 20. Another major warning about urban air quality came from Los Angeles. In the booming war years that sunny city, ringed on the north and east by mountains forming a stagnant atmospheric bowl when the air was warm and still, rapidly expanded its manufacturing and oil-refinery industries—and its automobile traffic and population—in response to wartime mobilization. Angelenos, familiar with dust in their air, began to notice a whitish haze tinged with yellowish brown and complained of eye and throat irritation. In time they called it "smog," a word coined in London when in December 1952 an atmospheric inversion trapped stagnant air over the city along with the dense fumes from industry and coal-fired boilers used to produce hot water systems serving neighborhoods. Four thousand Londoners died of respiratory distress, an event widely covered in the US media. Los Angeles public health officials found that their smog contained, among other things, health hazards such as sulfur and nitrogen dioxides, ozone, lead, and other pollutants with which Los Angeles and other cities would long struggle.

Water- and air-pollution episodes in local areas began by midcentury to add up to a national problem inevitably categorized as a natural-resource problem—though the conservation movement had yet to aggressively engage it. This would change in the 1960s, to the complete surprise of the political class who in the cold war–dominated years misjudged the growing strength and radicalization of three social movements—civil rights, women's rights, and conservation. All three movements expanded through the 1950s and 1960s.

The leaders of the conservation movement for the most part shared the lack of foresight of other elite classes, failing to anticipate the wave of energy about to transform and rename their own movement. The battle over Echo Park Dam aroused the movement, or part of it, in the 1950s and led to a coalition to launch a campaign for a wilderness act to provide a larger protective framework for the scattered wilderness areas within the national forests, but this seemed stuck in an unresponsive Congress. Among conservationists of all stripes, a certain pessimism and weariness seemed justified. The core national conservation groups in place at midcentury—Sierra Club (1892–), National Audubon Society (1905–), National Parks Association (1919–), Izaak Walton League (1922–), Wilderness Society (1935–), National Wildlife Federation (1936–), Ducks Unlimited (1937–), Defenders of Wildlife (1947–), and Nature Conservancy (1951–)—seemed to have stabilized in members by the 1940s. Then came expansion. The Sierra Club doubled in membership in the 1950s, allowed chapters to form in states other than California, and planned a move of its headquarters to Washington, D.C. By 1968 the club counted 68,000 members, ten times the membership of 1940 and still growing. The National Audubon and Wilderness Societies also doubled memberships in the 1950s, then tripled them by the end of the 1960s.

This grassroots renaissance spilled over into the 1960s and 1970s in the form of new organizations with more aggressive tactics—groups such as the Environmental Defense Fund (1967–), Friends of the Earth (1969–), and Natural Resources Defense Council (1970–).[64] At some point in the late 1960s people began to talk of a "third conservation movement," but the label did not stick. The differences between the old and new movements were too substantial to fit under the old conservation umbrella, even though concern for the natural world was a unifying theme. The new recruits and organizations—and many of the older groups, under younger leadership—were increasingly willing to take an adversarial stance against the government's natural-resource bureaucrats, challenging their data and goals and insisting on the participation of the new generation of citizen activists, dubbed the new "radical amateurs" by writer Stephen Fox. "Environmentalists" and "environmentalism" quickly became the dominant terminology for what Udall and Lyndon Johnson had wanted to label the "new conservation." Environmentalists tilted strongly toward the preservation commitment and were likely to have read or absorbed the ecological perspectives of Leopold and others, especially the acceptance of the place of Homo sapiens as only part of the universe.

Historian Samuel P. Hays, taking a careful look not only at the new national environmental organizations but also at grassroots groups sprouting in 1960s and 1970s at local and state levels, argues persuasively in Beauty, Health, and Permanence (1987) that the newly energized environmental movement reflected a new moral outlook taking root in parts of US society. The conservation-era stress on efficient development of material resources was giving ground to a stronger appreciation among an affluent middle class of the amenities and aesthetic uses of rivers, forests, wetlands, deserts, and suburban open space. That positive side of "quality-of-life" appreciation was matched by anger at exposure to noxious pollutants, a reflection of a growing concern for the impacts on human health of environmental change that had been only a small part of the early conservation movement. Hays found environmentalism especially strong in regions of the country characterized by high levels of education and rising incomes—for example, New England and the Pacific Coast—and among younger citizens everywhere, including substantial female activism and leadership.

The nation's political classes responded slowly in the postwar years to the potent new force being created by the confluence of the older conservationism and the quality-of-life uprising among people calling themselves environmentalists. As we have seen, three presidents after FDR offered hesitant and unimaginative leadership without sensing and responding to the ongoing shift in social values on human-environment issues. A full history acknowledges intermittent leadership competition from another arena—the legislative branch. Legislators on Capitol Hill in the early 1960s strongly caught the attention and changed the political agenda of some future presidents, which remains our main story line.

Of course, legislators have been a key part of the green story. That one-man army, TR, occasionally acknowledged and praised the skills and commitment to nature protection of House members John Pomeroy, William Lacey, William Kent, Glen Norbeck, John Saylor, not household names now, green legislators who receive little or no attention here. These and others like them are not the core of our story, kept on the other end of Pennsylvania Avenue so this book can be light enough to lift. We have made little or no room for Senators George Norris, Paul Douglas, Richard Neuberger, Henry Jackson, Wayne Morse, Gaylord Nelson, and many more. But we cannot understand the burst of clean-water and clean-air legislation of the LBJ/Nixon years without attention to two from Capitol Hill whose aggressive political leadership on air- and water-pollution problems played a large role in pulling the presidency back toward the Rooseveltian activism from which Truman, Eisenhower, and JFK in varying degrees had drifted away.

As difficult as it was for presidents to move the gears of national policy on controversial issues, members of Congress were even more unlikely as innovators. True, JFK won a prize for "writing" a book about eight influential and risk-taking senators (*Profiles in Courage* was drafted by Sorenson, with JFK supplying the organizing concept and some editing) even as he planned to move upward out of the US Senate to the ultimate leadership opportunity. Members of Congress he knew earned JFK's admiration for courageous votes or speeches, not for legislative innovation. A major reason was that a feature of post–Civil War politics was the long tenures in office of southern members of Congress from that one-party region, translating into the powerful and long-term grip of conservative (even when Democrats), rural-minded legislators upon the limited number of committee chair opportunities. Elderly senators chairing powerful committees, especially southern Democrats, were likely to be conservation resistors, rarely allies. FDR's presidency brought an era of Democratic majorities, but in his day and for some time after, the liberal, younger members with reform agendas were perpetually frustrated in their legislative ambitions by a bipartisan coalition of conservatives with a firm hold on committees, especially the House Rules Committee, with its stranglehold on floor discussion of bills.

In the 1950s, however, two junior Capitol Hill legislators nonetheless advanced from back-bench obscurity to national reputations by moving pollution-control legislation—a new federal assignment—within reach of enactment in the next decade. Blatnik, operating resourcefully as chair of the formerly not very active or important House Subcommittee on Rivers and Harbors, sensed an unorganized but growing constituency that could be mobilized to support clean-water projects. With the support of young and ambitious staffers, many with training in hydrology and biology, Blatnik made himself the master of this complex subject. Linking clean water to national as well as local economic development even more emphatically than as a public health issue, Blatnik guided the nation's first federal water-pollution-control program to Eisenhower's desk in 1956 and remained in the news through annual battles with the president about funding the federal-sewage-facility construction grants. As the 1960s arrived Blatnik enjoyed a national reputation, demonstrating the political rewards to be gained through this new way of sending public-works money into congressional districts and responding to justified public alarm about pollution.

A more influential example of pollution-control entrepreneurship by upwardly mobile subcommittee chairs was Maine's Edmund Muskie. A Democrat in a Republican state who would normally face an unpromising future, Muskie was outraged at the smelly pollution of the state's Androscoggin River by paper mills, and, as it turned out, so were Maine voters. He rode his reputation as "Mister Clean" to two terms as Maine's governor and won a US Senate seat in 1956. His ambitions were bottled up as a mere member of the Senate Public Works Committee until the 1963 death of its chair, Robert Kerr, led to Muskie's promotion to chair of the new Subcommittee on Air and Water Pollution. Muskie tackled these complex topics with energy. He collected a potent combination of staff and personal expertise in ecology and engineering and began drafting legislation, holding hearings, issuing reports on air and water pollution. Other legislators took up air- and water-pollution issues, but none matched Muskie's intelligence or flair for publicity. More than anyone else, the Maine senator made himself the key figure in pushing the nation's air- and water-pollution policies from state to national standards and enforcement in a series of laws stretching throughout the 1960s—air quality in 1963 and 1965 and five water-quality laws from 1963 to 1970. Two Democratic presidents were crucial allies, but Muskie concentrated on pollution and claimed a focal position in the national conservation limelight throughout the 1960s.

Blatnik was an unimposing figure on television and in public who developed no larger ambitions. Yet he demonstrated that a constituency existed for the new federal pollution-control assignment and that obscure legislators could become entrepreneurial pollution-control hawks and ride the issue upward. Reform of the House Rules Committee in 1961–1963 opened the door a bit wider. The tall, attractive, and likeable Senator Muskie faced a different future. He was acknowledged as a leading candidate for the Democratic presidential nomination in 1968 or 1972 or after. This was certainly the view of Nixon, the likely Republican choice. Cleaning up the nation's air and water, Nixon and others were concluding, was a winning issue the Republicans should adopt and might be one of the makers, or possibly breakers, of presidents.

Nixon envied JFK's reputation for new ideas and feared a permanent eclipse behind JFK's image as a catalyst of new energies. Tracking the two presidents' conservation records should have put the Californian's soul at ease. A three-decade burst of environmentalist legislation began after JFK, who now seems a politician of the Truman era. University of Texas policy historian Dennis Soden compiled for The Environmental Presidency (1999) a table of thirty major federal environmental laws enacted from 1945 to 2000. This historic burst of regulatory laws began not with JFK but with LBJ.

Environmentalism absorbed and supplanted conservation through the 1960s, and there was a moment in which it can be said to have arrived. On June 16, 1962, the New Yorker magazine published the first of three essays by Rachel Carson that would appear that year as the book Silent Spring. The book and its reception signaled a turning point in the human-nature engagement in the modern United States.

Carson was born in 1907 and raised on the edge of a small Pennsylvania town on the Allegheny River, nurtured by her parents in an appreciation of their forests, orchard, garden, and assortment of farm animals. And books. She moved easily through college to Johns Hopkins University graduate work in biology, conducted oceanic research at Woods Hole Marine Biology Lab, and wrote articles for newspapers and magazines on the human impact on the environment while working for the US Fish and Wildlife Service. Her first book, Under the Sea Wind (1941), was well received. Her second, The Sea around Us (1951), held a position on the best-seller lists for thirty-nine weeks and was translated into thirty languages. She followed this with The Edge of the Sea (1955), bringing more honors.

What does such a skilled marine biologist author do next? A friend living in Duxbury, a suburb of Boston, wrote to Carson of her complaints to local authorities that her farm, which included a large bird sanctuary, had been sprayed repeatedly in the summer of 1957 by DDT as part of a mosquito-control program and that songbirds had died in large numbers. Carson had proposed an article on DDT's effects on wildlife to *Reader's Digest* in 1945, and it was rejected. She knew DDT was first used in 1939 in the Pacific theater during the war for mosquito and other insect eradication and was also successfully used in malaria-control efforts overseas. Without definitive tests of the chemical's toxicology, DDT had been approved by the Department of Agriculture for widespread use in the civilian market in the United States in 1945. This chemical pesticide and others had critics, among them the National Audubon Society and a handful of scientists. After receiving her friend's letter in 1957 Carson urged several other scientists to take on an inquiry into the environmental and human health effects of the new chemical pesticides and write about them for the larger public. She met with no success. Carson then began the four years of research and writing for *Silent Spring*, in the last stages battling breast cancer and debilitating radiation.

The *Reader's Digest* editors who declined to encourage her proposal in 1945 can perhaps be forgiven for missing a major public-health issue beginning to arise out of scientific and technological breakthroughs made in US chemistry and physics, then brought into daily life by corporations. Experiments with the addition of fluoride to public water supplies by the US Public Health Service in the late 1940s seemed to show reductions in tooth decay, but much of the public was alarmed at this intrusion engineered by government and industry experts. In the mid-1950s it was revealed that US above-ground testing of nuclear weapons in the deserts of the Southwest and in the Pacific (by the mid-1950s, the United States had detonated sixteen atomic test weapons, the USSR thirteen, Great Britain one) produced radioactive fallout for hundreds of miles downwind, and government scientists were forced to concede that the particularly dangerous radioactive isotope strontium-90 did not harmlessly disperse but attached itself to calcium and was taken up by grasses and found in measurable amounts in cows' milk.

Chemical pesticides, herbicides, and fungicides, however, had made a vastly larger encroachment into daily life, especially when deployed in the agriculture from which people are nourished. The rural South made especially heavy use of pesticides, deployed aerially beginning in the interwar years to increase yields of cotton, corn, and wheat. Seventeen days before Thanksgiving of 1959, the US secretary of the Department of Health, Education, and Welfare revealed that traces of an herbicide that might cause cancer were found in cranberries grown in Oregon and Washington. Federal health officials, aware the public was especially fearful of cancer as longer life spans pushed that illness ahead of all infectious diseases as a cause of death in the United States, impounded 3 million pounds of cranberries, and some states banned sales.

This was the background for Carson's book on the side effects of DDT, the miracle pesticide of a growing group of what she preferred to call "biocides"—chemicals deliberately designed to kill plants, animals, and microorganisms. DDT was especially cheap and effective, seen as a magic bullet against insect carriers of disease and boosted by the respected scientists of the Department of Agriculture and the Public Health Service. By 1959, more than 100 million acres in the United States—croplands, parks, golf courses—had been treated with herbicides, pesticides, or both, and municipal authorities widely sprayed DDT for mosquito control. Carson wisely chose it as a case study in the health effects of manufactured chemicals coming into widespread use to kill parts of nature we did not like, with little thought as to the effects on humans and "wildlife" we liked.

Given this background of new human-made poisons entering the daily environment and mounting anecdotal reports of harm to humans, it is no surprise Silent Spring had a stunning impact—commercially, politically, intellectually.

Immediate book sales quickly reached 1.5 million, buoyed by a Book-of-the-Month Club selection. A Senate committee invited Carson to testify at hearings. JFK read the book prior to publication, acknowledged its importance at a press conference, and ordered his science adviser to arrange inquiries into the safety of pesticide use. Carson explicitly stated she did not call for an immediate end to chemical pesticides (the domestic sales of DDT were banned in 1972) but rather for research into biological alternatives along with rigorous scrutiny of the health effects of pesticides on humans. The chemical and food industries, led by corporations such as Monsanto, General Mills, and Gerber along with Department of Agriculture scientists, mounted a fierce campaign to discredit her as a popularizer of (bad) science and a threat to farmers' income. A Nobel Prize–winning scientist denounced her as the author of a "half-fiction novel" mounting "vicious, hysterical propaganda against pesticides," and a noted chemist charged that her questioning of the automatic link between "science" and "human betterment" meant the "end of all human progress." She was also accused of incompetence because she was a woman, even a "spinster," somehow disqualifying her for serious scientific work. Her corporate enemies rolled out an expensive public relations campaign and a lawsuit to discredit the book. CBS News planned a TV special for April 1963, and Carson overcame shyness to respond to her critics, as she did when invited to testify before hearings of a Senate committee.

Carson and Silent Spring won on all fronts. The president's Science Advisory Committee endorsed her position that the burden of proof of safety was on the manufacturers, and public opinion shifted decisively toward alarm about the public health and environmental impacts of the pesticides in such broad use. Her testimony before the Senate committee was masterful, offering no support to her critics. The conservation/environmental movement was energized by the book, angry, and afforded an education in the ecological viewpoint and vocabulary about "food chains" and awareness of the entire world as an ecosystem in which humans wielded awesome powers and must learn to be respectful partners. The impact of Silent Spring and the ensuing controversy nurtured a new skepticism about technology and the impartiality of scientific experts as well as government agencies with close ties to agribusiness.

The book began with a gripping scenario:

There was once a town in the heart of America where all life seemed to live in harmony with its surroundings. . . . Then a strange blight crept over the area and everything began to change. . . . Mysterious maladies swept the flocks of chickens; the cattle and sheep sickened and died. . . . The farmers spoke of much illness among their families. . . . There was a strange stillness. The birds, for example—where had they gone? . . . The feeding stations in the backyards were deserted. . . . It was a spring without voices. . . .

This town does not actually exist . . . yet every one of these disasters has actually happened somewhere. . . .

What has already silenced the voices of spring in countless towns in America? . . .

It was the "contamination of air, earth, rivers, and sea with dangerous and even lethal materials . . . synthetic creations of man's inventive mind, brewed in his laboratories . . . in an endless stream."

No witchcraft, no enemy action had silenced this stricken world. The people had done it themselves.

She found that almost 500 new chemicals a year, DDT now the most famous, were being sold as aerosols, dusts, and sprays designed to kill insects, rodents, weeds, fire ants, and other "pests" without concern for the
toxic accumulation of these new chemicals in the tissues of plants and animals, eventually threatening humanity. "Can anyone believe it is possible to
lay down such a barrage of poisons on the surface of the earth without making it unfit for all life? . . . The central problem of our age has therefore become the contamination of man's total environment with such substances
with incredible potential for harm."[65]

There are few examples of a single book both energizing and reshaping
the content of a social movement. Harriet Beecher Stowe's Uncle Tom's Cabin
comes to mind, but few others. Carson's account of the poisoning of the
food chain planted the "seeds of a new activism" and was an intellectual and
political turning point, offering "undeniable proof," in Vice President Al
Gore's words in the introduction to a 1994 reprint of Silent Spring, "that the
power of an idea can be far greater than the power of politicians."[66] In focusing citizens' attention upon the hazards of substances in daily use from
farms to cities and suburbs, Carson's book expanded environmental concerns beyond the most educated social classes to connect to the daily health
hazards faced by the entire range of the population, including racial and ethnic minorities and working-class people who had not yet responded to the
messages of conservationism.[67] Carson died in 1964.

7

*In short, a land ethic changes the role of Homo sapiens from conqueror of the
land-community to plain member and citizen of it.*
— Aldo Leopold, *A Sand County Almanac*, 1949

JFK selected Texan and Senate Majority Leader Lyndon Baines
Johnson (LBJ) as his vice-presidential running mate in 1960 in
an effort to gather some southern and western votes. He had
no expectation that he was picking a president. LBJ was riding
two cars behind him in the cavalcade through downtown Dallas on November 22, 1963, when JFK was shot and killed. LBJ
was sworn in on the plane that returned him to Washington,
D.C., now the thirty-sixth president.

LYNDON BAINES JOHNSON

He was born in 1907 on a farm in the hill country west of
Austin, Texas, the first of five children born to Rebekah Baines
Johnson, a college-educated reader of poetry and history, and
Samuel Johnson, a sometimes schoolteacher and jack-of-all-
trades who spent ten years in the Texas General Assembly. The
family moved from their harsh rural existence to nearby John-
son City when LBJ was five, and it was not much of a change.
Johnson City had a population of 323 people, no water or elec-
tric service, no paved roads or railway into or out of town.
There was not much in town or high school to engage the pre-

cocious young boy other than his father's political activities, which he found absorbing.

He graduated from high school at age 15, indifferent to his studies, then spent fifteen months as a vagabond and occasional worker in California. He yielded to family pressure and returned to Texas to attend a nearby small college, where he made an impression with his unquenchable ambition and overbearing manner but not for his classroom performance, in the B– range. He took a series of teaching jobs, one in a school for Mexican students, where he displayed a new and lasting sympathy for people more disadvantaged than himself. He married Claudia ("Lady Bird") Taylor, and the couple moved to Washington, D.C., where LBJ worked for a US representative from Texas. He was named Texas director of the National Youth Administration by Franklin Delano Roosevelt (FDR), who encouraged LBJ's ambitions, finding in him a new breed of southerner who embraced the New Deal and its commitment to an active role for the federal government in combating social problems. LBJ successfully ran for the US House in 1937, could not persuade the US Navy when World War II began to give him a combat assignment (he received a reserve commission), and served briefly on the West Coast and in the Pacific theater as an inspector reporting to the president. He narrowly won a US Senate seat in 1948 and became that body's youngest majority leader in 1955. A major architect of the Voting Rights Act of 1957, Johnson in 1960 was the only southerner who had emerged as a national political figure; he was offered the vice presidency and accepted.

The shock and sense of loss at the assassination of JFK were especially devastating to liberal Democrats, particularly those from the Northeast, who expected that the new, gangly, unpolished, indifferently educated Texan president would have no natural affinity with the JFK program, especially on civil rights, and would lack the persuasive gifts and rapport with the public the young president had established. The liberal reform era gradually taking form around JFK seemed abruptly ended by three shots from a sniper's rifle in Dallas.

They were quite wrong.

They did not anticipate that the surge of national remorse at JFK's assassination would produce a strong sentiment for enactment of much of "his program," if his successor asked for this, which LBJ did within days of assuming the office. Many people underestimated LBJ, whose instincts and voting record were somewhat to JFK's left. The new president was a master of the legislative process and driven by volcanic ambitions to leave a mighty presidential legacy. No one in 1963 could foresee that, as the social reform spirits of the 1960s intensified, the Republican Party would nominate conservative, anti–New Deal, Arizona senator Barry Goldwater for president in 1964. Goldwater steered the campaign toward a referendum on whether to repeal or extend the New Deal, accompanied by appeals to take a more aggressive stand in the cold war. The result was a landslide for LBJ and the Democrats, providing the new president the congressional majorities he would persuade, cajole, and browbeat into the creation of a legislative record unprecedented in US politics.

Would the agenda include conservation? That would have seemed likely in only token fashion and without enthusiasm. Liberalism in the 1960s had developed a long list of urgent, mostly city-centered problems in need of attention. Topping the list were the intensifying demands for a range of civil rights protections put forward by the increasingly formidable, well-led civil rights movements. Lined up after that urgent assignment was a chorus of calls for federal intervention to bring remedies to urban economic and social decay, economically faltering regions such as Appalachia, rising costs of health care, a struggling educational system. Ahead of these and other social issues on the liberal reform agenda and with the highest priority of all came the management of the recurrent and dangerous brush wars of the cold war, especially JFK's expanding commitment to the pro-Western government of Vietnam as it lost its grip on the country under siege by a communist-led insurgency.

How could conservation issues gain attention in this full-throated clamor for government-led "reform"? How especially, considering the background of this new president? His New Deal commitments were unquestioned but were grounded in programs to bring jobs to unemployed Texans and others. He was no outdoorsman, was born on a "ranch" but raised in a small town, and almost entirely evaded the sort of farm chores and rural rambles Harry Truman and Dwight Eisenhower knew. For recreation, young LBJ caroused in juvenile misbehavior with his high school friends or sat mesmerized in the gallery of the Texas legislature while his father pursued his avocation. LBJ had read none of the literature of conservation; indeed, his biographers agree that he read almost no books after college. It is difficult to discover an interest in nature or conservation issues in his political, intellectual, or recreational background.

What followed when LBJ entered the White House was a pleasant surprise for conservationists. He promised continuity with the entire JFK
agenda, which contained a modest commitment to natural-resource protection pressed forward by Secretary of the Interior Stewart Udall, who LBJ was
asked to reappoint. LBJ wasted no time in pushing the JFK agenda through
Congress—the Civil Rights Act of 1964 banning segregation in public accommodations, the tax cut JFK had proposed, federal aid to education, the
Immigration Act of 1965, and another important Voting Rights Act in 1965.

This was for LBJ only a start. Determined to run in 1964 on a record
mostly his own, the president pressed his staff, fourteen policy brainstorm-
ing task forces, and key members of Congress for policy reform ideas and
action. Johnson bragged in his presidential memoir that when his campaign
for reelection came to an end in November 1964, he had signed into law (and
was chiefly responsible for the passage of) thirty-six major pieces of legislation, with thirty-seven more moving toward his desk for signing. In his
speech to the graduating class of the University of Michigan in May 1964, he
offered a label—the "Great Society"—he hoped would give identity and coherence to his carload of programs. Journalists and historians accepted the
Great Society label, but coherence was elusive.

LBJ saw mandate and opportunity in the electoral results, and what followed in 1965 was aptly called the "perfect storm" by writers Calvin MacKenzie and Robert Weisbrot in *The Liberal Hour* (2008). Active, interventionist
government was the dominant political impulse of the time, confirmed by
the results of the 1964 elections.

The rest of the "perfect storm" came in 1965–1966. Historian Vaughn
Bornet counted 90 of LBJ's 115 legislative recommendations signed into
law—the Voting Rights Act, Medicare, a new Department of Housing and
Urban Development, measures on drug control and crime, a "War on
Poverty," federal support for the arts and humanities, a presidential disabil-
ity law, and much more—a lip-numbing list.[1] In his memoir, *The Vantage
Point*, LBJ proudly quoted journalist Tom Wicker: "The list of achievements
was so long that it reads better than the legislative achievements of most
two-term Presidents."[2] LBJ's achievements! The list of LBJ's allies and col-
laborators is left out by Wicker and many other biographers. Achievements
in politics are collective, but LBJ took the lead in claiming these (and others)
as his own.

And conservation? Most of the historians of LBJ's presidency barely men-

tion, if at all, that he was the president who embraced, built upon, and expanded JFK's proposed conservation commitments, then added enough new
emphases that he felt justified in inventing (or borrowing from his speechwriters or Secretary Udall) the phrase the "New Conservation."[3] LBJ's substantial conservation record has been hidden in plain sight, for reasons
themselves not hard to see. Southern politician LBJ guided the enactment of
two major civil rights laws in a time of acute interracial crisis intensified by
the assassination of Martin Luther King, Jr. He greatly expanded the welfare
state. Then he decided on military intervention in Vietnam and destroyed his
remarkable presidency. His conservation record has thus been virtually ignored by those who have been writing his place in history.

This was not for lack of effort by Secretary Udall in many speeches and in
a 1968 memorandum summing up the administration's conservation
achievements. "A general conclusion—quite inescapable—is that presidential leadership has changed the outlook of the nation with regard to conservation and has added vital new dimensions," Udall wrote to LBJ toward the
end of his presidency. "No longer is peripheral action—the saving of a forest, a park, a refuge for wildlife—isolated from the mainstream. The total
environment is now the concern, and the New Conservation makes man,
himself, its subject. The quality of life is now the perspective and purpose of
the New Conservation."[4]

This assessment of LBJ's "New Conservation" record came from a man—
Udall—whose job it was to nurture it, expand it, and brag about it. But LBJ
would not let Udall or anyone else outbrag him. He was incessantly promotional after he had signed something and had a vastly larger and almost
daily, even hourly, audience for his view of how it all happened. Reading in
his public papers the remarks LBJ made as he traveled through Ohio or Denver making speeches on the way as he dedicated a bridge or awarded a medal
to some worthy citizen, one finds a president who matched FDR in asser-
tions of his attachment to the land and his administration's conservation
achievements and aspirations.

On signing the Wilderness Act of 1964, for example, he praised the 88th
Congress but especially himself as the president who signed bills into law.
There was justification for this, but it was flawed as history. The immense
battle over the Echo Park Dam proposal in the 1950s had aroused environmentalists from all regions of the country, enlarging their numbers and influence beyond even that of the Colorado River Basin western states, whose

US representatives, senators, and chambers of commerce were stunned at the dam proposal's defeat. Convincing a majority of Congress that national parklands were sacred space, not dam and lake sites, was a mark of how far in numbers, political tactics, and grassroots mobilization conservationists had come from the Hetch Hetchy defeat four decades earlier. The Wilderness Act that LBJ signed on September 9, 1964, which set aside 9.1 million acres (now grown to 109 million acres and 757 wilderness areas defined in part as areas "where the earth and community of life are untrammeled by man, where man himself is a visitor who does not remain"), was the product of thousands of mobilized environmentalists responding to a powerful dual appeal—preservation of wild places and access to unique recreational experiences for those equipped to hike in and out. The wilderness system came in on the words and reflections of John Muir; Aldo Leopold; Wilderness Society founders Robert Marshall, Stephen Mather, and Howard Zahniser (drafter of the act); Sierra Club Executive Director David Brower; and the matchless western writer Wallace Stegner, who created the words: "Something will have gone out of us as a people if we ever let the remaining wilderness be destroyed."[5] The president would have done well to brag about their dedication and contributions along with his lesser one in signing a popular statute conveying a widely endorsed idea.

In remarks delivered in Portland, Oregon, in September 1964, LBJ attempted to explain his own conservation commitment more personally: "I grew up on the land. The life of my parents depended entirely upon the bounty of the soil. I devoted much of my public life to protecting for our children the great legacy of our natural abundance." In a preelection policy paper on November 1, he again took a long view. "We are at the close of the greatest conservation Congress in [our] history."[6] He went on, "Three changing forces are bringing a new era to conservation"—a growing population, the "darker side" of science and technology, and urbanization, which cuts humans off from nature. We must go beyond the "classic conservation of protection and development" to "creative conservation of restoration and innovation. . . . Above all, we must maintain the chance for contact with beauty. When that chance dies, a light dies in all of us."[7]

More policy achievement, flag-waving brags, and efforts to define the New Conservation lay ahead in his second term. One of the few historians to pay close attention to LBJ's conservation record counted nine task forces on natural-resource/environmental topics and twenty-two major laws passed. If one includes among "environmental measures" presidential proclamations and executive orders, Martin Melosi estimates that LBJ signed into law almost 300 conservation and beautification measures, "more . . . than had been passed during the preceding 187 years."[8] LBJ did not wait for the historians. On signing the amendments to the Clean Air Act in October 1965, he said, "When future historians write of this era, I believe they will note that ours was the generation that finally faced up to the accumulated problems of our American life."[9]

Many of his administration's conservation achievements were squarely in the footsteps of the Roosevelts—the expansion and protection of the number and acreage of national park, forest, and recreation sites and the Wilderness Act of 1964. To add to protected areas he signed the Wild and Scenic Rivers Act and the Land and Water Conservation Fund in the Rose Garden at the same time, providing almost $2 billion from outer-continental-shelf oil and gas receipts for federal and state public land acquisition. The US Fish and Wildlife Service created the Committee on Rare and Endangered Species, which compiled a list of shrinking species, and in 1966 and l969 Congress passed the first two of three Endangered Species Acts (ESAs), the most comprehensive in 1973. Careful readers will notice that the president who supported the 1973 law through the legislative process and signed it into law was Richard Nixon, a conservative Republican. The three ESAs seem an astonishing grant of federal authority in support of wildlife, easier to understand when we know that between 1968 and 1988 the total number of national conservationist organizations in the United States grew by 110 percent to 387.

The puny federal air- and water-pollution control efforts inherited from the Eisenhower administration were substantially expanded in Clean Air (1963 and 1967) and Water (1964, 1965, and 1966) Acts. LBJ signed, and as was his habit claimed more than his share of credit for, the National Historic Preservation Act of 1966, which went beyond steps taken by Congress under the 1935 Historic Sites Act to inventory historic buildings and sites. The 1966 law established a process by which all federal projects significantly altering or destroying historic properties and sites must be mitigated or abandoned. To some this would stretch the tent of conservationism over a fundamentally different effort—preservation of the built environment. To others the laws are kin because of sharing a common determination to resist the environmental destruction that has been the central dynamic of US capitalism.

By contrast to these policy battlegrounds familiar to both of the Roosevelt presidents, there was no exact precursor for the efforts of First Lady "Lady Bird" Johnson in promoting the Great Society's theme of urban (beginning with Washington, D.C.), and then national, beautification. High points here were the 1965 White House Conference on Natural Beauty and the Highway Beautification Act of 1965 aimed at reducing billboards and screening unsightly vistas. There were other innovations woven into LBJ's New Conservation—the newness of a significant urban focus, the broad antipollution effort, the pledge not to dam selected "scenic" rivers but to let their waters run to the sea. Several of LBJ's messages to Congress display a passion and sense of alarm unmatched by any of his predecessors. In his "Special Message to the Congress on Conservation and Restoration of Natural Beauty" on February 8, 1965, LBJ said:

> The storm of modern change is threatening to blight and diminish in a few decades what has been cherished and protected for generations. A growing population is swallowing up areas of natural beauty. . . . More of our people are crowding into cities and being cut off from nature. Modern technology can also have a darker side. Its uncontrolled waste products are menacing the world we live in. . . . To deal with these new problems will require a new conservation . . . a creative conservation of restoration and innovation. Its concern is not with nature alone but with the total relation between man and the world around him.[10]

A speechwriter drafted that statement, but LBJ authorized, edited, and delivered those words. It was rare for a president to tell a story, such as LBJ did in his memoir, of an atomic scientist who saw a small turtle in his walk through the woods, picked it up for his children, then explained to a friend why he returned to put it back: "It just struck me that . . . for one man, I have tampered enough with the universe."[11]

Another Johnsonian conservation innovation never grew much beyond the policy skirmishes and speculations of some of his top staff in the Departments of State and Health, Education, and Welfare (HEW) and the War on Poverty—inclusion of population limitation as a part of the policy agenda of the federal government. In the Truman years William Vogt and Fairfield Osborn had caught public attention in the late 1940s with books on the devastating environmental and social consequences of the acceleration of global and national population growth. For a growing number of conservationists these writers had succeeded in adding population limitation to the nature-protection perspective, if not to the federal government's political agenda.

US citizens in the twentieth century, these and other midcentury writers pointed out, lived in a time of stupendously accelerating global population growth. The 250 million humans on the globe in Jesus's time multiplied to 1 billion by 1830, then 2 billion in a scant 100 years (1930), then 3 billion in just 30 years (1960). This trajectory was unprecedented and alarming. A small but influential social movement grew to educate the public and explore policy options, managing to persuade President Eisenhower (as we have noted) to commission a report on the national-security implications. The (William S.) Draper report, *The Impact of Population Growth on the Strength of the Free World* (1959), warned that overpopulation was indeed a growing threat to global stability and thus to the national security of the United States. Eisenhower rejected the suggestion that government policy should attempt to curb the growth ("I cannot imagine anything more emphatically a subject that is not a proper political or governmental activity or function or responsibility," he wrote at the time, though he changed his mind about family planning when out of office). A determined cadre of population activists were soon busy on Capitol Hill as well as inside both the JFK and LBJ administrations. They persuaded agencies such as HEW, Aid for International Development (AID), and the directors of the War on Poverty to fund birth-control research and technology abroad and discuss initiatives at home, where more than 5 million women were said to be without access to contraceptive knowledge or technology. LBJ was well aware of this little-noticed policy discussion and experimentation within his administration but for political reasons resisted pressure to appoint a national commission. What he would do, cautiously, was insert one sentence on global overpopulation in his State of the Union Address in 1965 and again in 1967. Senator Ernest Gruening found four such Johnsonian comments in 1965, forty-one by the end of 1967. "I was breaking sharply with Presidential tradition," LBJ justifiably gave himself credit in his memoir. But comments about overseas population growth were as far as this president would go at his bully pulpit. "Population control was not considered a fit subject for the federal government" because the topic touched the "delicacies of the home and the dogma of the church."[12] The facts had moved him to utter a few high-profile sentences with no policy proposals to follow.

The historical record offers ample grounds for LBJ's hopes for a place in the two-Roosevelt conservationist pantheon. It also provides some critical perspectives to be weighed in the balance. Inevitably, there were occasions when LBJ was to environmentalists unnecessarily cautious. A leading example came at the end of his presidency, a moment when Grover Cleveland and Herbert Hoover, otherwise cautious and hesitant, boldly set aside protected public acreage before riding to the inauguration of their successors. LBJ, in the weeks before he was to leave office in 1968, was urged by Secretary Udall to use the Antiquities Act to set aside 7.6 million acres, increasing the acreage within the national park system by 25 percent. Johnson stalled in an extended fit of indecision, worried that congressional criticism might lead to a humiliating reversal. He also seemed motivated more by the fear of leaving office on a discordant note from congressional anticonservationists such as Wayne Aspinall than by the legacy of a final historic act enriching the endowment of future generations. As he dressed for the inauguration of his successor, he agreed to only 300,000 acres, infuriating Udall.[13] The episode reveals an occasionally timid LBJ who would not do his homework on the scenic and historic attractions of the sites proposed and was on personal terms with only one green lieutenant, the busy secretary of the interior.

Apart from a few uncharacteristically timid moments on particular issues, LBJ's administration can be taken to task for virtually ignoring several issues left to tomorrow: the growing dependency on overseas supplies of petroleum, for example, or the environmental and social devastation visited on the Appalachian region by mountaintop removal of coal by the Tennessee Valley Authority (TVA) and private electric utilities, memorably described in Henry Caulfield's *Night Comes to the Cumberlands*. Although LBJ was the first president to tell the US public that global population growth was a multifaceted problem that should be addressed, he not only declined to call attention to the environmental costs of the expansion of US population growth but in 1965 signed an immigration act that quadrupled immigration into the United States and by the mid-1970s was adding an additional 25 percent (and rising) to the nation's population growth—an environmentally unfriendly policy measure of major size and impact.

Among those who have been aware of the Great Society's impressive engagement with the "old" and the "new" conservation, there has been a fruitless dispute over LBJ's "sincerity." His life prior to 1963 revealed no interest in nature, and then out comes President Johnson as the prolific sponsor if not the father of the New Conservation, claiming that, in a normal world, it would have been his first priority. All the evidence points the other way. This late-in-life discovery of devotion to "the land" and the threatened creatures living upon it was a political decision by an unsurpassed tester of the political winds. LBJ certainly noticed conservation had proven itself in the JFK years a magnet for political allies, without much of an organized opposition. So LBJ was a late convert, unlike both Roosevelts, hunters and bird collectors launched into nature protection from childhood. The Texan seemed concerned about this and took head-on the problem of the source of his newly arrived concern for "the land." As president he frequently asserted his West Texas conservationist roots, tying it to growing up in the hill country west of Austin. "I grew up on the land. The life of my parents depended entirely upon the bounty of the soil," he told a Portland, Oregon, audience, which must have been puzzled to know what else one grew up on but land. If there had been no problems in education, race relations, or poverty, he wrote in his memoir, "I would have been content to be simply a conservation President. My deepest attitudes and beliefs were shaped by a closeness to the land."[14]

These platitudes convinced some people who worked with him and a few historians. White House Aide Joseph Califano wrote that LBJ's "respect for air, land, and water" was "rooted in his sense of the hill country's power."[15] Historian Hal Rothman expanded this theme into an entire book. Not only LBJ's upbringing in the hill country but his retreats to the ranch called the "Texas White House" "helped his restless soul find peace." LBJ said of the ranch: "These hills, these surroundings . . . provide the stimulation and inspiration that nothing else can provide."[16] It was all a game of political advantage. In his first year in the Senate, LBJ and (a reluctant) Lady Bird had bought a relative's modest ranch upstream from the house in which he was born. The 200 acres of alfalfa and a few sheep did not make it a "working ranch," and the puny Pedernales River was dry so much of the year that LBJ, to the irritation of his downstream neighbors, had the stretch of it near his house dammed and replenished by wells so that he could see some water.

Doubtless Senator and President Johnson much enjoyed vacations at his Texas ranch, just as George W. Bush cherished his time at another Texas ranch and Ronald Reagan spent a third of his presidential days at his ranch west of Santa Barbara. But LBJ's ranch was a midlife ornament bought to renew his image as a Texan with deep rural roots. There is no evidence that the young LBJ learned from or communed with nature in the hill country where he was raised. He did not hike or hunt or sleep at campfires in the hills green only after winter rains, knew nothing of the wildlife, and felt full joy when his convertible was fueled by both gasoline and beer. "By the time Lyndon Baines Johnson was born it was worn and poor," Theodore White wrote, the stands of cedar, juniper, and live oak ravaged for firewood and fencing and the tall buffalo grass depleted by overgrazing and seriously eroded.[17] His father was not a farmer but a cotton broker and politician whose family lived in a rural setting with a garden, chickens, and cows to milk. If Johnson learned any environmental lessons from his years in the hill country, they have not been recorded, though the lessons were there, and they were about land mistreatment by his ancestors. His strong conservationist attachment was not absorbed from the land in his youth or in later vacations at the ranch but was a political adoption of his senatorial and presidential years, beneficially tying him to FDR and the New Deal as well as to a political constituency of rising national influence. Yet what conservationists care how a president finds the way to their ranks? It should seem especially encouraging when the movement reaches such strength that politicians who long ignored it backdate their conversion.

A flaw in LBJ's record of substantial and impressive presidential leadership on natural resource matters was its distorted shape. His legislator's soul was attuned only to pushing legislation up to the presidential desk so that a bill could be signed into law—another notch on the gun. At this he had few peers, even taking account of the almost uniquely favorable circumstances created by JFK's death. He had virtually no concern for or skills in implementation, in making sure that programs made the desired changes on the ground. This is also a part of the executive's assignment—though it was not the interesting or history-making part for LBJ, who had virtually no management experience. So many new functions and agencies were authorized on his watch that the clogged and duplicative machinery sorely needed adjustment. Some in Congress and inside his administration encouraged the formation in 1964 of the Task Force on Government Organization, which recommended, among other things, a Department of Natural Resources, as did another task force in 1967. Interagency jealousies combined with LBJ's hesitation blocked these, as had happened in FDR's second term. This undermines his hope to be included in FDR's class of conservation leadership, for the second President Roosevelt, a naval official and two-term governor of New York, often turned his mind to new governmental mechanisms for the coordination of the government's expanding natural-resource-management assignment. One lesson from LBJ's law-passing presidential style seems obvious. US citizens who have much they want federal agencies to do in the way of steering society should select presidents who (among other things) have management experience and do not declare victory after the signing ceremony. New laws are only a starting point.

The Vietnam war continued to pull LBJ into political difficulties at home. In January 1968, the Communist Viet Cong mounted an offensive in twenty-seven key South Vietnamese cities, including the capital, Saigon. US military leaders asked for 200,000 more troops, and the home front surged with anti-war protests. The president's leadership became an issue in the party primaries that spring. Senator Eugene McCarthy challenged LBJ in the New Hampshire primary in March and won 42 percent of the vote. JFK's brother Robert Kennedy, now a New York senator, sensing presidential weakness, then announced his candidacy for the 1968 Democratic nomination. On March 31, LBJ, concluding that he could no longer lead the country or his party, announced that he would not be a candidate in November. Nixon was the Grand Old Party (GOP) nominee and defeated Vice President Hubert Humphrey. A strong showing by third-party candidate George Wallace cut Nixon's winning total to 43 percent of the vote, no mandate. Conservationists knew little about Nixon either before or after the 1968 presidential campaign, as it essentially ignored the natural environment.

RICHARD M. NIXON

Nixon's family history and his early years contained nothing exceptional in the way of civic leadership or distinction. The Nixon and Milhous families were Quakers. Richard's mother, Hannah, was a devout person entirely focused on family and church. His father, Frank, had dropped out of school after sixth grade and found jobs in the Los Angeles area as a street car conductor and oilfield roustabout before trying lemon farming in the small community of Yorba Linda, California, about thirty miles from Los Angeles. There Richard was born in 1913. The family moved to the small town of Whittier, where Frank Nixon and his five sons ran a filling station and general store. Richard was a diligent reader of the few books and magazines in the house and, with special pleasure, his Aunt Olive's *National Geographic*.

He attended public schools and little Whittier College, where he was an A student, debater, and student body president. From there he entered Duke University Law School, worked in the Office of Price Administration early in World War II, and then joined the US Navy, serving in supply duties in the Solomon Island campaigns and reaching the rank of lieutenant commander. After a brief postwar practice of law in Whittier, Nixon was elected to the US House, then the Senate in 1950.

His main and almost only theme as a member of Congress had been the pursuit of communists within the United States. In 1952 Eisenhower chose the intense, presentable, intelligent, untested Nixon as his vice president, still in those days a rather insignificant office. Eisenhower gave Nixon no assignments and met with him only rarely and briefly, so the vice president traveled abroad extensively, building a small and undeserved reputation as a foreign policy expert. A narrow loss to JFK in the presidential race of 1960 and a 1962 defeat in a run for governor of California appeared to end Nixon's political career, but he took the presidential nomination of his talent-short party in 1968. An electorate weary of a turbulent decade presided over by liberals sent Nixon to the White House, though a third-party candidacy cut Nixon's winning margin to 43 percent of the vote. The Democrats controlled both houses of Congress.

The environment was essentially absent from the presidential campaign. Democratic nominee Humphrey ran with conservationist Maine senator "Ecology Ed" Muskie but mentioned the environment only twice. Nixon briefly addressed natural resources in one of his eighteen radio addresses. The press showed even less interest in the topic.

Environmentalists, then, had flimsy hopes that this conservative Republican would offer even occasional presidential leadership on their issues. Nixon had an unimpressive congressional record on the environment; had voted for the Echo Park Dam, the conservationists' nightmare; and after election appointed as secretary of the interior Alaska governor Walter Hickel, a prodevelopment, oil-friendly politician who five days after his nomination stirred environmentalist protests with a comment to the media that he opposed "conservation for conservation's sake." Muskie admitted to "great apprehension" at the approach of the Nixon administration, worried that the "programs would be gutted."[18] However, Nixon could count, especially votes and lobbying budgets. Environmental organizations had flourished in the 1950s and 1960s—the Nature Conservancy founded in 1951,

Environmental Defense Fund in 1967, Friends of the Earth in 1969, Natural Resources Defense Council and the League of Conservation Voters in 1970. Throughout the 1950s and 1960s, the Sierra Club membership doubled four times, the National Audubon Society vaulted in size from 17,000 to 115,000, the Wilderness Society from 5,000 to 62,000.

Nixon was surprised by the fierce public opposition to Hickel's nomination. He knew environmentalists must be respected as a political force, but as his presidency began he had little feel for the issue and essentially no interest in any aspect of it. "A man of his generation," wrote J. Brooks Flippen in *Nixon and the Environment* (2000), "Nixon did not recognize the growing threat" to the environment, for he "had no personal experience" with urban-industrial pollution in his "idyllic" suburban Whittier [and] . . . enjoyed neither hunting nor fishing. Not once did he venture to the mountains and, rarely, to the ocean."[19]

Days after his election Nixon directed that several task forces be put to work on upcoming issues, on the domestic side such areas as taxation, health care, agriculture. Natural resources and the environment were left out and added to the list only later upon the intervention of a transition staff member who introduced the name of Russell Train as potential chair of a task force on natural resources and the environment. Train was an old-school Republican conservationist with impeccable social and academic credentials whose parents were on such good terms with President Hoover that the Train family enjoyed several Christmas dinners at the Hoover White House. Train had become a committed conservationist after two African safaris ignited a concern for wildlife. He left a federal judgeship in 1965 to head the Conservation Foundation. Nixon, without any recorded comment, agreed to the formation of the additional task force with the respected Train as head. The group met in December for less than two days and submitted a four-page report acknowledging widespread pollution of air and waters, urging that "improved environmental management be given high priority in the new Administration" so as to "begin the job of remediation." A position of special assistant for environmental affairs was recommended in order to provide a White House "focal point."

Environmental matters now had a tiny, management-oriented foothold in the new administration, for Nixon's designee as chief domestic adviser was Seattle land-use lawyer John Ehrlichman, who agreed with the Train report. On the environmental issue president-elect Nixon was receiving very cautious advice from essentially two lieutenants. He agreed to include in his In-augural Address a few greenish words: "In protecting our environment . . . we will and must press urgently forward."[20]

As it turned out, while the new administration in its first weeks was mov-ing a tiny distance toward environmental engagement, the environment was about to command intense national attention. On January 28, eight days af-ter Nixon's inauguration, crude oil began gushing from below a Union Oil Company drilling platform off the pristine beaches of Santa Barbara, Cali-fornia. It soon drifted onshore; a foul-smelling blanket of oil in places six inches deep and covering 800 square miles washed ashore along 30 miles of beach, killing marine life and soiling the harbor and waterfront of the resort community. The "blowout" released an estimated 100,000 barrels of oil, capped only after ten days. National television carried vivid pictures of drowned seabirds and seals, and the administration came under attack for inaction. Secretary Hickel delayed visiting the area for six days and initially refused local requests for a ban on oil drilling in the channel off Santa Bar-bara County. He then yielded to public pressure and suspended drilling for an unspecified time. The president did not inspect the area by air and ground until March, after Senator Muskie visited the scene.

The Santa Barbara oil spill was giving the new administration a public re-lations pounding. Later that year the notoriously polluted and debris-clogged Cuyahoga River in Cleveland caught fire. Although it burned for only twenty-four minutes and had caught fire twice before, the event was widely mentioned as an ominous warning sign that the environment would be the "issue of the year," according to *Time* magazine's January 1, 1970, cover.[21] The environment, Nixon's handful of conservationist advisers told the president, with supporting poll data, was now a leading political issue that had reached crisis proportions and could not be ignored. The Demo-crats in Congress, especially Senators Muskie and Henry Jackson (D.-Wash.), were easily seizing control of media coverage with proposals to end or more tightly regulate oil drilling off the California coast.

The administration's irresoluteness on the Santa Barbara oil spill was in one respect misleading. True, Secretary Hickel was not eager to criticize the drilling-permit processes of a major oil company, and the new president was temporarily visited by one of his spells of indecision. Yet Nixon did not intend to be a passive, Coolidgean, or Hooverian president. The assassina-tions of MLK and Bobby Kennedy, urban violence, and street demonstrations of the 1960s had convinced him that the nation and the presidency faced a crisis that could only be met by an activist, problem-solving president backed by a new political majority. When Nixon's five and one-half years as president were over, if we lift our eyes from the areas most associated with his time in office—foreign policy in general (especially opening relations with China) and the Vietnam War as well as the espionage leading to the Watergate scandal—we see that Nixon also had pursued with varying degrees of success an ambitious and far-reaching domestic reform agenda—initiatives in welfare reform; revenue sharing; government reorganization; national land-use planning; "wars" on crime, drugs, and cancer; expanded civil rights policy; greater coordination in urban policy. And environmental protection.

I list it last not because the administration's performance here was modest, for it was substantial and wide-ranging. It can be listed last because Nixonian environmental policy was so slow to take form, mostly because it had to be cobbled together by a few only modestly prepared aides working in the complete absence of presidential input or contact. The Santa Barbara spill exposed a near vacuum in the way of an environmental policy-making apparatus or capacity within the administration. Train sent the president the requested task force report on the environment and natural resources and was then sent off to the Interior Department to be undersecretary. That left no environmental expertise anywhere in the White House, though domestic counselor Ehrlichman claimed some experience in land-use law. The larger problem was that Nixon's determination to be an activist president was not backed up by a clear sense of what he wished to do, environmentally or otherwise. On the eve of his inauguration Nixon "was surprisingly unprepared for the presidency," wrote Washington, D.C., journalist Elizabeth Drew, a reflection not only of his skimpy governmental experience—four years as a junior member in the House followed by two in the Senate, and eight unchallenging years as a vice president often traveling abroad—but of the lack of even the broad outline of a domestic policy agenda in Nixon's mind.[22]

On environmental policy he had no ideas or even inclinations beyond the central conviction that he must not concede the issue to his opponents—most especially to his likely and to him most formidable opponent for the 1972 race for reelection, Senator Muskie. In a few months the president was to say to Ehrlichman that he intended to "strike a balance" between the "environmental radicals" and his political base in the business community. He did not know where that balance point might be and told Ehrlichman to "keep me out of trouble" on the environment, that is, not outmaneuvered by the Democrats, while he gave his own close attention to domestic issues that in his view had "political juice"—abortion, race, crime, drugs, welfare, and taxes.

To equip the White House to "take the offensive" on the environment, Ehrlichman, who had some vague environmentalist sympathies but little knowledge of current and past natural-resource-policy controversies, appointed thirty-year-old staff lawyer Egil Krogh to guide a task force to formulate a legislative agenda the president could present to Congress early in 1970. They had almost a year of startup time, but Krogh proved an unprepared lieutenant. The White House as summer arrived was moving very slowly on the environment, falling farther behind Democratic legislators. LBJ had signed a forest of measures, and a primary need in federal environmental policy was coordination and oversight. Senator Henry Jackson introduced legislation in 1969 to establish the Council on Environmental Quality to coordinate the work of the eighty departments and agencies with environmental responsibilities. He also explored possibilities for a National Environmental Policy Act to require evidence of environmental impacts before any significant federal program was launched.

Environmental policy making within the White House in that first year was fragmented and stumbling. The president in May had formed the cabinet-level Environmental Quality Council, which became a useless forum for departmental squabbles because the president almost never convened it. Separate committees studied problem areas in which the administration must decide whether to permit or terminate large projects with worrisome environmental implications—a supersonic aircraft; a waterway (Tennessee-Tombigbee) to be cut through a small range of mountains in northern Mississippi (possibly excavated by underground atomic blasts, an idea backed by several government groups) to allow barge traffic to float from the Tennessee River to Mobile, Alabama; a proposed new jetport southeast of Miami and encroaching upon the Everglades; a projected oil pipeline from Alaska's Prudhoe Bay across 800 miles of pristine wilderness. Summer months went by with mounting criticism and the administration nowhere on the environmental offensive.

An exception of considerable importance came when Daniel Patrick Moynihan, a liberal Democrat and staffer for JFK and LBJ hired by Nixon, who sensed his own need for policy innovation, urged the president to appoint a national commission to study the problem of overpopulation. Human population growth was at the heart of all environmental and many other social problems, Moynihan argued. The 3 million sales and twenty-two printings of Stanford University biologist Paul Ehrlich's book *The Population Bomb* (1969), in which he argued, "The human population of the planet is about five times too large," seemed proof that population growth was a mainstream concern. Congressional committees were studying population growth, and it was time, Moynihan said, for presidential leadership. Nixon, though wary of the political risks of sponsoring discussion of birth control and related issues, could not resist the chance to take the next bold step that the Democrats had not yet taken on this problem. On July 18, Nixon sent to Congress the first presidential message on population growth in the United States, promised increased funding for family planning (birth control) both abroad and at home, and asked Congress to appoint a national commission on population growth and the future of the United States. Congress agreed, and Nixon appointed John D. Rockefeller III chair of this pathbreaking inquiry.

The Nixon environmental offensive moved out of the trenches in August when Krogh asked to be relieved of his task-force assignment and was replaced by Interior Department geologist John Whitaker, an ardent outdoorsman and experienced Washington bureaucrat. Whitaker moved into the White House and collected a small working group of young aides borrowed from other natural-resource agencies. As they worked on the president's anticipated proposals to Congress scheduled for early 1970, they also began to send Nixon poll data showing rising public concern over threats to the environment. In 1965, water pollution was a worry among 35 percent of US citizens polled, rising to 74 percent by 1970. Early in 1969 only 1 percent of those polled ranked the environment the top domestic problem, but by 1971 the number had jumped to 25 percent. The end of the 1960s had not been a good time for the environment—the oil spill onto Santa Barbara beaches, thermal pollution from nuclear power plants killing fish in both eastern and western rivers, DDT imperiling the bald eagle, and the heavily polluted Cuyahoga River in Cleveland catching fire. At the end of 1969 the editors of *Fortune* magazine were finishing a special issue, to appear in February 1970, dedicated to an "immense transformation [that] has occurred in public concern about the environment." As Max Ways, one of the writers, put it: "Slowly as a poisoned snail, public concern over the physical environment crept forward during the first half of the century. In the 1950s anxiety began to quicken. In the 1960s . . . [it became] one of the major topics of discussion." "Looked at one by one, many of our present depredations seem relatively easy to correct," wrote the magazine's editors:

> But when we put the horrors in a row—the drab and clumsy cities, the billboards, the scum-choked lakes, the noise, the poisoned air and water, the clogged highways, the mountainous and reeking dumps . . . all [are] part of a single challenge to our civilization.
> Noisy, militant, litigious, growing in strength and numbers, the conservationists are on the march. . . . The number of conservation organizations and their size are growing too fast to tabulate.[23]

By Thanksgiving week of 1969, Nixon was presented a sixty-five-page report offering well-vetted policy recommendations on air and water pollution, outdoor recreation, and environmental policy reorganization. He took the report on vacation to Florida, and it provided a basis for his substantial environmental proposals in the State of the Union Address in January 1970 along with a special message to Congress in February.

But the Democrats had moved ahead of him and raised the bar. In early December 1969 Congress passed the Endangered Species Conservation Act, which Nixon signed at once, clearly playing a secondary role. They had sensed that public sentiment had decisively shifted on the matter of extinction of species. US citizens at the beginning of the twentieth century had known that the dodo bird was not just "dead" but extinct, as was the passenger pigeon, and, almost, the bison. By midcentury the bald eagle was clearly in decline, a prominent victim of the government's rodent-poisoning program. By the 1960s new technologies in ocean fishing and whaling added an international trade dimension to species extinction, and Congress in 1966 passed the first of a series of measures collectively called the Endangered Species Acts (ESAs). A second and stronger version was requested by Nixon in his 1972 State of the Union Address, and he signed it in 1973, though the Republican in Nixon must have flinched when signing into a law an elaborate, complicated, expensive, and controversial private-property-intrusive framework of science, law, and policy designed to list species as threatened and endangered, then to pursue the goal of recovery. Eighty nations convened in Washington, D.C., in 1973 to sign the Convention on International

Trade in Endangered Species of Wild Fauna and Flora (CITES), a trade embargo on endangered species. LBJ, Nixon, and their respective parties had
marched together on this one issue.

By December Senators Jackson and Muskie had reached agreement on a
historic "cornerstone law," the National Environmental Protection Act
(NEPA), requiring environmental impact statements before major federal
programs could be launched. Nixon had reservations but a veto invited an
override in Congress that might have branded Nixon antienvironmental. He
signed NEPA on national television on January 1, 1970, choosing a slow day
for distracting media events but a fine national holiday for a dramatic flourish by the nation's leading newsmaker. In an official statement, he began
with the efforts of his Environmental Quality Council so that he could point
out, "It is particularly fitting that my first official act of this new decade is to
approve the National Environmental Policy Act." It was "fitting," if you
missed the point, because he had led the way:

> By my participation in these efforts I have become convinced that the
> 1970s absolutely must be the years when America pays its debt to the
> past by reclaiming the purity of its air, its waters, and our living
> environment. It is literally now or never. . . . We are determined that the
> decade of the seventies will be known as the time when this country
> regained a productive harmony between man and nature.[24]

In neither his prepared text nor his verbal comments did Nixon explain,
let alone endorse, NEPA's unprecedented establishment of a framework of
environmental impact statements. He appears not to have grasped this central element, but he knew how to get to the head of the line in the legislative
process even though his limited personal engagement with the legislation
had been to raise vague doubts along the way that it was the right approach.

Still, the administration's floundering performance in 1969 had been replaced as the 1970s arrived with a president for the first time assuming the
role of a positive player on the environmental-protection stage. NEPA established the new three-person Council on Environmental Quality (CEQ), and
Nixon appointed dedicated environmentalists, with Train as chair. The president's first State of the Union Address in January devoted more space to the
environment than any other domestic topic and opened with oddly militaris-
tic language: "The great question of the seventies is, shall we surrender to

our surroundings, or should we make our peace with nature and begin to make reparations for the damage we have done to our air, our land, and our water?"[25]

His address reached an enormous audience, television viewers estimated at 20 million and others reached by print media. *Time* magazine characterized the speech as "eloquently limning the broad goals for the 1970s . . . inspiring in evoking the image of a refurbished and replanned America."[26] In this February 2, 1970, issue *Time* ran a lengthy cover story on environmental deterioration, and other magazines noted Nixon's address. Overnight, Nixon was in a leadership position. In historian Conrad Black's words, "In his State of the Union message on January 22, 1970, to the amazement of everyone, friend and foe, Nixon seized the initiative on environmental issues from the Democrats and ran away with it into a secret political rain forest where the Democrats couldn't find or attack him."[27]

Of course they attacked him anyway, but he was not the easy target on environmental matters they had assumed he would be. In his February 10 special message to Congress, he began with these words: "We in this country have too casually and too long abused our natural environment." He claimed that his message offered a thirty-seven-point program composed of twenty-three legislative proposals and fourteen administrative actions in the areas of water and air pollution, solid waste disposal, and urban parklands. Nixon's official statement accompanying the message boasted, "This is the most far-reaching and comprehensive message on conservation and restoration of our natural resources ever submitted to Congress by a president of the United States."[28]

Those words could have been written for LBJ by his writers; by JFK's booster in chief, Stewart Udall; or by Theodore Roosevelt's (TR's) top lieutenant, Gifford Pinchot. Nixon and his small corps of conservationist advisers did not yet belong in that company. In sending this one message to Congress (not a rare event; he sent thirty-three in 1970 alone) Nixon had not, as he claimed, vaulted ahead of the Roosevelts or LBJ as a tutor and prod to Congress. But in three national statements in January and February, with flashes of Kennedyesque rhetoric, he brought to mind his greenest predecessors. Significant results followed. The unfinished pollution-control efforts begun by the "clean air" laws of 1963, 1965, and 1967 had major failings in controlling harmful automobile and factory emissions, and Nixon's message acknowledged and addressed them with a proposal for national ambient standards, not a very Republican idea. On water pollution, Nixon also nudged federal involvement ahead by proposing a large grant program for sewage-facility construction and federal effluent standards for industrial pollution. The president also proposed a larger federal role in solid waste disposal and supported the expansion of a network of urban recreational spaces formed out of surplus federal properties. Nixon seemed genuinely enthusiastic and justifiably proud of this small "Legacy of Parks" program because it was hatched at a cabinet meeting and came out of the White House, not Congress. By the end of 1976 some 82,232 acres of federal property in fifty states had been converted into 642 parks, most of them close to or within cities.[29]

Most surprising of all, Nixon risked offending his Republican base by joining a bipartisan effort to explore the outlines of a national growth policy vaguely described in his January 1970 State of the Union Address:

For the past thirty years our population has been growing and shifting. The result is exemplified in vast areas of rural America emptying out of people and of promise [and] . . . the violent and decayed central cities of our great metropolitan complexes. . . . I propose that before these problems become insoluble, the nation develop a national growth policy. In the future, government decisions as to where to build highways, locate airports, acquire land or sell land should be made with the clear objective of aiding a balanced growth for America.[30]

This was all Moynihanish language, with no followup from Nixon. When Moynihan left the administration at the end of 1970, national growth policy submerged. A sibling was the idea of national land-use policy (NLUP) initially nurtured in the offices of several Democratic senators. The administration endorsed the idea of a nationally guided growth plan as a substitute for sprawl in each annual environmental message, though there was internal opposition. A Jackson bill passed the Senate in June 1973, proposing federal funding for state intervention to require effective zoning laws and land-use planning in rural as well as urbanized counties. To objections against a "federal takeover of local zoning," supporters from both parties pointed out that 10,000 acres of open land went under the asphalt of freeways and subdivisions every twenty-four hours in the United States, and national land-use planning merely meant effective local and regional zoning. By 1973, the election safely behind, the White House, supportive of NLUP for the previous three years, joined the critics, and the legislation faded away. That something called NLUP had been endorsed by the Nixon administration for so long was astonishing in a conservative Republican administration. In view of it, administration watchers could not have been entirely surprised when Nixon signed the Coastal Zone Management Act when it reached his desk in late 1972.

Nixon's embrace of environmentalism in 1970 may account for Secretary Hickel's sudden decision to firmly police resource extraction that same year. A fire on a Chevron oil platform in the Gulf of Mexico in March produced a substantial petroleum spill. Hickel investigated, then convinced the Justice Department to sue Chevron and nine other companies. "Let us find new ways of doing business," he told the National Petroleum Council in July, "so that our industries can prosper and our environment flourish at the same time. The right to produce is not the right to pollute." *Life* magazine wrote of Hickel in August: "Nobody in Washington seems to have come to so instant a realization that the environment is now as sacred as motherhood."[31] Nixon may have resented that the compliment had not come to him.

There were critics and dissenters to all of this, both within and outside his administration, and some hidden evidence that the president in this first winter was moving beyond his comfort zone. When Ehrlichman ordered a halt on construction of the Cross-Florida Barge Canal after a rigorous review of the environmental and economic costs against the benefits, and Florida Republicans bitterly complained, Nixon angrily "pushed my red call button and demanded to know why the hell I had stopped the canal." Ehrlichman stood his ground, citing a lengthy report that had convinced him, and Nixon did not want to spend the study time required to explain why he was reversing a top aide.[32] All the public knew was that the administration was no longer sending the Army Corps of Engineers to cut a ditch across Florida's ecosystems. When Nixon's February 18, 1970, environmental message made a strong statement for expanded environmental action, coming from a president who in his first year had not found a leadership role, the *Washington Post* called the message "forward-minded" and the *New York Times* applauded "the President's laudable purpose." "Has the president preempted the environmental issue?" CBS reporter Roger Mudd asked Muskie a week after Nixon's address. Muskie uncomfortably commented that it was not important who took the initiative.[33]

Then Nixon stumbled, badly. Senator Gaylord Nelson, impressed by the media impact of the campus "teach-ins" in opposition to the Vietnam War, began to plan for a "national teach-in on the environment." He recruited twenty-five-year-old Harvard graduate student Denis Hayes as organizer, and against all odds "Earth Day" took place across the country on Saturday, April 22, 1970. Students on an estimated 2,000 college and 10,000 high school campuses as well as in urban settings rallied with banners, listened to speeches, held panel discussions, flattened automobiles with sledgehammers, held mock burials for the internal combustion engine, threw birth-control pills into crowds, and passed around replicas of a blue-green globe. Both houses of Congress adjourned for the day so that members could participate if they wished, which leading Democrats did. Senator Humphrey spoke at an Indiana high school, Senator George McGovern at the University of Indiana, Senator Ted Kennedy at Harvard.

Estimates of participation ran to 20 million people, making Earth Day the largest national protest demonstration in our history. Environmentalism had for a day taken over the schools and streets, and it was unexpectedly large, deep, and unhappy with the status quo. The organizers of Earth Day were divided on whether the event should be bipartisan. Senator Nelson insisted that Republicans be asked to participate, but Hayes and the students refused an invitation to meet with Ehrlichman in the White House. The president's advisers were split. Hickel and Train urged Nixon to join the movement, declare a national holiday, and urge federal employees to participate in Earth Day events. Nixon chose what Ehrlichman thought was a middle course. Key administration staff would agree to speak around the country, hailing the administration's commitment to environmental quality. Some White House staffers participated in a symbolic cleanup of the Potomac River.

The media, however, rarely give space to White House staffers, especially when large public events are unfolding. Attention went to the Earth Day activists, with some directed to the president, in this case to his absence. Nixon chose not to take part in any way, though some of his aides urged that if he did not give a speech, he should at least issue a proclamation on April 22, such as he had recently done in proclaiming National Archery Week. The president declined to express in any way that he shared the concern and hopes of the Earth Day activists. The news media and other commentators, predictably, did not present the administration's stance as a middle path.

The Earth Day crowds were "predominantly anti-Nixon," reported CBS *News* anchor Walter Cronkite. Writer Kurt Vonnegut told a New York City gathering, "If we don't get our President's attention, this planet may soon die."[34] A strong case could be made that environmental issues indeed had his attention. In midsummer 1970 Nixon's Advisory Council on Executive Reorganization discovered that forty-four separate federal entities in nine different departments were involved in pollution issues, rejected the idea of a new department of environment and natural resources, an idea narrowly defeated in FDR's day, and recommended the independent Environmental Protection Agency (EPA), with jurisdiction over pollution abatement and all monitoring, research, and standard setting. Nixon sent the proposal forward as a reorganization plan and became one of the architects of the EPA. Senator Muskie, who had proposed such an agency in 1969, grudgingly called it a "useful beginning." The president took the credit for an innovation in executive branch reorganization. His appointee to head the EPA was the respected Indiana environmental lawyer William Ruckelshaus.

Looking back, the summer of 1970 had been Nixon's high-water mark in environmental leadership. Running disputes over a set of proposed environment-damaging projects—the Alaska oil pipeline, pressures to allow the US Forest Service (USFS) to penetrate wilderness areas to increase timber production, a pro-mining report of a public land commission, the old issue of grazing fees in the high mountain West—fueled continuous battles between environmental organizations and the Republican administration's growth-oriented constituencies. Nixon sometimes wound up on the green side of such issues in part because he had appointed some environmentalist counselors such as Train and Ruckelshaus. Whitaker, in the White House, had an environmentalist leaning, though Nixon did not much enjoy his company. The most important green lieutenant was former land-use lawyer Ehrlichman, who had a broad range of duties and much influence. Ehrlichman told journalist Wicker that Nixon once remarked, when signing off on a substantial increase in EPA authority recommended by Ehrlichman, that his own attitude toward environmental issues was: "When in doubt, make it a park."

The president agreed in late spring to meet with leaders of the top environmental groups to discuss funding of birth-control programs, but he was not in a friendly mood and opened the meeting with these words: "All politics is a fad. Your fad is going right now. Get what you can, and here's what I can get you." He was going to cut funding for family planning. The thirty-two-year-old new head of the Sierra Club, Philip Berry, aggressively responded, "I don't believe what you believe in." A heated argument ensued, and Nixon ended the meeting, probably vowing not to meet with environmentalists again. That fall the media correctly portrayed Muskie's anti–air-pollution bill as stronger than the one the administration preferred in the House, and when Nixon eventually signed into law Muskie's Clean Air Act amendments in December, he refused to invite the senator to the signing.

The rivalry for environmental leadership between the president and the Maine senator seemed to continue through 1971, but research in the papers of Nixon and his aides, pulled together especially well by Flippen in his book on Nixon's environmental-policy performance, reveals that Nixon was shifting ground through 1971 and into the election year as he soured on the environment as an issue and generally tilted his administration to the right.

The public could begin to see this in February 1972, when Nixon offered his third environmental message to Congress, barely going through the motions. He called for purchase and completion of the Great Cypress Swamp and enlargement of the endangered species list. This time he had nothing more to say about national land-use planning, and that complex and daring idea died in late 1974 as White House backing became weaker. Muskie commented that the 1972 environmental message was a "sham-attack on pollution," taking issue not only with the details of the speech but also Nixon's sincerity.

He was right on the latter count. Internal documents and aides' memoirs make it quite clear that Nixon was increasingly unsure that he wanted to continue on the environmental offensive—which should probably be termed a counterattack because he was trying not to lose ground to his "enemies." In comments to his staff during 1971 Nixon questioned whether all this attention to the environment was politically justified, after all the only reason he was engaged with it. Whitaker had been sending him poll data for months, showing that public concern over air and water pollution had jumped from tenth place in mid-1969 to fifth place a year later, and the president knew that *Time* magazine named the environment the "issue of the year" in January 1971. Nixon conceded these measures of public environmental concern but told staff, "I don't believe the public interest is deep," just "wide in some areas." "The environment is not a good political issue," Nixon told John Haldeman in February. "I have an uneasy feeling that perhaps we are doing too much. . . . We're catering to the left in all of this."[35]

Gradually, Nixon began to curb his handful of environmental aides and to encourage others in the administration, especially Commerce Secretary Maurice Stans, to raise questions about the costs of environmental regulations lest they injure economic expansion. His Interior Department moved ahead on the Alaska pipeline, and Nixon agreed to speak at a groundbreaking for the Tennessee-Tombigbee Canal. "Environmentalists are a group of people that aren't really one bit interested in safety or clean air," he grumbled to aides. Their interest was in "destroying the system." He seems to have concluded that the political gains from his occasional environmental "offensives" were minor and that his reelection depended upon a "southern strategy" appealing to voters concerned with "traditional values" in matters of crime and race relations, upon firming his probusiness base, and above all upon making headlines for his foreign policy successes. In a nationwide speech in July he announced that his national security adviser, Henry Kissinger, had arranged for Nixon to be the first president to visit Communist China. Nixon's visit came in February 1972, with much fanfare. "International affairs is our issue," Nixon told aide Charles Colson. By the end of 1971 the president led Senator Muskie in the polls by 12 percent, his approval ratings at a peak. That autumn he began to speak publicly about the hazards of environmentalism. "How many jobs is it [regulating auto exhaust] going to cost?" he asked a Detroit business gathering in September. Muskie commented: "It appears that the administration has undergone an environmental metamorphosis, emerging from the cocoon not as a butterfly but as a moth."[36]

In March came another Nixonian retreat, at immense ultimate cost to the nation. The Rockefeller Commission reported:

> We have concluded that no substantial benefits would result from continued growth of the nation's population. . . . The gradual stabilization of our population would contribute significantly to the nation's ability to solve its problems. . . . Recognizing that our population cannot grow indefinitely, and appreciating the advantages of moving now toward the stabilization of population, the Commission recommends that the nation welcome and plan for a stabilized population. . . .
>
> From an environmental and resource point of view, there are no advantages from further growth of population. . . . Indeed, we would be

considerably better off . . . if there were a prompt reduction in our
population growth rate.[37]

Instead of endorsing at least the major thrust of the findings of a commission he had requested, Nixon perfunctorily thanked the members for
their work, refused to invite Rockefeller to deliver the report to the White
House, and in two days made his only comment on the report, selecting two
of the group's sixty-two recommendations for repudiation—liberalized
abortion laws and the availability of birth-control information to minors. By
1972 winning over the blue-collar Catholic vote normally claimed by the
Democrats weighed heavily in shaping his negative response to the unique
population study he had requested two years before. No advice would have
been of more benefit to all US citizens, and to their natural environment,
than to have a president agree with and recommend for thought and action
the basic counsel that the nation "welcome and plan for a stabilized population." Such an opportunity had never come before and will be painfully late
if it ever comes again.

For the rest of the year the environment continued to recede from public
view and political news. An exhausted Muskie broke down under hostile
press questions about political activities of his wife and himself, was accused of weakness under fire, and soon dropped out of the race. The National Wildlife Federation pried loose a statement on the environment from
both Nixon and the Democratic nominee McGovern, and their staffs produced similar homilies, Nixon's one page long. "We should force the candidates to face up to the environment," the Sierra Club editorialized just weeks
before the November election, but its members never found a way. While
Nixon dodged, Vice President Spiro Agnew was apparently encouraged to
express support for some of the most controversial development projects.
Opposition to the Alaska oil pipeline, Agnew said in August, was "inconsistent with the adventurous spirit of the frontier."[38]

Environmental policy making in Congress continued in the election year,
and the Pesticide Control Act of 1972 (an ocean-dumping-control law), the
Marine Mammal Protection Act, and the Coastal Zone Management Act all
came to Nixon's desk that autumn and were signed. Nixon was far ahead in
the polls and had reservations about all four bills, but he played it safe and
continued his "partner" role with one large exception. The 1972 amendments to the Clean Water Act passed by overwhelming votes—74–0 in the

Senate, 366–11 in the House. The bill carried an $18 billion price tag, and when it reached Nixon's desk in October he vetoed this popular measure because of its "budget-busting" costs. The veto was immediately overridden. Nixon then made use of a novel presidential maneuver he would use frequently in his second term, "impounding," or refusing to spend, half of the $18 billion authorized. The public and some of the news media found all this intragovernmental conflict confusing and hard to follow.

Nixon's reelection, by this time, was a foregone conclusion, the candidates' environmental records apparently a nonissue. With his activist performance from 1970–1971, Nixon had successfully prevented his and his party's "ignore the environment" inclinations from becoming a political liability. He was reelected with 60.7 percent of the vote and the electoral votes of all but one state.

With Muskie driven off the stage and a second term won, Nixon's repudiation of his first-term environmental activism strengthened. As part of a postelection cabinet and staff shakeup, Nixon pushed his handful of environmentalist aides further to the perimeter by sending Whitaker back to the Interior Department and inserting as natural resource counselor (i.e., gatekeeper expected to keep the topic out of Nixon's office) Earl Butz, a seasoned defender of the nation's soil-eroding, pesticide-drenching agricultural policies who would write in an early internal memo: "There are many more important things than the environment."[39]

The president's third environmental message in 1973 essentially declared victory in the environmental campaign. "I can report to Congress that we are well on our way to winning the war with environmental degradation."[40] Alarmed by the unjustified optimism, a group of environmental organizations requested a meeting with the president. No reply came for three months, and then a refusal. Environmental honeymoon over.

In 1973 Nixon careened toward what would turn out to be impeachment and resignation from office. The catastrophe began in early 1972 when a group of Nixon loyalists operating out of the White House basement began a series of illegal "dirty tricks" against Nixon's political enemies. Exposure and revelations of a presidential coverup and obstruction of justice, collectively called the "Watergate" scandal after the apartment complex where police discovered a break-in of offices of the Democratic National Committee, created a crisis atmosphere. Tape recordings in the Oval Office revealed the presidential conspiracy to break the law and obstruct justice. Nixon was impeached, resigned in August, and returned to California.

Is Watergate illegality and removal of a president dramatically important stuff but a detraction from our topic? Harvard historian Arthur Schlesinger, Jr., in his timely *The Imperial Presidency* (1973), had nothing to say about environmental policy but described an administration swollen beyond manageability, its premier occupant and closest aides far removed from contact with the public and increasingly disrespectful of constitutional limits established in the balance of powers. His book was about Nixon but more importantly about the directions in which the presidency was as well as was not taking us, a major theme here.

Some assessments of Nixon's environmental record have been startling in their claims. To Train's recollection, Nixon's environmental agenda "was so wide-ranging, and yet so comprehensive, as to be without precedent in the history of the U.S."[41] Train's enthusiasm for the Nixon record, partly generated by his own role in it, went too far. Although Nixon's agenda can be called unusually "wide-ranging" because new environmental protection avenues had been opened in the decades separating him from TR and FDR, chiefly in the areas of industrial and urban pollution, one important contrast is seen when we remind ourselves that we do not have to say of the two Roosevelts what we must say of Nixon. The chief executive's conservation commitments and achievements came not from inside his head and heart but were in large part forced upon him by the political power of an expanding social movement and an environmentally conscious Congress. Nixon's leadership, even in his early, green period, was decidedly not in the Rooseveltian class.

This may be an overall if not presidential improvement, reflecting a maturing social movement and public education. Nixon took a leadership position for two years because he was driven by the desire to keep himself abreast of the environmentalist legislators whom he regarded as his chief rivals. It was on his presidential watch that the many cornerstones of modern US environmental law and administration were put into place, though they had been incubating for years in the care of congressional sponsors and organized environmentalists.

From the point of view of Senators Muskie, Jackson, and possibly others, their congressional committees were the real architects of the new core institutions, NEPA and CEQ. These legislators nominated themselves as first in line for credit, with the actual signer of legislation in line behind them. But the metaphor is misleading. Presidents do more than sign bills the White House may not have had a hand in drafting. After NEPA was signed, the future of the new agencies it created would be given early direction by appointments and decisions, budgetary and otherwise, of the head of state.

Take for example CEQ, and in particular how President Nixon used the tools no senator had at his disposal—the chief executive's verbal backing of the agency and then nomination of Train and two other qualified council members—to nurture several international agreements that were important first steps toward a global regime of environmental law.

Oceanic oil pollution was a growing environmental problem virtually ignored by the conservation movement until the 1960s. Harbor and coastal oil spills and ballast discharges from tankers and industry had attracted the attention of Secretary of Commerce Hoover as early as the 1920s, but he could make no headway. Because oceanic oil pollution arose mostly from oil-tanker ballast discharges as well as accidents, it begged an international solution not forthcoming as long as the sea was universally regarded as too vast for human pollution. By the 1960s the growth of oil-tanker traffic to the industrialized West from Middle Eastern and South American exporters in ever-larger ships led to routine ballast wastewater discharges in port waters and occasional tanker groundings and huge spills. On March 12, 1967, the oil tanker *Torrey Canyon*, with a full load of 120,000 tons of oil taken on in Kuwait, ran aground and broke apart off the West Coast of Cornwall, England, coating fifty miles of shoreline with crude oil and killing an estimated 15,000 seabirds. A comprehensive water-pollution bill with stiff penalties for oil spills died in conference in the waning days of the LBJ administration. Then Nixon was elected president, and twelve days after his inauguration, Gulf Oil Platform A blew out off the coast of Santa Barbara, California, coating the beaches black.

The problem of ocean pollution was thus in the thoughts of Nixon and his handful of environmental advisers, especially Train. "This country can no longer afford to squander valuable time before developing answers to pollution and oil slicks from wells, tankers, or any other source," Nixon said on his first, February 11, visit to Santa Barbara after the spill.[42] Action would require international agreements, his cup of tea. In March he proposed that NATO create the Committee on the Challenges of Modern Society and suggested oil pollution as among the "problems of the modern environment" the new body should address. In October he released the report *Ocean Dumping*, prepared by staff from CEQ with the participation of the Departments of State, Interior, Transportation, and other agencies. In his February 1971 environmental message and a subsequent May message solely on ocean dumping, the president announced a basic national policy and called for legislation and an international conference on the problem.

This was a great deal of presidential activity in six to eight months. Then the White House seemed to lose interest in the topic. Still, momentum had been generated. Administrators and staff from CEQ, the Coast Guard, the Department of State, and other branches of the government were vigorously carrying out their president's marching orders to seek an international regime for control of ocean dumping. An international conference was held in London in 1972 leading to the Convention on the Prevention of Marine Pollution by Dumping of Wastes and Other Matter (for some reason dubbed MARPOL), taking effect in 1975 with fifteen nations (seventy-eight today) as signatories. The treaty left many loopholes. The Nixon administration shrank from requiring double bottoms to oil tankers, and ocean dumping problems continued with slight abatement as ever-larger cruise ships gradually became worse polluters than oil tankers. But a start was made at a time when Nixon was presidentially engaged, and his chief contribution was agreement to use public language that empowered parts of the federal bureaucracy coordinated by Train at CEQ. In this case, presidential rhetoric probably had little impact on public opinion but did authorize role expansions by entrepreneurial bureaucrats in search of a mission. The moving force arousing the public was the media coverage of oil spills and oil-strangled seagulls and seals.

Train was becoming a sort of lesser version of Pinchot, though of course he did not box or hike or brainstorm in the White House late at night with Nixon, as Pinchot had with TR. Train was the chief moving force behind the anti–ocean-dumping agreement forged in London and headed the US delegation to the first UN Conference on the Human Environment in Stockholm in 1974, the International Whaling Convention also in London, and the 1973 Convention on International Trade in Endangered Species. When Train returned from these birthing places of international environmental law he was never invited to the White House for a debriefing. But in some sense this unprecedented international activity goes also on the scorecard of President Nixon, though he had little interest in it.

Nixon's environmental record includes a promising shift in party align-
ments on environmental issues that might have lasted longer but for the surprising emergence on the national political scene of antienvironmentalist
movie actor, Reagan. For a brief time, Nixon led the Republican Party toward
reembracing TR's identification with nature protection in the interests of future generations. Contrast the unenthusiastic three sentences under the
heading "Neglect of Natural Resources" in the 1964 Republican Platform on
which Goldwater ran with the substantial promises of protective actions "in
the tradition of Theodore Roosevelt" in the 1968 platform behind Nixon,
then the expansive and lengthy brag about wilderness areas, wildlife protection, and pollution-control laws in the 1972 version of that document. The
greening taking place here is one measure of the tenure and brief political
engagement of Nixon.

Nixon's absolute lack of intellectual and emotional engagement with any
part of the vast environmental preservation agenda made it difficult for
many contemporaries with conservationist sympathies to fully credit his
short period of robust and unexpectedly positive leadership. If "motives" are
suspect, performance is often devalued, even ignored. Whatever Nixon's
motives, there is something else not to like behind the official rhetoric. Historians with access to presidential documents, tape recordings, staff memoirs, and diaries reveal to us a Nixon not only emotionally unstable, obscene
in expression, bigoted, and obsessed with "enemies" but also contemptuous
of, among other things, the environmental movement and its leadership.
Several people who worked on natural resource issues with Nixon concluded
that he had no views on the environment just as he had no fixed opinions on
anything except on the importance of his political success.

This seems, unfortunately, not entirely true. During Nixon's presidency
and afterward he repeatedly expressed—privately—opinions on conserva-
tionism/environmentalism (he never understood the difference) grounded
in profound historical ignorance. In a cabinet meeting on energy policy and
air pollution, Train reports that the secretary of commerce urged the president to "emphasize the ethic of conservation," to which Nixon responded,
in genuine puzzlement: "What's that?"[43] He regarded environmentalism, as
he had conservationism before it, as somehow both a leftist, "system-
destroying" part of contemporary radicalism and a "rich person's game," a
temporary fad in which elitist leaders refused to appreciate economic realities. After early receptivity, he allowed a muddled conception of environmen-

talism as an illegitimate ideological enemy to guide him toward complete alienation from a constituency he once courted. This was ignorance compounded by paranoia. A president's education is a powerful thing the voting public only superficially explores when the selection of a leader is being made. Nixon disengaged from his brief and productive environmentalist phase as his reelection challenge approached. He admonished his cabinet and staff in 1972 to "get off the environmental kick." He followed his own advice, moving on to matters that were not "fads" and "political losers."

In 1991, after a speech in New York, ex-president Nixon encountered William Reilly, once one of his staffers as head of the EPA. "I know you. You're at EPA, and I founded EPA. I'm an environmentalist too."[44] No he wasn't and never had been. In his post–White House years Nixon wrote seven books, gave innumerable speeches and interviews, and never once mentioned natural-resource or environmental issues except for that comment to Reilly. What he might truthfully have said to his former staffer would have been: "I was never an environmentalist, proud to say, but for a while as President I marched in the front of their ranks, for they seemed for a time to be moving in my political direction, which was reelection." Better he should join their ranks for a short, strategically productive time, and for self-serving reasons, than never at all. Nixon died on April 22, 1994, the twenty-fourth anniversary of the first Earth Day.

GERALD R. FORD

Every previous president was elected to that office or to the vice presidency, which under certain unpleasant circumstances amounts to the same thing. The sole exception was Gerald R. Ford, appointed vice president and sworn in as president on August 9, 1974, as Richard and Pat Nixon flew back to their home in San Clemente. The US electorate had not chosen Ford for either office. He served 896 days in the White House before failing to be elected president on his first attempt, and his less than a full term in office was so devoid of major policy or political change that he commands little space in histories of that office or studies of the leadership performance of its occupants.

The occasion of his succession, with government in disarray and disrepute, was not a promising one for innovation in any policy agenda. The situation did offer an opportunity for a president to restore public trust and calm, to some degree. In that role of healer, Ford must be judged a success. Along the way he made little innovative mark in any sector of policy, and historians (and the public) have tended to accept this as all historical circumstances permitted. It was Ford's destiny to serve briefly as a caretaker, almost a placeholder, some people thought.

This assessment is a lenient misjudgment. No twentieth-century president, with Calvin Coolidge arguably an exception, could be merely a calming figure warming a chair in the Oval Office. The federal government's engagement with society is so pervasive that the chief executive necessarily makes decisions of considerable national influence, even if some are forced on him. This is true even with regard to policy areas for which the caretaker president has no enthusiasm and in which his instinct is to curb the federal role, such as the conservation cluster—natural resources and the environment.

Ford biographers and historians of his tenure have adopted his combination of lack of interest and opposition regarding environmental policy during his two years and not quite two and one-half months in office. The small number of histories of his presidency have almost nothing to say on any aspect of the large array of environmental issues receiving policy attention during his time in the White House—with the exception of the sudden arrival in 1973 of the "energy crisis," a policy cauldron centered on a suddenly scarce (or artificially overpriced) natural resource, petroleum. A book-length bibliography of writings on Ford's presidency contains only one citation under "environment" but ten on the swine flu scare of 1976 and fourteen on the 1976 presidential television debates with Jimmy Carter. A pair of memoirs from two Nixon environmental aides tell us most of what we know about Ford's environmental-policy performance. His memoirs touch on no environmental issue apart from the energy component of natural resources.

Of course, a modern president necessarily engages environmental-policy topics with some frequency because parts of the administrative branch are engaged daily in matters of natural resources or pollution, and some of these reach the White House. Ford's presidency is an especially interesting part of our larger study of the environmental issue because he was the first president after TR who, though a Republican, saw environmental protection as at odds with the more important goal of steady economic growth and thus in need of curbing.

Ford was born in 1913 as Leslie King, Jr., in Omaha, Nebraska. His mother soon moved herself and the boy to her family town of Grand Rapids, Michigan, to escape a wife-beating husband. There she remarried, and Leslie King, Jr., took the name of his adoptive father, a paint salesman.

Young Gerry attended public schools and conceded in his autobiography that he "struggled" to make "average grades in science and Latin" in high school. However, he somehow worked his way into the top 5 percent of his graduating class. His single enthusiasm was athletics, especially football. Grand Rapids was surrounded by lakes and cutover forests, and although Gerry became an Eagle Scout and spent part of one summer at a scout camp on Mackinac Island, there is no record in any biographies, or in his own memoirs, that he formed any emotional or intellectual connection to the natural world. His father bought a share in a cabin on the Pere Marquette River and did some fishing there, but Ford mentions only that the family often went along. His favorite outdoor place was the football field at his high school and then the one at the University of Michigan. At both schools he was an outstanding center and linebacker, even receiving not-very-lucrative offers to play professional football. He worked from 1935 to 1939 as an assistant football and boxing coach at Yale. In the summer of 1936, he worked for several weeks as a park ranger at Yellowstone, which he describes in his autobiography as supervision of tourist traffic and monitoring the daily tourist photo opportunity when the bears were fed. He had nothing to say about the grandeur of Yellowstone.

Always a hardworking though not an exceptional student, Ford was allowed to take courses part-time at Yale Law School in 1938, was then admitted, and graduated in 1941. Ford as a law student was a "decent sort, of average ability," observed law professor Eugene Rostow.[45] In all accounts of his youth and education there is not one mention of any book he read. (That is also true of his presidency, although he cowrote three books after he left public office.)

Ford joined the US Navy in 1942 and served as a junior officer in training and athletic coaching assignments in the United States, then on an aircraft carrier in the South Pacific. He was discharged in 1946, returned to law practice in Grand Rapids, and was elected to Congress as a Republican representative in 1948. He became friends in Congress with, among others, JFK and Nixon and took note of their presidential ambitions. His own highest goal was to become speaker of the House, and he was elected minority leader in

1965, as close as he would come to his aspiration. As a US representative Ford was a center-right, balance-the-budget, Republican loyalist who never wrote any legislation but excelled in personal relations. He was a "solid, inertial guy" who never made enemies, his Republican colleagues recalled. In the House he voted with Nixon's preferences more than 80 percent of the time and was rewarded with the vice presidency when Agnew, in October 1973, pleaded no contest on charges of tax evasion and was forced to resign.

It was not the end of Ford's ascent, and the only environmentalist at a high level in the Nixon government, Train, wondered how a Ford administration would handle the environmental issues that, like it or not, no president could entirely avoid. Train was encouraged when Ford reappointed him as head of the EPA and invited him to resume cabinet attendance. Not encouraging was Ford's message to Congress on legislative priorities a month after taking office, in which he offered a small list of bills deserving priority attention and placed the most emphasis on the need to reduce the federal budget by $700 million, which turned out to be bad news for the EPA budget.

Train was in the audience in November to hear Ford use these inconclusive words at a conference in Portland, Oregon: "We cannot enrich our lives by impoverishing our land. We can raise both [the] standard of living and the quality of life."[46] In December the president received the annual report of the CEQ, out of which his aides crafted for the president a message to Congress congratulating the United States for its "crusade to improve the quality of our human environment." He continued that we must "accept the need for balance" with other "energy and economic goals at the same time." At a meeting on energy policy in Vail, Colorado, late in December, Ford volunteered in a social moment at the mountain retreat that he was a poor fisherman and did not enjoy it and had never been a hunter. One of his top aides, former head of a large corporation Roy Ash, remarked that he had "never fished in his life." Train mused to himself, "It seemed surprising and unfortunate to me that so many people in leadership positions had so little exposure to the outdoors."[47]

At a conference in Cincinnati in 1975 when Train was in the presidential party, Ford agreed to meet with a large group of environmentalists and hear their concerns. The next day he gave a speech that made Train and his friends uneasy when he endorsed environmental goals but, reversing his view expressed in Portland, insisted economic growth must always come first. Train had tried to teach Nixon to argue that there was no necessary conflict between the two goals, and now he had to start over again. However, his office was not in the White House, which among other things isolated him from Ford's speechwriting staff. In any event that staff was mediocre after one of Ford's new aides, Robert Hartmann, fired the Nixon speechwriting team that had produced much of the "Kennedyesque" rhetoric. Ford's speeches were pedestrian and poorly organized, especially unfortunate because his delivery was sometimes awkward.

The binge of environmental-protection legislation that began with LBJ tapered off in the late 1970s as Ford served out Nixon's second term. In part it tapered off because Ford set presidential records in vetoing bills Congress sent to him. He vetoed forty-six acts of Congress while president. His annual average of vetoes was 15.3, nearly four times the yearly mean for presidents from 1889 and 1985.

Some environmental laws survived Ford's instinct for telling members of Congress they were too active. He signed two major pollution-control laws gestating for several years that had developed considerable support, including the "in principle" leaning of the Nixon White House—the Resource Conservation and Recovery Act (RCRA) of 1976, regulating municipal solid and oil wastes. He also reluctantly signed the Toxic Substances Control Act (TOSCA) of the same year, with which he was especially unhappy because it authorized the EPA to regulate the production, use, and disposal of a range of hazardous chemicals. He objected to the bill's requirement of pretesting new chemicals, a costly step for industry. A veto, however, was made politically risky when in February 1976, national news media reported that twenty-eight workers in a Virginia chemical plant making the pesticide Kepone had been hospitalized. Not long afterward the pesticide was found in the bottom sediments of the James River. In this period the public learned that a General Electric plant in New York had for some time been discharging toxic polychlorinated biphenyls (PCBs) into the Hudson River and, as Rachel Carson had warned, into the food chain, including fish and therefore also including people who ate the fish they caught. Ford signed TOSCA, which was to have a troubled future.

But on other matters Ford's basic probusiness outlook, reinforced by corporate lobbyists and an economic recession tilting policy toward curbing federal expenditures, soon led to conflict with environmentalists on several fronts. Under heavy lobbying pressure from a tiny group with strong ties to western politicians—sheep ranchers—Ford in 1975 modified Nixon's 1972 executive order banning use of poisons against predators on public lands and permitted the use of sodium cyanide. He was also not sympathetic with the environmentalists' attack on strip mining, a mountain-scalping way of producing cheap coal and thus cheap electricity for US consumers that brought horrendous costs to the natural environment and human communities in the mountain regions of the Appalachians and Rockies. Nixon had proposed a Mined Area Protection Act in his 1971 environmental message to Congress but lost interest, so the flaws of the old 1872 Mining Act were still there when Ford took over—and when he left. The White House was pressured by the Interior and Energy Departments to oppose an anti–strip-mining bill backed by Representative Morris Udall on the grounds that it would raise energy and other costs at exactly the wrong time. Ford let his opposition be known behind the scenes, pocket-vetoed the Udall legislation in December 1974, submitted a weaker substitute in February, and vetoed it because Congress had restricted the coal miners (which included the TVA) more than he liked. An override failed by three votes. Feelings ran high because an anti–strip-mining law was a prime goal of many environmentalists that year as well as a lightning rod for hard-line opponents of any federal regulation of toxic (or any other kind of) industrial wastes. "I am in hysterical opposition" to the Udall bill, stated Representative Sam Steiger (R-Ariz.), for it raises the specter of having the "EPA, an advocate of pristine atmospheric hypogenic values . . . administering these kinds of ambiguous regulations [that] would guarantee the destruction . . . of the land itself and would fall like an overripe fruit in the hands of the waiting Communist hordes." To the contrary, argued Representative Kenneth Hechler, the bill was a "very loose series of band-aids on a very serious cancer."[48]

This veto termination of a popular environmental regulatory program reminds us presidents sometimes matter a great deal. Ford had twice derailed a natural-resource–protection law with a lengthy history and large majorities in favor. This was leadership, shortsighted and costly. As Ford settled into private life in California, where no strip mining was allowed, the practice that produced 37 percent of US coal output went on defacing the ridgelines and polluting the streams of pieces of the landscape that if gathered together would match the size of Connecticut. Brower once said, after he made the mistake of agreeing to the dam that would flood Glen Canyon, that one should not decide the fate of a place one has never seen. A two-hour trip out of Washington, D.C., would have taken President Ford into West Virginia to see strip-mined mountains and the polluted and silt-clogged creeks below them, but Ford's friends did not include a modern Muir eager to guide him there.

Another promising measure was squashed, this time permanently, when Ford held a cabinet meeting in late 1974 to discuss the legislation to enact NLUP, a proposal initiated by congressional Democrats and endorsed by Nixon. Finding only the Interior Department, EPA, and CEQ in favor of even a modest version of the legislation, he justified withdrawing his support by citing the need for budget discipline at a time when, as he said in his first State of the Union Address: "I should say to you that the State of the Union is not good" because of an unprecedented combination of inflation and recession.[49] The proposed act, which should have been called the Federal Support for State Zoning Reform Act, was intended to push states to fight urban sprawl and protect ecologically sensitive sites through federal financial aid for and strict oversight of local zoning laws, with new attention to preservation of prime agricultural lands.

Summing up the domestic policy record of the Ford presidency, historian John Robert Greene concluded, "Environmental policy received short shrift."[50] His forgiving explanation was that priority had to be given to economic troubles afflicting the US economy in the 1970s, which for any president would crowd out many other opportunities. One must have some sympathy with the three presidents of that decade, who suddenly found themselves at the official helm of a national economy inexplicably running too slowly (high unemployment, low growth rate) yet at the same time too fast (inflation) as a result of the increase in petroleum prices that began in the early 1970s and accelerated with the Arab oil boycott of 1973. Ford himself cited these economic maladies as the reason for his resistance to expanded environmental protection. "I pursue the goal of clean air and pure water," he explained, "but I must pursue the goal of maximum jobs and continued economic progress."[51] The two were apparently, in his mind, in eternal conflict, and "economic progress" came first, leaving the other short.

Seeing the domestic policy agenda in that light, unlike FDR, who found conservation compatible with the search for jobs and economic progress, Ford's presidency made no political use of environmentalism's collective agenda of natural-resource preservation, environmental amenity, public health gains, and public works benefits. Ford apparently had not been listening on the many occasions LBJ talked about enhancing the "quality of our lives" through environmental protection as an augmentation of national material well-being. Ford displayed no interest in environmental issues out of unexamined assumptions about hard tradeoffs between job growth and environmental protection, along with a conservative, Republican dislike of government program expansion. It is not clear whether, while in the White House, Ford was aware that his upcoming 1976 national election contained a substantial environmentalist vote he had never had to consider in his campaigns for his House seat from Grand Rapids. The result was a replay of Nixon's second, "brown" term, the president ignorant of the conservation movement around him, dismissing its agenda as an expensive frill.

One might say there are no mysteries here, that this could have been predicted by anyone who scrutinized Ford's education and life experiences. But then what are we to make of the example of Nixon? With no youthful exposure to the outdoors and its creatures, trained in the law and shaped by years in the Congress, where foreign affairs held all his interest, he matched Ford in lack of experience in and education about the environment and the need for conservation. Yet Nixon still asserted a brief though policy-shaping leadership role, converting himself for two or three crucial years into an environmentalist president for the political gains he (correctly) saw in it. So with Ford we seem to need another factor to explain his obstructionist environmental record beyond poor education and total absence of any exposure to the conservation ethic or arguments.

Perhaps, as some said during Ford's ascent in politics, he was not very bright and thus incapable of a Nixon-like theft of environmentalist clothes. Surrounding Ford there had long been questions about his basic intellectual gifts for any complex management job, especially for the big one he was never trained or elected to do. "Can you imagine Gerry Ford sitting in this chair?" Nixon asked Nelson Rockefeller on one of the latter's infrequent visits to the Oval Office. LBJ, once irked by the plodding discourse of Representative Ford, commented: "That's what happens when you play football without a helmet." White House Aide Robert Hartmann told Ford his largest problem was that "you don't suspect ill motives of anyone." Representative Charles Goodell found Ford "genuinely naïve."[52] Others saw a lack of intellectual firepower. "It is fair to say that Ford is slow, unimaginative, and not very articulate," wrote journalist Reeves in an early biography. "His success was a triumph of lowest-common-denominator politics, the survival of a man without enemies, the least objectionable alternative." Reeves reached back to the insights of a classic book on the mediocre political leadership at the presidential level of the US system in the decades between Abraham Lincoln and TR. "The methods and habits of Congress," Englishman James Bryce had said in his classic *The American Commonwealth* (1888),

> and indeed of political life generally, seem to give fewer opportunities for personal distinction, fewer modes in which a man may commend himself to his countrymen by eminent capacity in thought, speech or in administration. Eminent men make more enemies, and give those enemies more assailable points, than obscure men do. . . . Who now knows or cares to know anything about the presidency of James K. Polk or Franklin Pierce? The only remarkable thing about them is that being so commonplace they should have climbed so high.[53]

Reeves, returning to the Ford record in an article in 1996, "I'm Sorry, Mr. President," softened his judgment. Maybe "dumb" was always too harsh a judgment about Ford, Reeves conceded. I agree, after reading much of Ford's public output, especially press conferences where no speechwriter could put the best face on what he had to say. Ford was capable, occasionally, of talking about complicated policy issues but undeniably awkward and somewhat lacking in confidence when on television. Reeves, in any event, shifted the grounds for his assessment. After reconsidering the Nixon pardon, Reeves assessed it as the right thing for the country. "Whatever his failings as a leader . . . he was right about the big one."[54]

But Reeves's reassessment on the basis of one Ford decision cannot go unchallenged. Ford served for almost two and one-half years, about the same amount of time as JFK, and as with all presidents, the historical appraisal must encompass all the large things he engaged or failed to tackle. This book asks about resource/environmental issues, regarding which Ford was a retreating and mostly wrongheaded leader who wasted precious time. In any event, the voters, this once, share no blame for a flawed selection process. It was a unique process, Nixon inviting advice from the public, his staff, and Congress and then carrying this avalanche of opinion to Camp David, where he reluctantly agreed upon Ford, though he strongly preferred Texan John Connelly—and this only after Ford agreed to step aside for Connelly in 1976. "Congress made Gerry Ford President," declared House

Speaker Carl Albert, by which he meant that a handful of leaders from the Hill made it firmly clear to Nixon that only Ford would go through without objections.[55]

Indeed, US voters' poor record as selectors, evident so often in this account, could have been more painfully demonstrated if the man they did select to be the vice president behind Nixon, the ignorant and corrupt Agnew, had not fortuitously been convicted of tax evasion and, just in time, moved out of the line of succession. Only in this perspective are we grateful, in retrospect, for President Ford.

When Ford stood for reelection in 1976 the stakes for environmentalists were high. Would the Democrats, now seen as the party with stronger environmentalist leanings, replace Ford with someone who, whatever his other commitments and talents, might resume the progress on environmental protection made by the Democratic presidents of the 1960s and, briefly, Nixon?

In our national beginning, most of the land within national boundaries was public domain—almost four out of every five acres in the continental United States. At our bicentennial in 1976, when official policy ended the great era of transferring public lands to private control, more than 1.1 billion acres had been transferred to individuals, states, corporations. The federal government still owned, in the name of the whole people, 635 million acres of land, or almost 28 percent. The retention of that land for public use as parks, forests, wildlife refuges, and other sites has been the starting point of our more than a century of stories.

JIMMY CARTER

President Ford's renomination for the 1976 presidential campaign was routine, but the Democratic primaries produced a surprise nominee, Georgia governor James Earl Carter, Jr., who insisted on being called Jimmy.

Born in 1924, Carter was raised on a farm near tiny Plains, Georgia (population: 550), in a house that lacked indoor plumbing and electricity (which came when he was 13). "My most persistent impression as a farm boy was of the earth. There was a closeness," he wrote in one of his several books about his Georgia roots, "almost an immersion, in the sand, loam, and red clay that seemed natural, and constant." He and his companions "led an active life outdoors, spending our days in the fields and woods. . . . Throughout my young life, I was obsessed with hunting and fishing. . . . I had a fishing pole in my hands as early as I can remember."[56] He was also a "voracious reader" not only of hunting and fishing magazines but also of "adventure books" by Zane Grey and Jack London as well as the "flowery writing" of Muir and Henry David Thoreau.[57]

He and his three siblings could also draw upon middle-class assets. His mother, Lillian, was a trained nurse and avid reader. His father, called Earl, was a prominent local farmer and owner of a farm-supply company. Jimmy attended high school in Plains, where he was an ardent reader (a habit formed at home for all the Carter children) and good student. Though three or four inches less than six feet tall when I met him at the Woodrow Wilson Center in 1983, he played on the school basketball team. Influenced by postcards from foreign ports visited by an uncle, Carter made an early decision to attend the Naval Academy. This required extra courses in scientific and technical subjects, which he took at Georgia Southwestern College and, briefly, at Georgia Tech. He was admitted to Annapolis in 1943, was graduated in 1946 toward the top of his class, and shortly thereafter married Rosalyn White, beginning a remarkable partnership that strengthened him both personally and professionally.

In the navy he had served on surface ships and diesel-electric submarines and spent some time in the fledgling nuclear submarine program run by the legendary Admiral Hyman Rickover. Upon the death of his father, Carter resigned his commission in October 1953, after seven years and four months of service. Despite Rosalynn's reluctance, he returned to the family farming-based business on the outskirts of Plains.

Carter plunged at once into volunteer civic roles, was elected to the Georgia Senate for two terms (1962–1966), and lost a race for governor in 1966. He ran again and won in 1970, soon establishing himself as a rare southern liberal by declaring that racial discrimination had no place in the future of Georgia and working on educational and civil-service reforms. His ambition aimed higher, and the Democratic Party was leaderless after McGovern's disastrous candidacy in 1972, carrying only two states. Few national pundits gave Carter, a Georgia farmer and "born-again" Christian who taught Sunday school at his local Baptist church, any chance when this southern governor with 2 percent national name recognition decided to enter the Democratic presidential primaries. However, his campaign was well planned and staffed, and his basic "I am an outsider" strategy proved a good fit for the public mood of the mid-1970s. To further introduce himself to the public, Carter wrote *Why Not the Best?* (1976), an autobiography ending with a frank explanation of why (and how) he was running for president and an affirmative answer to the questions: "Can our government be honest, decent, open, fair, and compassionate? Can our government be competent?"[58] Yes, he argued, with the right leadership.

He jumped into an early lead by winning the Iowa caucuses and the New Hampshire primary and had visited thirty-seven states before other candidates took him seriously. His key advantage, exploited from the beginning, was his identity as an outsider, no part of the "inside the beltway" Washington that had produced an unpopular war and a president driven from office for impeachable offenses. "I will never lie to you," Carter found several ways to say, with or without explicit references to Nixon. Sandy-haired, often flashing a toothy grin, intense, and effective in small groups, he took the nomination on the first ballot and defeated President Ford on November 2, 1976, by a narrow 50.1 to 48 percent margin, becoming the first candidate from a Deep South state to win the presidency since 1848. Both houses of Congress were in Democratic hands, but there was no claim that the new president had any sort of electoral mandate because the election had not turned on one or two issues, and the turnout was the lowest in recent years. Carter was fifty-one years old.

On the night of Carter's election my historian friend Robert Kelley and I were driving home from a meeting and, hearing that President Ford was about to concede, pulled the car into a lot overlooking a Pacific sunset to listen. Carter was on the way to the White House, and we shared anticipations of a successful presidency for this new sort of centrist Democrat, whose intelligence and verbal skills brought to Bob's mind another southerner coming from a governorship to the White House and a notable presidency—Wilson.

As it turned out, we had much company in misjudging what was ahead for President-elect Carter and his country. But Carter on his election night had already made a mark on presidential history. For the first time, a new president's strong environmental stands were a key part of his winning electoral strategy, carrying him to the nomination. His record as governor won him the support, or at least the sympathetic ear, of every environmentalist in Georgia. He had created the new Georgia Department of Natural Resources, increased natural-resource–protection spending, and strengthened enforcement procedures leading to stiffer penalties for violations of air- and water-protection laws. He took a special interest in the protection of the Chattahoochee River north of Atlanta, withholding zoning permits for highway and bridge construction. His preservationist instinct reached beyond rivers and nature's special places to include historical sites protected by his creation of the Georgia Heritage Trust Commission.

Governor Carter's most acclaimed conservation accomplishment was to stop the Army Corps of Engineers' planned Sprewell Bluff Dam on the Flint River, which would have flooded and transformed a twenty-eight-mile part of the river revered by canoeists, anglers, and hikers. Carter had at first favored the dam but listened to environmentalist objections, visited the river twice by canoe and twice by helicopter, and declared his opposition not just to this dam but to the "construction of unwarranted dams and other projects at public expense." "The Army Corps of Engineers," he said later, "ought to get out of the dam-building business." This episode received national media attention and allowed Carter to emerge as more than a regional figure, especially among those people who preferred free-flowing rivers to dams. State governors did not normally oppose federal proposals to spend money on water projects in their states, and Carter's stance "gained him near-celebrity status among environmentalists" around the country, in the words of historian Jeffrey Stine, as a result of his environmentalist achievements.[59]

While contemplating his run for the Democratic Party's nomination in 1976, Carter and his advisers knew that his environmental record as governor could help him create what he lacked, a national following gathered from all regions and across party lines. As early as 1974 he began by asking Georgia environmentalists for their help, and it was forthcoming in the form of Conservationists for Carter (CFC), a group that produced supportive mailings and, in the middle of the Democratic primaries of early 1976, contacted environmentalist supporters of the presidential candidacies of Representative Udall and Senator Jackson to urge them to shift their support from their lagging candidacies to Carter. Many national environmental organizations, most influentially the League of Conservation Voters, cited Carter's Georgia record in endorsing him over Ford.

There had been no precedent for this in US history—a presidential candidate who rallied the support of virtually every part of the national (and Georgian) environmentalist apparatus and won the nomination with that as a contributing factor. Environmentalists in Georgia were easily rallied by Carter's record during four years as governor, and he found a novel way to reach voters in every state. At the urging of aide Hamilton Jordan, Carter in 1974 began to write his "campaign biography" and finished *Why Not the Best?* in October 1975, just before the presidential primaries. This brief book about the life and career of an eighth-generation Georgia farmer who rose to become governor met with sensational success, selling more than 1 million copies and having an "electrifying effect in the New Hampshire primaries," in the words of historian Douglas Brinkley.[60] Carter's prose conveyed a candid, scrupulously honest personality of high moral purpose and an unexpected narrative ability. His detailed description of life on a Georgia peanut farm (they grew other crops and raised cattle, but peanuts were the money crop) communicated an affection for rural life quite different from the negative accounts of Harry Truman and LBJ and prepared the reader to credit Carter's assessment that he "spent more time [as governor] preserving our natural resources than on any other one issue." Readers learned in the chapter "Government and the Outdoors" that he and Rosalynn were over the years frequent visitors to favorite natural sites across the South, "rode the wild rivers on rafts and in canoes and kayaks, . . . studied the wildlife programs on our isolated game preserves, . . . observed alligators and Pileated Woodpeckers and fished for bass in the freshwater lake that is, in all the world, closest to the sea." The nuclear engineer finished this chapter on the outdoors by quoting from Sidney Lanier's *The Song of the Chattahoochee*: "Out of the Hills of Habersham, Down the valleys of Hall, I hurry amain to reach the plain, run the rapid and leap the fall."[61]

Campaign autobiographies almost never have any impact on presidential (or other) elections, but *Why Not the Best?* vastly expanded Carter's national following and was a decided asset as he entered primaries in states where he was unknown. The role of his conservation background in the general election is less clear, but for the million or more readers of his book, especially conservationists, he gained an edge in the contest with Ford. The media coverage during the campaign and the debates did not sharply contrast the candidates' environmentalist views, concentrating on broad economic or foreign policy differences.

Yet when environmental organizations' magazines or journals devoted to natural-resource policy made comparisons of the two candidates' views and records, readers easily saw a clear choice—evident also in the two candidates' responses to a questionnaire from the American Society of Mechanical Engineers. On energy policy Ford "basically endorsed the historical annual growth rate of 5 percent in energy consumption," concluded the author of an essay on the election and environmental issues. The president had no interest in energy efficiency, had vetoed two anti–strip-mining bills, cut spending for the EPA and for water-pollution controls in the 1977 budget, and favored easing of clean-air regulations on automobiles and coal-fired power plants. He also turned a deaf ear on environmental matters, giving Soviet Premier Leonid Brezhnev a wolfskin coat as a present and accepting in return some whalebone carvings imported illegally into the United States in violation of the Endangered Species Act. Carter tried to highlight the environmental-policy differences between himself and his opponent, occasionally bragging about canceling that Georgia dam, opposing strip mining, and placing a major emphasis on energy conservation. Both were enthusiastic about the future of nuclear energy, though Carter was more cautious about the hazards.[62] Neither of them talked, or was asked, about climate.

Carter won a narrow victory with 51 percent of the popular vote and a 297–240 Electoral College margin. As Inauguration Day approached, the emerging perception of President-elect Carter offered expanding reasons for environmentalist enthusiasm. Not only had readers of *Why Not the Best?* learned of his emotional and personal engagement with the outdoors (which Carter had actually understated, as readers would learn when he published *An Outdoors Journal* in 1988) and from his conservation record as governor. The national media gave considerable attention to the activities of the president-elect's transition team, which included a "cluster" of advisers on natural resources and another on energy. These advisers met frequently with environmental leaders, many of whom Carter hosted for an all-day meeting in Plains.

Beyond these signs that the upcoming administration promised to be extraordinarily engaged with natural-resource protection, the scribes and commentators who shaped the media perception of new people in the nation's political life were forming, on the whole, a positive assessment of the Georgia governor and president-elect. "He is probably smarter, in the College Board sense, than any other President in this century," commented journalist James Fallows, who had agreed to join Carter's speechwriting team. CBS White House Correspondent Robert Pierpont told Carter biographer Betty Glad, "Intellectually, Carter is the smartest President I've covered."[63]

Carter had long been a serious reader of three or four books each week. In the 1970s he shifted from foreign affairs and economics to "histories and biographies concerning our nation and the presidency." These included James MacGregor Burns's *Leadership*, with its stress on the moral dimension of great presidential leadership.[64] Had Carter read Schlesinger's *The Imperial Presidency* (1973)? Indeed so, and although he shared the national dismay at Nixon's cultivation of the presidency's dark side, he was touchingly convinced that the right Washington outsider (a farmer from Plains, Georgia?) could put all that behind the nation without the presidency-weakening measures contemplated by many in the Congress. In an interview with journalist Bill Moyers in early 1976, he spoke of the need for strong presidential leadership in our oft-paralyzed political system, mentioning both Roosevelts, Wilson, and Andrew Jackson. Carter said:

> There is only one person in this nation who can speak with a clear voice to the American people. There's only one person who can set a standard of ethics and morality and excellence and greatness or call on the American people to make a sacrifice . . . or answer difficult questions or propose or carry out bold programs. . . . In the absence of that leadership, there is no leadership, and the country drifts.[65]

The Moyers interview did not bring out the other side of Carter's conception of the presidency, the "balance" with the other powers, which took the form of a near contempt for the role of legislators in Congress. If the president was the trustee of the national interest, members of Congress to Carter were "politicians" who at best only pretended to seek the good of their districts and in fact worked unwaveringly for their own individual survival and advancement. "He doesn't like politicians," presidential scholar Tom Cronin said in expressing a widely held view of Carter: "He really just doesn't like them."[66] This would cause Carter serious difficulties when he began as president to govern jointly with people at the other end of Pennsylvania Avenue, who were, in most cases, smart enough to detect that he just did not like or, worse, did not respect them or what he saw as their motivating values.

So there were many early signs that Carter meant to lead and strongly believed the country not only was in need of a strong presidency but eager for it. The final chapter of his campaign biography foreshadowed his campaign speeches. An era of reform, he argued, must begin with closing the "chasm between people and government," the establishment of honesty and openness where government had become "isolated from the people," the shift from drift and lack of planning to long-range goals and national purposes. He hinted at policy areas in need of most attention—welfare, health care, education, and an end to the "wasting of our energy resources and other precious raw materials as though their supply were infinite. We must even face the prospect of changing our basic ways of living. . . . We are still floundering and equivocating about protection of our environment. . . . What does come next [out of Washington] must be a firm commitment to pure air, clean water, and unspoiled land."[67]

At the close of his campaign biography Carter sided with both schools of the early conservation movement, lining up with Muir in wishing to keep a Georgia river free and on the same page using the resource-efficiency language of Pinchot and the resource-exhaustion themes of TR. There was also a hint of the fundamental change in values called for by Leopold. The stage seemed set for an expansive and creative period of environmental public policy.

Head of the National Association for the Advancement of Colored People (NAACP) Benjamin Chavis first became interested in the connection between pollution and race when in 1982 he visited the predominately African American residents of Warren County, North Carolina, and learned from their bitter experience with toxic wastes in neighborhood air and water and from the writings of sociologist Robert Bullard of the rise of an anti–pollution-based social movement among racial minorities. Six hundred people gathered in Washington, D.C., in October 1991 to launch and encourage a national movement for "environmental justice."

Four years after Kelley and I imagined a successful presidency for the Georgia naval engineer and peanut farmer, Carter was fired by the voters and sent back to Plains. A book published as Reagan made plans to replace Carter in the White House, Clark Mollenhoff's *The President Who Failed* (1980), used an adjective that soon attached itself to Carter's four years. It had been a "failed presidency." Memoirists followed by biographers and then the first wave of historians agreed on the "failure" analysis although not on the explanations. These were shaped by the relative weight given to Carter's shortcomings in the face of the "events that overwhelmed" his presidency.

Of the first, much was made of his poor relations with Congress, his immersion in details (he once told historian White that just before their meeting he had read the entire Air Force budget), and his unmelodious speech delivery.[68] Carter was an "oratorical mortician," commented Senator Eugene McCarthy, but Carter rejected suggestions that he hire a speech coach. One of his speechwriters, Fallows, lamented Carter's "passionless presidency" and his inability to communicate to the public a coherent or compelling vision of where he meant to take the country. Passionate and disappointed liberals in the president's party complained that Carter failed to convey a sense of strong liberal leadership.

The second broad explanation held that the problems and political circumstances of the second half of the 1970s probably would have undone any president. Carter's difficulties were caused by overwhelming external circumstances—a sluggish yet also inflationary economy, petroleum shortages engineered abroad, a set of intractable foreign-policy dilemmas allowing no decisive resolution, and a rightward drift of US political sentiment that Carter sensed but his party's liberal leadership would not acknowledge. Another version of the "external circumstances" interpretation was that US governing institutions and public confidence in them had been so eroded by the turbulence of the 1960s and 1970s as to make the nation almost ungovernable.

Carter's presidency did not begin as one a majority of the voters would four years later reject. He started with strong public approval, true of all new presidents. To signal a reversal of the trend toward an "imperial presidency," Carter wore a suit rather than formal clothes to his inauguration; then he and Rosalynn walked from the Capitol to the White House. Carter ended the custom of having the Marine Corps Band play Hail to the Chief at presidential appearances, curbed the use of limousines for top White House staff, and sold the presidential yacht anchored in the Potomac. During an unusually cold Washington, D.C., winter he set a pattern of wearing cardigan sweaters for TV appearances, turned thermostats down to 65 degrees in the White House, and installed solar panels on the roof. The symbolism was obvious—our new president was not a Washington political insider and could set an example of frugality and the common touch.

Then the hard work began—setting the agenda of important tasks and the priorities among them. Despite his thin majority, Carter put before Congress a large reform agenda based upon a booklet listing his 115 major campaign promises—reforms in educational policy, Social Security, health care, taxation, deregulation of transportation, transfer of the Panama Canal to that country, and much more. In early 1977 this added up to a formidable thicket of problems, and his top staff began to concede that there was no organizing principle or slogan—no Carter New Deal or new frontier.

Perhaps a rallying concept could be found in energy-policy reform. Carter well knew of the historical turning point reached without any notice when in 1948 the United States, the world's largest producer and consumer of oil, became a net importer, increasingly buying oil from the Middle East. This slow shift of power was abruptly demonstrated in 1973–1974 by the OPEC price increases and disruptive embargo. The Nixon and Ford governments floundered, then tried to reassure the public with talk of increased drilling, mining, and building more nuclear reactors at home. Carter decided to persuade the United States to explore another path—energy conservation and the development of renewable energy sources.

On April 20 he delivered an energy speech to a joint session of Congress and the nation. "Tonight I want to have an unpleasant talk with you," Carter began, "about a problem that is unprecedented in our history." He reported the grim facts of an increasing dependency upon foreign petroleum at rising costs. We must make fundamental changes in our energy uses and sources, he said, accepting the reality of energy-supply limits and learning to conserve ("our first goal is conservation") and to innovate. This would require a commitment to social change that Carter, reaching into our history, likened to what philosopher William James in a 1906 essay had called the "moral equivalent of war."

Public opinion polls indicated that Carter's speech, to an audience of 80 million, was generally taken as commendable leadership, the Gallup Poll recording 71 percent approval of his presidency that spring. It seemed an auspicious beginning. The president was in strong command of issues and facts in early press conferences, and Rosalyn was turning out to be an impressive asset, standing in for the president by chairing meetings when his calendar was clogged or some crisis required all his attention.

But the energy initiative did not go well. He had not put forward the details of the promised energy plan conceived by a small working group. When delivered in July, it had 113 separate provisions, a mixture including petroleum price controls, research on synthetic fuels, excessive profit taxes on oil companies, and the new Department of Energy. The ensuing three and one-half years of intense lobbying over complicated energy-policy choices gave an uncomprehending public no sense of governmental competence on either end of Pennsylvania Avenue.

In retrospect, Carter's great gamble on energy policy as an organizing goal for his administration was admirable executive leadership, except it was a political mistake because it required the unwelcome language of limits and making do with less of something formerly thought unlimited and cheap around which the United States had built its transportation systems, its housing, its metropolitan form. The public was resentful and complacent— and ignorant. A CBS poll in October 1977 found that only 43 percent believed there was a "real" energy crisis, with 47 percent convinced shortages were a profit-boosting plot by oil companies. Congress wrangled over the energy plan for most of Carter's term, eventually giving him, in pieces, a weak version of what he had asked. "The energy bill," a White House aide conceded, "was the single greatest political mistake we made in our first six months. When we couldn't pass it, people got the impression that the President just couldn't manage the government."[69]

Carter's early reform agenda brought him other political difficulties. As a governor he had been critical of what he called "unnecessary dams and water projects" as the "worst examples" of the "pork barrel problem."[70] Forced by the budget cycle to make an early decision without consulting individual members of Congress, Carter sent to the Hill a budget proposal in February that eliminated 19 of the 320 water projects Ford's budget had proposed. He soon announced other cuts for a total of 32, eliminating incoming federal grants expected by one-third of the House Democrats. These representatives were outraged at this unanticipated executive leadership, which they saw as an intolerable intrusion into their pork-barrel spending. Carter persisted in his critical scrutiny of water projects throughout his four years and had the courage to challenge the juggernaut of federal water projects, including energy-producing dams, but paid a high political price.

This ruckus with mostly southern and western members of Congress overshadowed Carter's remarkable May 23 environmental message to Congress, which included more than a dozen new legislative proposals but nonetheless placed the emphasis less on new legislation than on enforcement of the laws passed in previous years. Carter's message displayed the "administrative presidency" in full-court press—five executive orders and a wide variety of policy statements and directives to coordinating committees and federal agencies, most of which had not existed twenty years earlier. The competence of the environmental parts of the permanent government and the new president, detail-oriented and habitually sleeping only six hours a night, were on display in this lengthy message the press found difficult to summarize. Reporters and editorial writers much preferred new laws to administrative reforms. One line was frequently quoted: "The discovery of toxic chemicals in the environment is one of the grimmest discoveries of the industrial era."[71]

Carter inherited from Ford the same inflation-prone but sluggish economy, and he irritated liberal Democrats by fighting the inflation side of the nation's economic maladies with budget cuts to reduce the deficit. He devoted enormous time to foreign-policy issues too complex for the public to readily follow—such as the Strategic Arms Limitations Talks (SALT II) with the Union of Soviet Socialist Republics (USSR) to extend the 1972 agreements to limit and shrink nuclear stockpiles. He had some modest legislative successes with uncertain long-term benefits—the new Department of Energy, the new Department of Education, significant deregulation of transportation. Still, inflation and unemployment climbed, the congressional wrangling over his proposals went on, and internal disarray surfaced when Carter's key adviser, Bert Lance, director of the Office of Management, was forced in the summer of 1977 to resign and return to Georgia because of allegations of earlier financial improprieties.

These circumstances gave Carter the worst first year of any modern president, in the view of political scientist Charles O. Jones.[72] His legislative record that year was thin because he was at odds with the liberal-labor members of his party along with those irate over the water-project cancellations. He slipped downward in the "approval rating" polls throughout 1977. In his State of the Union Address in January 1978, Carter appealed for a "new spirit," a phrase that "went nowhere," one of his speechwriters said, because it could not serve as a "unifying idea" for the twenty-one items Carter identified in that speech as needing congressional attention. The Republicans made small gains in the autumn 1978 elections, and Carter tried again in his 1979 State of the Union Address for an organizing slogan—this time a "new foundation." It was another easily forgotten phrase.

That year was dominated by international events, such as the Camp David Accords averting a conflict between Egypt and Israel and the beginning of a lengthy ordeal when fifty-two hostages were seized by an Iranian revolutionary mob that broke into the US Embassy in Tehran, Iran, in February. The "hostage crisis" provided front-page print news and prime-time–dominating television footage of blindfolded and taunted hostages for fourteen months as President Carter's diplomatic (and one aborted military) efforts failed to produce their release.

National attention in July was unexpectedly pulled back to domestic politics when Carter, returning from an economic conference in Tokyo, found that rising gasoline prices and long lines at service stations, combined with inflation running at 12 percent, had driven his approval rating to a new low (for him) of 30 percent (Truman had the approval of only 26 percent as he left office). Carter canceled a planned energy speech and sequestered himself at Camp David for ten days of thought and consultation. He asked advice from many people. From inside the government the most influential documents were memos from pollster Pat Caddell affirming that the nation was in a historical "crisis of confidence" and that this was an opening for presidential greatness. Caddell guided Carter to the writings of influential contemporary social critics, such as Robert Bellah, Christopher Lasch, and Daniel Bell, whom the president invited to Camp David along with almost 150 religious, business, labor, and political leaders, with good representation of women and minorities. He even visited two nearby "ordinary" families by helicopter.

Carter then returned to Washington, D.C., to give a televised speech to the nation on July 15 in which he followed Caddell's advice, to the dismay of other aides who thought the "crisis of confidence" idea sounded too much like a sermon. He told the public he had set aside the idea of a fifth speech to the nation on energy issues and "decided to reach out and listen to the voices of America." What he had discovered was that US citizens had drifted into a "crisis of confidence, a turning point in our history. . . . We've learned that piling up material goods cannot fill the emptiness of lives which have no confidence or purpose." His own efforts to carry out his campaign promises had not addressed this larger problem, pointedly characterized in a comment to Carter made by a southern governor who bluntly told him, "Mister President, you are not leading the nation, you are just managing the government."

Speaking with what a number of listeners called unusual passion (for engineer Carter) and even at times eloquence, the president promised to lead the way out of the national funk (the media soon were referring to this as his "malaise" speech, picking up a label offered by Senator Ted Kennedy, who was challenging Carter for the 1980 nomination): "We are at a turning point of our history. There are two paths to choose. One is a path I've warned about tonight. . . . All the promises of our future point to another path, the path of common purpose and the restoration of American values."

To steer the public along that path, Carter offered a tangible goal: "I am tonight setting a clear goal for the energy policy of the U.S. Beginning this moment, this nation will never use more foreign oil than we did in 1977—never." On the "battlefield of energy we can win for our Nation a new confidence. . . . Energy will be the immediate test of our ability to unite this nation." He proposed various steps to restore energy independence—import quotas, an energy security corporation to invest in new energy sources, an energy mobilization board, and a "bold conservation program." With these and other steps, the "solution of our energy crisis can also help us to conquer the crisis of the spirit in our country."[73]

"Perhaps no President since Lincoln has probed so deeply into the metaphysics of spirit that makes America a nation as Jimmy Carter tried to do," wrote White.[74] Early indications from polls suggested that the public responded well to Carter's remarkable speech, and phone calls to the White House were three-to-one favorable. Then in subsequent days he made what turned out to be a large political error, asking for the resignation of his cabinet and accepting the resignation of five. This changed the subject from his analysis of the underlying national problem and his proposed remedies, shifting public attention to governmental disarray. Public opinion about the Carter administration returned that autumn to a downward curve as the inflation rate reached 13.3 percent and the election year 1980 loomed just ahead.

With the passage of time Carter's dramatic "crisis of confidence" speech is increasingly seen as a farsighted and even courageous effort to be what FDR had called a "preaching president," educating and rallying the public to deal with major problems too long ignored. That commendable (in principle) effort was undercut by Carter's ill-timed and dubious decision to follow it with firing cabinet officers. The nation did indeed need to begin a fundamental reorientation of its energy-consumption patterns, and Carter was the first president who understood this, breaking with the Nixon-Ford framing of the issue as a shortage of supply that could be managed by the usual technological fixes.

Many politicians and pundits, however, and even some of Carter's aides, concluded that putting the historically unprecedented energy problem at the center of the agenda of a presidency had been a fatal political mistake, however courageous. It would lead inevitably to pessimistic talk of "limits to growth" (title of a best-selling book of 1972 reporting computer-based predictions that rates of growth would bring global crisis by 2100), which implied lifestyle changes critics could assail, turning the issue into a "third rail" for any national politician or party. Carter's unflagging attention to the nation's emerging energy crisis became a central part of his presidency, one dogged by low and declining public approval ratings. Ambitious politicians dreaming of the White House took the lesson from the Carter years that voters did not want presidents who frequently brought them bad news, as Carter had done in his third month in office by bringing up "unpleasant" subjects.

Does knowing that the Carter presidency "failed," at least in the judgment of the 1980 voters and most commentators to this day, tell us that he would necessarily have made little headway on the many and large environmental policy issues to which he called attention in his 1976 campaign? Presidential history to this point suggests that only strong overall presidential performances have made room for substantial environmental advances. The presidents ranked highest on conservation/environment matters were TR, FDR, and LBJ, three who happened to successfully sponsor large liberal reform measures generally, along the way registering large gains in environmental education and policy. In each case this substantial environmental policy achievement happened when the president not only was a personally committed conservationist but combined this with unusual communicative gifts and a strong base of popularity (TR, FDR) or, in one case (LBJ), the momentum afforded by an accident of history, the assassination of his predecessor. Carter, who brought a strong and long-standing environmentalist commitment into the White House, enjoyed none of these other advantages—no mandate for change, no Congress-intimidating popularity, no united party, and, as it turned out, limited personal ability to communicate the urgency of environmental protection and the lesson that the benefits of environmental stewardship offset the costs.

So his failed presidency would necessarily leave behind minor if any environmental-policy advances? Surprisingly, not so. The environmental record of the troubled Carter-led government is strikingly impressive. At the outset he gathered talented and committed lieutenants, such as former Capitol Hill staffer Katherine Schirmer, who led the "natural resource cluster" on his transition team; Douglas Costle, who was picked to run the EPA; James G. Speth, senior environmental attorney with the Natural Resources Defense Council, who was picked to head the CEQ. Carter named as secretary of the interior Idaho governor Cecil Andrus, who made considerable progress in reining in the development-oriented agencies beneath him.

In May 1977, as we have seen, Carter sent Congress an environmental message of unprecedented scope (and length, at thirty-six pages). The intellectual quality of the message surpasses even the environmental messages of LBJ. Reflecting the shift from the forest- and wildlife-protection impulses of conservationists, Carter began with pollution and human health, then moved to problems and policies affecting energy and the urban environment, turning then in rich detail to new plans to increase wilderness, designate wild and scenic rivers, and expand wildlife protection. He called attention to another new problem, "introduction of exotic animals and plants into the United States," and closed with attention to population growth as a "major environmental problem," promising a major study of "probable changes in the world's population, natural resources, and environment." Significantly, Carter opened the message by making a case that no president had consistently made (with the exception of FDR): "environmental protection is consistent with a sound economy" and pollution-control measures "have generated many more jobs than they have lost."[75] Calling the presence of toxic chemicals "one of the grimmest discoveries of the industrial era," he proposed stronger efforts against toxic wastes and a large increase in the EPA budget. Environmental messages are not read by citizens at the breakfast table or by more than a handful of members of Congress but are primarily a statement to the rest of the executive branch about White House policy. "The various (environmental) agencies," said a reporter for *Congressional Quarterly*, "have got the word that the man in the White House is an environmentalist."[76]

Before that May message, Carter became the first president to signal that the old dam-building commitment of conservationism must now be held to environmental as well as cost-effective tests. Federal water projects that had coasted out of the Hoover-Roosevelt years as popular pork-barrel projects benefiting western and southern members of Congress and the three large federal dam-building agencies for the first time ran into White House objections based upon environmental as well as cost concerns. The former Georgia governor knew many water projects were ecologically harmful and economically wasteful, and he proposed in his second month in office a "hit list" (media language) of nineteen projects that should not go forward. Some US representatives rallied to the defense of the nineteen projects and produced water legislation Carter reluctantly signed, but federally funded dams, river channelizations, and wetland drainage projects now had their first presidential critic.

Environmentalists who grumbled when Carter compromised on the water projects he targeted for elimination were even more disappointed when the president, after torturous interagency and legal battles, finally allowed the completion of the Tellico Dam in eastern Tennessee despite findings that it would ruin the riverine habitat and cause the extinction of a small fish almost nobody had ever heard of (the snail darter) and perhaps fatally weaken the new Endangered Species Act.

In 1979 Carter sent Congress another environmental message making a strong defense of the administration's record, including the 1977 amendments to the Clean Air and Water Pollution Acts some environmentalists thought unnecessarily industry-friendly. He struck the same tone of conciliation in his administration's environmental record in his 1980 State of the Union Address. The president was charged with being insufficiently courageous on environmental matters in the Democratic presidential primaries that year, where he faced challenges from Senator Kennedy and former California governor Jerry Brown. In the fall election third-party candidates John Anderson and Barry Commoner tried to make Carter's environmental-protection performance an issue but found little public support.

As the president took the field against Reagan, twenty-two different environmental groups with 10 million members, most of them with nonpartisan traditions, endorsed Carter in September. One environmentalist called him the "most environmentally minded President in history."[77] There is something to be said for that view if one excludes the two Roosevelts. Carter's environmentalism was a deep commitment rooted in his attachment to the outdoors, and athough his administrative and public education efforts were earnest and frequent, his legislative achievements were limited by an unfavorable economic setting and well-funded and organized business lobbies.

Yet Carter closed strongly. In a short period at the very end of his presidency, he signed two important laws environmentalists had almost despaired of ever enacting. The RCRA of 1976 had required industry to store, treat, and dispose of hazardous industrial wastes and keep "cradle-to-grave records" of such materials. It was a fundamental building block in the nation's slowly emerging regulation of industrial pollution. However, improved current disposal habits did not address past dumping, which had poisoned the nation's waterways and air and littered the landscape with often leaking hazardous waste ponds and burial sites. Private owners of waste sites open to all dumpers willing to pay a fee rarely kept records of those who used the facilities, universally of shoddy construction, allowing wastes to leak during heavy rains and leach into nearby water supplies. Public alarm at these time bombs was fanned by news of large hazardous waste and leaking dump sites, such as the "valley of the drums" on the Kentucky side of the Ohio River, where a wartime synthetic rubber industry had been hastily constructed with the river as a dump; the Stringfellow Pits in Southern California; and the town of Love Canal near Niagara Falls, New York, which became the largest such story in the late 1970s. In the early 1940s Love Canal permitted tract homes and a school to be built over a trench used to bury rusting barrels of toxic wastes generated by the Hooker Chemical Company. In subsequent years residents complained of foul smells from the trench after heavy rains, and in the 1970s these wastes began to ooze upward to the lawns and streets of part of this suburban town, with reports of serious illness among the horrified residents. These and other media-covered discoveries of the nation's unknown toxic legacy buried out of sight spurred the formation of grassroots environmental advocacy groups whose members added economic, gender, and racial diversity to the national environmental movement.

Congress began to recognize that RCRA did not deal with the effects of past dumping, and pressure built behind a proposal to enact the Comprehensive Environmental Response, Compensation, and Liability Act (CERCLA to insiders, Superfund to others). After his November defeat Carter might have been expected to lose interest in legislative struggles, but his lobbying for Superfund (and concessions to the petroleum lobby, agreeing to exempt oil spills) made the difference in the law's passage in December. CERCLA represented a major commitment to toxic-waste cleanup, empowering the EPA to locate and clean up abandoned hazardous-waste dumps and charge the clearly responsible companies for the costs. When several dumpers were involved and responsibility was hard to pinpoint, the cleanup was to be paid for out of an "orphan fund" financed by corporate excise taxes. Superfund engaged the EPA in a highly technical, complex, and litigious regulatory commitment that over the years came to have a durable level of public support despite critics of the costs.

Another of Carter's finish-line environmental achievements came in early December 1980 when he signed the Alaska Lands Act, providing varying degrees of protection to 104 million acres of federal land coveted by developers. The law was drifting toward defeat when Carter threatened to issue a bold executive order designating most of the targeted land as national monuments. It was a TR moment. Carter issued the order on December 1 and was burned in effigy in Fairbanks by people who regarded their public lands as owned by Alaskans, not the United States. Congress concluded that on a matter of this size a legislative act was better than a presidential order, and Carter signed the Alaska Lands Act on December 2. Representative Udall recalled the occasion in memorable terms: "Jimmy Carter signed this 419-page piece of paper, and with one stroke of the pen . . . he had doubled the National Park System, tripled the Wilderness Preservation System, and more than doubled the refuge acreage."[78]

In his last days in office. Carter received and commended to the public a report he had commissioned from the CEQ, *The Global 2000 Report to the President*. The group had been asked to "study the probable changes in the world's population, natural resources, and environment through the end of the century." It was the first effort to look ahead on such a scale and famously concluded in a forty-two-page summary of a three-volume report, "If present trends continue, the world in 2000 will be more crowded, more polluted, less stable ecologically, and more vulnerable to disruption than the world we live in now. . . . Time for action is running out." The report forecast growth of world population from 4.5 billion to 6.35 billion by 2000 and 10 billion by 2030. No projections of US population were offered, and the 1972 Rockefeller report was never mentioned. The group confirmed the beginning of a new era of intensifying worldwide problems and disruptions. One of these problems would be both planetwide and almost unknown to the public. The burning of fossil fuels, especially coal, "may contribute to . . . increased concentration of CO_2 in the earth's atmosphere, possibly leading to climate changes" with "highly disruptive effects." Climate change was a new hazard discovered on the presidential watch of Carter.

A small group of members of Congress, impressed by this report, prepared legislation establishing population policy and improved ecological "early warning" planning, to await the president who would take the oath in January, but that would not be Carter, so there was no institutional followup.

HOW GOES THE PROJECT? END OF THE 1970S

The decade of the 1970s surpassed even the 1960s as a watershed of progress for the national environmental-protection enterprise. Presidential leadership is not the place to find a sufficient explanation. Presidential sponsorship as an element in the expansion of the environmentalist project shrank somewhat from the unsustainable level achieved in the 1960s by the grand legislator, LBJ. Nixon was for two years a fellow traveler—or, more accurately, a competitor for the green voter—but after 1971 he was ideologically hostile to the environmental movement and its aspirations. Ford had the same ideological objections to environmental protection and, with rare exceptions, blocked or resisted environmental initiatives. Carter was an informed and committed environmentalist politician but could not bring to the environmental cause a popular base and was in political difficulty from his first months in office forward.

Given unsympathetic or weakened presidents, the environmentalist project might have been expected to weaken and even lose ground by the end of the 1970s. That was the gist of a prediction by a highly respected political scientist writing just two years after Earth Day was born. Anthony Downs, in the influential article "Up and Down with Ecology: The Issue-Attention Cycle," argued that "American public attention rarely remains sharply focused upon any one domestic issue for very long," but the issue "leaps into prominence, remains there for a short time, and then . . . gradually fades from the center of public attention."[79] Environmentalism seemed to him in 1972 just such an ephemeral issue. He was quite wrong. The environmental-protection movement became more robust and produced more results as the 1970s went on.

Why would people increase their attention to environmental protection and appreciation rather than, as Downs and others predicted, lose interest in what critics saw as a rich people's fad, ill-suited as the basis for a mass movement? The forces drawing new converts into the movement and holding the loyalty of others were the same basic social forces Samuel Hays had identified as expanding the elite ranks of conservationism into the broader-based environmentalism—rising education levels, affluence, and appreciation of the values of a clean natural environment for recreational and aesthetic outdoor experience. Environmentalism's educational machinery added converts—brilliant books by Leopold and Carson, outdoor nature excursions arranged by the National Audubon Society's millions of birders, and that reliable and periodic teacher and recruiter, environmental crisis—days of smothering smog in Donora, Pennsylvania, Los Angeles, and Denver; the oily wastes in the Cuyahoga River in Cleveland catching fire; the black globs of oil suffocating the seabirds on Santa Barbara beaches.

These and other forces drove expansion of membership in national environmental organizations throughout the 1960s and 1970s along with proliferation of local groups upset by toxic-waste dumping into their air or water. Claiming one-half million members in the mid-1960s, environmental organizations surged to more than 3 million ten years later and sustained the growth into the 1990s. The Sierra Club grew from 31,000 in 1965 to 124,000 by the mid-1970s; the National Wildlife Federation from 256,000 to 540,000; the National Audubon Society from 40,000 to 115,000. The national environmental organizations all had Washington, D.C., offices and rallied their members with national magazines and an effective combination of direct-mail fund-raising and lobbying. The movement's social base had broadened from the white, male elites of TR's day to include the millions of students who responded to the call for Earth Day in 1970 and after. Grassroots activism was spurred across the country by toxic-waste discoveries such as the one in Love Canal, New York, in 1978. "The environmental cause," White wrote in his account of the 1972 election, "has swollen into the favorite sacred issue of all politicians, all TV networks, and all good-willed people of any party."[80]

Thus when Carter's time came, the movement had attained impressive size, organization, and public acceptance. It was not solely dependent upon a president's commitment but could also find allies and leadership among congressional entrepreneurs who had learned the publicity and vote-gaining power of environmental protection and pollution controls. The movement was also beginning to aggressively make use of the judicial branch through environmental lawsuits. Environmentalists were also engaging state and local governments, where environmental battles had become the daily fare of local politics.

The movement's political and intellectual growth beginning at the end of the 1960s is the starting point for understanding why Downs (and others) misread the prospects of environmentalism for the decade after Earth Day 1970. In 1983, a poll of historians ranking presidents on overall performance placed Carter twenty-fifth, down in the company of presidents such as William Henry Harrison, John Tyler, Zachary Taylor, Millard Fillmore, James Buchanan, Andrew Johnson, and Coolidge.[81] These ranking historians deserve a dismal assessment for apparently ignoring Carter's environmental record, which, if alone considered, would have placed him closer to the company of two Roosevelts and a Texan. Considered along with all else, he moves far above the dismal mid-nineteenth-century men who watched the war come.

The political and intellectual potency and legitimacy achieved by the environmental movement by the end of the 1970s seemed to be accepted with varying degrees of enthusiasm (or reluctance) by all of the national politicians in both parties who in 1980 mounted organized campaigns to run for president against or instead of Carter. The environmental-protection impulse was by the 1970s a very large and well-organized constituency that politicians with national ambitions were careful not to offend, but as the presidential primaries acquainted the public with the candidates, was there sixty-nine-year-old California governor, running for the GOP presidential nomination for the third time, was not just indifferent to conservation but hostile.

To start with, Reagan was the acknowledged standard-bearer of the antigovernment or "conservative" crusade launched by Senator Goldwater in his 1964 run against LBJ. In the Republican primaries of 1980, Reagan liked to arouse audiences with this one-liner: "The nine most terrifying words in the English language are: 'I'm from the government, and I'm here to help.'" He made no exceptions for the park rangers, foresters, or pollution fighters from the EPA. Presumably, their help was dangerous also. In 1980 environmentalists reminded each other that Reagan, following a 1966 speech to the Western Wood Products Association, was asked what he thought about the most recent efforts to "save the redwoods." He responded, "There is a common-sense limit. I mean, if you've looked at a hundred thousand acres or so of trees—you know, a tree is a tree, how many more do you need to look at?" The media recognized this as a major gaffe, and soon the quotation was repeated in conversations from California to the East Coast. It was usually shortened to: Reagan is the guy who once said, "If you've seen one redwood, you've seen them all."[82] Three years after that long-lived comment he made another much-quoted remark, saying within reporters' hearing that the Santa Barbara oil spill was "no big deal." A case could be made that the media exaggerated the spill's biological impacts, but Reagan had made no such nuanced comment. His bad habit of self-inflicted one-liner wounds was repeated in October 1980, in the heat of the campaign, when Reagan was quoted as saying, "Trees cause more pollution than automobiles."[83]

The author of those easily remembered lines dismissing environmental concerns won the Republican presidential nomination in 1980. The campaign almost ignored the environment, but Reagan went off script on the issue at least once, asserting that the EPA was too aggressive in pursuit of a clean environment. His handlers worked hard to keep candidate Reagan from saying anything at all about the environment and were generally successful. Reagan took the lead in polls after the 1980 GOP convention, but by October the race was quite close. Surveys revealed that a large part of the public had no enthusiasm for either man (or for Independent Party candidate John Anderson). The public "was tired of Carter and embarrassed by his failures," wrote the author of an early history of the 1980 campaign, but "it feared Reagan for his lack of experience and his quick-draw pronouncements on matters of great sensitivity."[84] Carter and Reagan debated once, and conservation was squeezed into one question on energy. Neither man had much to say, and the debate moved on to Social Security, plodding toward the dramatic moment at the end when Reagan asked the audience, "Are you better off than you were four years ago?" Neither at the debate in Cleveland nor in the candidates' major speeches did the environment emerge as an issue. Vice President Walter Mondale tried once or twice to make much of Reagan's dislike of the TVA but without success. The political process for picking a president in 1980 failed again to clarify for voters the environmental positions of the candidates, who seemed to have sharply different views. To avoid environmental topics was a deliberate decision by the poll-guided campaign managers on both sides. The US public, polls were said to have revealed, did not rank environmental protection anywhere near the top of its concerns. The campaign managers for both candidates accordingly kept environmental issues off the television screens.

Carter was burdened in his campaign for reelection by a poorly performing economy, the absence of an enthusiastic base, and, fatally, by the long, vividly televised ordeal of the hostages in Iran, punctuated by a failed effort at a military rescue in April 1980. Reagan swept into office with 489 electoral votes and a 51 percent majority (Carter took 41 percent, with 7 percent for Anderson). Carter returned to Plains in January and, with Rosalynn's active partnership as always, began a multifaceted postpresidential life of public service, operating out of the Atlanta-based Carter Center (and library) when he was not overseas. His efforts in promoting human rights and economic development, and especially his diplomatic interventions to resolve international conflicts, led to a Nobel Peace Prize in 2002. He and Rosalynn rarely passed up a chance to go flyfishing or canoeing, and, drawing upon his continued outdoors activities, Carter published more than a dozen articles in sports magazines. By 2010 he was the author of twenty-two books, at least four of them memoirs focused upon his life in rural Georgia.

In early 1981 James Hansen, director of the National Aeronautical and Space Administration (NASA) Goddard Institute for Space Studies, published in Science a paper arguing that greenhouse gases were rapidly building up in the atmosphere and predicting that the coming decade would be unusually warm and the 1990s warmer still. The New York Times story ("Study Finds Warming Trend That Could Raise Sea Levels") on this scientific article was the paper's first front-page coverage on climate change, and Hansen quickly became a frequent expert asked to testify before Congress and address numerous audiences. Carbon dioxide, he pointed out, is being pumped into the atmosphere ten times faster than natural process can remove it. He told a Senate committee in 1988 he was "99 percent certain" that the unusually hot summer of that year meant climate warming was under way. "The scientific evidence is compelling," said Senator Tim Wirth, a Democrat from Colorado, and it was now time for Congress to act.[85]

8

Our natural resource heritage is generally being preserved adequately and managed well.
— Ronald Reagan, 1987

Nelle Wilson Reagan gave birth to Ronald Reagan on February 6, 1911, in an apartment over a bakery in Tampico, Illinois. His father, John E. "Jack" Reagan, an alcoholic and intermittently employed shoe salesman, moved the family through a series of midwestern towns before settling in the small community of Dixon, Illinois.

In his autobiography *Ronald Reagan: An American Life* (1990), he remembered Dixon as an idyllic place to be raised, small town at its best, even in the Great Depression. The town was situated on both sides of the Rock River, which he remembered as "my playground," a place for swimming and fishing and hikes. He also depicts himself as an avid reader of nearly anything, but especially, for a time, books (he does not name them) on the wildlife and birds of Dixon. He claimed, unconvincingly, to have become, at least for a time, a sort of "naturalist." In fact his autobiography depicts the young "Dutch," as he preferred to be called, as a summertime recreational user, without curiosity, of the natural world around Dixon.

Reagan was happiest when engaging in human group activities, especially when he could be the center of attention. In high school and at nearby Eureka College, where he lettered in football and was a C student in his major, economics, he began to show a strong interest in acting. He worked for a time as a radio announcer and then took a train to Los Angeles in 1937, the fourth year of the Depression. In the first of a lifetime string of lucky breaks, Reagan found an agent who arranged an audition leading to a contract with Warner Brothers. He began to appear in Hollywood B movies at a furious rate, recalling that he once made thirteen B pictures in one and one-half years.

When World War II came he joined the US Army and, disqualified from combat duty because of astigmatism, was assigned to a motion-picture unit in Hollywood. After the war he worked as president of the Screen Actors Guild and found some minor TV and movie roles. When his movie career slackened, he began in 1954 to tour the country as a spokesperson on public affairs for General Electric, visiting 139 plants to deliver "the speech," a Reagan combination of patriotic boosterism and his newly acquired hostility to "big government."

Few in the 1950s noticed that this low-profile former actor had undergone a political transformation from his admiration of Franklin D. Roosevelt (FDR) in the 1930s (he voted for FDR four times) to a Goldwater conservative. He endorsed Dwight Eisenhower in 1952 and Richard Nixon in 1960, and in 1962 he changed party affiliation to the Grand Old Party (GOP). "I didn't leave the Democratic Party," he explained when asked about his trajectory. "The party left me," he continued, implying that FDR would have agreed with him had he lived into the 1960s.[1]

Reagan, broad-shouldered, affable, and gifted with a honeyed voice, in 1964 gave a nationally televised appeal for funds for the Goldwater campaign and with Goldwater's crushing defeat became the chief national spokesperson for the conservative movement. In one view, he had moved outside of the center of US politics and into futility. However, the center was moving rightward, and Reagan's actor background made him the master of television-oriented campaigning. He was elected governor of California in 1966 and then reelected.

Then in 1980 he was elected president by an impressive margin, receiving 50.7 percent of the votes to Jimmy Carter's 41 percent (John Anderson took 7 percent). Reagan had revived, and ridden into the White House on, the anti-liberal-government social movement launched by Barry Goldwater in 1964.

The environmentalist community expected only unspecified bad things from a Reagan presidency. "It will be a long winter" for us, Representative Morris Udall commented after the election. The Republican platform passages on "conservation" were brief and promised "revision" and "reform" to ensure "environmental protection must not become a cover for a no-growth policy and a shrinking economy." The Democrats affirmed their commitment to "stewardship of an irreplaceable environment." Reagan in his speech accepting the nomination criticized a "tiny minority opposed to economic growth and who were responsible for 'obstructionist campaigns' of regulation." Although "we will not permit our . . . environmental heritage to be jeopardized," he argued, economic prosperity comes first. Here he said in public what he often said privately—that environmentalists were a tiny minority.

Those who had paid close attention to Reagan's two terms as governor might have acknowledged that he made in Sacramento a surprising record as an environmental moderate. In his impressive book *Governor Reagan* (1980), reporter Lou Cannon explains Reagan's sometimes proenvironment performance in the capital as a sort of accident not likely to be repeated. His secretary of staff appointments in the early days was a conservative Republican who thought the new governor's cabinet-level appointments should go to people who knew their subject matter and recommended for secretary of natural resources a progressive lumberman and avid backpacker, Sierra Club member Norman "Ike" Livermore, whose hero was John Muir. Livermore hit it off with Reagan from the start. Because the California public was showing a rising enthusiasm for environmentalism, and Livermore and a handful of other conservationists were framing the issues, Reagan as governor took some notable positions on nature protection. He was guided by Livermore into supporting the establishment and expansion of Redwoods National Park, opposing a US Army Corps of Engineers plan for a massive Dos Rios Dam on the Eel River, signing a law expanding coastal zone protection, and signing the California Environmental Quality Act. He lined up with the forces working to create regional entities to protect San Francisco Bay and Lake Tahoe from pollution and led the opposition to a trans-Sierra highway. A skillful Livermore guided Reagan toward these positions with timely help from other trusted aides who happened to be TR conservationists—Chief of Staff Bill Clark and California Parks Director William Mott.

When Reagan left Sacramento, he also left behind the environmental moderate. He gave more than 1,000 addresses between 1976 and 1980, writing two-thirds of them himself. His core beliefs dominated these addresses—warning of the "communist conspiracy," calling for buildup of national defense, and indicting the growth of government taxation and reg-

ulation. Environmental matters made only a sprinkling of appearances under the category of excessive governmental regulation. He defended the City
of Los Angeles for dumping sewage into Santa Monica Bay, ridiculed the de-
lays in building a dam in Maine because of worries about the survival of the
furbish lousewort, and complained that a dead tree was "pure waste" lumberers could have eliminated but for governmental interference.[2] With Livermore and his handful of environmentalist allies left behind in the California
capital, Reagan was listening to other advisers who were invariably prodevelopment Republicans ignorant of environmental matters and contemptuous of environmentalists.

The most important adviser in the transition period after Reagan's election turned out to be Senator Paul Laxalt of Nevada, a close friend who asked
Reagan to let him name as secretary of the interior a westerner of Laxalt's
choosing and to let him play a set on the White House tennis court. Reagan
agreed to both the serious and the trivial requests, and Laxalt finally settled
on lawyer James Watt, head of the Colorado-based prodevelopment Mountain States Legal Foundation, funded by oil and extractive mineral companies and dedicated to the "wise use" rather than the preservation of public
resources. Watt knew the Interior Department from a tour there during the
Nixon and Gerald Ford administrations, and as a public speaker he had become a prominent figure in the "Sagebrush Rebellion," the name given to a
revival in the Nevada Legislature in 1978 of the "great land grab" in the West
that Bernard DeVoto had pilloried in national magazines in the 1950s. These
Nevadans' core demand was the same—either privatization of public lands
or ceding them to the states. This movement was reignited by Carter's termination of many water projects and more restrictive policies on hard-rock
mining and grazing permits. It took form in Nevada in 1979 when the legislature passed a bill claiming title to all public lands within the state. Watt's
Colorado stirred with similar sentiments, and he at once allied himself with
the bold demands of the region's ranchers, miners, and timber cutters.

Because President Reagan continued to be the hands-off leader he had
been as a governor, lieutenants mattered a great deal. In putting forward
Watt, Laxalt had brought on board at the cabinet level a man who would become, at least for two turbulent years, a major architect of Reagan's environmental policies. Moderate (and unpredictable) "conservationist" Governor
Reagan had in the late 1970s morphed into a presidential candidate given to
dismissive comments on environmentalism and, as president, now had a

key public land adviser who shared his boss's basic leanings as well as his misjudgment of the nation's long-running environmental awakening. Watt, like Reagan, mingled with the rebellious westerners and shared without reservations his views of who owned the public lands—local exploiters or a national constituency. "I renew my pledge to work toward a 'Sagebrush solution' of public lands issues in the West, either privatizing public lands or turning them over to the states," the new president telegraphed one of the movement's leaders.[3] Both Watt and Reagan were misjudging the political implications of a major demographic shift to the West after World War II, bringing to the region a more metropolitan population with appreciation for the national parks and forests and no real commitment to the counterclaims of the ranchers, miners, and timber users who attended such meetings.

Watt soon claimed center stage on public land issues and, inevitably, the new administration's larger environmental outlook. Yet his aggressive performance does not mean Reagan's natural-resource and environmental policies had been unpredictable until the Watt appointment provided firm direction. After Reagan left Sacramento, all of his close advisers, or "kitchen cabinet," were ignorant if not misinformed on environmental matters and reinforced his instinct to see the conservationist/environmentalist agenda as just another problem of swollen and intrusive government. The new president's base was the right wing of a party of which the western elements were believed to be sympathetic to a Sagebrush Rebellion that actually spoke for a shrinking set of interests.

Still, administrative appointments in the areas of natural resources and the environment were especially important in a Reagan government. As governor he had revealed a habit of giving lieutenants in environmental matters a loose rein because it was not one of his core concerns, and his knowledge was skimpy and unreliable. Although he had his own leanings in all areas involving governmental regulation, he had already, in Sacramento, proven remarkably pliable and unpredictable on environmental matters as well as remarkably unaware of historic conservationist battles.

A proud westerner and horseman who had owned four ranches before he bought his favorite and final one, the 688-acre Rancho del Cielo up the West Coast from Santa Barbara, Reagan actually claimed to see himself as an "environmentalist" because he enjoyed the Rock River in his youth and all of his ranches as a "haven and refuge." However, he had a deaf ear and blind eye—or no curiosity—for the living nonhuman creatures in those habitats. Rea-

gan's relationship to nature was an incoherent combination of romantic no-
tions, leaving much room for contradictory behavior and the influence of advisers who knew more or felt more strongly than he did. He was a man who,
in Lou Cannon's words, was "strangely insensitive to the magnificence of
the redwoods."[4]

More important than his aesthetic insensitivity was Reagan's stubborn
belief in the basic outlook Teddy Roosevelt (TR) and the first generation of
conservationists (and all subsequent ones) had rejected—that the United
States was a place of superabundant, even inexhaustible, land and resources.
Although Livermore and one or two other conservationist lieutenants briefly
steered Governor Reagan away from his basic indifference to nature protection, as he approached the presidency he found himself surrounded by anticonservationists. Reagan quickly veered to a different path closer to his
ideological outlook. Lieutenant Watt did not so much invent the administration's environmental-policy leanings—sure to lean toward weaker business
regulation and less nature preservation no matter who ran the Interior Department—as become their chief spokesperson and, ironically, their most
visible subverter.

Reagan and his allies brought to Washington, D.C., in January 1981 an
imposing, some would even say revolutionary, agenda. He intended to replace the prevailing liberal political philosophy in order to launch an era of
conservative political dominance and policy reform—to restructure the taxation, regulatory, and fiscal policies put in place by FDR and subsequent liberal regimes, to sharply prune if not dismantle the welfare state, to reverse
the trend toward larger federal percentage of the gross domestic product
(GDP), to rebuild US military power, and to win the cold war. Priorities
would be necessary, and Reagan had his "core concerns," in historian Hugh
Davis Graham's term—strengthened national defense, defeat of the global
communist conspiracy, reversal of the growth of government, lower taxes,
deregulation of business.[5] Environmental policy was not one of these core
concerns for Reagan—only one recognized as important to a small segment
of the public he seemed to think could be dissuaded by ridicule. If the Environmental Protection Agency (EPA) had its way, he once said, "You and I
would have to live in rabbit holes."[6] The environment made almost no appearance in the 1980 campaign, though Reagan had occasionally gone off
script to make well-reported "one-liner" remarks. Air pollution in the
United States was "substantially controlled," he once asserted. As for the

"over-population problem," the Reagan campaign tossed off the judgment that the "earth could support 28 billion people."[7]

President-elect Reagan appointed a task force on the environment that included Russell Train and William Ruckelshaus, EPA administrators under Nixon and Ford, along with respected environmental scientists, but only three copies of their cautiously reformist report were ever made, and Reagan and his transition team ignored it—which meant ignoring the advice of the Republican Party's most knowledgeable conservationists. In December, the conservative think tank Heritage Foundation presented the incoming administration a bulky, 1,093-page report, *Mandate for Leadership*, containing two dense chapters of needed reforms in the Department of the Interior and the EPA.[8] *Mandate for Leadership* was too thick to be of much use to top policy makers, but it expressed an idea of rising appeal to governmental professionals—the "administrative presidency." This referred to a growing trend in the White House, under both Republicans and Democrats, of seeking policy change primarily through key appointments, executive orders, budgeting, executive branch reorganization, and signing statements—rather than pressing Congress for legislative changes that faced a clogged path to substantial reform. Reagan in his first week in the White House took two early, easy steps, displaying the role of symbolic presidential gestures in the sweeping policy changes he had in mind, when he cut the staff of the Council on Environmental Quality (CEQ) by half and ordered the removal of the solar panels Jimmy Carter had placed on the White House roof.

The emphasis on administrative rather than legislative strategies in the effort to dismantle or shrink the existing environmental regulations and protections gave unusual importance in early 1981 to Reagan's (or Laxalt's) choice of interior secretary. Watt could be expected to staff the department with "Reagan revolutionaries" drawn from the western Sagebrush Rebellion and eastern free-market think tanks. Beyond that, Reagan gave Watt virtually no direction. Their first meeting lasted only twenty minutes. The new president-elect offered Watt the job and then the two agreed on five vague objectives for the Interior Department, the tall, angular, articulate forty-three-year-old Coloradoan apparently taking the lead. There was "instant rapport," a Watt-friendly author wrote.[9]

Watt must have seemed an ideal choice to head the Interior Department, which Reagan and his top aides knew nothing about. Raised in Wyoming, Watt was valedictorian of his high-school class, a straight-arrow, nondrinking, good student who earned a law degree after college and worked in Washington, D.C., as a staffer for his Republican senator. He then spent several years in the Nixon-Ford Interior Department before becoming the first director of the Denver-based Mountain States Legal Foundation, which turned corporation donations, most prominently from the wealthy conservative brewer Joseph Coors, into legal assaults on "bureaucrats and no-growth advocates who create a challenge to individual liberty and economic freedoms."

Watt saw his leadership of the Department of the Interior as a chance to do what he regarded as God's work, reversing to the degree possible the policy errors institutionalized, as he saw it, since TR had so dramatically expanded its assignment to manage most of the public lands. "We are on a crusade," he said after he was chosen. "I kind of feel that mission."[10] The Interior Department had custody of all but the national forest part of the nearly 700-million-acre public domain—the 455 million mostly high, arid acres of the Bureau of Land Management (BLM), with its ranching-mining clientele; the 48 national parks; and the 286 national monuments, historic sites, and national seashores. Most important to Watt were the BLM parts of the public domain rich in coal, natural gas, petroleum, and nonfuel minerals. "Wise use," a phrase churned up by some of the more PR-savvy in the Sagebrush movement, meant immediate and unrestrained use, ignoring the toxic residues of extraction and other environmental costs.

No knowledgeable person would have argued that there was zero room for reform within the Interior Department or in its statutory underpinning. Indeed, environmentalists had long been the most vocal critics of the long-standing "clientele capture" of the department by western ranching, mining, and drilling interests since before Albert Fall embarrassed President Warren Harding by earning a jail term. There was no decade in the twentieth century when conservationists had not complained that fees for grazing on public lands were too low, protection of the public lands in the high grasslands from overgrazing woefully inadequate, the terms of energy leasing too favorable to oil drillers and miners. Friends of the national parks worried about overuse and underprotection. Even the addition or expansion of national parks conservationists were always inclined to favor was known to have an objectionable side. The process for establishing new parks could sometimes take on a pork-barrel cast when influential members of Congress exerted pressure, and the system needed corrective scrutiny. The federal gov-

ernment sometimes acquired parcels with little historic or ecological signif-
icance often surrounded by private properties and difficult to manage as
public lands, and a case could be made even among conservationists for
some limited privatization.

These "improve the system" reforms in public land management were of
minor interest to Watt. His objectives, he told an early meeting of top Interior Department staff, were much larger: to "mine more, drill more, cut
more timber, to use our resources rather than simply keep them locked
up."[11] He was not hesitant in quoting President Reagan as the leading partner in pursuing these reforms. Shortly after his confirmation, Watt began to
fire all but a handful of the department's top officers and replace them with
people who shared his sense of mission. Soon he announced the first of his
new directions. He proposed a moratorium on acquiring new land for national parks, opening more public land to mining and logging, and increasing offshore leasing for mineral extraction. By the spring of 1982 he was able
to announce the largest coal-lease sale in history, in the Powder River Basin
of Wyoming and Montana, as well as proposing the same for many wilderness areas, and he had vastly expanded the oil and gas leasing on the outer
continental shelf. He created the interagency Property Review Board, which
began planning to offer as many as 35 million acres of wilderness areas for
sale to private individuals, a shift from the Sagebrush Rebellion idea of giving the lands to western states. He also suggested that states be given responsibility for strip-mining regulation and called for "zero-budgeting" the
entire historic preservation program. Watt's door was closed to environmentalist leaders after six weeks in office.

Each proposed or actual Watt reform seemed to signal a broad-front retreat from public-land–protection policies commenced under Benjamin
Harrison and accelerated thereafter. His language declared war. "I never use
the words Republican and Democrat. . . . It's liberals and Americans."
"What is the real motive of the extreme environmentalists? . . . Is it to simply
protect the environment? Is it to delay and deny energy development? Is it to
weaken America?"[12]

The secretary met immediate resistance, first from the "environmental
community," normally not a very cohesive collection of organizations sitting
atop a scattered but growing national membership. Environmentalists were
galvanized into action by Watt's plans and rhetoric, and by July 1980 the National Wildlife Federation with its 4.5 million members, along with the

Sierra Club and the Wilderness Society—seventeen organizations in all—had mounted a well-organized counteroffensive. A barrage of books and pamphlets came off the presses of environmental organizations in 1982 and 1983, and membership in these groups surged between 1980 and 1983—the Wilderness Society grew 144 percent, the Defenders of Wildlife almost 50 percent, and the Sierra Club 90 percent, bringing new funds for staff and program expansion.[13] Ten of the largest groups ranging from the National Wildlife Federation to the National Audubon Society published *An Environmental Agenda for the Future* (1985) in an effort to move beyond indictment to agenda setting.[14]

Watt must have anticipated some organized opposition, perhaps relishing it as a sign that he was striking at the heart of the environmentalist empire. He could not have anticipated that environmental organizations would capture a rising level of media attention and turn his actions into a source of their own organizational strength and energy. All the national organizations and many smaller ones launched membership drives and mobilization campaigns keyed to the threat posed by Watt with huge success. The Sierra Club, for example, warned its members, "Unless you and I act immediately, we shall surely see the destruction . . . of our national parks, the invasion of our irreplaceable wilderness lands, and the demise of habitat for our nation's wildlife." Sierra Club members sent 1 million "Replace Watt" petitions to congressional offices and the White House.

The media gave ample coverage to these normally obscure natural-resource and public land disputes the interior secretary had generated, and increasingly the story was framed as a controversy over Watt, who liked to give speeches and frequently lashed back at environmentalists, calling them "zealots" and a "small group of extremists."[15] He seemed to welcome environmentalists as enemies, thinking them a small minority, but he could not have welcomed comments by congressional leaders expressing considerable resistance to his "mine more, drill more, cut more timber" policy proposals. His proposed expansion of outer-continental-shelf oil-lease sales off the West Coast brought stiff opposition from a bipartisan group of California representatives to Congress, and the State of California joined several environmental groups in a lawsuit to block the policy. Influential Wyoming senators Alan Simpson and Malcolm Wallop sponsored legislation to ban oil drilling in their state's wilderness areas, a break with Watt by key Republicans.

The troubled, short career of Watt can be quickly summarized. In 1981 the White House had more important issues than public lands—including an assassination attempt in March that left the president hospitalized for several weeks. In Reagan's Inaugural Address the president placed environmental protection in a stark, new perspective when he pronounced, "In the present crisis, government is not the solution to our problem. . . . Government is the problem."[16] The government's focus must now be unwaveringly on an "economic affliction of great proportions." By summer, the media attention to Watt's reforms began to surface in press conferences. "Are you ever going to let Jim Watt up here?" a reporter asked. "Jim Watt has been doing what I think is a common-sense job," Reagan responded, "in the face of some environmental extremism that we've suffered from. . . . People are ecology, too. We have some needs, and there has to be provision for us to live."[17] This was not Reagan at his verbal best, but he would get more practice in responding to questions about one of his cabinet members. On January 20, 1982, a reporter from the Los Angeles Times asked the president, "You appointed a guy Interior Secretary who is perceived to be the extremist on the development side. Do you have second thoughts?" "No, not at all. . . . Let me remind you of something. I fancy myself an environmentalist," at which point he bragged about his record in California. "What happened in our own state was . . . that the environmental movement—there hadn't been such a thing before our administration. It started during my terms as governor . . . but it got out of control. And we had environmental extremism that was going beyond all bounds of reason."[18] "Environmentalists, for example," he responded to a question from a St. Louis radio interviewer, "I'd never heard the word, but . . . before I left as governor, the environmental movement was under way nationwide."[19] Was this a claim to have been one of its leaders? As for Watt, "I think he's an environmentalist himself, as I am."[20]

These are astonishing exchanges, revealing a president whose verbal skills could not always compensate for his substantial ignorance and misconceptions when environmental issues were raised. In his major state papers he continued to have almost nothing to say on environmental matters. His State of the Union Address in January 1982, on domestic issues, was focused on economic recovery, "returning power to the people," and other such Reaganite staples, with only one brief reference to the need for "Clean Air legislation . . . to increase jobs."[21]

With the congressional elections of 1982 not far off, White House senior staff began to worry that Watt's notoriety might hurt the ticket. Polls found a negative image attached to Watt among all voters, though he continued to draw enthusiastic audiences from the new-right movement, and White House advisers were divided about his effect on the 1982 and eventually the 1984 elections. Watt struggled through 1982 and into 1983 to win over the public and expand his constituency. "In a conflict between the preservationists and the sportsmen, we're going to the sportsmen," he told readers of *Field and Stream*. He had not hunted in more than twenty years.[22]

His role in the Reagan presidency ended, fittingly, when he made news again because of a flippant remark to a chamber of commerce audience in September 1983. Asked about affirmative action, he said he had an advisory committee on that subject. "I have three Democrats and two Republicans. I have a black, I have a woman, two Jews, and a cripple."[23] The audience chuckled at the remark, but the media gave it much negative publicity, including the disapproval of Reagan's daughter Maureen, and the president was forced to downplay it. Several influential Republican senators either withheld support for Watt in this latest episode or were critical of him. Watt resigned on October 9, 1983. Reagan appointed his friend William Clark to head the Interior Department, and the war over the public lands receded from the Reagan agenda.

Another lieutenant from the West—like Watt, personally unknown to the president-elect and added to his top administrative ranks by others—further compounded Reagan's self-inflicted problems with environmental matters. The transition team ran into unexpected difficulties finding a "qualified" Republican to head the EPA, and again Reagan wound up appointing a Colorado warrior hardened by engagement in that state's political battles over natural-resource and federalism issues. Anne Gorsuch earned a law degree from the University of Colorado when she was 22 and was elected to the Colorado General Assembly in 1976, where she became a key member of a coalition of conservative lawmakers called the "House Crazies." Both enemies and friends conceded Gorsuch was smart, articulate, and formidable, indeed unyielding in argument. These assets came with one shortcoming that somehow did not block her ambitions to head the EPA. Her only real work experience, after one year in the Peace Corps, was as a legislator who had never run any organization. In 1980 she joined the Reagan transition team in Washington, D.C., and emerged as the most verbally impressive of the candidates contending for the challenge of leading the EPA. Her nomination and confirmation took four months. It was late spring when she took charge of a major battlefront in the "Reagan revolution."

The EPA in 1981 was just ten years old, a large and growing bureaucracy of 11,500 employees with a budget of $1.35 billion charged with oversight of nine major pollution-control statutes including the Clean Air and Clean Water Acts. It was expected to control and reduce air pollution from 150 million motor vehicles and many factories and power plants. Within its purview also was the nation's annual production of 500 billion pounds of hazardous wastes and a billion and a half pounds of pesticides.

This brief and partial summary understates the assignment ambitiously framed by Congress for the EPA, which by 1981 was much in need of some basic reforms. Burdened with a vast assignment in establishing national air- and water-quality standards and regulating hazardous wastes, pesticides, and other toxic substances, including noise, the EPA was swamped. It was not meeting its own deadlines, early permits had expired without renewal, and compliance was spotty (predictably) given the vast size of the US economy and the breadth of its mandates. Friendly critics who wished the EPA well were urging Congress to permit the agency to drop the policy of "uniform rollback," requiring all plants and industries to reduce emissions by the same amounts in the same ways, when regulatory flexibility promised greater efficiencies. The phrase used for the EPA's guiding idea after one decade was "command and control" across the board, a strategy that maximized conflicts with industry and, in the view of friendly critics, failed to explore incentive-based approaches. In short, the new Republican administration had good cause to explore reforms of the EPA's approach to pollution control, and indeed the Carter administration had shown some receptivity to modest lessening of command-and-control regulation and more incentive-based strategies.

The Reagan administration was not without intellectual guidance in accelerating this tactical policy shift. A blueprint for reforms in pollution-control policy was delivered to a not very interested presidential transition team by the Task Force on the Environment in late December 1980. White House political operatives were not at all interested in environmental policy except to have less of it. Reagan, who would prove a "hands-off" president, was especially hands-off in 1981 because he was seriously wounded in an assassination attempt in March and required time to recover. Gorsuch was thus unusually free to choose how to "reform" the central pollution-control agency of the US government, though she soon learned that others in the White House—the Office of Management and Budget (OMB) and the White House–based Task Force for Regulatory Relief, chaired by Vice President George H. W. Bush—would pressure her to move rapidly ahead in the basic assignment of making the EPA smaller and more "industry-friendly."

For her part, Gorsuch was unwaveringly determined to "reform" the EPA, but the tedious work of shifting away from "command-and-control" directives and habits and replacing them with greater use of market signals while still achieving pollution prevention and cleanup was beyond her education, patience, and sense of mission. Just after her confirmation she told top EPA staff that she intended to shift the decision-making process from Washington, D.C., to the state capitals, to save taxpayers' money by streamlining (shrinking) the agency, to cut paperwork, and to "keep a lid on those unnecessary regulations which have created hardships on our national industries, driving up the cost of consumer goods."[24] Not a word about finding better ways to carry out the original EPA mission, reduction of pollution of the environment.

Gorsuch looked forward to budget cuts that not only achieved the larger Reagan goal of shrinking government but that she would use as a rationale for firing senior career employees who had the Carter rather than the Reagan outlook on environmental protection. She expressed no concern at the deep cuts in scientific research, the foundation for setting standards on permissible exposure to toxic chemicals. However, even Gorsuch was shocked when the OMB under David Stockman demanded the doubling of her proposed 28 percent in cuts for fiscal year 1982. A cheerful President Reagan backed Stockman and forced Gorsuch to accept an EPA budget closer to the OMB's draconian numbers than her own.

She soon began a set of industry-friendly, or as some said, pollution-increasing decisions. Superfund strategy underwent a transformation under Gorsuch and Assistant Administrator Rita Lavelle, former public relations flak for two California chemical companies who had secured the post of EPA assistant administrator for solid waste through White House intervention. Lavelle substituted self-certification of hazardous chemicals by the manufacturing companies for EPA rule making, loosened rules governing permits for hazardous waste facilities, and proposed to delay indefinitely the regulation of toxic pollutants released into public water-treatment plants. Negotiated settlements of Superfund cases were touted as supplying needed income to the US Treasury by Gorsuch and Lavelle but were denounced as "sweetheart deals" with polluting companies by critics in Congress. Gorsuch in 1982 exposed her basic outlook when she declared there would be no need to continue the Superfund program of toxic-waste-dump cleanups beyond 1985.[25]

She was pushed hard in these directions by the OMB and the Task Force for Regulatory Relief. Predictably, her zeal for relaxing regulations on industry led to occasions of undue corporate influence. A key aide to Gorsuch, serving as a consultant to the EPA pending his own confirmation, received payments from a solid-waste-disposal firm in Colorado for arranging for Gorsuch to lift a ban on dumping barrels of liquid wastes, Love Canal style, into landfills. Blatant favoritism to polluting industries came to the attention of congressional committees, and by the end of 1982 six separate committees were investigating the Gorsuch EPA's management of the new Superfund program.

Inside the EPA, employees (not including political appointees) grumbled not only of her basic hostility to the agency's mission but also about her remoteness in her twelfth-floor command post. Gorsuch did not consult widely, was aloof even in social gatherings, and reportedly offended some in the agency by certain lifestyle habits offensive to Washington elites in general and environmentalists especially—her fondness for wearing fur coats and polluting meetings and the air in her office by smoking two packs of Marlboros a day. As expected, she quickly replaced many senior staff political appointees with people with close ties to polluting industries or the Republican Party. Senior career staff began in 1982 to retire or leave the agency in rising numbers, anticipating layoffs or slow advancement. Those who remained leaked reams of material to Congress, environmental organizations, and the media.

Gorsuch, like Watt, soon became a story of something larger within the Reagan administration—a major effort to undermine and if possible eliminate the environmental regulations constructed over the previous two decades. Agency morale and effectiveness were said—in Washington circles, and then in the media—to be eroding, and "managerial problems at the EPA" became a repeated story. A rising number of EPA regulatory actions were behind schedule or canceled in 1982, a year in which the agency managed to clean up only two Superfund sites. At the end of 1982, six congressional panels were looking into allegations of "sweetheart deals" between polluting industries and EPA employees.[26] Alarmed at the news from inside the EPA, Train wrote in the *Washington Post* in February 1982 of his "profound concern of what is happening at EPA today. The budget and personnel cuts, unless reversed, will destroy the agency as an effective institution for many years to come."[27]

A House committee at the end of 1982 charged that the EPA had mishandled the $1.6 billion toxic-waste Superfund and subpoenaed 700,000 EPA documents. Gorsuch obeyed orders from the White House to refuse the subpoena on grounds of executive privilege and was cited for contempt of Congress as the Justice Department essentially abandoned her defense. Embattled on all fronts and recognized by the White House as a political liability, she resigned in March 1983 (she had divorced David Gorsuch and married Robert Burford in February 1982, so the media reported Anne Burford as resigning from the EPA). Twenty of the EPA's top administrators also left the agency under pressure from Congress. Lavelle was forced out of office and spent several months in jail.[28] Asked by a reporter in a question-and-answer session on March 11, 1983, if he still held that Burford had "done nothing wrong . . . [and] can leave EPA with her head held high," President Reagan at first dodged the question, then stated, "I did regret very much" her resignation. "She was doing a job. And we, this administration, can be very proud of our record in environmental protection." The reporter persisted: "The Republican polls now show that your policies are perceived by the public . . . as being more favorable to the polluters than to the public. Are you going to change any of your environmental policies now that Mrs. Burford has gone?" Reagan responded, "In (my) eight years as governor, California . . . led the Federal Government in environmental protection." The questioner noted that Reagan had "been quoted in the past as talking about environmental extremism." Reagan's response brought a group laugh and ended the exchange: "Well, there is environmental extremism. I don't think they'll be happy until the White House looks like a bird's nest."[29]

The administration retreated on environmental policy reform after Watt and Burford were forced to resign from their offices. Within a week of the press conference announcing Burford's departure, Reagan appointed Ruckelshaus again administrator of the EPA, praising his record of environmental protection. On June 11 the president gave a short radio address from Camp David on "Environmental and Natural Resources Management." "I believe in a strong environmental policy that protects the health of our people and a wise stewardship of our nation's natural resources. But that's enough about me." He then cited Watt's improvement of national park visitor facilities, gave figures on his administration's expansion of wilderness areas, and claimed, "Our country . . . is growing more healthy and more beautiful each year," of which "we can all be proud."[30] Later that month came his brief message to Congress transmitting the CEQ annual report, expressing again a feeling of pride in his administration's record on the preservation of scenic beauty, expansion of wilderness areas, control of pollution, and all those fine things in which he had always believed (because he said so).

The Reagan revolution, an effort to radically shrink the federal government except on the national-security side, pursued its reform goals through two terms with mixed results viewed either as a radical, government-reducing change in the US political and policy landscape or bold reformist rhetoric followed by many fumbled opportunities. The revolution went forward after 1983, however, essentially without an environmental-policy component. Reform through the appointment of top administrators devoted to the Reaganite dismantling of environmental regulation had led quickly to unanticipated political troubles, and the White House chose in 1983 not to devote major energies to the pursuit of a different, legislative route to the same ends. An official at the US Chamber of Commerce that year reminded Reagan's aides of considerable business enthusiasm for a substantial legislative weakening of the Clean Air Act and Superfund but was told legislative change must wait until "after we finish the tax and budget issues." That time never came. Reagan's environmental-policy reforms took an administrative form from the first—key appointments to run natural-resource agencies at which budgets were severely reduced and maneuvers such as Executive Order 12291 requiring agencies to perform "regulatory impact analyses" of their activities for scrutiny by the OMB, which often rejected them as more cost than benefit. The White House never got around to a serious effort to push through Congress (where Republicans controlled only the Senate) revisions of the basic Clean Air, Clean Water, and Superfund laws.

Two prominent experts on environmental policy in the Reagan years, Michael Kraft and Norman Vig, argued at the end of 1984 that by using administrative rather than legislative change, "the President has gotten most of what he wanted" in environmental-policy reform. As evidence, they noted that EPA staff numbers were cut by almost 3,000 in Reagan's first term; Burford presided over a reduction by half in EPA research funding; new hires to top positions were almost exclusively from the private sector and regulated industries; Watt weakened enforcement of strip-mining, mineral leasing, and other laws by cutting jobs in regulatory offices and by hiring from regulated industries; and Reagan fired most of the staff of the CEQ and cut its budget by 72 percent. Overall, the president presided in his first term over a 32 percent reduction of federal spending on natural-resource and environmental programs.[31] More than one scholar has called this "hollowing out" of the environmental regulatory apparatus Reagan inherited from the 1970s.

Some support for this conclusion about Reagan's achievements came from the volley of "indictment books" published in 1982 and after by environmental organizations, piling up a list of environmental harms permitted by the industry-friendly Watt/Burford regimes. Pamphlets and books such as Friends of the Earth et al. (ten environmental organizations), *Ronald Reagan and the American Environment: An Indictment* (1982), Common Cause, *Who's Minding the Store?* (1982), and Jonathan Lash et al., *A Season of Spoils* (1984) angrily argued that the miners and ranchers operating on public lands and industrial polluters everywhere in the United States enjoyed an almost free hand when the Reagan administration took over the Interior Department and the EPA.[32]

The pro-Reagan Heritage Foundation, in its continuing *Mandate for Leadership* series, seemed at first to agree that Reagan was making a large difference at least in public land management, noting with satisfaction that oil and gas leasing in the outer continental shelf increased almost threefold under Watt's new proindustry agency, the Minerals Management Service.[33] Yet this early view of Reagan as a successful dismantler of environmental protection soon gave way to a more restrained view. Budget cuts and top personnel changes were important tools of the "administrative presidency," but their implementation by Watt, Burford, and an overworked White House staff had only a short-term effect. After public and congressional complaints drove Watt and Burford from office, the administration then had to give up ground gained in order to calm the uproar. Ruckelshaus insisted on a significant budgetary restoration for the EPA as a condition of accepting the appointment, and by 1985 he had achieved a modest funding increase. The EPA completed 102 Superfund site cleanups in Ruckelshaus's first six months and an additional 597 sites by 1985. Ruckelshaus, finally weary of battles with the OMB and the White House, retired after the 1984 election, but Reagan's appointment of veteran administrator Lee Thomas was welcomed by most environmentalists, despite his lack of enthusiasm for Superfund. The wars between the Reagan revolutionaries and the environmentalist community had been intensely felt by both sides but by the end of Reagan's first term were essentially in the past. The president accepted the advice of his Interior Department and signed laws establishing the Great Basin National Park and the Mount St. Helens National Volcanic Monument. He was forced to accept larger congressional appropriations for wilderness and forest service programs (except for road building) than he had proposed and glumly signed a 1986 law requiring industries to report their toxic releases. The White House no longer talked about the Sagebrush Rebellion or its more intellectually substantial successor, the wise-use movement.

Thus it can be said that in his two terms Reagan presided over a brief shrinkage of federal environmental enforcement while conspicuously losing the more important public opinion battle over the direction of our national environmental policy. Conservative think tanks and pundits who paid attention to environmental policy admitted to a mood of disappointment and frustration. In return for short-term budget cuts and a few months of regulatory laxity the president, in the view of some conservative intellectuals and policy wonks, let slip past an apparent opportunity to make fundamental changes through legislation. Instead of pushing for regulatory easing of the Clean Air and Water Acts and Superfund as well as in the basic strategy and working mode of the EPA itself, Reagan, in the view of the 1984 and 1989 editions of the Heritage Foundation's *Mandate for Change*, "failed badly" to offer a persuasive new vision of a prodevelopment, market-oriented environmental policy.

The causes of Reagan's defeats in the environmental-reform arena began with hastily made key appointments and include Reagan's detachment from the work of his top administrators. The debate goes on as to whether Reagan lacked the mental power to carry through any complex management reforms, including the environmental-policy revision he wanted—when he thought about it. Many biographers and historians have questioned his cognitive abilities. He was a "complete airhead" (biographer Edmund Morris), an "amiable dunce" (Clark Clifford, aide to several Democratic presidents). "He lived life on the surface where the small waves are, not deep down where the heavy currents tug," wrote Republican speechwriter Peggy Noonan. "He knows less than any president I've ever known," concluded Speaker of the House Thomas "Tip" O'Neill. He worked "three to four hours on most days," wrote biographer Richard Reeves.[34]

Others find in his published letters a clear mind and a tenacious student of political affairs. Perhaps Laurence Barrett in Gambling with History strikes a balance. Reagan was a "useful simplifier who knew what he wanted," but outside his core concerns—which did not include stewardship over natural resources—he was "lax and largely inattentive."[35] Whatever one thinks about Reagan's mental capacities and work ethic, it seems undeniable that his close counselors fundamentally misinterpreted Reagan's 1980 election as a strong mandate for the evisceration of all environmental regulation as an important part of all that he wished to do.

He and his team also underestimated the depth of conviction and expand-ing base of the environmental movement. The Sierra Club's membership re-mained static at 180,000 until late 1982, when it surged to 335,000, and the organization collected more than 1 million signatures on a petition demand-ing that Watt be fired. Membership growth was experienced by all national environmental groups. Although only four claimed 100,000 members in 1980, fifteen did by 1990. With membership expansion came a stimulus for fund-raising. Watt served for more than two years as a lightning rod drawing out environmentalist energies and mobilization, essentially a gift to environ-mentalists from the most unfriendly president they had ever faced. When Reagan said, "There are environmental extremists," as he frequently did, he was not factually wrong, depending on what he meant by "extremists." Probably he had not read but perhaps had heard about Edward Abbey's widely read novel The Monkey Wrench Gang (1975), a story about a small group of desert lovers in the mountain West who, dedicated to throwing wrenches in the gears of US development, sabotaged brush- and tree-clearing bulldoz-ers, chainsaws, and lumber-company and law enforcement helicopters and made plans to dynamite the Glen Canyon Dam. Abbey's fictional wrench throwers reminded some observers of the tactics of the organization Earth First!, pledging "no compromise in defense of Mother Earth." Reagan's large error was to confuse this fringe with the immense, growing, and bipar-tisan social movement surging in TR's lifetime and thereafter. In this mis-judgment the president had much company among conservative Republicans. The Republican Study Committee based in the House of Rep-

resentatives in 1982 published the report "The Specter of Environmentalism" depicting the movement as a "culture" war against property rights in
which liberals made common cause with "revolutionaries" and the "coun-
terculture."[36]

Reagan's episodic reform campaign had the unintended consequence of
giving new energy to environmentalism, though events outside politics were
perhaps more influential. Spectacular pollution episodes, widely reported in
the media, also intensified public environmental worries. The Missouri
town of Times Beach had to be evacuated and eventually abandoned when it
was discovered in 1983 that its unpaved streets had been oiled by wastes
from local chemical plants containing, among other things, the toxic chemical dioxin. The oil tanker *Exxon Valdez* ran aground in Prince William Sound,
Alaska, in March 1989, spilling up to 750,000 barrels of oil, fouling local waters and beaches, and killing large numbers of wildlife. In March 1986 a rup-
ture at a nuclear power reactor in Chernobyl, Ukraine, sent a plume of
radioactive fallout across large regions of the Union of Soviet Socialist Republics (USSR) and forced the evacuation of some 335,000 people.

Such incidents were part of the background against which, for the first
time, a president attempted to dismantle or nullify the US structures of environmental protection constructed in the 1960s and 1970s. The result was to
strengthen the entire green community. Activated by a new sense of urgency
and growth in membership and budgets, the "big ten" environmental organizations began to meet weekly to coordinate strategies, and their lobbyists found congressional offices increasingly receptive. Public opinion polls
tracked the rise in environmental group membership growth. A Roper poll
in September 1982 found that 69 percent of the public believed environmental-protection laws "are about right or haven't gone far enough," and a Har-
ris survey late that year reported 76 percent of those polled thought
"disposal of hazardous wastes" was a "serious problem."[37]

Thus the Reagan revolution in environmental policy amounted to first-
term budget and staff cuts for environmental regulation and a regulatory tilt
in favor of extractive industries. Even this was moderated midway through
the first term, and the agencies "hollowed out" were finally put in the hands
of experienced people who believed in the mission of the basic environmental laws. The outcome of this struggle has to be assessed both as a Reagan
defeat as well as a surprising rallying moment for modern environmentalism facing for the first time a fundamental challenge from a popular presi-

dent. Sierra Club Director Carl Pope wrote in 1988, "It is clear that the past eight years have not turned out to be as disastrous as [we] feared."[38]

Pope doubtless credited the derailing of Reagan's sweeping reform effort in environmental policy and public perception to the passionate counterattacks of environmental groups such as the Sierra Club. Public opinion polls tell a more important, larger story of a broad and deep shift in national opinion toward strengthening support for the pollution-control measures enacted in the 1960s and 1970s. Reagan and his policy advisers badly misjudged the environmental views of the voters, taking as a "mandate" to repeal all environmental regulation what was only the permission to replace Carter. Still, to emphasize Reagan's defeat as an environmental-policy reformer leaves something out that makes his presidency a considerably browner and more consequential one. We must look beyond what Reagan as president was not able to do in weakening environmental regulation and discrediting the larger movement and ask what he was able to prevent Carter from doing in a second term.

Here the antienvironmentalist achievement of Reagan was substantial and accomplished in one single day—when he received more votes than Carter on the first Tuesday in November 1980. In the last weeks of the presidential campaign the editors of the Sierra Club magazine, *Sierra*, worked hard to arrange a debate presenting the views of both Carter and Reagan. Reagan's managers seemed open to the joint coverage, but in the end *Sierra* magazine had to print a Carter interview followed by a staff-written summary and critique of what they thought were the Californian's views and policy proposals on the environment. Most interesting in this uneven exchange is what Carter told *Sierra* he intended to do in the area of environmental protection if reelected for another term. He had already proposed and intended to press for, among other things, the Alaska Lands Act, stronger hazardous-waste cleanup efforts, and progress toward a sustainable-energy future. "Studies" had been done providing the ground for new protections against soil erosion and for coastal resources. Most important of the Carter administration's studies was *Global 2000*, an ambitious report on world population, natural resources, and environmental challenges through the end of the century. Reagan's second-term agenda, with the major exception of tax reform in 1986, was increasingly taken up with international issues—US military intervention in Lebanon, the administration's covert interventions against the communist regime in Nicaragua, two summit meetings with Soviet premier Michael Gorbachev. At home, the year 1984 was, of course, dominated not by policy formation but by the presidential election campaign that returned Reagan with a vote of 59 percent and a sweep of forty-nine states.

It would be difficult to designate another presidential campaign in the modern United States conducted in such a sea of trivialities. Reagan on the stump (more accurately, on television) made very short talks and repeated code words such as "hope," "future," "opportunity," and "America's back." Democratic nominee Walter Mondale delivered boring speeches on the deficit, Medicare, and the arms race, promising a presidency unlike Reagan's in its devotion to "fairness." The environment made virtually no appearance even in the televised debates, where journalists had some opportunity to frame important questions. The candidates said nothing on the topic, in part because Reagan and his handlers were determined not to allow this policy area to again make him more enemies than friends. Mondale, who had no environmental interests, failed to connect Reagan with the legacies of Watt and Burford. He had primed himself for the campaign by reading thirty books on contemporary issues and social trends, not one of them addressing the environment. The president made a few gestures designed to associate himself within the environmental mainstream, scheduling speaking engagements in two national parks where he delivered platitudes about "morning in America."[39]

In his second term Reagan rarely had anything to say on the environment, certainly nothing suggesting that he any longer had a reform agenda there. His State of the Union Addresses got longer, but any comment on the environment was brief and mildly bragging. Every year the CEQ wrote for his signature a presidential cover message noting "with pride" the fine work the administration was doing in protecting our natural heritage. The annual index to his public papers after 1983 shows more references to Guatemala, education, Portugal, and Israel than the environment. Some earlier policy positions curbing environmental regulations were continued without comment. The president opposed moving from research to regulation of acid rain generated by power plants. He vetoed the Clean Water Act reauthorization twice, and his veto was overridden. Reagan reluctantly agreed with congressional pressures to establish a new national park in Nevada and add several million acres to the national wilderness system. Secretary of the Interior Donald Hodel quietly continued Watt's efforts to expand energy and mineral access on public lands.

There was, however, an important behind-the-scenes environmental controversy engaging the administration throughout the second term, and here he surprised us with one last puzzlement—his behavior on the issue of the "ozone hole." General Motors discovered in 1931 a new class of chemicals called chlorofluorocarbons (CFCs)—hailed as "perfect chemicals" because they were inert, nontoxic, noncarcinogenic, and nonflammable. They were ideal for refrigeration, air conditioning, and aerosols, and their production surged throughout the second half of the twentieth century, quadrupling in the 1960s as they were widely adopted as solvents by the booming electronics industry. By the mid-1980s, 3.5 million metric tons of CFCs were produced in the United States, which consumed one-third of the world's total output.[40] Then in 1974 two University of California researchers concluded that CFCs, after their industrial uses, rose to the stratosphere, where they broke down into chlorine, which made a chemical assault on the ozone layer, a thin layer of vapor around the earth protecting humans as well as some plant and marine life from harmful ultraviolet solar radiation. British researchers ten years later discovered a "hole" in the ozone layer over the southern polar ice cap. Media coverage of the threat to the ozone shield generated growing concern, and a series of international conferences and research efforts began in 1977 to seek a global solution. What would be the US position, after taking the limited step in 1978 of banning CFCs in domestic aerosol cans?

Although much was unknown in the science of ozone in the atmosphere, the mass media reported a consensus among scientists that CFCs played a role in the depletion of the ozone layer with resultant harmful effects on plant and human health, including an item the media chose to emphasize— skin cancer. Congressional interest intensified, and a battle was waged inside the Reagan administration. International meetings began in Montreal in 1986 with the possibility of some sort of treaty—or none at all. The State Department, the EPA, and the National Oceanic and Atmospheric Administration (NOAA) urged support for a strong international treaty, whereas within the OMB and the Departments of the Interior, Commerce, and Agriculture ideological opponents of business regulation pressed the White House to take a position producing a weak treaty or an indefinite postponement of the negotiations in Montreal. CFC-producing companies, DuPont in the lead, initially presented a solid front in opposition to strict international controls or bans.

Would Reagan exert leadership as the Montreal meetings approached a critical point, and in what direction? The record of his administration on international environmental issues was not encouraging. The research of a *Washington Post* staff writer in 1983 led him to generally agree with an indictment by ten environmental organizations finding the Reagan administration "indifferent to hostile" toward proposals for international cooperation in environmental protection. The Reagan government cooperated in holding an international conference on whaling and another on the earth's biological diversity, but in the case of other and more important international efforts to create some sort of global regulation (on acid rain, carbon dioxide buildup in the atmosphere, law of the sea, trade in hazardous substances, international sale of nuclear materials, and the UN World Charter for Nature) the Reagan government was "largely negative." So it was a surprise when the president who had presided over that record sent, on September 18, 1987, an "eyes-only" personal cable from the White House to the lead negotiator for the United States endorsing the strong position taken by the State Department. The internal bickering within the administration, which had received considerable press coverage, was over. The Senate then voted unanimously for ratification. Reagan publicly said, "This is an historic agreement," and left it at that. He received much praise and very little criticism. Years later (2010) one could find on the Internet revisionist blogs arguing that Reagan should be seen as another TR for his backing of the Montreal Protocol, which "was the work of the Gipper."[41]

This is a large exaggeration. The president had not played any direct role until the eleventh hour and before that had appointed all the top aides who opposed the position he eventually supported. True, no other country's executive (except the United Kingdom) had personally taken a stand on the issue as he finally did, and the fact of an international treaty tackling the issue was indeed an "achievement," but a flawed achievement, as time would tell. EPA officials and independent scientists concede that the early results of the Montreal Protocol included an international contraband trade in the banned Freon gas coolant, and there is almost no recycling of this banned coolant frequently released into the atmosphere. It is hard to say whether a poorly enforced ban on formerly harmful though widespread industrial practices should rank among the apex achievements in the "environmental diplomacy" of the twentieth century, which includes international agreements to curb ocean dumping, ban trade in endangered species, and control transboundary air pollution.

Why, at this critical moment in the history of international ozone diplomacy, did we suddenly encounter Governor Reagan, the sometimes environmentalist, again? A short sentence in his diary was all Reagan ever had to say on his Montreal Protocol decision, and other records are sparse.[42] He seems to have been moved in part by awareness that many in Congress sensed the public wanted US leadership to fix the ozone-hole problem. Key figures such as Senators Max Baucus and John Chafe and Representative John Dingell held frequent hearings and urged a strong US leadership role in banning the manufacture of CFCs and halons. A Senate resolution urging a strong treaty passed by 80 to 2 in the summer of 1987 as the administration's ultimate position remained in doubt. It also had to be a large factor behind Reagan's decision when, toward the end, DuPont—recognizing that consumers were moving away from CFC-based products and that its own research gave the company an advanced position in the development of substitutes for CFCs— led a group of producers toward a change of position toward favoring an international regulatory framework as preferable to a patchwork of state and national regulations or bans. It mattered also that the proposed ban on the production of ozone-depleting chemicals did not take the form of curbing the extraction of some useful and otherwise harmless resources used to build the United States and produce profits, such as forests and minerals. It was also important that CFCs produced a global pollution problem affecting everyone, and the science behind the indictment was impressive. It may also have been important, perhaps very important, that Reagan had experienced the removal of two skin cancers in 1985 and one in 1987.[43] Then there was the role of close friends and advisers—trusted lieutenants. A strong Montreal Protocol had unwavering support from two of Reagan's most astute and experienced advisers, Chief of Staff Howard Baker and, most forcefully in the crucial last days, Secretary of State George Shultz. One might add to the lieutenant factor a person who was Reagan's equal rather than a top subordinate—close friend and prominent conservative, British prime minister Margaret Thatcher, who reversed herself after a rigorous review of the scientific information and urged Reagan to support a strong treaty. Again, in helping a president sort things out, lieutenants mattered.

Here we should expand our attention to the role of presidential lieutenants to include blunderers who unintentionally aided those they saw as the president's enemies. Just as fate gave environmentalists a Watt and his incendiary mouth in the year a new President Reagan put his crosshairs on

302 | CHAPTER EIGHT

protected public lands, in 1987 the administration's internal struggle over ozone policy was influenced by another top appointee, Hodel. Like many Reaganite conservatives, Hodel was given to describe any cancer attributed to ozone depletion (which they regarded as unproven) as a "self-inflicted disease" brought on by lifestyle preferences freely chosen by people who decided to lounge on the beaches, play golf, or move from Michigan to live in sunny Florida. This was Hodel's view, frequently expressed. In the summer of 1987 he was quoted as saying in a White House meeting (and earlier to the *Wall Street Journal*) that people would not be bothered by UV radiation coming through any ozone hole if they would just wear sunglasses, wide-brimmed hats, and sunscreen. His remarks were met with ridicule and mocked in cartoons and other press comments, increasing the pressure on Reagan to endorse the strong treaty position his negotiators had painstakingly staked out for the United States.[44] Thus Reagan, at the end, when many factors aligned favorably, added one final green moment to his skimpy total and buoyed the spirits of the Republican heirs of TR. Signing the Montreal Protocol was essentially the end of the Reagan presidency's turbulent environmental-reform engagement.

In signing a treaty to eliminate ozone-depleting chemicals, Reagan reluctantly engaged a new type of environmental problem, transboundary atmospheric pollution. With his luck, ozone destruction moved first onto his desk—a difficult pollution puzzle—but worse was coming. Elsewhere in Washington there was arriving in the 1980s a second, more potent, and far-reaching environmental disturbance destined to baffle and vex all of Reagan's presidential successors. Climate change had evaded broad notice because people are interested in weather, not climate (writers on this topic have used several terms, most frequently global warming or climate change; I will use the terms interchangeably). The science of climate change was in considerable doubt, and fluctuations in both weather and climate were not unusual in human history. No one took a course in college on climatology— except Al Gore and some of his Harvard classmates, where he learned from atmospheric scientist Roger Revelle that humankind had apparently been stirring up planetary trouble over the past few centuries as people shifted energy sources from wood to coal to oil and gas as part of industrialization. The result, Swedish scientist Svante Arrhenius argued in an 1896 paper, was the dumping of new and, so far as we knew, unprecedented loads of human-produced carbon dioxide into the atmosphere. He calculated the result of carbon-dioxide–trapped infrared radiation as a nine-degree warming of earth's climate, with rising seas and withered crops. His idea "floated in obscurity for a very long time," wrote Bill McKibben in The End of Nature (1989)—about a century, actually, as other scientists identified a wider range of atmospheric troublemakers (a term I first saw in Michael Oppenheimer and Robert Boyle's Dead Heat [1990]) released into our planet's atmosphere by human action, principally carbon dioxide from burning fossil fuels, but also ozone, nitrous oxide, and methane. "Greenhouse gases" have always held a portion of the sun's warmth from reradiating back into space, keeping planetary temperatures on average 59 degrees Fahrenheit warmer than otherwise. These gases allowed humanity to evolve on an otherwise much colder planet despite unpredictable weather and a climate subject to large and puzzling variations, such as the Medieval Warming Epoch from 800–1250 and the Little Ice Age from 1550 to 1850.

Arrhenius and others suspected human activities were warming the earth. Scientific interest was quickened by atmospheric observations begun in the 1960s from the 11,000-foot peak of Mauna Loa Volcano on the Island of Hawaii, finding atmospheric concentrations of carbon dioxide increasing annually. A National Academy of Sciences report in 1983 found "reason for concern but not panic," arriving at the same time an EPA study found that the nine warmest years of the century had occurred in the previous fourteen years. The atmospheric-pollution debate was now breaking out of science into politics and policy on two fronts—global warming and ozone depletion. Within the decade of the 1980s the Montreal Protocol seemed to have reduced if not ended the atmospheric pollution of the ozone-destroying CFC chemicals causing cancer and other negative consequences. Global-warming worriers laid out a vastly more costly set of possibilities—rising sea levels as a result of melting ice caps, drought and flooding, agricultural disruption, the spread of tropical diseases. Skeptics in the ranks of atmospheric and oceanic sciences doubted the climate models predicting catastrophic warming, arguing that the oceans would absorb most carbon dioxide and that greenhouse gases could be buried deep in the earth. A great experiment in global climate change was under way and generating emotional debate.

Reagan's speechwriters prepared for him a Farewell Address delivered on January 11, 1989, just before Air Force One took the Reagans back to California. The United States, he insisted, should aim to be a shining city "upon a hill . . . built on rocks . . . teeming with people . . . doors open to anyone with the will and heart to get there."[45] This vision of an ever-expanding metropolis built upon such unpromising environmental foundations was Reagan's profoundly misguided intellectual legacy to a nation in need of modifying its inherited growth path. His presidency left behind a conundrum—environmental concern was increasingly popular in Reagan's nation, and yet so was he, arguably the most environmentally illiterate president since Harding.

The Republican nominee in 1988, no surprise, was Vice President George H. W. Bush, who had held a wide range of career assignments but remained somewhat elusive. After being nominated by his party, the loyal vice president sensed a need to distinguish himself from the Reagan, a task beyond his verbal and conceptual abilities. His two autobiographies do not explain why Bush in the first days of his campaign decided to distance himself from one of Reagan's serious political blunders—the Watt/Burford campaigns to roll back decades of environmental protection. The first indication the 1988 presidential race might give environmental protection unprecedented salience in the appeals of both parties came in a Bush speech in Detroit, where he declared himself a TR-type conservationist, promised a plan to curb acid rain, said it was time to end solid-waste dumping in the oceans, and pledged to end the loss of wetlands to development. More media attention came when Bush took the press on an excursion boat around Boston Harbor and gleefully pointed out the floating solid waste and sewage, which he blamed on daily discharges of 500 million gallons of wastewater for which Governor Michael Dukakis, his opponent, was responsible. The Dukakis camp seemed surprised by this turn in the campaign and later attempted lamely to blame President Reagan. The press reported Bush claiming to be a "Republican president in the Teddy Roosevelt tradition, a conservationist. An *environmentalist*. I am an environmentalist and always have been and always will be."[46] Either, like Reagan, he did not know the meaning of his words or he had convinced himself that he had the verbal and mental abilities to square the nature-protection proenterprise circle as only TR among Republican presidents had done.

GEORGE H. W. BUSH

George Herbert Walker Bush was born in 1924 in Milton, Massachusetts, the son of Prescott Bush, a Wall Street investment banker and US senator from

Connecticut. He was raised on the family estate fronting the beach at Kennebunkport, Maine, where he "started fishing at the age of five or so, in the cold waters along the Atlantic Coast of Maine" and later acquired a decent game of tennis. His out-of-doors time was mostly spent sailing, and none of his biographers record any curiosity about the region's wildlife beyond where the fish were biting in the surf near his home.[47]

He was on a silver-spoon path through Andover toward Yale when World War II interrupted and gave him a chance to show a gritty, even heroic side. He enlisted in the US Navy in 1942 at age 18, then trained as a pilot and flew combat missions in the Pacific, earning the Distinguished Flying Cross. After the war he entered Yale, graduating with a Phi Beta Kappa key and a major in economics. His two memoirs and many biographies convey little information on his intellectual development at Yale. We know little of what he read outside of economic texts, what hobbies and interests he pursued.

Married to Barbara Pierce and with a growing family, Bush relocated them westward where he entered the oil business, choosing to establish a home in Midland, Texas. It was a sprawling, treeless boomlet town planted on the dry flatlands of West Texas without "mountains, . . . ocean fronts, . . . fishing holes," or other natural endowments, in the words of a lawyer friend.[48] There they led the backyard barbecue, friends-over-for-bridge life, Bush helping to found a bank, coaching Little League Baseball, and teaching Sunday school. He soon became a millionaire, and, restless for the next step up the ladder toward prominence and achievement, he ran successfully for Congress in 1966. After losing a Senate race in 1970 he served as ambassador to the United Nations under Nixon, then envoy to China, then director of the Central Intelligence Agency (CIA).

This balanced and busy portfolio and unusual New England–Texas political base led to his selection as Reagan's vice-presidential running mate in 1980. Eight years as vice president created for Bush a political image as Reagan's lightweight, which may have persuaded him and his handlers in the 1988 presidential race that he needed a bold image makeover. In any event all were astonished when, in a speech in Detroit in August, Bush promised support for the Clean Air Act stalled in Congress and stricter enforcement of toxic-waste laws.[49] Closer to inauguration, the new president-elect surprised environmentalists by appointing World Wildlife Fund head William Reilly to manage the EPA and promising to strengthen the CEQ, which Reagan had virtually closed.

After winning the election with the electoral votes of forty states, Bush promptly met with representatives of some thirty environmental organizations, who gave his transition team a list of 700 proposals to consider. He then struggled to reauthorize and strengthen the Clean Air Act Amendments of 1990. This had the potential to be a joint presidential-congressional achievement stalled in Congress for thirteen years. When he signed the Clean Air Act reauthorization into law, his role as legislative manager was inflated by some of his friends (such as White House lawyer Boyden Gray), who called the 1992 Clean Air Act the "most sweeping environmental statute ever passed."[50]

After signing, Bush veered in a brown direction, appointing a new White House Council on Competitiveness chaired by Vice President Dan Quayle, a predictable friend of corporations eager to externalize the costs of production. He tacked green again when he increased funding for the national parks and the enforcement of the Endangered Species Act and promised to "plant a billion trees" a year, another off-the-wall Bush impulse with little follow-up. The environmental president continued to veer brownward. His Inaugural Address contained nothing on the environment, and a 1989 White House "Fact Sheet" meant to brag on the administration's green achievements began by boasting about reforestation projects. On the fast-rising global climate-change issue, Bush showed no interest, adopting Reagan's policy—more research before more enforcement.

As president, Bush never entirely broke off contact with environmentalists as Reagan had. An example was his acceptance of an invitation to speak at a symposium held by Ducks Unlimited at which he said several green-sounding and inconsequential things: "Our natural heritage must be recovered and restored"; "Sound ecology and a strong economy can coexist"; "We need more parks"; and "Polluters will pay." When swearing in Reilly to head EPA, he added: "I want to broaden the consensus for a clean environment."[51] The prose was sophomoric, and the president's actions could run counter to his occasional platitudes about environmental stewardship. A prominent example was his role in the much-publicized June 1992 Earth Summit (the UN Conference on the Environment and Development) in Rio de Janeiro, another UN forum at which the rich nations would be pressed to agree to sharp reductions in their greenhouse gas emissions (i.e., their economic growth) while poor societies desperate to industrialize insisted they be exempt from such limits. But even Western constituents and governments recognized Rio as a rare international opportunity to support a negotiating mechanism to promote future agreement on some middle ground. Bush came under pressure from the green left to attend and propose some conciliatory middle ground, but there was equal influence from his own party to ignore the meeting. The path he took satisfied no one. He hinted up until the opening day that he would not attend (172 governments participated and 108 sent their heads of state). Then he went and stayed only three days, made a speech claiming that the United States had the world's best environmental policies, and refused to sign a climate-change convention as well as a biodiversity pact to protect animal and plant life from extinction. Sharp criticism was heard around the world and at home.[52]

For Bush there were a few more minor speeches to environmental groups, but the president's skimpy record on the environmental protection front was closed. With Democrats controlling both Houses, this was not a surprise, but Bush showed no interest in many trouble zones—climate change, strip mining, the endangered bald eagle and other waning critters, crowding and pollution in national parks. He seemed to possess considerable energy for his job, his multitude of speaking engagements and appearances filling two fat volumes a year. Environmental/conservation events were vastly outnumbered on his calendar by visiting foreign dignitaries, offering disaster condolences, congratulating winning sports teams, handing out medals to military heroes, and meeting delegations of Sunday school teachers from Oregon. The president in the 1990s talked, celebrated, and welcomed seemingly without letup. When he had something to say on nature protection, President Bush reminded no one of the White House speechwriters such as Wallace Stegner and Stewart Udall, whose drafts brought Henry David Thoreau, John Burroughs, John Muir, and Rachel Carson into the Oval Office or pressroom for JFK and LBJ. Bush seemed decently served by his writers, but to read him ad libbing or on the fly was to endure again the dull vocalizations and tone-deaf ear of Harding. In the autumn of 1989, he uttered this Harding-speak: "If the earth is an altar, we must make it an altar not of security but of celebration."[53] His approval ratings spiked upward when he ordered the invasion of Panama and again in January 1991 when he launched a war called Operation Desert Storm to unseat Saddam Hussein. Then his ratings sagged toward his last months in office.

Bush was not a very good president when all things are lined up, but disappointed environmentalists were possibly wrong to conclude he had brazenly lied to them that early autumn of 1988. He had thought so infrequently about the meaning of the phrase "environmental president" that he may well have thought a few Earth Day speeches and a new national park in New England ought to satisfy the tree-huggers. That it meant presidential leadership toward a society significantly transformed was beyond his education or ambition. Even if, like the two Roosevelts, Bush had harbored any impulse toward the range of societal changes contemplated by environmentalists, this Bush lacked the ability to communicate it. As he and we learned many times when he talked of a nation illuminated by a "thousand points of light," bafflement radiated outward. In an astute 2006 essay, Katherine Langford pointed out that journalists following Bush mentioned his visionlessness as early as August 1988 and frequently thereafter. Soon Bush himself was talking about the "vision thing," which "bothered him a lot," commented White House Press Secretary Marlin Fitzwater.[54] Bush mentioned the word "vision" 277 times in his public statements over his four-year term, about half the time referring to others (George Washington, US astronauts, athletes) and half to himself. Revealingly, because he never developed a master narrative for US history or his own presidency, each mention of vision in his presidential speeches and remarks was a forgettable cluster of fragments. "Ask me what my vision is," Bush wrote in his diary in his first week in office. "Third World debts, politics in Central America, Soviet accountability, nuclear cleanup, budget deficit, and the savings and loan. . . . How does that grab you?"[55] He offered a list of generalities in his 1992 State of the Union Address and one frosty March 1992 day in Camp David drew up another list of examples of his vision for his speechwriters—mentioning health care, strong families, world peace, and other worthy-sounding elements that did not cohere as a political program.[56] Ev'rybody talkin' 'bout vision ain't goin' there.

When Bush was voted out of office in 1992, the author of the influential book *Earth in the Balance*, Gore, expressed wonderment that the same Bush who displayed so little political courage on environmental matters as president stood so staunchly, in his career in the Congress and as the ambassador to the United Nations, in favor of human-population limitation, the key to the achievement of all environmental protections. Bush sponsored appropriate legislation and made "eloquent" speeches in those days, Gore recalled. In a foreword to a 1972 book on the population crisis, Bush attributed his passion on the birth-control issue to his father, who lost one election because of his own stance on the controversial policy. "Full of courage on the issue then," Gore wrote, "his courage has vanished"[57] when a second term as president was at stake. Bush seemed in a strong position in early 1992, mostly as a result of favorable events in Soviet relations and the Middle East. Several strong Democrats declined to run. This opened the door for a little-known outsider of modest beginnings—Arkansas governor Bill Clinton.

BILL CLINTON

William Jefferson Clinton was born in 1946 in Hope, Arkansas, to a troubled family, yet excelled in public schools (his high-school principal refused to let him run for senior class president because he had run for top offices every year and usually won). He disliked being alone, biographer David Maraniss noted, and especially liked crowds when a good time was under way, such as when he was making a speech or playing his saxophone.[58] He attended Georgetown University and Yale Law School, where he met, married, and shared political ambitions with Hillary Rodham.

A tireless campaigner and talented public speaker, Clinton in 1978 was elected the youngest Arkansas governor. He lost and then regained the office, holding it from 1983 to 1992 and combining that with his service to the Democratic Leadership Council to become a seminational figure with a moderate image as an education reformer who seemed to know everyone in the state. People who knew him almost uniformly predicted that he would become president one day, though—like most men who have become president—seeking the office for no particular reason. An unfriendly journalist from the *Arkansas Democrat-Gazette* (the only statewide newspaper), Paul Greenberg, called Clinton "Slick Willie" and said there was "no there there."[59]

As governor he had little—or talked little about—environmental issues, reflecting the weak mobilization of the state's environmental forces and his own lack of interest. Governor Clinton once felt the anger of the poultry industry, more than was deserved, when he decided not to keep a campaign promise to allow their trucks to increase from 72,000 to 80,000 pounds, but usually he managed to look the other way when the poultry industry disposed of untreated animal wastes in local waterways. In the words of

Maraniss, he "often . . . gave large corporations large tax breaks to stay in Arkansas" and accepted rides in the Tyson Foods corporate jet nine times.[60] Early in the 1980s the West Coast–based Weyerhaeuser Lumber Company had begun clear-cutting timber in the state's Ouachita Mountains and some of the scenic stretches of highway from Little Rock to Clinton's hometown of Hot Springs, nestled in a small national park. Clinton viewed the areas from a helicopter and appointed a timber-management task force headed by an outraged environmentalist whom the governor then reluctantly fired under pressure when he advocated an end to clear-cutting. In speeches, Clinton could comfortably hit a green note. "For as long as I can remember," he said in his first gubernatorial Inaugural Address, "I have loved the land, air, and water of Arkansas, and I will do what I can to protect them."[61] However, "protecting them" often was not, Governor Clinton calculated, worth the animosity that came from efforts at strict environmental enforcement on large corporations like Tyson Foods.

"What I can to protect them" was a political throwaway line. Neither Bill nor Hillary or apparently any of his top aides in the governor's Little Rock command post had a strong interest in nature—no green lieutenants. In his long autobiography Clinton said nothing about the landscape or wildlife of Arkansas, with one exception. He briefly noted in *My Life* that the "beautiful" Buffalo River running eastward out of the Ozarks "recently had been named the first river protected by Congress under the Wild and Scenic Rivers Act." He was not entirely pleased. "I supported protecting the river," he recalled, but then he agreed with the objections of the families owning homes or structures on or near the riverbank, feeling that they and their heirs should have been spared purchase by eminent domain and allowed to keep riverine properties in perpetuity. Some wild and scenic river that would have been, forever surrounded by immovable owners and their descendants! Fortunately, the canoeists and other wilderness advocates who shaped the Wild and Scenic Rivers Act had not needed Clinton's influence, for he was probably a dubious ally.[62]

Clinton won the White House in the 1992 election with 43 percent of the popular vote against Bush's 37 percent, with 19 percent going to third-party candidate Ross Perot. No environmental issue had come to the top of campaign debates and polls, though Clinton in his speeches had made several green promises—to fight pollution aggressively, invest in renewable energy, give the EPA cabinet status, and even to make his administration the "greenest in history." Some thought Clinton's choice of Senator Gore as his running mate would serve as a test as to whether a substantial pro- or antienvironment voter bloc existed in the United States. Gore's environmental activism, reaching back to family dinnertime discussions about Carson's *A Silent Spring* and capped by his best-selling book on global warming, *Earth in the Balance* (1992), was unmatched on any presidential ticket in US history. Gore went into the 1992 campaign expecting as much because "one of the main reasons I ran was to try to elevate the importance of the crisis as a political issue," he wrote in that book. "Little did I know that even a more seasoned . . . candidate than myself would have had a difficult time keeping his campaign focused on issues considered exotic at best by pollsters and political professionals. . . . Worse, I started to wonder whether the issues I knew to be important really were peripheral after all." So "I discussed what everybody else discussed," and when he tried to stress global environmental issues in the small, semiprivate meetings with media editorial boards he found their minds closed, his green issues ignored. He does not mention what we may assume, that Clinton doubtless exerted immense pressure on Gore to talk about the issues judged central by the campaign's political professionals.[63] President Bush thought Gore's "greenness" a potential handicap for the Democrats and frequently referred to Gore as the "Ozone Man," once commenting, "This guy is so far out in the environmental extreme we'll be up to our necks in owls" and predicted the future would be "outta work for every American" if the Clinton-Gore ticket succeeded. "This guy's crazy."[64]

The Republican ridicule of Gore apparently had no effect on the outcome of the election, though it may have helped Gore sell a few more copies of *Earth in the Balance*. As Clinton had assumed, the head of the Democratic ticket set the campaign's tone and substance, and Gore was careful to establish no independent voice. The Democrats had not fielded Clinton and an environmentalist but a pair of youthful, attractive, southern-border-state, Ivy League–educated moderates with impeccable civil rights records and a steady focus on economic issues. After the election, environmentalist hopes vested in the new administration began to materialize as Clinton announced top appointments—President of the League of Conservation Voters Bruce Babbitt to head the Interior Department and Gore aide Carole Browner as head of the EPA. By the count of environmental writer Mark Dowie, Clinton picked two dozen prominent environmentalists for top posts in agencies not thought of as directly related to natural-resource matters, such as the OMB, the National Security Council, and the State Department, where Secretary Warren Christopher added global environmental concerns to his speeches and overall agenda. The election of Clinton and Gore plus the appointed "green team" produced euphoria among environmentalists. (Sierra Club Director Pope said we were seeing the "best and perhaps last hope to help move the country from devastation to stewardship," encouraged by Clinton's early promise to lead a US government that would be the "greenest in history.")[65]

Greenest in history? Clinton's Inaugural Address in January 1993 had no environmental elements, and his only environmentalist speech that year was a directionless Earth Day ramble at a botanical garden, in which a president after ten weeks in office had almost no policy changes to report, bragging only about an executive order promoting recycling at government offices. A year later he again delivered an Earth Day talk, this time with a weak effort to express a discernible theme, doubtlessly urged by Gore. "Preserving the environment is at the core of everything we have to do in our own country, building businesses, creating jobs, fighting crime, raising our children. . . . As we renew our environment, we renew our national community." Another forgettable effort to take environmentalism on the political offensive came as he launched his Council on Sustainable Development in June 1993: "A healthy economy and a healthy environment go hand in hand."[66] After more than a year, real environmentalists in high places in the administration realized Clinton had to be pushed. Secretary Babbitt made a full record of his own green lieutenant activities, writing a little memoir and feeding inside stories to journalists. Vice President Gore's prodding was kept under the wraps of his presidential ambitions and doubtless now rests in sealed boxes in the William J. Clinton Presidential Library in Little Rock.

Part of the problem was that Clinton's list of objectives was so long and unfocused, no one could be sure of his priorities. He put pressure on Congress to strengthen the Clean Water Act and Superfund, conveying no sense of their relative importance. Executive orders were signed encouraging federal recycling and (vaguely) discouraging the "environmental injustice" of toxic dumping in poor and minority neighborhoods. Hillary and Chelsea installed recycling bins and new, more efficient refrigerators in the White House kitchen. In the second Earth Day speech Clinton put his political spin on very modest substance: "We are trying to bring a new spirit of community to the work of protecting and restoring the environment" because "govern-

ments alone cannot save the environment; people and communities must."
Or "government is a partner, not an overseer."[67] The greenest opportunity in
the 1990s, many believed, was to make progress on what was emerging as
every country's fearsome, big problem—global warming. Clinton and Gore
in the campaign had promised to "cut greenhouse gases to 1990 levels by
2000." In his second Earth Day speech, Clinton reported that a plan was "in
the works."[68]

Environmental groups and activists reserved judgment but did not like
much of what they saw in the early Clinton era—especially the signing of a
1995 law disappointing environmentalists in the Pacific Northwest in their
sustained battle with loggers. Several green organizations did what they
were expected to do—express impatience at the pace of the environmental
component of Clintonism.[69] Most seemed to concede that it was unrealistic
to expect an early burst of Clintonian policy reform successes on any front.
His winning margin had been less than half of the total votes cast because
there was a third candidate contending for votes. Political division quickly
became worse when Republicans in the 1994 congressional elections rallied
around Newt Gingrich's "Contract with America" and took back the House.
The "contract" only indirectly threatened existing environmental programs
but challenged their funding and regulation in general. Clinton's hand was
not a strong one for any of his hopes, and his own nomination and election
confirmed that the public mood in the 1990s contained much skepticism toward the sort of liberal activism associated with FDR, LBJ, and JFK. Clinton
inherited a particularly high level of ideological and partisan gridlock, and at
pivotal moments in his presidency he navigated between disagreeing "stakeholders" by "triangulating" a middle position between hard disagreements.
For his part, Clinton was an intelligent and gifted orator given to hyperbole,
prone to sloppy management, occasionally indecisive, and plagued by earlier (and future) sexual indiscretions. He and (after 1994) an aggressive Republican majority in Congress wrangled inconclusively over reauthorization
of basic laws on clean water, Superfund, and the Endangered Species Act.
Policy gridlock between legislative and executive branches, a longtime feature of US politics, seemed to intensify as the twentieth century approached
an end. In his first year the only significant green legislation Clinton signed
was the 7-million-acre California Desert Protection Act. Secretary Babbitt
and Clinton (in that order) then proposed a package of public land management reforms intended to raise grazing and mining fees and institute tighter

controls over rangeland conditions, including termination of use of pesticides. At once they learned something about environmental politics in the rural West. The Sagebrush Rebellion of the Reagan/Watt years had folded, but mining, smelting, lumbering, and other wood-product industries encountered material shortages in the booming housing markets of the 1990s, spawning a "wise-use" movement expressing passionate resistance to the Babbitt-Clinton restrictions on access to public rangelands.[70] Babbitt and Clinton shared their small piece of the credit with a bipartisan crowd of governors, members of Congress, and environmental lobbyists who signed off on a $7.8 billion, forty-year Everglades Restoration Plan in Clinton's final days in office. The League of Conservation Voters gave Clinton a C+ at the end of his first year but revised that slightly upward in his second term. Babbitt gave himself what I take to be an A– and Clinton what felt like an "Absent" (or was it a D+?) in the interior secretary's memoir-like *Cities in the Wilderness* (2005), an interesting book in which the historic Everglades deal and every other major public land innovation was administered without Clinton's involvement.

A climate-change-control program finally was introduced in a Rose Garden announcement on October 17, 1993, an ambitious fifty-point plan for reducing the emissions of greenhouse gases to their 1990 levels by 2000. Many of the new policy interventions soon disappointed the planners, even though some produced a portion of the intended energy efficiencies or shifts away from fossil fuels.[71] The president's hopes were undercut in part by the robust economy of the 1990s, bringing population growth Clinton could have reduced at two opportunities: when an immigration-reform package was presented to him in 1995 by a commission chaired by US Representative Barbara Jordan and when he received policy suggestions from the Council on Sustainable Development including immigration reduction (among other things). With immigration running at the highest levels in US history, between 1990 and 2000 the country added 30 million people and 25 million more cars, major forces in pushing greenhouse emissions 15 percent above the levels of 1990.

In Babbitt's view, Clinton needed an environmental challenge in which his "scant" first-term record could show some wins, and the secretary reached back to TR to hand Clinton a conservation scorecard of TR's public land set-asides. Clinton responded with zest.[72] Having discovered the Antiquities Act, the president in 1996 set aside the 1.8-million-acre Grand Staircase–Escalante National Monument in southern Utah and twenty-two other national monuments (more land in national monuments in the lower forty-eight states than any president since TR), forty-two new wildlife refuges, the Northwestern Hawaiian Coral Reefs Reserve, and road-building prohibitions in several national parks and forests. Clearly, however, Clinton's main interests were elsewhere, chiefly in welfare reform and Hillary's special passion, health-care reform. The 1994 State of the Union Address was eighty minutes long, with three sentences on the environment. In 1995 the State of the Union Address devoted 50 of 38,000 words to the environment. Yet it was some achievement by lieutenants Babbitt, Gore, and Browner that Clinton in his second term was often heard insisting at budget time that there must be special protective efforts for health care, education, Social Security, and the environment.[73]

Ironically, Clinton early in his first term agreed to pursue an environmental cleanup effort where the public and environmental organizations could be expected to be unaware of the problem or the results—on military installations. Here he deserves credit for continuing the efforts of recent commanders in chief. In 1975, President Ford's Defense Department established the Installation Restoration Program, and President Carter subsequently issued an executive order, widely ignored, requiring all federal facilities to comply with subfederal environmental regulations. The Reagan administration—beginning, surprisingly, with the Defense Department—established the Defense Environmental Restoration Program (DERA). This looks like a sturdy little tradition of a self-greening military, but an important driver was Congress, which in 1992 passed legislation signed by President Bush requiring the Defense Department as well as the rest of the federal government to comply with environmental laws. Bush announced on the twentieth anniversary of Earth Day that his administration's environmental and defense roles had been integrated, and Secretary of Defense Dick Cheney pledged to make his department a "model of environmental protection." First came an estimate and description of the problem, which one study described as a "costly legacy of decades of the Cold War . . . an environmental problem of enormous, almost immeasurable magnitude." Military operations produced thousands of toxic landfills, buried storage tanks, and polluted groundwater—by 1985 an estimated 400–800 sites requiring remediation, 12,000 by 1989, and 20,000 by 1993—implying a cleanup program costing $30 billion. Clinton as commander in chief accepted the costly, low-profile assignment for which there was no grateful constituency except sometimes the communities surrounding those polluted military installations. More frequently they were angry at the delays in cleanup, and in his first summer Clinton announced the Fast-Track Cleanup Program on military installations.[74]

All presidents lust for a high historical ranking among their elite peers. Clinton had a slow start but presided over a strong economic performance in the 1990s and became the first Democratic president since FDR to be reelected and serve a full second term. How, in the second term, could he further enhance his chances for an eventual above-average, or even near-great, ranking on the historians' periodic ranking of presidential performance? We now know that the first piece of advice from those who knew Clinton would be short and simple: for starters, confine your sexual activities to your wife or do not lie, or both. This avoids impeachment and scandal and clears the way for achievement. The Clinton fresh from reelection at the end of 1996, with another term at hand and contemplating how he might gain everhigher achievement rankings, apparently dismissed that sort of advice, if he heard it. A serious student of the presidency, he knew well that high rankings among presidents come when events give them a crisis—a civil or world war, a depression, or at least some smaller challenge to meet, just as Truman navigated through the dangerous early cold war or LBJ steered through the racial crisis.

We are especially interested in his opportunities and performance as an environmental leader, and to some degree so was Clinton, an insatiable resume builder for whom any opening for a policy success was not to be overlooked. He made good use of executive orders under the Antiquities Act in expanding protected public lands—important but not legend-making achievements. Environmentalists were of several minds about Clinton's record, some coming to the end of his two terms, in the words of James M. Burns and Georgia Sorenson's *Dead Center* (1999), "disenchanted by . . . centrist and weak leadership . . . reduced to thwarting the GOP" in its efforts to brown what had been greened.[75] The only environmental crisis on a major scale Clinton inherited or encountered was global warming—a scientifically complex, conflict-generating, slowly emerging, and widely denied problem on the edges of scientific discussion for a century. It was drawn forward by the discussion of the other atmospheric ailment demanding attention, ozone-layer damage by chlorofluorocarbons, and by the news that the 1980s had been the warmest decade on record, with monster storms, widespread forest fires, and widespread drought. Atmospheric concentration of several greenhouse gases (carbon dioxide receiving the greatest attention) were traced to human activity, especially combustion of fossil fuels. A scientific consensus on the reality of climatic warming and its mostly human causation had formed by the end of the 1980s, along with widespread uncertainty and argument about its likely effects—crop-killing heat and droughts, violent weather events, arctic ice melting, and rising sea levels producing large human refugee flows from low-lying shores and islands. Gore, in *Earth in the Balance*, estimated (with supporting citations where such numbers were obviously speculative) that 10 million of Bangladesh's coastal residents would be displaced in the "next few decades," along with 60 percent of the population of Florida.[76]

By the 1990s a president could assume the public was exposed to a substantial number of stories on global warming. In 2001 a big newspaper in New York City published 508 such stories, more than it devoted to Iraq or Social Security.[77] According to a Gallup poll in 2001, 31 percent of the public believed global warming posed a "serious threat," but 66 percent did not. What should be done, if anything? Some engineers argued for dumping enough iron shavings in the ocean to allow it to absorb green-house gases (GHGs). A more widely held idea was to persuade humans to curb or end the emission of such gases, which suggested an international conference and treaty. One was convened in Kyoto, Japan, in December 1997 to write a protocol requiring all signatory nations to make significant reductions in order to stabilize GHG emissions, with advanced industrial nations in the lead. President Clinton signed the Kyoto Protocol but knew the Senate would refuse to ratify it. The senators unanimously informed him in 1997 they would do so only as long as developing nations (such as giants China and India) were not required to make reductions. Clinton accepted this reality and did not submit the treaty. At the end of his presidency only twenty-nine nations had ratified the Kyoto Protocol.

Clinton liked to talk, late at night or any other time, and he especially liked to talk about how he could continue to expand his political achievement and reputation. He was also a rapid and avid reader, mostly of history and biography, but it is unlikely he knew or had been told by some erudite aide that a bloc of five modern presidents had qualified for extra credit from presidential rankers for their quiet leadership in an almost hidden but vastly important subfield of environmental protection—I will call it population stabilization policy (PSP). If Clinton had been told this, one can readily imagine his appetite for more information on this little-discussed opportunity for president-led innovation. He perhaps remembered that Nixon in 1969 commissioned a population-growth study from a group chaired by one of the Rockefellers and that there had been some sort of political kickback when the report was delivered that made the news. Some historian perhaps told Clinton that Nixon was the fifth of five to go down that population-stabilization-policy path. An impressive heritage, many environmentalists believed.

FDR, we well know, was concerned about resource shortages, but he did not devote any time to human-population-growth worries as a component of the larger conservation problem (as some earlier conservationists had done) because it seemed in his thirteen-year presidency to be solving itself through declining birthrates and the virtual end of immigration. However, global birthrates and larger immigration flows accelerated after World War II, attracting the attention of five presidents from Truman to Nixon (though not in that order) who incrementally and cautiously took the lead in public education and public-policy reform on the demographic dimension of environmental protection. Clinton, as far as we know, did not learn this PSP history at Georgetown University, Yale Law School, or Oxford University. There is evidence that at some time, maybe early in his second term, he may have encountered this story. How did demography—population numbers and how they are trending, with what costs and benefits—get on the agenda of these five presidents? How not! There were 4 million US citizens at the time of George Washington's presidency, 151 million when Truman took the oath, and the numbers mounted on. The global population numbers and trends were even more alarming. Two 1948 best-selling books by William Vogt and Fairfield Osborn, respectively, told the nation where the global numbers were going and their grim implications. Truman did not read these books, as far as we know, in which he would have learned some stunning numbers. The global human population reached 1 billion by Jesus's day, doubled to 2 billion by 1830, accelerated to add a third billion again in 100 years (1930), and a fourth billion in 30 years (1960).

A social change that momentous should come to the attention of society's leaders, including our president. Indeed, it did in 1958, though the pathway to the mind and engagement of Eisenhower was cluttered and difficult. The 1950s was the decade filled with the challenges of the cold war, which all of Washington was intensely preoccupied with winning. How could we win if the impoverished third world was hampered in economic development by relentless population growth? Several members of the Senate Foreign Relations Committee pressed Eisenhower to appoint a special group to study the work of the rudderless military assistance program, to which he appointed Wall Street investor William Draper, who just happened to be close to John D. Rockefeller III, who just happened to be a passionate worrier about population growth and a supporter of birth control, who converted Draper, whose report endorsed an expansion of US foreign aid to include contraceptive technology and education. Eisenhower's first thought about government engagement with population size was negative, and he forcefully rebuffed this suggestion, but Draper and his report were persuasive and launched a change in the tools employed in US foreign aid—"birth control," or "family planning," or other euphemisms. Eisenhower explained his change of mind in a September 1963 article in the *Saturday Evening Post*: "It may be that I was carrying that conviction too far. . . . We should tell [aid-receiving] nations how population growth threatens them and what can be done about it." Just months before this article came out, JFK, responding to arguments from his own State Department, announced his view that population increases "were of serious concern." Foreign-aid legislation under JFK began to include family-planning assistance, and LBJ, pressed by Secretary of State Dean Rusk, added this sentence to his State of the Union Address in 1965: "I will seek new ways to use our knowledge to help deal with the explosion in world population." In 1964, Eisenhower had convinced Truman—who had also changed his mind—to join him in serving as honorary cochairs of Planned Parenthood.

How many presidents had publicly expressed concern about and commissioned studies of global overpopulation and, to a lesser degree, the exercise of reproductive choice (limiting family size) for US women? Three so far, if we do not count Truman's Paley Commission, reporting in 1951 on supplies of raw materials. Congressional leadership was also engaging the global population situation. Senator Ernest Gruening, braver than all of all his colleagues, held Senate hearings in 1965 on birth-control availability in the United States and opened the hearings with a supporting letter from Eisenhower. Gruening expressed the idea that the United States should aim part of its foreign aid toward population stabilization in the third world and also support birth-control access for women in our country. These new population policy impulses were strengthened by the enormous impact of Paul

Ehrlich's 1968 book *The Population Bomb*. As we have seen, the environmental movement quickly took to the idea that curbing population growth was a central key to the protection of nature and learned the I = PAT formula created by Ehrlich and John Holdren: (environmental) impact (I) = population (P) × affluence (A) × technology (T). Also remember writer C. P. Snow's chant before an Earth Day crowd in 1970: "Peace! Food! No more people than the earth can take!"

One more president was then added, like the others cautiously nervous that "overpopulation" concerns might be politically hazardous. In 1969 newly elected President Nixon's aide Daniel P. Moynihan convinced his boss to take what could have been the largest (yet) presidential step on the population-growth question. Nixon agreed to appoint (as we have seen) the Commission on Population Growth and the American Future, chaired by Rockefeller, and sent a special population message to Congress.

Now we count five presidents who cautiously explored a new strategy for winning the global struggle against communism and for environmental protection—restraining population growth. The Rockefeller report carried a line that would have been useful for to-be-president George W. Bush: "A new vision is needed—a vision that recognizes man's unity with nature." The report pivoted on the memorable recommendation that the "Nation welcome and plan for a stabilized population." The report expanded the focus to include immigration, which the study found to its surprise was bringing 400,000 new people a year into the country (this was an undercount), or 25 percent of our annual growth. Clearly, a stable population would require lower levels of immigration, a discovery that came just seven years after Congress passed a major immigration expansion in 1965.

Then Nixon, believing himself threatened with political reprisals by the Catholic hierarchy anchored overseas, decided "birth control" might be politically toxic from the point of view of a significant portion of the US electorate, declined to receive the report, and fatally undermined his own leadership claims. The report was widely circulated and discussed, but not from the bully pulpit. Five presidents had warned about population growth. Soon there were six. Nixon, the fifth, backed away on political grounds, then in April 1974 ordered a study of the national-security implications of population growth. When the report, *National Security Study Memorandum 200*, arrived in the Oval Office in 1975 the president (the sixth to approve of population control) behind the desk was Ford, who endorsed the report findings and called for the United States to exert world leadership in population control, including stabilization of our own population by 2000.

Quickly came the seventh president to care about this issue, when Carter in May 1977 launched a joint CEQ/State Department study, published at the end of 1980 as *Global 2000*, with the memorable announcement, "Environmental problems do not stop at national boundaries," and this summary:

If present trends continue, the world in 2000 will be more crowded and more vulnerable to disruption than the world we live in now. Serious stresses involving population, resources, and environment are clearly visible ahead. Despite greater material output, the world's people will be poorer in many ways than they are today.[78]

The report offered the US government's best projections on population worldwide as of 2000, an immense effort of data gathering and extrapolation leaving no time, the authors decided, for policy recommendations that in any event would rest in the hands of the world's independent governments. "Action" was urgently needed to preserve the "carrying capacity of the earth." But no reader could miss the point that population—the first topic addressed—was the basic driver of the shortages and "global problems of alarming proportions" ahead.

Now it was six times, in the years 1958–1981, that an alarm had been sounded from the White House concerning the triad some called by its fancy French term the *problematique* or "problem cluster"—population, resources, and the environment. If Clinton was told of this historic seven-president agreement and public-education project, one can imagine that he would have been a touch envious and sensed a leadership opportunity. He could be the eighth to take the lead in educating policy makers and the public on the costly implications of what until lately had always been taken for granted as a good thing—global (including US) population growth in perpetuity. If he needed encouragement, it could have come close at hand from at least two of his top green lieutenants who had frequently written on the hazards intensified by global population expansion. The two were the president's science adviser, Holdren, who had been in his academic days a frequent writer (often jointly with Ehrlich) on the hazards of global overpopulation, and that fellow down the hall, Vice President Gore.

It is thus easy to imagine some lieutenant(s) advising Clinton to continue the tradition and become the eighth president to form a working group to explore policy responses to the population-growth component of environmental protection and national security. Someone near Clinton may have nudged him in this direction. The truth seems more bureaucratic than inspirational. In Clinton's early months, someone in the State Department discovered the United States was party to an agreement reached by all signatories to the 1992 Rio Earth Summit to report in 1997 on progress made toward sustainable development (SD) and to have national sustainable-development strategies in place by 2002. It was either keep that pledge or make a fuss, so Clinton signed an executive order in 1993 establishing the President's Council on Sustainable Development, a collection of some twenty-five business executives, government officials, and community leaders whose assignment was to "advise the President on sustainable development," much less than the Earth Summit dreamers had in mind.

What, exactly, was SD? A 1987 UN Commission chaired by Norwegian prime minister Gro Bruntland had defined SD, in its book *Our Common Future*, as "development that meets the needs of the present without compromising the ability of future generations to meet their own needs." The phrase caught on as a concise and "balanced" statement of goals for human societies, with a vocabulary of "fairness" and "sharing" that appealed to those on the left and younger generations. The phrase multiplied rapidly during the 1990s. Communities, states, companies, philanthropic organizations, and social reform groups declared that they were sustainable or intended to be by some date certain. Seattle established an Office of Sustainability under pressure from citizens' group Sustainable Seattle, and when that city's mayor issued a call for other cities to follow, six responded at once; 250 cities were officially engaged in sustainability planning by 2006, the number still rising. Sustainability institutes proliferated on university campuses, such as the University of California–Santa Barbara, boasting thirty-five student organizations working on sustainability. Sustainable high schools in Oregon built hay-bale–lined classrooms to control air quality (yes, a strange idea). Residents of the Island of Santa Catalina off the California coast, running out of water in 2011, found that their search for a consultant on the water problem turned up an impressive firm called Sustainable Communities, based in Colorado. Sustainability was a full-service term of many uses and at the outset had no enemies. Yet even the fans of sustainability admitted it was a fuzzy term much in need of clarification.

Clinton had launched such an exploration with his Council on Sustainable Development. Task forces were formed, meetings were held, several task force reports were published, and we can assume advice was given to the president at some time during the six years. A closing national town meeting was held in Detroit May 2–5, 1999, and a final report published (*Toward a Sustainable America*), presenting ten goals from a "healthy environment" through "stewardship" and "education," with the fourth goal being "conservation of nature" and the eighth being simply "population," followed by the seven words, "Move toward stabilization of U.S. population." The media did not know what to make of this list of good things the nation was urged to want—though the council website expressed a desire to "catalyze a national movement" that would commit all governments, federal to local to state, and all communities and stakeholders to "sustainability planning." News outlets gave the rollout of the final report of the sustainability project one day of skimpy coverage, then moved on.

No one saw Clinton's council assignment as the writing of an eighth chapter of a slowly moving book project undertaken by a string of presidents starting midcentury. They knew nothing of their predecessors and, perhaps, mercifully so. It turns out to be no easy thing for seven of our presidents over a span of nearly three decades to sponsor the writing of pieces of a new global story (lacking a title) of which the main theme was surging human numbers, depleted resources, and endangered environments. Each drafting committee was only dimly aware (if at all) of the chapters (reports) that had gone before, and seven chapters by multiple authors on a gloomy topic is not a formula for large sales and broad social discussion. The "What is to be done?" policy question occupied some of the seven reports more than others and one (Carter's) not at all.

Some excitement internal to US administrations, however, can be seen or sensed as we look over this fragmented, eye-opening, half-century effort to discern the future. Rockefeller's report to Nixon insisted US population growth must be curbed, which turns out to mean limiting immigration because it accounts for one-quarter of the nation's continued growth. This, along with family-planning support, drew internal and some external dissent. The end-of-century report of Clinton's council was laced with internal divisions on the "sensitive issue" of population and immigration, reluctantly acknowledged to be connected. Council staff (or the White House) at first attempted to prevent discussion of population entirely by assigning it to the dark limbo of no task force. Some sort of internal complaint forced the formation, a year after the task forces were launched, of the Task Force on Population and Consumption. That group's separate report, presumably read by few, pointed out that legal and illegal immigration together were the source of one-third of US population growth, which is "now at an all-time high." What to recommend? Because "reducing immigration levels is a necessary part of population stabilization and the drive for sustainability," we recommend "policies that reduce illegal immigration." What of legal immigration? This was a sensitive issue. This language may be found in the slim report of the Task Force on Population and Consumption. The final Council on Sustainable Development report recommended the United States "move toward the stabilization of population," a puny commitment with no goals or timetables contradicted by other language stating that the world and US populations "will grow," but what "must not grow" are "pollution, waste, and poverty." So despite the decision of the late-formed Task Force on Population and Consumption to recommend population stabilization through immigration reduction, the council report at the end omitted such words and ideas.

In any event, with this 1999 report, Clinton had joined the other seven presidents. He may have regretted it because it generated language vulnerable to criticism. But it was child's play for Slick Willie to express thanks for the council's good thoughts on what must be done to achieve sustainability and avoid the questions on immigration limitation and population stabilization unwisely raised (in his view) by a rogue task force. He was well practiced at ignoring immigration-reform recommendations—a subject he timorously treated as a third rail when Representative Jordan visited the White House in 1995 to deliver to the president the report of her national Commission on Immigration Reform. He said he agreed with her report recommending substantial cuts in immigration, which he did not. Her death of cancer in 1996 allowed Clinton to ignore her commission as well as his own council. So the council was thanked for its thoughts on moving the nation toward sustainability, its peripheral recommendations for population stabilization through illegal immigration reduction ignored to sink from sight.[79]

Had the population growth problem left the stage because the numbers had finally begun trending down? On the contrary, global population growth was churning up a steep twentieth-century climb that would continue—5.2 billion by 1990, projected to rise to between 7.8 and 12.5 billion by 2050. As for the demographic trajectory of the United States, it had behaved erratically as the twentieth century unfolded, confounding projections and predictions. Fertility rates—one of the drivers of population size—declined steadily from 1900 to midcentury, experienced an unexpected "baby boom" from the 1940s to the 1960s, and then resumed a decline to the total fertility rate of 2.1 in 1972, allowing demographers to announce the coming of a stable population in two generations if the second, big driver of population size, immigration, remained at the low numbers experienced from 1914 to the late 1960s. The expansion of legal immigration signed into law by LBJ in 1965, with lax border and interior enforcement, allowed the annual immigration flow to climb past 1 million through the 1970s and 1980s. When Clinton set his council to work in 1993 searching for sustainability, the population problems warned of years earlier by Vogt and Osborn (1948) and Ehrlich (1967) were at record-high levels. Between 1970 and 2000, the US population soared by 70 million people, or 33 percent.

This was very big demographic news, unwelcome to many environmentalists. It seemed a cruel turn of affairs when US families had by 1970 voluntarily brought their average family size down to parents plus 2.1 children—or "replacement-level fertility"—only to have these historic gains erased by immigration expansion signed into law by politicians and the illegal immigration permitted by them. Several environmental groups made room in their lobbying for immigration reduction. Zero Population Growth (ZPG) in the late 1970s devoted one full-time senior staffer to coordinating a campaign to cut back on immigration, and the Sierra Club testified before the Hesburgh Commission on Immigration Reform in 1980 that immigration policy was, in effect, an expansive population-growth policy. At the end of that decade the Sierra Club leadership urged Congress to tie immigration admissions to the goal of population stabilization.

However, these and other environmental organizations were feeling pressure from liberal staff and funders who were uneasy in any role as immigration reformers lest they be charged with racism, inadequate commitment to "diversity," and involvement in politically incorrect activities. By the end of the 1980s the leadership of these and other (not all) environmental groups ended their lobbying and policy support for lower levels of immigration. Clinton was not yet governor of Arkansas when environmentalists disappointed with the ZPG and Sierra Club abandonment of immigration restriction took the lead in creating the Federation for American Immigration Reform (FAIR, 1979–), hoping to curb the large numbers of legal immigrants permitted by the 1965 immigration law and the growing numbers of illegal immigrants virtually allowed to enter and remain in the United States. The base of this new immigration restriction movement was composed of the same elements as in the era of TR—environmentalists, allies of workers hurt by foreign labor competition, and a sprinkling of conservative intellectuals concerned about national cohesion. The post-1960s buildup of both legal and illegal immigration energized immigration reformers, many of whom were environmentalists, and began to drive a wedge inside some green organizations, the Sierra Club and ZPG foremost among them. As Clinton's council fended off the "p" word (population) and the "I" word (immigration) in the 1990s, the Sierra Club's staff was dropping immigration restriction from its agenda.

The inner history of Clinton's Council on Sustainable Development and its fumbling of the core question of population growth will one day be illuminated by memos and emails in not-yet-opened boxes at the William J. Clinton Presidential Library in Little Rock. Clinton on more than one occasion had proven himself timid and fearful when population and immigration issues surfaced, and he may have been behind the sanitizing of the council's reports. Clinton, busy with Kyoto Protocol details, turned over the direction of the council to Gore, who was preoccupied with positioning himself for a 2000 presidential run when he would not want his environmental passions or the administration's association with "population-control" language to unnecessarily offend any voters. Whoever carried the message that the council was not to endorse or even mention the population size/immigration connection, it has to be seen as a Clinton decision and stands as a presidential setback to the ongoing environmentalist project.

In the years from Reagan to Clinton something innovative on the green side had been happening within national security circles. Where did you find the government-employed professional environmentalists in Washington, D.C., as the 1980s began? In the EPA, the National Park Service (NPS), the US Forest Service (USFS), certain congressional staff—anyone can start and extend the list. At the end of the 1990s? In those places, but one has now added the Pentagon, Defense Department, State Department, National Security Council, CIA, and military academics. The rapid greening of the skill base and interests of the nation's national-security professionals inside and outside government was arguably the big environmental policy news of the last two decades of the century.

A leading scholar on this expansion of the influence of environmental knowledge and perspectives in the field of national security, Richard A. Matthew of the University of California–Irvine, dates the birth announcement to the 1994 publication in the *Atlantic Monthly* of the immensely influential article "The Coming Anarchy," by journalist Robert Kaplan.[80] The root cause of failing states and social conflict in Africa, the Middle East, and elsewhere, Kaplan argued, was increasingly environmental and resource degradation, replacing the cold war as a major threat to US security. Other national security specialists—Lester Brown, Richard Ullman, Jessica Mathews, and Norman Myers made the case that environmental and resource monitoring was underused intelligence deserving of more attention from our national-security apparatus. Urged on by Gore, Secretary Christopher gave a "corner-turning speech" at Stanford University in 1996 insisting on the importance of environmental knowledge and initiatives in formulating US security policies. The greening spread into the military as Congress began to finance base and hazardous-waste cleanup, land restoration, and recycling and to emphasize strict fuel efficiency. Gore and Clinton, neither with military experience, were relentless sponsors of this multifaceted expansion of interest in the environmental dimension of security policy and national defense planning. Clinton, in a speech at the National Academy of Sciences in 1994, quoted both Kaplan and Thomas Homer-Dixon, a leading writer on future "water wars," ecological collapse, overpopulation, and cross-border pollution as predictors of both intrastate and interstate violence.

Clinton and Gore, the "green hope," had in eight years made no historic "legacy" contribution in the last decade of the century—unless one justifiably acknowledges what Clinton call his impressive "land legacy"—50 million acres of newly protected public lands capped off in December 2000 with the largest nature preserve in US history in the Northwestern Hawaiian Islands Coral Reef Ecosystem Reserve, sprawling over nearly three-quarters of the nation's coral reefs—a strong ending.[81]

9

If you are against a dam you are for a river.
— David Brower

Vice President Albert Gore was nominated by the Democrats to be their party's presidential candidate in 2000, and on November 5 he received 543,896 more popular votes (for 48.4 percent of the total) than his Republican opponent, George W. Bush (at 47.9 percent). A complicated and contested recount of votes in Florida led to a Supreme Court decision in December that Bush had won the electoral vote and thus the election.

George W. Bush was the first son of Barbara and George H. W. Bush and, with the exception of the war hero part, followed a similar educational and career path as his father—public and private schools in Houston, then Phillips Academy in New England, higher education at Yale and Harvard Business School, brief service in the Texas Air National Guard, marriage to Laura Welch, business ventures in oil and baseball in Texas, elected governor in 1994. A mediocre though popular student, Bush described his adult reading habits as inclined toward political biography, but he rarely mentioned particular books or anything the books taught him. As a young man he was a hard drinker, helped to stop the habit shortly after his fortieth birthday by his wife's skillful intervention and his religious faith—a story that reflects well on both Bushes and had a second benefit of being a political asset.

He was raised in the two West Texas towns of Odessa and Midland, places he fondly described in his memoir *Decision*

Points as similar towns subjected to "frequent dust storms" where "native trees did not exist" and the "ground was flat, dry, and dusty." More important to the Bushes, "beneath it (Midland) sat a sea of oil."[1] Young George rode bikes on the treeless streets and played baseball, and his memoir finds him out of doors only when jogging. He said nothing in the brief account of his youth in West Texas about water, as in lakes, rivers, creeks, or even the lack of them. He had no interest in the outdoor hobbies of many affluent Texas males—hunting, fishing, hiking, horseback riding. Yet later in life there emerged a limited and trendy conservationist side to Bush, or to Laura. His speechwriter David Frum recalls the president's irritation at finding lamps left on after meetings in the Map Room and grumping when noticing brightly lit vacant offices in the Executive Office Building. The home he and Laura, who may have been substantially behind this, built on their Crawford ranch property reused all bathwater, grass was replaced with western wild grasses, and the ranch vehicles ran on propane. Frum referred to this side of Bush not as environmentalism but "ancestral Puritanism."[2]

Bush lost a congressional contest in 1978 and then ran successfully for governor in 1994, his agenda a cluster of unfocused reform proposals in education, welfare, and law enforcement. Environmentalists in Texas gave him a dismally low ranking over the course of his two terms (1994–2000), unimpressed with his campaign brags that he had signed a law (sponsored by others) providing a subsidy for wind-powered electricity.

If we ask why young Bush pursued the presidency, there seem two contradictory answers, each containing truth. He ran, like his father, as a Bush, that is, for no particular reason other than a family heritage of running for ever-higher offices with an intention to serve honorably, enjoy power, and relish the spotlight. There were larger ambitions inside his party and what was called US conservatism as a political and social movement. Barry Goldwater first mobilized the Sunbelt Republicans whose mission was to rebuild the Republican Party with western leadership focused on the goal of reconfiguring US politics and uprooting the New Deal. Bush's father answered that call, even though he proved to lack Ronald Reagan's abilities to communicate the mission.

Could this second George Bush be shaped to be the man to complete the grand project launched by Goldwater and Reagan—making the Republican Party the majority and a reformist instrument of ending the New Deal? The

330 | CHAPTER NINE

2000 campaign did not define Bush very well before the national electorate. A sunbelt, probusiness Republican, he described himself as a "compassionate conservative," which he explained in his acceptance speech at the GOP convention in 2000 by combining two phrases—"big government is not the answer" with the "alternative to bureaucracy is not indifference."

His narrow election victory over Gore combined with general economic prosperity and the absence, at first, of any sort of recognized crisis, foreign or domestic, to give President Bush no mandate of any kind for his diffuse agenda. This new chief executive, who was known well only in Texas and within the inner circles of the Republican Party, gave his short Inaugural Address, surprisingly eloquent (Bush had hired good speechwriters), though marked in delivery by touches of verbal awkwardness that would stay with him always. His remarks on environmental matters were confined to two sentences pledging attention to the safe topics of the Land and Water Conservation Fund and the national parks.[3] During the campaign he had made his father's error with slightly different wording, declaring that he would be our first "eco-friendly" president. A few weeks earlier he had made senior environmental appointments, drawing people primarily from business backgrounds or conservative think tanks. The secretary of the Interior Department, Gale Norton, had close ties with James Watt and the rightist Mountain States Legal Foundation. The new secretary of energy, Spencer Abraham, was on record as favoring the abolition of the department he was chosen to head. Vice President Richard "Dick" Cheney, who most recently had worked for Halliburton, an oil-services corporation, chaired the Energy Task Force appointed by Bush on his ninth day in office. The media gave this task force, asked to draft an energy plan, much (thin and arms-length) coverage because its agenda, membership, and consultants were "secret," yet known to include a heavy representation of "stakeholders," which to Cheney meant oil companies. The press attention was justified because the group's report, delivered to Bush in May, embodied the core policy ideas on energy shaped and nurtured from the days of Reagan and Watt. The Energy Plan was the latest version of a long-standing GOP hope to end US dependence on foreign oil with expanded production of fossil fuels and nuclear energy at home. The tools would be industry-favorable tax incentives, regulatory relief from the Clean Air Act (1970–) controls over harmful atmospheric dumping, and storage of nuclear wastes.

The role of conservation? Cheney expressed the administration view.

"Conservation might be a sign of personal virtue, but it is not a sufficient basis for a sound, comprehensive energy policy." Not sufficient, he believed, and not even one useful tool among many. Bush had his own way of putting this conviction: "You cannot conserve yourself to energy independence."[4] The goal of the plan was hugely ambitious—to dismantle or neuter the apparatus of environmental and energy policy going back to Jimmy Carter's 1970s—terminating or weakening regulations of that era; opening up new sources of fossil fuels in western public lands and through mountaintop removal in West Virginia and Tennessee; resuming the expansion of nuclear energy; and on the foreign/military policy side, projecting US strength abroad, especially in the Persian Gulf region. That Bush established his Energy Task Force on his ninth day in office suggests the media was right to sense a major policy departure and to press for access or leaks. Something of large importance was afoot in the name of energy policy, designed and guided from the White House. It was all secret, but not really. Veteran energy-policy watchers in Washington, D.C., discerned the stakes. Representative Edward Markey of Maine called the Bush plan a "Trojan Horse to take health and environmental laws passed in the last generation off the books."[5]

The Energy Task Force was an early and leading example of the administration's embrace of "administrative presidency" tactics in recognition of the discovery of all recent presidents of both parties that "passing a law" had become extraordinarily difficult. Environmental and other policy under Bush would follow a familiar trend, frequently being shaped in the White House in the form of budgetary cuts in fiscal 2002, 8 percent reductions for environmental programs (the largest for any sector), and executive orders generally easing clean-air, water-waste-disposal, and endangered-species regulation in response to industry complaints or suggestions.

The Kyoto Protocol, which Bush called "fatally flawed" in early 2001 as he withdrew the United States from the discussions, was indeed flawed primarily by failing to impose any greenhouse gas (GHG) limits on China and India, but withdrawal from the process generated justified criticism abroad and at home. Bush also began his administration by denying climate change was "real" and human-made. Most poll results most of the time showed a public ignorant and unengaged on this invisible international problem clothed in scientific language. One study found that only 20 percent knew of Bush's Kyoto decision, 28 percent of his reversal on carbon dioxide.[6] This suited members of the administration whose central thrust on energy was exactly wrong—expanded consumption of fossil fuels. Bush released a skimpy, two-paragraph message on Earth Day, April 21, 2001, containing these vague words: "We have made progress. . . . There is much more to do."[7]

It was not clear at the end of summer 2001 what would become of the administration's plan on energy policy, then tangled up on the Hill. Its environmental implications seemed wholly negative, and green organizations and critics generated a small din of complaint. Bush responded as had other presidents under green attack, visiting national parks, putting in motion executive orders that would create four national monuments and the world's largest marine reserve northwest of the Hawaiian Islands in the Pacific Ocean, and having his White House spokesman, Tony Snow, cite in 2007 these actions along with Bush's earlier decisions to slightly increase park budgets as a sign that the president was, like Teddy Roosevelt (TR), "keenly committed" to conservationism and environmentalism from the start.[8]

Then his presidency, and the history of the United States, was decisively changed by the terrorist attacks in New York and Washington, D.C., on September 11, 2001. Bush began to refer to himself as the "war president," leading the nation in a "war on terror" in which the enemy terrorists were located in parts of the Middle East and in what he called the "axis of evil"—Iran, Iraq, and North Korea. Combat operations—new wars—began in Afghanistan and Iraq.

The war on terror is not our story, except that it conferred popular approval on Commander in Chief Bush sufficient to make possible passage of some of his legislative proposals, such as Medicare prescription-drug coverage (2003), education reform ("No Child Left Behind," 2002), and five tax cuts (2001–2007). These were flawed in different ways and shared the result of enlarging the deficit but were touted by the White House as presidential achievements, paving the way for his close reelection in 2004 and doubling his time in office. Terrorist attacks had given Bush what he entirely lacked before September 11, 2001—a purpose for his high office and its powers.

Even wartime presidents daily engage domestic channels of policy in which decisions must be made—among them in the Bush years a looming Social Security system bankruptcy, an ominous and growing federal deficit, large-scale illegal immigration, and financial collapse in the banking and auto industries. Environmental/natural-resource issues sometimes pushed forward, including that increasingly central one someone called the problem from hell—climate change.

Bush came close to having no personal interest in any environmental issue, with the exception of energy resources, where he had a lifetime devotion to oil production with coal just behind. Yet no part of the arid western
landscape where he grew up, none of the nonhuman creatures living on, in,
and through it seemed to stir his curiosity or sympathy. He lived most of his
life in the Southwest, a region littered with the ruins of civilizations driven
into extinction by severe and sustained droughts. His early presidency coin-
cided with damaging wildfires stretching across a drought-stricken belt of
states from New Mexico to Colorado to southern Oregon, blackened landscapes he visited in July 2002. Yet he left no record of any personal interest in
water issues and drought cycles in that overpopulated region or anywhere
else.

Bush's father left him one example of environmental policy activism—
the Clean Air Act of 1990. Young Bush accepted without argument his father's assumption of the undesirability of the toxic chemicals spewed into
the country's air by utility and industrial smokestacks, trucks, and cars. In
his 2000 campaign he recalled the first Bush president's successful sponsorship of clean-air legislation meant to streamline and prune preexisting protection of public health from toxic elements. On the stump, young Bush
promised only minor and incremental improvements, requiring power
plants to reduce four emissions harmful to public health, including carbon
dioxide—and then changed his mind as his administration started to work
on "clear skies" legislation and realized that he was almost sure to lose the
electoral votes of at least coal-dependent Ohio and West Virginia if he did
not yield on carbon dioxide, which was also a greenhouse gas. He thus waf-
fled on climate change while crafting legislation on familiar pollutants, and
polls showed him losing ground on environmental stewardship. He reluctantly acknowledged a climate change problem in February 2002 when he
endorsed more climate research, which seemed far too timid a response to
environmentalists and to the growing ranks of convinced climate scientists.

In the absence of presidential leadership, neither political party on Capitol Hill attempted to muster a majority on climate-change policy. In the resultant policy vacuum, state and local governments began to pass their own
GHG regulations—California governor Arnold Schwarzenegger declared,
"The debate is over. We know the science, we see the threat, and we know
the time for action is now." He signed a law requiring that state's emissions
by 2020 to be lower than levels of 1990.[9] By 2007 thirty-six states had "cli-

mate action plans," and mayors in 522 cities had signed their agreement to the Kyoto Protocols. Such uneven regulatory proliferation was the last thing wanted by businesses selling across state lines and left the United States out of the conversation of the body of nations that had ratified the Kyoto Protocol and sought broader and more effective consensus. A few months before his reelection in 2004 Bush moved to a more positive position and pledged that his administration would join a UN-led effort to reach some global accord, if China and India joined the effort. In 2004 this would have been an admirable position to take by the head of the nation annually producing one-third of the world's GHG emissions. Bush apparently recognized that scientific and public opinion seemed to be shifting toward the view that global warming was "real" and substantially human-caused. "Mr. President, is global warming real?" a reporter asked him on May 13, 2008. Finally, no reference to scientific doubts. "Yes, it is real."[10]

Many close watchers of the politics of climate change detect a "tipping point," the title of a best-selling 2000 book by Malcolm Gladwell in 2007, in the long-simmering discussion of atmospheric warming. That year held a number of opinion-changing events. Gore narrated a low-budget documentary, An Inconvenient Truth, described by critics as a "man, a message, and a scary slide show." The emotional film won an Emmy Award and two Oscars, and Gore shared a Nobel Prize that year with the climate scientists on the UN Intergovernmental Panel on Climate Change (IPCC). That organization rang the alarm bell in 2001 that global warming was "likely," then declared in 2007 that it was "unequivocal." "Suddenly what had seemed to many an abstract and remote danger took on the foreboding aspect of an existential threat," said Newsweek in a special issue, "Save the Planet," in April 2007. The main story there was not so much new scientific information but a sea change of opinion not only among members of the public but on behalf of many corporate deniers. Environmentalist Bill McKibben urged a goal to focus public attention—it was 350 parts per million (PPM) of carbon dioxide in the atmosphere, which he acknowledged to be too high but had been urged by the respected James Hansen, the National Aeronautical and Space Administration (NASA) chief climatologist, who thought it could be reached from today's 450 PPM. Preindustrial levels had been 275.[11]

As a youngster, Gore had been given a lifetime passion by reading a book—by Rachel Carson. His documentary had an equal or surpassing effect on the young. When I saw the film in 2007, two teenage girls sobbed audibly at the sight of a baby arctic polar bear weary of swimming and unable to cling to a melting, shrinking piece of ice. The melting was human-caused, the film told us.

President Bush, perhaps unhappy with his ranking by the League of Conservation Voters as the "most anti-environmental president in our nation's history," or taking note of the Gallup poll on Earth Day 2007 ranking the "environment" as a public concern ahead of terrorism, health care, and Social Security, heralded the 2007 IPCC report as a "landmark." As Bush's speechwriters prepared his State of the Union Address in 2007, the CEOs of ten major corporations appealed to him to set a federal ceiling on GHGs to end the policy uncertainty. He had only one year left in the White House, now free of reelection concerns. The Kyoto Protocol had now been ratified by enough countries to go into effect, requiring member industrialized nations to reduce their emissions 5 percent from 1990 levels by 2012. The United Nations estimated these goals would not be met, and experts predicted GHGs would climb 50 percent above 1990 levels by 2050.[12] Bush in June of that year, apparently recognizing that public and business opinion had shifted, asked the fifteen countries with the largest GHG emissions to meet and adopt a goal sufficient to "control" their releases. The European Union applauded, but the governments of China and India, or at least the peoples, had not seen the Gore documentary, had not "tipped," and nothing came of the president's effort at leadership, though some months later he committed the US government to join a UN-led process to produce a new global climate plan. When former New Jersey governor Christie Todd Whitman resigned from her leadership of the Environmental Protection Agency (EPA) in 2003, citing her unhappiness at being "often at odds" with the White House, Bush appointed a scientist with strong environmental credentials to fill the post. The administration had, sort of, turned in a green direction at the end.

On the sixth day of Bush's last month in office, he designated 195,280 square miles of uninhabited Pacific islands, reefs, and atolls near Samoa as marine national monuments—the only conservation move not thought of by TR. Yet even as some presidential staff in the West Wing were working on marine national monuments in the far Pacific, others were making the last-minute gifts to oil companies in the spirit of "drill baby, drill" by opening oil leases for auction bidding near three national parks in Utah.[13]

"As George Bush's last year in office comes to a conclusion," wrote Harvard professor and six-year senior staffer in the Office of Management and Budget (OMB) John D. Graham, "critics declared that our forty-third president was a failure" from every angle.[14] This oft-heard judgment was also reflected in the public opinion polls. The Gallup approval rating in his last year dropped to a sixty-year low of 28 percent, marking him as the second-most unpopular president in the modern era (Harry Truman sank lower during the Korean War). Knowing that Truman's low standing with the public in his day has moved upward among historians as time and archival access work their revisions, some historians remind us that the book on Bush (and all presidents) is not closed. However, there is an impressive record of error and deficiency on his watch—the bungled military occupation of Iraq, the ill-advised invasion of Afghanistan, surging public debt, mismanaged handling of emergency relief during and after Hurricane Katrina struck New Orleans in August 2005, unpopular proposals for mass amnesty for illegal immigrants, and reinvigorated "imperial presidency" expressed in bold (mis?)uses of executive power, such as creation of detention centers at Guantanamo Bay, Cuba, and in secret locations in the Middle East where suspected terrorists termed "enemy combatants" were subjected to "enhanced interrogation" (i.e., torture) beyond the reach of US law.

The second Bush's environmental record we have reviewed is memorably bleak, including obstructionist leadership on climate change, a White House–based contempt for science, a habit of looking the other way on offshore oil exploitation, unrestrained mountaintop removal, and the new "fracking" technology used in and after the 1990s to exploit oil-shale deposits in virtually half the states. Environmental policy analysts Byron Daynes and Glen Sussman have compiled an Index of Greenness comparing three presidents—the two Bushes and Bill Clinton. Adjusting for years in office, George H. W. Bush made four times the number of references to environmental issues in public statements as his son, and Clinton surpassed both. Clinton set aside more than 11 million acres, whereas the combined (nonoceanic) acreage set aside by the two Bush administrations was 680,000 acres. Bush the son was more sparing with environmentally protective executive orders than his father and, by a wide margin, Clinton. The "environmental presidency" of the older Bush "never really emerged," and the "eco-friendly" approach promised by the younger Bush "was not reflected in his environmental agenda."[15]

BARACK OBAMA

The Democratic Party in August 2008 conferred its nomination for president on a forty-seven-year-old junior US senator from Illinois (he had served in Washington, D.C., for only four years). On November 4, 2008, he was elected with 52.9 percent of the popular ballots and 332 electoral votes against 206 for his opponent, former prisoner of war and respected veteran Senator John McCain. Obama was inaugurated as the forty-fourth president on January 20, 2009. "Who is this guy?" many asked of this new, meteoric figure in US politics.

Barack Hussein Obama was born in 1961 in Honolulu, Hawaii, to a Caucasian anthropologist mother and a Kenyan economist father who not long after his son's birth left Hawaii. Young Barack (called Barry until he began college in California) was raised, in turns, by his mother and grandparents. For a five-year period he joined his mother in Indonesia, where she remarried and had career opportunities. He then returned to Honolulu for the advantages of the best precollege education, attending Punahou School, where he was a B student. He began his college years at Occidental College in Los Angeles, and was graduated from Columbia University and Harvard Law School, where his selection as president (their odd term for editor in chief) of the *Harvard Law Review* was hailed as elevating the first "African American" to that position. This terminology was politically but not biologically correct because Obama was of mixed blood, once termed "mulatto" in the English-speaking world. The Hawaiian term for this, *hapa*, was not known in the mainland United States.

After law school Obama worked briefly for a firm in New York, moved to Chicago to engage in church-based social work, which he called community organizing, married law school classmate Michelle Robinson, and settled his family in the Hyde Park section of the lake city. He also taught constitutional law as a lecturer at the University of Chicago. Those who knew him tend to agree that he was, in the words of biographer David Mendell, an "extraordinarily ambitious, competitive man with persuasive charm." "He's always wanted to be president," said close friend Valerie Jarrett.[16] He was elected to the Illinois Senate in 1997, served three terms, and won a seat in the US Senate in 2004. He gave a mesmerizing speech before a large national audience at the Democratic National Convention in July 2004. "The reaction to his speech was overwhelming," wrote two historians. "He was now a national celebrity and began to build the helpers for the presidential run he seems to have been pondering for some time."[17]

Obama's national exposure was enhanced by two memoir-style books. The first, *Dreams from My Father* (1995), was an account of his upbringing and his search for a racial identity and mission in the United States. It drew modest sales. The second, *The Audacity of Hope* (2006), was a call for a new national politics rising above bitter partisanship to "begin the process of changing our politics and our civic life." He admitted that he did not "know exactly how to do it. . . . In this book I suggest in broad strokes the path I believe we should follow."[18]

There was a national audience for such a book, such an author, and such a combination. It at once became a best seller, attracting praise for its author, called by the chair of the National Endowment for the Arts, Rocco Landesman, the "most powerful memoirist since Julius Caesar."[19] Chicago newspaper columnist Clarence Page saw a political vacuum ready to be filled by a leader of African ancestry articulating his social unity message: "The whole country right now is looking for that kind of a come-together kind of feeling."[20] "You are uniquely suited for these times," campaign adviser David Axelrod told Obama in the fall of 2006 as his presidential run geared up. "No one within our party is as well positioned to rekindle our lost idealism . . . and pick up the mantle of change."[21]

This was early daydreaming from the inside because Obama "had yet to propose anything philosophically new" in his books, Mendell pointed out. He was a "wiry, intense, out-of-nowhere state legislator with an arresting story and a gauzy vision," in the view of journalist Joseph Lelyveld.[22] Yet Obama's fuzzy promises of "change you can believe in" moved many voters, especially the young. With his message combining multiculturalism and optimism and his attractive image, Obama outlasted chief Democratic rival Hillary Clinton in the run through the Democratic primaries and then in November won a solid victory (365 to 173 electoral votes) over McCain. "He had come from nowhere," observed Jonathan Alter, the "fastest, farthest journey in modern American political history . . . largely by himself."[23]

McCain had a substantial environmental legislative record and, compared with other Republicans, a faintly green one. Obama's record was virtually nonexistent in state office, where he focused on racial and urban issues. As a US senator he briefly had a position on an environmental committee in which he had no real interests and on which his voting record was made skimpy by frequent trips home to Chicago.

It says something about the length of Reagan's shadow that the presidential election of 2008 was the first since 1976 in which environmentalists had something positive to say about both candidates, though almost all tilted toward Obama and against the party of former presidents Bush and Bush. Both candidates in 2008, recognizing that public opinion on climate change had become more concerned, acknowledged that human-caused climate change "is real and urgent." Both seemed open to energy policies that induced cuts in heat-trapping gases, differing on methods. The Obama campaign's white papers for media consumption were long and enthusiastic lists of promises and reflected a strong attraction to energy issues. The League of Conservation Voters complained with good reason that in the presidential debates and other major interviews of candidates by five top television news anchors, only 8 of their more than 3,000 questions mentioned global warming, reflecting the candidates' agreement not to focus on the issue.[24]

After Election Day, Obama's attention shifted to appointments and plan making, and thirty major environmental organizations were invited to send in their suggestions. From Washington-savvy environmentalists Obama informally earned approval for his choices of who would share his administrative powers—Carol Browner as "climate czar," Lisa Jackson as head of the EPA, Nobel Prize–winning physicist Steven Chu as secretary of energy. A "green dream team," some called his choices. Still wondering what sort of environmentalist this new president was (or was not), I started by reading his two memoirs.

Obama lived most of his growing-up years in Honolulu, on the leeward and more densely urbanized side of the Island of Oahu. Judging by his account, the geography and climate of the place made no great impression on him; life in Honolulu (or Jakarta, where he lived for five years) never seemed to pivot on island landscape or wildlife but overwhelmingly on individuals and his urban activities with them—his mother, grandparents, younger sister, and schoolmates. He and biographers tell of basketball games, long walks through the city, movies seen, hanging out at Mr. Burger's Drive-In, dabbling in beer, cocaine, marijuana. It might as well have been Topeka, Kansas, where his mother was raised.

This was a surprise to me—and also disappointing for what was not in his story. I lived on Oahu for three years in my twenties (1958–1960) while posted at the Marine Corps Air Station at Kaneohe Bay. I returned to the mainland a few months before Obama was born and visited Oahu again to teach for a semester at the University of Hawaii–Manoa when he was a toddler. I kept a diary during my Hawaii years, and these island impressions sharply contrasted with Obama's narrative in *Dreams from My Father*. To me Oahu, except for the acres of pineapple rows planted in fields of red, powdery dirt on the dry central plain, was a sensory delight in all days and seasons. The fragrances of plumeria, night-blooming jasmine, and white and kahili ginger were carried everywhere in the warm, humid air. The dominant spine of mountains spilled instant waterfalls when ocean winds pushed low-flying clouds to the altitude where they must release their moisture. Landscape more richly dictated the very language of direction than in the other states. One could ask which direction was North or South in the forty-nine states, but the locals in Hawaii had terms they preferred—one either went or looked *mauka*, toward the top of the ridgelines and peaks, or *makai*, toward the beaches and the sea.

Fragrant, moist, and warm, Honolulu was also crowded and becoming distressingly more so, its streets and especially the aging main artery, Lunalilo Freeway, jammed at all daylight hours. The first jet airline service to Oahu came in 1959, the tourist crowds expanded, and Waikiki responded by permitting the growth of a skyline of steel and glass hotels and apartments, the owners of the Foster Towers Building bragging that it was the first to reach twenty-five floors. One of Obama's biographers, David Maraniss, found an outraged 1961 comment by radio host Arthur Godfrey, longtime Hawaii booster and visitor, who grumped that "if you really want to get sick, go out about five miles on a catamaran, and just take a look. Why, this place looks just like Pittsburgh."[25] Most of the "natives," and some visitors such as Godfrey, complained of the surge of unwelcome growth menacing paradise, but city planners responded to the traffic by building a second freeway over the mountains to Kaneohe on the windward side. In my time there, small knots of intellectuals wrote letters to the newspaper and held meetings to discuss how to cap the growth. There was brief interest in requiring all but a quota of visitors to leave after a short tourist stay. A pioneering land-use law in 1961 earned for Hawaii in the 1960s and 1970s a reputation as a leading state in what was called the "quiet revolution in land-use control." There is no evidence constitutional lawyer Obama ever mentioned this policy innovation years later in his writings or lectures. Antipoverty policy interested him, not urban sprawl's visual and environmental scars. The growth-control debate flickered out in Hawaii, and the "planners for inevitable growth" prepared in 2014 to break ground on construction of an above-ground "bullet train" from downtown Honolulu (ultimately, Waikiki) northwest around Pearl Harbor to Kapolei and Barber's Point, an ugly defacement of the island skyline.

Obama grew from birth to eighteen (minus five years in Indonesia) in an Oahu he did not see (or, at least, hardly in his memoir) as the fragrant, verdant, blue-ocean-cradled, space-limited, crowded place I found it to be in those years and into the future. He described it as the city in which the basic story was his interaction with family and friends and puzzling over his place in society. He did not see perpetual and space-clogging growth on a small island as one of the defining core narratives and reform agendas around him. What he saw and pondered was human interactions, and he seemed to like what he saw. He would write, in the language and tone of multicultural popular culture: "Hawaii offered a variety of cultures in a climate of mutual respect" that "became the basis of my values." Of course, he was writing in his late twenties about the recollections of a teenager. I had perhaps unrealistically hoped for an Obama at least slightly resentful of the climb of suburban sprawl up the slopes of the Koolau Mountains behind Punaou School. I did find this passage upon my second reading of *Dreams from My Father*:

Even now, with the state's population quadrupled, with Waikiki jammed wall to wall with fast-food emporiums and pornographic video stores and subdivisions marching relentlessly into every fold of green hill, I can . . . (be) stunned by the beauty of the islands. The trembling blue plane of the Pacific, the moss-covered cliffs, and the cool rush of Manoa Falls, with its ginger blossoms and high canopies filled with the sound of invisible birds . . . the shadows off Pali's peaks, the sultry, scented air.[26]

My disappointment eased a bit; my hopes went up a slope. He *did*, at least that once and in a book meant to present his best side, see the Hawaii that I and many others saw and cherished: a fragile, growth-pressured, inherently unsustainable gem. That passage has no match anywhere else in his two memoirs, in which he moved to the concrete canyons of Chicago and New York, where only the people and political institutions, not the Great Lakes or the mighty Hudson River, interested him. Years later he recalled a trip with his mother and grandmother to Yellowstone, which he found "immense," "grand," and "diverse," but he never returned and seems to have visited only this one national park. "Obama was no tree hugger. Nature wasn't something he felt in his gut," wrote Michael Grunwald.[27]

As for Obama's education in books and academic settings, he and his biographers tell us mostly of a self-selected though important reading list—the classic racial-grievance-focused writings of W. E. B. DuBois, Langston Hughes, Ralph Ellison, Richard Wright, Malcolm X, James Baldwin, Martin Luther King, Jr., and Taylor Branch. This is an indispensable list but begs considerable augmentation even if social reform movements are your "major." Obama told Mendell he read other things—the Christian bible, Shakespeare, Nietzsche, Herman Melville, Toni Morrison. But what did he *not* read, or not remember reading? Apparently Occidental and Columbia (Harvard Law School is not in the business of general education) did not also expose him to a list of authors addressing past and present environmental problems—such as Henry David Thoreau, George Perkins Marsh, John Muir, Aldo Leopold, Rachel Carson, Wallace Stegner. As biologist Garrett Hardin would have put it, Obama was literate, not demonstrably numerate, and not ecolate at all. A small attempt at expanding his education was made by a handful of writers asked by the *New York Times Book Review* in June 2008 to recommend books for presidential candidates. Barbara Kingsolver steered Obama (and the others) toward a handful of environmentally informed and informing authors and books. She recommended Gore, McKibben, E. O. Wilson, and Wendell Berry, authors engaged with our national and global future.[28]

In the 2008 campaign Obama seemed to outpromise McCain on environmental stewardship, though neither made it a major theme. The League of Conservation Voters analyzed the 2008 presidential debates and major news interviews and found that of more than 3,000 questions, only 8 were on global warming.[29] Still, most polls showed that the voters had concerns about clean air and water, and both final candidates put on their version of a green face—though McCain's running mate, former Alaska governor Sarah Palin, was a "drill, baby drill" western Republican. McCain produced campaign material calling TR his "hero" and pledging to work for clean air and to deal with global warming. The differences between the candidates "tend to be a matter of degree," concluded the *Los Angeles Times*, begging the question.

Environmental writer Mark Hertsgaard attended Obama's victory speech in Grant Park, Chicago, where he heard his "first black president" say of our "planet in peril" that we should "hope" because "Yes, We Can." In the general euphoria Hertsgaard quotes a German scientist telling his US friends, "This is the hour of leadership." Hertsgaard agreed.[30] Obama's Inaugural Address on January 20, 2009, was about his "hope" and "change" themes again, offering few details. He put a label on his growing cluster of projects—a "new foundation" for "growth and prosperity over the long term." The label did not catch on with media or public, though he used it several times thereafter.

Economic stimulus and budget bills were sent out on the legislative conveyor belt, along with a plan for health-care reform. Many environmental-protection promises had also been made. An oft-quoted campaign promise was, "When I enter the White House," as Obama said in June 2008, it will mark the "moment when the rise of the oceans began to slow and our planet begins to heal."[31] Environmentalists responded to such language with exhilaration at the prospect of an Obama regime. "A new era begins January 20," exulted Sierra Club executive director Carl Pope, who expected a "battle" but was "hopeful" because Obama was "elected in a genuinely transformational moment."[32] A coalition of environmentalists quoted him in his first month in office as saying that "few challenges facing America—and the world—are more urgent than combating climate change."

An early decision was made to link the two biggest domestic problems. The administration's central remedy for high unemployment was an economic "stimulus plan" in the form of a Keynesian jolt of federal spending, the thinking went, so why not aim much of the new federal stimulus—after industrial and financial bailouts—toward spurring the decarbonization of the national energy economy, gradually replacing fossil fuels with renewable sources and thereby reducing dependence on Middle East petroleum? Grunwald's detailed (and lengthy) *The New New Deal* (2012) describes the "stimulus plan" (the American Recovery and Reinvestment Act, signed February 17, 2009) as a sprawling package of measures beginning with energy but including changes in education, health care, transportation, and other parts of the economy, all aiming not solely at jobs but shifting much of the economy toward cleaner, renewable energy and more efficient uses. It took form in 100,000 projects bringing 3 million jobs and reminded Grunwald of a "new New Deal," by which he seemed to mean the Works Progress Administration public works component of the vast Rooseveltian reform program but without Franklin D. Roosevelt's (FDR's) conservation projects in soil conservation, reforestation, and wildlife habitat. He interviewed an administration insider who effused, "We probably did more in that one bill than the Clinton administration did in eight years."[33] The Obama administration's initial year of work on the slowly evolving green agenda was underwhelming to most environmental organizations based in Washington, D.C., who put on a smiley face at first and understandably blamed Republicans for obstructionism. Spurred by 100,000 petitioners from a "victory garden" movement, Michelle Obama and their daughters broke ground on a part of the White House lawn for an organic vegetable garden. Eleanor Roosevelt's gardening during World War II was said to be her model.

Obama's appointments began to be named and to show progress in fulfilling some presidential promises, as when new Interior Secretary Ken Salazar promptly reversed a George W. Bush decision to grant oil leases on seventy-seven parcels near Dinosaur National Monument. All very commendable, but what of the global problem from hell? Based on presidential speeches and informal remarks, an initial case could be made that policy to combat climate change was important to the new president. The former law school professor was a good promiser with respect to arguably the largest and most complex environmental malady to reach any president's desk, but he was not turning out to be an impressive global climatology teacher when not speaking from prepared text. He lacked command of the science and seemed unwilling or unable to offer the public an educational narrative of industrializing nations' GHG emissions followed by the already arriving climatic changes that would in time destabilize all human societies—warmer weather, icepack melting, ocean rising, displacement of millions of refugees from coastal cities, severe droughts along with violent storms, disruption of agricultural economies, spread of tropical diseases, acceleration of species extinction. Reagan-style one-liners seemed to Obama's liking, as when he told a Seattle fund-raising audience that if China and India consume energy the way the United States has, "we'll be four feet under water."[34] Admittedly, global warming was a grim narrative for a president to occasionally bring before a public thirsty instead for the good news and for a Congress told the solution had already been formulated.

In the 2008 campaign Obama, McCain, and Clinton had all endorsed some version of a cap-and-trade system for curbing GHGs, an idea with many sponsors in the cities and states. Energy executives at a West Coast meeting that spring preferred almost any national system of regulation (the cap-and-trade notion seemed to qualify) to the "hell" of current, contradictory federal, state, and local rules. When nominated, Obama backed bipartisan cap-and-trade legislation stalled in the Senate after failing in a 2004 vote. Some informed environmental and energy experts thought a cap-and-trade system was formidably complicated and much inferior to a simpler carbon tax. A cap-and-trade bill passed the House in 2009 but was festooned with unpredictable complications some members did not pretend to understand, and it could not muster the sixty Senate votes to defeat a Republican filibuster. Public concern about climate change seemed to soften under a well-financed campaign by climate-science deniers, energy-industry lobbyists, and the tenacious partisan objection that even the cap-and-trade approach would raise the cost of electricity on coal-fired power plants and send inflationary and job-killing ripples through the economy. Obama's allies hoped the president could somehow improve the outlook for reductions of GHGs by resorting to his bully pulpit, and in his first 233 days in office he gave 266 formal speeches, with climate change a frequent theme.

All the administration's plans as they rolled slowly out in 2009 and after were impeded to one degree or another by a formidable cluster of economic maladies inherited from the George W. Bush second term—741,000 jobs lost in January 2009 alone, stocks careening downward, housing forfeitures in record numbers, mounting public debt. All this together "takes all the oxygen out of the room for virtually anything else," commented a Sierra Club lobbyist.[35] "This thing we're in doesn't yet have a name," wrote Nick Faumgarten in the New Yorker. "The financial crisis, the recession, the Great Recession . . . this thing is enormous and all-pervasive . . . [and] is pretty much the only subject of conversation."[36] There were many Obama loyalists among the reporters covering the Washington policy beat who, like Ryan Lizza of the New Yorker, allowed themselves to see economic recovery on the near horizon and to claim (in Lizza's words) that the president's "first two years stand as one of the most successful legislative periods in modern history."[37]

This glowing assessment rested mostly on "Obamacare," the national health-care plan the new president was able to sign on March 20, 2010, though it was threatened by Supreme Court scrutiny. It survived that, as well as the creative hazards of implementation. There was also a disappointing response to the stimulus package, criticized for being too large or too small to produce the desired recovery. The year brought no climate-change legislation, only the souring realities of partisan gridlock on the next year's budget and Republican control of the House.

How much Obama administration floundering had its roots in partisan resistance by Republicans and how much in Obama's caution and occasional uncertainty? Was he far better at running for president than at being one? Commentators asked why Obama did not make greater use of a president's unique tools for shaping what the public hears and takes to be the administration's agenda.[38] Gore allowed himself to be quoted as critical of Obama in an essay in *Rolling Stone*: "He has never presented to the American people the magnitude of the climate crisis."[39] Gore's experience in the White House and as a climate-change educator gave weight to his criticism, at least in green and Democratic circles. Other commentators expressed the view that what some saw as Obama's hesitancy about launching an all-out campaign to win a complete and effective energy policy with public backing reflected a justifiable preoccupation with the puzzle of what to do about the wars in Afghanistan and Iraq and the Iranian nuclear project. Critics of slow progress on the green (and nongreen) agenda had to acknowledge the results of a 2011 poll from the Pew Research Center reporting that "global warming" and "protecting the environment" had both slipped down in the list of voters' concerns.

The Nobel Prize Committee in Norway made its own early judgment on Obama's climate-change efforts by awarding a prize to him in October 2009 for having "captured the world's attention" and "playing a more constructive role" (than his predecessor?) "in meeting the great climatic challenges the world is confronting."[40] Gore called the prize "extremely well deserved," but it was not. The large Natural Resources Defense Council (NRDC) can be taken as an example of the early optimism of one of the nation's larger environmental groups whose leadership decided for purposes of the 2012 election that the glass was at least half full, but it was not—yet. The NRDC hailed the administration for a "remarkable number of actions" amounting to varying degrees of "progress across a range of environmental policies" designed to result in "jobs, . . . sustainability goals for federal agencies, . . . new fuel economy/greenhouse gas emissions standards, . . . [and] reducing large ship emissions" along with "saving Chesapeake Bay," canceling Bush administration gas and oil leases on public lands and mountaintop removal permits—and so on for ten pages of "actions" and "progress," admittedly "leaving much to be done."[41] There was no measurable progress on most of these, such as "saving" the Chesapeake Bay. Could Obama do more? Greens and liberals asked what FDR had done in the 1930s to persuade Congress to enact and the public to endorse his recovery program amid a more crippling economic slump than Obama faced. FDR had a vision of where the country ought to go, some said, and a catchy name for all the frenzy of dam building and other public works, banking/stock exchange reforms, and social insurance system—the "New Deal." The phrase caught on in 1933, but Obama's "new foundation" did not, though he gave it a good try in his Inaugural Address—"one of the best of his presidency," Axelrod said to writer George Packard, "honest . . . inspired speaking" but "hardly anyone remembers it." Indeed, it is hard to think of a single line from an Obama presidential speech that had caught on. "He gives a speech and moves on," Axelrod told Packard, "spending little time moving the narrative forward." He "has no larger vision," concluded Bill Clinton's chief of staff John Podesta. Even if he did, how would we know, when the bully pulpit is now swamped by blogs, talk radio, and Twitter?[42]

Looking back, the high point for Obama in the first term may have been in the autumn of 2009, when he claimed his Nobel Prize and made headlines in the *New York Times* in late November, telling delegates to an international meeting in Copenhagen that the United States would reduce GHG emissions by 17 percent below 2005 levels by 2020 and 83 percent by 2050. This bold pronouncement was more a hope than a policy-backed target because he was referring to language in a House bill that would never be confirmed by the Senate.[43]

Then came a presidential speech devoted, finally, to telling the public what the plan was—or was going to be. In his January 27, 2011, State of the Union Address Obama surprised both environmentalists and the energy industry by recommending a sort of legislative "Plan B" package constructed out of renewed support for nuclear power, clean technologies for continuing

to burn coal, and a limited expansion of offshore drilling—all without uttering the words "global warming." The cap-and-trade structure was now leg-
islatively dead, and what remained was unfocused and unnamed.[44]

There were other signs Obama's overall plan was now quietly focusing on
reelection in 2012, bending environmental and energy policy toward a cautious, "I'm for everything" center. The administration had initially been wary
about the plans for landscape-scarring and aquifer-invading construction of
the Keystone XL Pipeline, proposed to carry Canadian "dirty" petroleum derived from oil sands across the United States to refineries on the Gulf of
Mexico and from there to foreign markets. Obama began to see merit in it,
promising no decision until after the election and more extensive study. Environmentalists admitted to "heartburn" over the administration's softening
on the Keystone XL Pipeline and permission for drilling again off the Gulf
Coast.[45] In a year with record-breaking temperatures, arctic ice melting, and
drought, three presidential debates hardly touched global warming.[46] Environmentalists opening their mail from the House Committee on Energy and
Commerce were told of a report (sponsored by committee Democrats) finding that, on a set of environmental measures, 94 percent of Republicans
"voted in favor of the antienvironment position." The message was that if
Obama's environmental record was nothing to write home about, it should
be chalked up to partisan obstructionism. The Obama campaign letter to my
household in August 2012 talked much about the recovering economy but
said nothing at all about population or resources or environment.

As the election year shortened, Obama's GHG policies had to be disappointing to liberals who recalled his 2009 promise that when he walked into
the White House, it would be the "time when the planet began to heal." In
the first presidential primary debate in September 2012, the words *global
warming* were not uttered. Obama's green efforts were wide ranging and
substantial by contrast with the president just before him and also with his
2012 opponent, former Massachusetts governor Mitt Romney. When the National Wildlife Federation (NWF) a month before voting asked each candidate to state his position on key environmental issues, the contrast was
pronounced.[47] The Romney campaign declined to respond because of lack
of time, so NWF staff drew his answers from campaign publications, and it
all boiled down to less regulation and more fossil-energy production—and
not a word on global warming one way or another. The Obama campaign
submitted a polished if short list of "steps I will take to reduce GHGs," list-

ing steps already taken—higher fuel-efficiency standards for US vehicles, investments in clean energy, reduced government-produced emissions. On the stump, Obama almost never raised this issue on his own initiative, presumably detecting that much of the public found it boring and tedious—a scattering of small conservation "programs."

Some environmentalist Democrats, unsurprisingly, openly broke with Obama in the fall of 2011. Responding to a call from respected environmental writer McKibben and others, many younger greens showed up outside the White House in substantial numbers (an estimated 12,000) in the first week of November for "sit-in protests" taking the form especially of speeches objecting to the Keystone XL Pipeline. Some were arrested and did jail time. Obama made no recorded comment.[48]

When his reelection moment came in 2012, green organizations, as he must have expected, rallied to him with no exceptions that I could find. The Sierra Club endorsement of early October was hailed by a club staffer as earned by "historic victories" during which "President Obama had our backs." (Does that mean he was safely in the rear as they fought?) If elected, then, Obama "will have a clear mandate."[49]

However, reelection conferred no mandate for anything. His campaign slogan—"Forward"—meant nothing in particular. At a September 2012 meeting of his closest aides—"Obamans," someone called them—Obama suggested that the agenda for the next meeting ought to be "what I think about everything." A week later they listened to the president read from ten yellow-pad pages of his notes. It was an extraordinary exposure for him and did not go well. He wished "they had done more" in general, though they had "done a lot," starting with climate change (which deserved and did not attract discussion). Down through a long and disorganized list, he repeatedly "cared a lot" and wished he had "done more." This for immigration reform, poverty, Israel, the prisoners at Guantanamo, predator-drone strikes, gay marriage, and so on. If anyone had hoped it would all add up, awaiting only a compelling label, this had not happened. Worse, Obama's inability to pull it all together was leaked and became known to a large uninvited audience. Two writers, Mark Halperin and John Heilemann, in their 2012 campaign chronicle *Double Down*, reported that Obama was furious when his private remarks that September were leaked and suggested that we could call Obamaism "Pragmatic Progressivism." Having either heard (or heard of, and leaked?) the president's list, Halperin and Heilemann concluded, "He needed help, he needed focus." The episode revealed much about Obama and Washington politics.[50]

Yale professor David Bromwich spoke for me and I think many after the 2012 national elections: "Lower, meaner, duller campaigns there have been, but never one in which so many issues were treated with such studious avoidance." He singled out as the most important avoided issues the Middle East wars, taxation, and the "environment and pollution," which seemed to slip under the campaign-issue radar more frequently even than wars and taxation. Certainly the palette from which the 2012 presidential election was colored had little green in it, and the responsibility for that rests at least half with Obama, who seemed to have concluded that the campaign against climate change had a dangerous capacity to be a negative element preventing his reelection.

After one term, he probably would have objected indignantly to such an interpretation, and with some reason. His administration had allocated billions of dollars of recovery funds to energy efficiency and renewable-energy programs and ordered federal agencies to reduce GHG emissions from government buildings and vehicles by 28 percent by 2020. However, the president made only half-hearted efforts to tell a large global and national story about the US struggle to end the reckless and costly atmospheric experiment we (and all humans) had launched in ignorance and denial, and he quietly acquiesced in the legislative gridlock preventing a national program with firm targets. By 2012 environmentalist complaints were increasing. Obama "isn't doing bloody much on climate change" and is "censoring it from his major speeches," blogged Joe Romm, without evidence (on www.think progress.org). July 2012 was the hottest month in US records, and rising sea levels threatened coastal cities and property.[51]

Audubon printed this in August and could not know that the immense Hurricane Sandy would devastate low-lying portions of coastal New York and New Jersey the weekend before the November voting, inflicting damages of $10 billion in early estimates, revised in a month to $42 billion for New York and $29.4 billion for New Jersey. Surging waves from seventeen to thirty-two feet moved inland, the entrances of major tunnels to Manhattan were filled with water, some runways at John F. Kennedy International Airport were for a time under twenty-five feet of water. "This may be that sort of Cuyahoga River moment for climate change," commented a Penn State climate scientist. "It has galvanized attention to this issue."[52] The tides pushed by Sandy's monstrous winds first inundated Manhattan's subways and store basements and then perhaps convinced the public (for a while) that the warnings should be heard now and behavior changed. Two days after Sandy came across the beaches, the media discovered that the public and leaders had ignored detailed warnings from a 2009 seminar of New York region civil engineers that a devastating storm surge into the region was "all but inevitable" given rising ocean levels and more violent storms. New York governor Andrew Cuomo told President Obama in October, "We have a hundred-year flood every two years now." Sure enough, nature made more ocean water and less ice after humans changed the chemistry of the atmosphere, and ashore the water came. The director of a research group on sea levels in Princeton, New Jersey, told reporters, "Three of the top ten floods at the Battery since 1900 happened in the last two years.[53]

Obama achieved the reelection won by only seventeen presidents of the forty-four who have held the office. Yet there were months throughout much of 2012 and even into the final weeks of the campaign when this seemed in question. A struggling economy was an unfavorable background for all incumbents. On top of this, Obama performed poorly in the first presidential candidates' debate, and had Romney not turned out to be a wooden candidate prone to verbal errors, Obama might have been sent home to Chicago or Honolulu. Polls showed that those who had voted strongly for him in 2008, especially racial/ethnic minorities, women, and the young, had lost some of the edge of excitement generated by his arrival on the scene as our first half-black president. "Nobody madly loves Obama anymore," wrote Maureen Dowd a month before the election.[54]

In those uncertain days when Obama's defeat seemed entirely possible, one of the central questions for political watchers drew well-deserved attention: how to account for the mediocre—and sometimes not even that—performance of our president, this young and (millions thought) promising, new political figure? "What was wrong with Obama?" The beginning of an answer wove back and forth through his second book—that the US political system and social bonds were broken. Everyone knew that, but it was a new perspective that Obama's misjudgments were now acknowledged by many as part of the problem. He admitted in an interview with Charlie Rose that his "biggest mistake" had been "thinking that this job was just about getting the policy right. That's important, but the nature of this office is also to tell a story to the American people that gives them a sense of unity and purpose and optimism." On this score he had fallen short, he conceded to Rose. Citing this episode, columnist Thomas Friedman in July 2012 argued that Obama was indeed at the hub of the problem. "He needs a narrative" to tell the people, an optimistic one, of course, Reagan-like but also "infused with values." He needs a big idea," agreed environmental writer Timothy Egan in December 2010. "He has lost control of his political narrative," concluded correspondent Richard Stevenson in January 2010. Obama "told me" in a February 2011 interview in the Oval Office, author Ron Suskind wrote two days after the election, that the "coin of the realm" is telling a story that will make US citizens "optimistic." "Still Waiting for the Narrator in Chief" was the title of an article by Matt Bai in the *New York Times* two days before the election. The new president's advisers, Bai went on, were wary of "too much speechifying," with the result that Obama did not speak to the people enough and the "narrative really got away from the president in those early days of 2009–10." This assumes Obama once had an effective story line and lost it by lack of practice or some other reason, a theory backed by no evidence.[55]

There are two dimensions to this oft-heard "he needs a narrative" interpretation. One is the view that Obama once had a winning story for purposes of coming out of nowhere in 2004 to become a winning candidate in 2008, but that narrative turned out to be an empty run of cliches that could serve as an election formula but not a governing story either for him or the people he led. A different version of this comes in George C. Edwards's book *Overreach* (2012). Obama, in Edwards's view, had a serviceable if not riveting life story for a candidate, but once in the White House he soon proved so frequently passive and unguided that unfriendly pundits and Republicans no longer believing him a globalist socialist shifted to a new theory—Obama had always lacked an adequate vision to undergird national leadership for the turbulent contemporary era.[56] Friedman added an essential insight into the composition of a story any president could, or must, take to the people. The story must be "infused with values . . . the most obvious in our case" being "sustainability . . . growth that lasts."[57]

Obama's second term began with two major addresses in 2013. Again, environmentalists listened for their themes. In his second Inaugural Address, delivered on January 21, 2013, Obama spoke eight sentences on climate change, "more than he devoted to any other specific area," the *New York Times* counted. The president pledged to use administrative tools such as

BUSH II AND OBAMA | 353

EPA rule making and "have the federal government itself produce less carbon pollution. . . . We will respond to [the] threat of warming," Obama continued. For those who deny this problem, the evidence is in "raging fires, crippling drought, and powerful storms." After this, the main themes were the "economy, . . . jobs, . . . [and] growing the middle class."[58]

The president's State of the Union Address in February focused again on economic matters, telling citizens they should ask three questions each day, two of them about jobs. He asserted a liberal agenda on social programs including an increase in the minimum wage, immigration liberalization (including what amounted to amnesty for the 20 million illegal immigrants in the country), and gun control. Somewhere below that came the Gifford Pinchot–like intergenerational commitment: "For the sake of our children and our future, we must do more to combat climate change. The fact is that the 12 hottest years on record have all come in the last 25," along with record-making heat waves, droughts, wildfires, floods. If Congress will not come up with "market-based solutions, I will . . . come up with executive actions we can take."[59]

These brief and isolated comments on climate change as an important agenda item for the second Obama term initially attracted less attention from the media than the topic of the minimum wage. Journalist Elizabeth Kolbert of the *New Yorker* must have been tempted to repeat her comment of December: "As Obama embarks on his second term," more economists and energy experts are endorsing a carbon tax, and more than 100 large corporations, including Royal Dutch Shell, called in December for lawmakers worldwide to set a "clear, transparent, and unambiguous price on carbon emissions. . . . It's time for him [Obama] to take some risks."[60] Why not tax carbon, now that some of the big energy companies had changed their minds and invited it? His two major presidential speeches in early 2013 declared no such risk-taking in environmental policy. Obama simply reaffirmed that he was still against climate change and wanted Congress to "partner" with him in raising the price of carbon—or he would turn to his administrative powers. He and the Republicans in the House fought instead the familiar war of the budget, intensified somehow by the presence of Obama, who seemed to bring out the unyielding instinct in GOP leadership and rank and file—or they brought out the same fundamentalist passions in Obama and his party's militant base, or both. Clearly, both. The result was stalemate and a sense of political gridlock throughout the rest of his term, with environmental issues in varying degrees of inching sideways. An expected presidential decision on whether to permit building of the 2,000-mile Keystone XL Pipeline brought the environmentalists out of their offices in February to picket around the White House again.[61]

Obama's relationship with the environmental community, correctly called "complicated" in early 2012, remained very edgy throughout 2013 and 2014, the environmentalists eager for signs of a more resolute and persuasive performance, especially on global warming.[62] Perhaps, like other presidents, he had decided to wait until something changed in the political atmosphere to allow him to invest more capital and time on that difficult problem. Nature might have been said to be cooperating. Two-thirds of the country remained locked in drought, arctic ice melted over the 2012 summer at record-making levels, global GHG emissions were at a historic high in 2011, and *Science* in March 2013 published a study finding that global temperatures had not been this high for 4,000 years.[63] When critics charged that Obama had a poor record on public land policy, favoring permits to drill and mine much more often than protecting the land from exploitation, former Clinton interior secretary Bruce Babbitt calculated that presidents George H. W. Bush and Clinton both protected one acre of public land for every acre leased for hydrocarbon extraction, whereas Obama's record so far was 6 million acres leased compared with 2.6 million acres set aside as parks, monuments, or wilderness areas. Obama hastened in March 2013 to set aside five new national monuments.

The centerpiece of Obaman reforms was said to be "Obamacare," a sweeping health-care insurance system enacted in 2010 and engulfed in the summer and fall of 2013 by unexpected rollout disarray and computer-system design flaws. Computer systems did not function smoothly in enrolling millions of clients, and Obama was pounded in the media for months for falsely assuring citizens on the details of their medical insurance shift, in particular denying that many would lose coverage. Millions did lose coverage. Other elements of his agenda were still blocked—an ill-defined immigration reform giving "pathways to legal status" for those who had broken the law, stricter controls on firearms, and an increase in the minimum wage filled out his wish list as 2013 moved on.

In June 2013 Obama gave a major speech at Georgetown University on climate change said to "thrill" environmentalists by offering a new plan, called by Gore the best plan of any president. Obama seemed to have moved away from what some called his "half-a-loaf centrism" with a pledge that he would not approve the Keystone XL Pipeline if it would "significantly exacerbate the problem of carbon pollution."[64] Four leading Republican administrators of the EPA who had served under presidents Nixon, Reagan, George H. W. Bush, and George W. Bush joined in an August 2013 *New York Times* op-ed commending Obama's recent "climate action plan" for controlling GHG emissions and urged an "overdue debate about what bigger steps are needed."[65] Nothing came of this bipartisan opening for planning talk on climate change.

Environmentalists wanting stronger White House leadership were reminded that "hope" was what Senator Obama had promised in his 2005 book, in which he admitted that he did not know exactly how to get what he and we were hoping for. "Hope was the good theme, but it was not specific enough," wrote an environmentalist critic of his presidency. "We need to commit to some specific goals."[66]

A group of historians was invited to a dinner at the White House shortly after Obama's reelection, where most were said to have attributed the persistence of our national policy floundering not to their host, Obama, but in large part to the lame-duckism that came in all presidents' second terms and inevitably shrank their influence to some degree. "Almost no second term turns out well," commented historian of the presidency H. W. Brands, apparently expressing a consensus.[67] Obama, who is not often quoted expressing in public worries about his "legacy," displayed in other ways the nervous activity of a reelected leader frustrated by skimpy legacy-improving prospects in his second term. He traveled incessantly, speaking to friendly audiences around the country, and announced in July 2013 in unfresh language the elements of a new "strategy" to focus on the economy. The rest of his list was becoming stale. Was he "running out of juice," one reporter asked? "I am doing what presidents do," he responded. Without mentioning the bully pulpit directly, he embraced it: "I can put pressure on them [the Republicans]. I can rally the American people."[68] In the next six months it seemed evident that he could not. The US electorate had elected and reelected a celebrated orator who turned out not to be a gifted communicator, though the policy gridlock had many sources.

A *New York Times* reporter in May wrote that "now we see the paradox" of a president "who to critics appears ever more intrusive" as he presides over Internal Revenue Service (IRS) scandals and a government "snooping into reporters' phone records," while Obama, the sponsor of many reform ideas, "comes across as something of a bystander occupying the most powerful office in the world."[69] If he was a bystander as the summer of 2013 began, things only got worse. By late fall, with the "rollout" of Obamacare stalled by malfunctioning computers and underestimated costs, the president was forced to express regret that his promises about Obamacare had been broken by some insurers. The news media talked of a "crisis of confidence," and two polls in November reported that a "majority of Americans no longer trust [sic] the president." "This is Obama's 'Bay of Pigs,'" wrote Joe Nocera in the *New York Times*.[70] "Where's Obama the manager?" editorialized the *Wall Street Journal*. He seemed "bored by the daily tasks of governing."[71] By December 2013 Obama's approval rating slumped to 37 percent, a low point for him. "The president is a very muddled and entrenched figure who needs to get out of a defensive crouch and get some new ideas," wrote Peter Baker, who covered the White House for the *New York Times*.[72] Obama responded by shaking up his top staff, bringing in Clinton's former chief of staff, Podesta, and acknowledging weariness yet "hopes for action in 2014" as in December he boarded the plane for the first family's annual Hawaii vacation.

At the close of 2013 the most visible and (apparently) influential leader of US environmentalism, McKibben, wrote for the *Rolling Stone* website a ten-page assessment, "Obama and Climate Change." "Cynics who said Obama and his insiders were too closely tied to the fossil fuel industry" may have been right. The United States will shortly be the world's biggest oil and gas producer, which makes us a "global-warming machine," according to McKibben. In a speech in Oklahoma in 2012 Obama hailed this new energy independence and "backed fracking to the hilt," apparently unaware that "most of the coal and gas and oil that's underground has to stay there," in McKibben's view. What does our president "really believe?"[73] Historian Douglas Brinkley shed some light on this after a 2013 interview with the president. He reported that Obama's "main goal" and legacy aspiration was building a defensive "firewall" around the progressive/New Deal inheritance. Toward the end of 2013 the president affirmed that he was a strong admirer of the Hoover Dam, evidently unaware that increasing numbers of environmentalists were no longer fond of it.

OBAMA AS PRESIDENT

Acknowledging that he has two more years in office as I write, it can be said that Obama's pulpit was never very green, emotionally or intellectually, at a time when the environmental challenges were becoming unprecedented in global impact and the ecosystem costs were steeply rising.

One positive assessment, shared by him and the voters, will surely stand up to scrutiny and time—that a man of mixed race, almost universally called "black" to maximize the transcendence of the occasion, had been elected (decisively, and twice) at all was a historic achievement in a very large and important sense, apart from his subsequent record. Like the bear riding the bike, it was astonishing to see him doing it at all in a country so long run by white males at the top. The benefit to the nation of this precedent is huge. It stands as a permanent enlargement of our eligibility pool, not one ounce diminished if we conclude that his environmental (and other) leadership was on the low end of mediocre at a time in our national history when the cost of electing not very strong or well-prepared presidents is rising.

10

We have to arouse something akin to a war psychology . . . if we are really to make this a Permanent Country.
— Morris L. Cooke

The raging monster upon the land is population growth. In its presence, sustainability is but a fragile theoretical construct.
— E. O. Wilson, *The Diversity of Life*, 1992

Counting back from this year, twenty-two presidents over a 125-year span (beginning in 1891) have engaged what was to be called conservation of natural resources, ranging from national park, national forest, and wildlife refuge designation and management to air- and water-quality regulation and much else familiar to readers of this book. These "conservation" (later, environmental) issues had not been understood and experienced as an ongoing part of their work by the presidents who had gone before—George Washington through first-term Grover Cleveland. Then in the 1890s a new theme in presidential history was added to their preexisting duties in peace and war. Benjamin Harrison and his immediate successors thought the new assignment had only to do with forests they would never see. Theodore Roosevelt (TR) expanded it hugely.

To gain perspective on the twenty-two presidential stories that commenced in 1891, I sorted them by their leadership (or not) toward this growing federal engagement in nature protection. It is not a story without noncooperators. Early on we encounter TR's sad discovery that not all presidents were going to welcome this nation-preserving work. His handpicked successor, William Taft, had seemed a conservationist but after he was in office displayed deep and disabling reservations. Presidents began to divide on conservation, beginning when Taft broke with TR on this issue (and some others). Beginning with Benjamin Harrison and all the way to Barack Obama, there formed two clusters—facilitators/expanders (twelve) and skeptics/opponents (ten) of this new cause. These roughly equal clusters of presidents suggest stalemate. There was much of that but also many occasions of movement in the course of more than a century as the nation evolved, slowly, from no vision or plan for its vast public domain to federally administered spaces not destined to be given or sold like the rest of the United States—59 national parks covering 150 million acres; 155 national forests and related units covering 192 million acres; 560 wildlife refuges sheltering the habitats of birds, fish, mammals, and reptiles; 79 national monuments; 78 historic sites; 15 national rivers; vast ocean protected and endangered species zones; a huge air- and water-regulatory apparatus; and more. Writer Wallace Stegner had all of this in mind when he called the national parks the "best idea we ever had . . . us at our best." Thanks to (among others) the green twelve, it could be said that many, if not most of these "public goods" would not have become a part of our collective national life. The Donald Trump high-end hoteliers or the religious, ethnic, and other private groups would have bought and controlled access to Yellowstone, Yosemite, Grand Canyon, Crater Lake, and many others.

Harrison was not the initial conservation president because he thought of this new idea on his own but because he was asked by respected friends to take it on. Following his cooperative but limited role, only the two Roosevelts among the twenty-two presidents robustly and with sustained enthusiasm took up the challenge of nature protection, producing large and beneficial effects on the nation's physical history. Nine more (Grover Cleveland, Woodrow Wilson, Harry Truman, John F. Kennedy, Lyndon B. Johnson, Richard Nixon, Jimmy Carter, and Bill Clinton) were frequent or at least occasional leaders in the conservation cause, making up a most-of-the-time greenish presidential cadre. Obama is not finished as I write this and thus far has been cautiously and irregularly green. So, a shaky twelve.

Eleven others I found uninterested in nature protection, indifferent, or negative—William McKinley, Taft, Warren Harding, Calvin Coolidge, Herbert Hoover, Dwight Eisenhower, Richard Nixon, Gerald Ford, Ronald Reagan, George H. W. Bush, and George W. Bush—with Nixon in both lists. Eleven plus twelve does not quite add up to twenty-two, but when you are dealing with Nixon you can expect some funny math. Twelve and ten, twenty-two. (Should we count Al Gore rather than George W. Bush, since he received more popular votes in 2000?)

That vast transformation in natural-resource protection required more than a century for half our presidents and their allies to put in place. Our story is a virtual tie moving in and out of the White House, presidents leading at cross purposes as often as making sequential policy advances in a sustained nature-protection direction. By this policy accounting, the voting US citizens (or the politically active percentage of them) have, since Harrison, sent us an almost even number of varying shades of green and brown presidents. The national forests, national parks, wildlife refuges, national monuments, pollution laws, and international treaties all had many parents and custodians in and out of government, but one or more of twelve presidents signed off on almost all these protected sites as well as the Wilderness Act, federal pollution controls, and much else. As we move into a more crowded, warming, earth-transforming century, the question animating this book becomes how to do vastly better—greener—in selecting, influencing, and serving the chief of the executive branch.

Many books scrutinize parts or the whole of the institutions and opinion foundations of US environmental policy history—the "green state," in the felicitous phrase used by Christopher Klyza and David Sousa in *American Environmental Policy*.[1] The focus of the book in your hand is on the president and the presidency twenty-two times over more than a century and the instructive stories of how presidents led toward nature preservation, or not.

To TR and those who shared his activist view of the presidential office, the answer started with stronger leadership from the president and his branch in an expanding conservation agenda. The forest reserve lobbyists of 1891 went to see President Harrison rather than other influential people, such as the senator who chaired the Interior Committee or the chief justice of the Supreme Court, because Harrison as chief executive was thought by the Boone and Crockett Club members to have certain powers needed to initiate forest and watershed protection. It does not sound like much, and Harrison did not think it warranted calling in the lawyers. Enough for him that presidents could sign (or not) congressional bills into law and issue a few executive orders that he or his top appointees enforced. He appointed administrators and was expected to supervise the senior ones. On rare occasions he acted as chief diplomat—who else? He also influenced the budget.

These chores hardly seemed like a full-time job, especially when its occupants tended to be deferential to the antimonarchical heritage of this fledgling republic in its first century. It never occurred to presidents in the days of, say, Taylor, Fillmore, or Pierce (Abraham Lincoln was a special case) to conceive and push hard for his own or his party's "program" or to find novel ways to educate and mobilize the public or to press Congress hard to submit to his views with the argument that the president's views are those of a majority of the nation and deserve greater weight than those of legislators, who represent only localities and sections. Setting aside a piece of public land as a national forest did not to Harrison seem to stretch his powers.

The nineteenth-century tradition of presidential deference and passivity toward Congress and precedent was rapidly changing as Harrison set aside the first forestlands. The assertive TR was in the wings, soon to provide remarkable creative energy to the history of presidential enlargement in the twentieth century. Students of our political history speak of the evolution of the "modern presidency," arriving by stages at first almost trivial. Cleveland was the first president to have his own White House office phone, which he answered personally. Soon thereafter, McKinley commanded a staff of six, who did that sort of thing for him, and an office manager to bring order to the records. President Wilson expanded his audience and intensified his influence over the national agenda by, among other things, delivering the State of the Union Address to a joint session of Congress. His successor, Harding, not thought of as an innovator, gave that speech to a vast audience on the radio. More to the point of presidential expansion, two new departments, the Federal Reserve Bank and two regulatory commissions, were added to the executive branch before involvement in world wars required further enlargements. The Brownlow Commission Report of 1937 concluded that "the President ["still" might have been added] needs help" with the expanding duties of Depression-era activist government, and in response Congress established the Executive Office of the President, which cold war presidents (and Congresses) expanded. Expectations and functions of presidents grew throughout the twentieth century, a story we have followed through only one policy cluster—natural resources.

A necessary constitutional rearrangement, TR and those who shared his views would have said of Progressive Era and subsequent presidential-power strengthening. But a slowly enlarging executive branch—rapidly expanding in wartime—did not necessarily translate into adequate natural-resource protection located in Washington, D.C.

Looking back at the first three presidents after Harrison signed the law creating national forests, we see that almost nothing was learned or taught by them as they expanded this new assignment TR would later call conservation. Creating national forests had not been these three presidents' idea in the first place. Harrison, Cleveland, and McKinley took the minimal steps required, persuading and educating few citizens as to what should be done next after an obscure new law signed by Harrison allowed some forested public lands to be "reserved." It was a very sluggish start.

Then came TR, and what he taught was so vast and irreversible that it could not be contained in the 896 pages of Douglas Brinkley's biography *The Wilderness Warrior* (2009). A lesson on what one big thing *not* to do when you are TR and hold the apex US public office is: do not give that office to your unsympathetic friend Taft without many late-night discussions.

Moving along the learning curve we encounter the post-Taft stretch of four nature-ignorant politicians who slipped into major party presidential nominations, election, or succession in the 1920s. (Taft could be called the first of these, if we may start the 1920s early.) Wilson taught us that a talented writer and orator was of very modest use to the conservation cause if he neither understood nor cared about it. His interior secretary, Franklin Lane, was selected because he was aligned with western developers, and Wilson himself frequently complained that conservation too often meant "locking up" resources. Harding, in addition to being ignorant on all policy matters, appointed the most corrupt interior secretary in our history, Albert Fall. Then came Coolidge, who had no policy goals beyond lower taxes and was praised for his comment that US citizens' only purpose in life was "business," and Hoover, who could not find coherent or compelling language to explain why conservation was and ought to be the "settled policy of the country." Whatever TR taught, after him the national political machinery for years piled up White House nonleadership in environmental as well as most other national policy areas. Harding was fit for no part of the presidency but ceremonies, and Coolidge excelled only in long naps and short workdays containing no part of TR's conservation agenda. Engineer Hoover also decisively proved that White House conferences of industrialists do not bring an end to industrial wastes and that a president who looks at his shoes as he talks does not move listeners to remedial action, though he sometimes rec-ommends it. Together, they were five early nonconservationists, a brown start to the twelve greens.

Greener presidents came in and after the 1960s as environmental organi-zations expanded their membership and influence. Yet the public was not yet reliably green. Note that neither Roosevelt had gained the office because of his conservationist record and commitments. Franklin D. Roosevelt (FDR) as New York governor had long spoken frequently and with passion about trees, soil, and rural life and often repeated a story of a once-verdant Chinese valley devastated by deforestation. It was or should have been well known in 1932 that no presidential candidate in either party matched FDR's rurally grounded economic recovery policy ideas and experience. Yet the Demo-cratic presidential convention came just minutes away from handing the 1932 nomination instead to a near-illiterate governor of Texas who stood for nothing but ending prohibition on bourbon. It was a rare event when Carter's winning margin in 1976 came from conservationists who knew that he floated rivers.

Are there reliable clues to future greenness in some of these life sketches? One element of early education has been said to forecast a nature-respecting career, but it turns out to have erratic predictive power. Rural upbringing made him a strong environmentalist president, LBJ claimed, as did (with more reason) Carter. Nature-appreciating wives were a factor in both cases. A farm upbringing did not have that effect on Coolidge, Eisenhower, or Tru-man (or their wives) and in any event is the early life experience of a small and shrinking handful of future US presidents. It seems to sometimes de-velop a person's nature appreciation when a river runs through the family's land, presumably teaching watershed and wildlife lessons—though the large impact of the Hudson on FDR was not matched by Ronald Reagan's days of lifeguarding on the nearby Rock River. Future presidents were not of-ten avid readers and shortsightedly preferred patriotic military and political histories to wildlife and nature books. Only a few reported the shaping influ-ence of even one of the classic green writings—the "end of the frontier" es-say by Frederick Jackson Turner, the nature writings of Henry David Thoreau, John Burroughs, John Muir, George Perkins Marsh, Aldo Leopold, Marjory Stoneman Douglas, Rachel Carson. More directly and daily influen-tial on presidents than books were the intellectual mentors I have called con-servation lieutenants—among them TR's Gifford Pinchot and W. J. McGee;

FDR's Rex Tugwell, Irving Brant, and Harold Ickes; Eisenhower's brother Milton; JFK's and LBJ's Stewart Udall, Orville Freeman, and Wallace Stegner. Female potential lieutenants with the highest nature-writing credentials met Truman (Douglas) and JFK (Carson), but both women were near the end of life when they encountered two presidents unaccustomed to working with highly skilled females.

Learning how to get a consistently green Nixon rather than the brown one we had to endure during much of his tenure seems straightforward. Schedule an election that Nixon might lose against a popular senator acknowledged to be Mister Clean on the Hill, and Tricky Dick revives the TR tradition. Even the politically secure Reagan can in his second term be substantially unbrowned if environmental organizations grow to unprecedented numbers and public relations skills just as Reagan appoints two foot-in-mouth top aides to visible environmental posts.

Then there is that most reliable toolbox for those who would be presidential green makers—the beneficial disaster. Expect quick action from presidents whose morning news briefing tells of large and disfiguring petroleum spills on populated coasts; rivers catching fire as they pass through industrial sites; blistering summers draining water reservoirs and causing wildfires in the West; waves of refugees beginning to arrive in Australia, Canada, and the United States from ocean-inundated Pacific atolls and the coastal lowlands of Bangladesh and India.

OBAMA, WHO HOPED TO TRANSFORM

The president we know both the most and the least about is the last one, Barack Obama. He came to the office with an audacious goal larger than taking over the White House. "I want to transform this country," Obama told an audience in Iowa and repeated it several times.[2] This second ambition, the "transformation," was hopelessly grandiose and not very original. Voters responded not to his presumptuous "transformation" promise but rather to a chance to atone, somewhat, for racial crimes. Obama spent his terms in the White House casting about for his mission among many causes with the liberal bent he had absorbed at home. He early on visited Selma, Alabama, to honor the legacy of Martin Luther King, Jr. He signed into law "Obamacare" medical insurance reform, adopted the open-border aspirations of Hispanics and others illegally immigrating into the United States, endlessly coped with Middle East crises while careful not to use the words "Muslim terrorist," and frequently with modest effect, urged US citizens to join the battle against climate change. No conspicuous legacy in sight.

True, he inherited an unusually fragmented political system and society, a discovery his memoirs will surely emphasize. He may have had time on plane rides to realize that the two apparently most promising legacy-making opportunities that seemed to come his way were an environmental crisis taking the form of invisible and climate-changing "emissions" collecting in the cold, dark skies, and a reform of health-care funding. Both presented formidable problems as policy reforms, especially the former. To the surprise of many, the experience-light organizer of disorganized Chicago neighborhoods and self-confident speech giver turned out to lack key qualities for pursuing those "legacy-making" achievements.

We are most interested in this book in the global-warming disorder and what Obama's almost two terms might illuminate. No environmental disruption of this enormity and estimated costs has ever been forecast and described by so many credible scientists, the disruption said to be already in the early stages. Obama engaged global warming promptly and intermittently with more energy than his predecessors (Bill Clinton and George H. W. Bush), who left him a low bar. To explain the modest scope of climate-change remediation in his two terms, Obama and supporters blamed Congress, climate-change deniers, and fossil-fuel producers. Rightly so, to a point, but there is much evidence that the environmental agenda in general was never near the top of Obama's list, possibly for expedient political (re-election) reasons. After a carbon tax was found politically unreachable in 2009, Obama was active in sermonizing on warming, including it in major speeches such as the State of the Union Address. But his attention was remarkably divided, and he frequently confessed to or chose other compelling priorities. He told interviewers early in his second term, and again in his State of the Union Address in January 2014, that his main strategic goal now was to condemn and if possible narrow the gap between rich and poor.

Although the inevitable cost of climate warming was a persistent theme of the administration, few onlookers discerned an Obama strategic assault guided by the White House. Climatologists reported summers longer and hotter, California's drought more severe. The 150 ice sheets once in Glacier National Park had melted to 30, reason to rename it "Glacier Memorial

Park." Obama was occasionally bold, signing with China in the fall of 2014 a mutual reduction of greenhouse gases and steering the Environmental Protection Agency (EPA) toward more stringent global greenhouse emission (GGE) curbs that Congress would not confirm. He delayed for six years a decision on the Keystone pipeline. In a series of executive actions, he proposed amnesty for illegal aliens, the largest national population increase ever sponsored by a US president.

SORTING OUT THE OBAMA PRESIDENCY—PREMATURELY

Appraising his not-quite-finished regime without abundant memoirs, unpublished papers, and the passage of time that enriches judgment, I guess historians will gravitate toward a below-average ranking for Obama. Average seems likely also for his environmental leadership.

Obama was and is what his mother and grandfather taught him to be before he started teaching himself in that same direction—a conventional, urban liberal, civil-rights-oriented "neighborhood activist" of familiar views and no managerial experience or instincts, who wishes many causes well. Environmentalists should look elsewhere for a leader who has slept under the stars and, if Hawaiian, knows and cares that the islands' coral reefs are dying underneath the Pacific's emerald waters as they slide upward across the beaches.

In recruiting our governing elites, we should give the edge to those who have managed sizable institutions where science is respected and elevate to top leadership those who agree with Robert F. Kennedy, Jr.'s decision to leave "social justice causes" and "go green since green is the ultimate civil rights and human rights agenda"[3] and who have strong ties to a future-engaged social movement that surged out of the 1960s, generating Earth Day gatherings in every state and city, passing around green-blue globes they admonish each other to take care not to break.

NOTES

CHAPTER 1. THE NEW NATION'S PUBLIC LANDS

1. William Cronon, ed., *Uncommon Ground* (New York: Norton, 1995), 23.

2. M. B. Livingston and C. A. Rich, *A Treasure on the Trace: The French Camp Story* (1996), 1–2.

3. Thomas D. Clark, *The Greening of the South* (Lexington: University Press of Kentucky, 1984), 2.

4. Ibid., 36.

5. James B. Trefethen, *An American Crusade for Wildlife* (New York: Winchester Press, 1975), 73; Henry Clepper, *Origins of American Conservation* (New York: Ronald Press, 1966), 23.

6. John F. Reiger, *American Sportsmen and the Origins of Conservation* (Corvallis: Oregon State University Press, 2000), 69.

7. George Catlin, *Letters and Notes on the Manners, Customs, and Condition of the North American Indians*, vol. 1 (London: Author, 1841), 2–3.

8. Thomas Jefferson, *Notes on the State of Virginia* (1767; New York: Harper and Row, 1964), 17.

9. Henry David Thoreau, "The Maine Woods," in *The Writings of Henry David Thoreau*, vol. 3 (Boston: Houghton Mifflin, 1906), 212.

10. See Donald J. Pisani, "Forests and Reclamation, 1891–1911," *Forest and Conservation History* (April 1993): 68–79.

11. Dayton Duncan and Ken Burns, *The National Parks: America's Best Idea* (New York: Knopf, 2009), 8–11; Donald Worster, "John Muir and the Modern Passion for Nature," *Environmental History* (June 2005): 19.

12. James P. Warren, *John Burroughs and the Place of Nature* (Athens: University of Georgia Press, 2006), 1.

13. John Muir, *Our National Parks* (Boston: Houghton Mifflin, 1901); Muir, *The Yosemite* (New York: Century, 1912), 255.

14. John Muir, *My First Summer in the Sierras* (Boston: Houghton Mifflin, 1911).

15. George Perkins Marsh, *Man and Nature; or Physical Geography as Modified by Human Action* (Cambridge, MA: Belknap Press of Harvard University, 1865).

16. *Annual Report of the Secretary of the Interior* (1877), 94.

17. Carl Schurz, *Reminiscences*, vol 1 (New York: McClure, 1907–1908), 93–95.

18. E. Louise Peffer, *The Closing of the Public Domain: Disposal and Reservation Policies, 1900–1950* (Stanford, CA: Stanford University Press, 1951), 15; Roderick Nash,

Wilderness and the American Mind (New Haven, CT: Yale University Press, 1967), 101, 102.

19. Duncan and Burns, *National Parks*, 8.

20. Ulysses S. Grant, *Personal Memoirs of Ulysses S. Grant, Major General U.S. Army*, vol. 2 (1885; Lincoln: University of Nebraska Press, 1996), 322.

21. Daniel J. Phillipon, *Conserving Words* (Athens: University of Georgia Press, 2004), 58–59.

22. Duncan and Burns, *National Parks*, 73.

23. Michael Cohen, *History of the Sierra Club, 1892–1970* (New York: Random House, 1988).

CHAPTER 2. BENJAMIN HARRISON, GROVER CLEVELAND, AND WILLIAM MCKINLEY

1. John Ise, *The U.S. Forest Policy* (New Haven, CT: Yale University Press, 1924), 120–139; Harold K. Steen, *The U.S. Forest Service: A History* (Seattle: University of Washington Press, 1976); Harold Socolofsky and Allen B. Spetter, *The Presidency of Benjamin Harrison* (Lawrence: University Press of Kansas, 1987), 70–73; Samuel T. Dana and Sally Fairfax, *Forest and Range Policy* (New York: McGraw-Hill, 1956), 91–101.

2. Marion Clawson and Burnell Held, *The Federal Lands: Their Use and Management* (Lincoln: University of Nebraska Press, 1957), 28.

3. Thomas Wolfe, "The Four Lost Men," in Wolfe, *From Death to Morning* (New York: Scribner, 1932–1935), 121.

4. Anne C. Moore, *Benjamin Harrison: Centennial President* (Hauppauge, NY: Nova Science, 2009), 1; Dennis L. Soden, ed., *The Environmental Presidency* (Albany: State University of New York Press, 1999), 31.

5. Daniel Ruddy, ed., *Theodore Roosevelt's History of the United States* (Washington, DC: Smithsonian Institution, 2012), 222–223, 340.

6. See Donald J. Pisani, "Forests and Reclamation, 1891–1911," *Forest and Conservation History* (April 1993): 68–79.

7. Steen, *U.S. Forest Service*, 26–28; and Harold K. Steen, "The Beginning of the National Forest System," in Char Miller, ed., *American Forests* (Lawrence: University Press of Kansas, 2010); Paul Russell Cutright, *Theodore Roosevelt: The Making of a Conservationist* (Urbana-Champaign: University of Illinois Press, 1985), 178.

8. Benjamin Harrison, *This Country of Ours* (New York: Scribner, 1897), 278–279.

9. Harold K. Steen, *Origins of the National Forests: A Centennial Symposium* (Durham, NC: Forest History Society, 1992), 204.

10. Philip C. Dolce and George H. Skan, eds., *Power and the Presidency* (New York: Scribner, 1976), 58.

11. Allan Nevins, *Grover Cleveland: A Study in Courage* (New York: Dodd, Mead, 1934), 224–225.

12. Steen, *U.S. Forest Service.*

13. Henry Graff, *Grover Cleveland* (New York: Holt, 2002), 40–42.

14. William Allen White, *Masks in a Pageant* (New York: Macmillan, 1928), 156.

15. John Muir, "A Plan to Save the Forests," *Century* (1895): 631; Samuel P. Hays, *Conservation and the Gospel of Efficiency: The Progressive Conservation Movement, 1890–1920* (Cambridge, MA: Harvard University Press, 1959), 42.

16. Char Miller, *Gifford Pinchot and the Making of American Environmentalism* (Washington, DC: Island, 2001), 120–125.

CHAPTER 3. THEODORE ROOSEVELT

1. Edmund Morris, *The Rise of Theodore Roosevelt* (New York: Coward, McCann, and Geoghegan, 1979), 387.

2. Paul Russell Cutright, *Theodore Roosevelt: The Making of a Conservationist* (Urbana-Champaign: University of Illinois Press, 1985), 202–207.

3. Douglas Brinkley, *Wilderness Warrior: Theodore Roosevelt and the Crusade for America* (New York: HarperCollins, 2009), 526–527; Mary Beth Lorbieckie, *Aldo Leopold: A Fierce Green Fire* (New York: Oxford University Press, 1999).

4. Brinkley, *Wilderness Warrior*, 13–15.

5. Timothy Egan, *The Big Burn: Theodore Roosevelt and the Fire That Saved America* (Boston: Houghton Mifflin Harcourt, 2009), 71, 240, 247.

6. Theodore Roosevelt, Opening Address, *Proceedings of a Conference of National Governors*, May 13, 1909.

7. Fred L. Israel, ed., *State of the Union Messages of the President*, vol. 3 (1790–1966).

8. Theodore Roosevelt and Hermann Hagedorn, *The Works of Theodore Roosevelt*, vol. 4 (New York: Scribner, 1926), 29.

9. Gifford Pinchot, *The Fight for Conservation* (New York: Doubleday, 1910), 42–44.

10. See Gifford Pinchot, *Breaking New Ground* (New York: Harcourt Brace, 1947), 322–326; Pinchot, *Fight for Conservation*, 41, 48.

11. Quoted in Edward Way Teale, *The Wilderness World of John Muir* (Boston: Houghton Mifflin Harcourt, 1976), 316–317.

12. Israel, *State of the Union Messages*, vol. 2, 2026.

13. John Muir, *The Yosemite* (New York: Century, 1912), 262.

14. Quoted in Carl Buchheister and Frank Graham, Jr., "From the Swamps and Back: A Concise and Candid History of the Audubon Movement," *Audubon* (January 1973): 19.

15. Carolyn Merchant, "Women of the Progressive Conservation Movement: 1900–1916," *Environmental Review* 8 (Spring 1984): 78.

16. Roy Robbins, *Our Landed Heritage: The Public Domain, 1776–1936* (Princeton, NJ: Princeton University Press, 1942), 354–355.

CHAPTER 4. WILLIAM TAFT, WOODROW WILSON, WARREN HARDING, CALVIN COOLIDGE, AND HERBERT HOOVER

1. Henry F. Pringle, *The Life and Times of William Howard Taft*, vol. 2 (New York: Farrar and Rinehart, 1939), 815.

2. Rachel Scheuring, *Shapers of the Great Debate on Conservation* (Westport, CT: Greenwood, 2004), 15.

3. James Penick, Jr., *Progressive Politic, and Conservation: The Ballinger-Pinchot Affair* (Chicago: University of Chicago Press, 1968), 47.

4. Gifford Pinchot, *Breaking New Ground* (New York: Harcourt Brace, 1947), 392–393.

5. William Howard Taft, *Our Chief Magistrate and His Powers* (New York: Columbia University Press, 1916), quoted and discussed in Gene Healy, *The Cult of the Presidency* (Washington, DC: Cato Institute, 2008), ch. 2.

6. Michael Bromley, *William Howard Taft and the First Motoring Presidency* (Jefferson, NC: McFarland, 2003), 198–199.

7. Fred L. Israel, ed., *State of the Union Messages of the President*, vol. 3 (1790–1966), 2536–2537.

8. Ann Vileisis, *Discovering the Unknown Landscape: A History of America's Wetlands* (Washington, DC: Island, 1997), 155.

9. Michael Genovese, *The Power of the American Presidency* (New York: Oxford University Press, 2001), 7; Kendrick A. Clements, *The Presidency of Woodrow Wilson* (Lawrence: University Press of Kansas, 1992), 7.

10. Arthur S. Link, *Wilson: The New Freedom* (Princeton, NJ: Princeton University Press, 1956), 4.

11. Arthur S. Link, ed., *The Papers of Woodrow Wilson: 1913* (Princeton, NJ: Princeton University Press, 1978), 149; Israel, *State of the Union Messages*, vol. 3, 2549.

12. Francis N. Lovett, *National Parks* (Lanham, MD: Rowman and Littlefield, 1998), 81.

13. E. Louise Peffer, *The Closing of the Public Domain: Disposal and Reservation Policies, 1900–1950* (Stanford, CA: Stanford University Press, 1951), 132.

14. Link, *Wilson: The New Freedom*, 127.

15. John Ise, *The United States Oil Policy* (New Haven, CT: Yale University Press, 1926), 334.

16. Franklin K. Lane, *The American Spirit* (New York: Stokes, 1918), 4.

17. Donald Swain, *Federal Conservation Policy, 1921–1933* (Berkeley: University of California Press, 1963).

18. Samuel P. Hays, *Conservation and the Gospel of Efficiency: The Progressive Conservation Movement, 1890–1920* (Cambridge, MA: Harvard University Press, 1959), 175.

19. Link, *Wilson: The New Freedom*, 126.

20. Robert Gottlieb, *Forcing the Spring* (Washington, DC: Island, 1993), 47.

21. Arthur S. Link, *Wilson: Road to the White House* (Princeton, NJ: Princeton University Press, 1947), 20–22.

22. Clements, *Presidency of Woodrow Wilson*, 4–5; Alice Hamilton, *Exploring the Dangerous Trades: The Autobiography of Alice Hamilton* (Boston: Little, Brown, 1943), 194.

23. Pinchot, *Breaking New Ground*, 417.

24. John Opie, *Nature's Nation* (Boston, MA: Wadsworth, 1998), 419.

25. *New York Times Magazine* (July 13, 2014): 32.

26. Israel, *State of the Union Messages*, 84, 69.

27. William E. Leuchtenburg, *The Perils of Prosperity* (Chicago: University of Chicago Press, 1958), 93.

28. William Ridings and Stuart McIver, *Rating the Presidents* (Secaucus, NJ: Carol, 1997), 191.

29. Edward A. Ross, "Controlled Fecundity," *New Republic* (January 25, 1922), 243.

30. Robert Sobel, *Coolidge: An American Enigma* (Washington, DC: Regnery, 1998), 144.

31. Claude M. Fuess, *Calvin Coolidge: The Man from Vermont* (Boston: Little, Brown, 1940), 317; Robert H. Ferrell, "Calvin Coolidge: Man and President," in John Earl Haynes, ed., *Calvin Coolidge and the Coolidge Era* (Washington, DC: Library of Congress, 1998), 132.

32. Quoted in Ferrell, "Calvin Coolidge," 141.

33. Israel, *State of the Union Messages*.

34. Philip Moran, ed., *Calvin Coolidge Documents, 1872–1933* (Dobbs Ferry, NY: Oceana, 1970), 128–132.

35. Ibid., 132.

36. Calvin Coolidge, *Foundations of the Republic* (New York: Scribner, 1926), 325.

37. Herbert Hoover, *The Memoirs of Herbert Hoover: Cabinet and Presidency, 1920–1933* (New York: Macmillan, 1952), v–vi, 29.

38. See Ellis W. Hawley, "Herbert Hoover, the Commerce Secretariat, and the Vision of an 'Associative State,' 1921–1928," *Journal of American History* (June 1974): 118.

39. Douglas C. Drake, "Herbert Hoover, Ecologist: The Politics of Oil Pollution Control, 1921–1926," *Mid-America* (July 1973): 214.

40. For Hoover's view, see Hoover, Memoirs, 60–65.

41. Michael Cooper, "McCain Reverses Himself," New York Times, April 11, 2008, C28.

42. Kendrick A. Clements, Hoover, Conservation, and Consumerism: Engineering the Good Life (Lawrence: University Press of Kansas, 2000), 76.

43. Ibid., 24.

44. Hal E. Wert, Hoover, the Fishing President: Portrait of the Private Man and His Life Outdoors (Mechanicsburg, PA: Stackpole, 2005), 69.

45. Kendrick A. Clements, "Herbert Hoover and Conservation, 1921–1933," American Historical Review (February 1984): 69.

46. William Hard, "Giant Negotiations for Giant Power: An Interview with Herbert Hoover," Survey Graphic (March 1924): 577.

47. William E. Leuchtenburg, Herbert Hoover (New York: Macmillan, 2009), 75–79, 114.

48. Wert, Hoover, xii–xiii.

49. Irving Brant, Adventures in Conservation with Franklin D. Roosevelt (Flagstaff, AZ: Northland, 1989), 1.

50. Mary Beth Lorbiecki, Aldo Leopold: A Fierce Green Fire (Helena, MT: Falcon, 1996), 68.

51. Aldo Leopold, "The Wilderness and Its Place in Outdoor Recreation Policy," Journal of Forestry 19, no. 7 (November 1921): 718–721.

52. Loomis Havemeyer, ed., Conservation of Our Natural Resources Based on Van Hise's "The Conservation of Natural Resources in the United States" (New York: Macmillan, 1930), 514–519, 356–358.

53. Edward A. Ross, Standing Room Only? (New York: Century, 1927), 186, 193.

54. Havemeyer, Conservation, 526.

55. Thomas Dunlap, Saving America's Wildlife: Ecology and the American Mind, 1850–1990 (Princeton, NJ: Princeton University Press, 1988), 87.

CHAPTER 5. FRANKLIN D. ROOSEVELT

1. Kendrick A. Clements, Hoover, Conservation, and Consumerism: Engineering the Good Life (Lawrence: University Press of Kansas, 2000), 191.

2. Edgar B. Nixon, ed., Franklin D. Roosevelt and Conservation, 1911–1945 (Hyde Park, NY: Franklin D. Roosevelt Library, 1957), 112–113.

3. Walter Lippmann, Interpretations, 1931–1932 (New York: Macmillan, 1932), 260–262; Ronald Steel, Walter Lippmann and the American Century (Boston: Little, Brown, 1980), 291.

4. Geoffrey C. Ward, "Franklin Roosevelt: Builder and Bibliophile," paper presented at Oberlin College, November 2, 1991, 3.

5. Ibid.

6. See Nixon, *Franklin D. Roosevelt and Conservation*, vol. 1, 17–18, 299.

7. Ibid., 17, 71–81.

8. Sarah T. Phillips, *This Land, This Nation: Conservation, Rural America, and the New Deal* (Cambridge, UK: Cambridge University Press, 2007).

9. Franklin Delano Roosevelt, "Acres Fit and Unfit: State Planning of Land Use," in Samuel Rosenman, ed., *The Public Papers and Addresses of Franklin D. Roosevelt* (New York: Random House, 1938), 485–495.

10. Ibid., 697; Kenneth S. Davis, *FDR: The New Deal Years, 1933–1937* (New York: Putnam, 1979), 386.

11. FDR's "Brains Trust" of academic advisers would today be called the president's intellectuals. In his *Intellectuals and the American Presidency* (2002), Tevi Troy traces this enhancement of modern presidents' power from John F. Kennedy to George W. Bush.

12. David M. Kennedy, *Freedom from Fear: The American People in Depression and War, 1929–1945* (New York: Oxford University Press, 1999), 99–101.

13. Raymond Moley, *After Seven Years* (New York: Harper,1939).

14. Nixon, *Franklin D. Roosevelt and Conservation*, vol. 1, 151, 333.

15. Neil Maher, *Nature's New Deal: The Civilian Conservation Corps and the Roots of the American Environmental Movement* (New York: Oxford University Press, 2007), 5–16.

16. Rexford Guy Tugwell, *Roosevelt Revolution* (New York: Macmillan, 1979), 68–72.

17. Arthur M. Schlesinger, Jr., *Coming of the New Deal, 1933–1935* (New York: Houghton Mifflin, 1958), 341–343.

18. Ibid., 339–340.

19. Tugwell, *Roosevelt Revolution*, 183.

20. Schlesinger, *Coming of the New Deal*, 342–343.

21. William Harbaugh, "The Limits of Voluntarism—Farmers, County Agents, and the Conservation Movement," in John Milton Cooper and Charles E. Neu, eds., *The Wilson Era: Essays in Honor of Arthur S. Link* (Arlington Heights, IL: Harlan Davidson, 1991), 91.

22. Sarah Phillips, "Law, Policy, and Planning the New Deal Roots of Modern Environmentalism," in H. L. Henderson and D. B. Woolner, eds., *FDR and the Environment* (New York: Palgrave Macmillan, 2009), 112.

23. Nixon, *Franklin D. Roosevelt and Conservation*, vol. 2, 3–6.

24. Aldo Leopold, *The River of the Mother of God and Other Essays* (Madison: University of Wisconsin Press, 1991).

25. Nixon, *Franklin D. Roosevelt and Conservation*, vol. 1, 469.

26. Schlesinger, *Coming of the New Deal*, 554.

27. Phoebe Cutler, *The Landscape of the New Deal* (New Haven, CT: Yale University Press, 1985), 95.

28. Nixon, *Franklin D. Roosevelt and Conservation*, vol. 1, 130.

29. See Paul S. Sutter, *Driven Wild: How the Fight against the Automobile Launched the Modern Wilderness Movement* (Seattle: University of Washington Press, 2002).

30. Curt Meine, *Aldo Leopold: His Life and Work* (Madison: University of Wisconsin Press, 1988), 302–303, 317.

31. Ibid., 320.

32. Albert W. Atwood, "Is This Conservation?" *Saturday Evening Post* (September 25, 1936): 23.

33. Jay "Ding" Darling, "Conservation: A Typographical Error," *Review of Reviews*, 35–38.

34. Rosenman, *Public Papers and Addresses*, vol. 4, 62.

35. Sherwood Anderson, *Puzzled America* (New York: Scribner, 1935), 71.

36. Clinton Rossiter, *The American Presidency* (New York: Harcourt Brace, 1956), 2–3.

37. Jean Christie, "Morris L. Cooke," in Otis L. Graham, Jr., and Meghan Wander, eds., *Franklin Roosevelt: His Life and Times—An Encyclopedic View* (Boston: G. K. Hall, 1985). See also Morris L. Cooke, "Is the U.S. a Permanent Country?" *Forum and Century* (January–June, 1938); Rosenman, *Public Papers and Addresses*, vol. 5, 61–65.

38. Nixon, *Franklin D. Roosevelt and Conservation*, vol. 2, 632.

39. Michael Beschloss, *Presidential Courage 1789–1989* (New York: Simon and Schuster, 2006), 191.

CHAPTER 6. HARRY TRUMAN, DWIGHT EISENHOWER, AND JOHN F. KENNEDY

1. Harry S. Truman and Robert F. Ferrell, *The Autobiography of Harry S. Truman* (Boulder: University of Colorado Press, 1980), 6, 30.

2. David McCullough, *Truman* (New York: Simon and Schuster, 1992), 74–75.

3. Dennis Merrill, ed., *A Documentary History of the Truman Presidency*, vol. 15 (Bethesda, MD: University Publications of America, 2011), 25–27; Gerald D. Nash, *World War II and the West: Reshaping the Economy* (Lincoln: University of Nebraska Press, 1990), 150–151.

4. Kevin Powers, "Franklin D. Roosevelt," in Kathleen A. Brosnan, ed., *Encyclopedia of American Environmental History*, vol. 4 (New York: Facts on File, 2011), 1142.

5. Thomas Wellock, *Preserving the Nation: The Conservation and Environmental Movements, 1870–2000* (Hoboken, NJ: Wiley-Blackwell, 2007), 211.

6. Richard Severo, obituary of Douglas, *New York Times*, May 15, 1998, A18; Jack Davis, "Conservation Is Now a Dead Word," *Environmental History* (January 2003); Davis and Raymond Arsenault, eds., *Paradise Lost? Environmental History of Florida* (Gainesville: University Press of Florida, 2005), 301–312.

7. Louis W. Koenig, ed., *The Truman Administration* (New York: New York University Press, 1965), 134–135.

8. Karl Brooks, "A Lesson in Concrete," in Richard S. Kirkendall, ed., *Harry's Farewell: Interpreting and Teaching the Truman Presidency* (Columbia: University of Missouri Press, 2004), 304–305.

9. Elmo Richardson, *Dams, Parks, and Politics: Resource Development and Preservation in the Truman-Eisenhower Era* (Lexington: University Press of Kentucky, 1973), 56.

10. Roderick Nash, *Wilderness and the American Mind* (New Haven, CT: Yale University Press, 1967), 212.

11. Wallace Stegner, "Wilderness Letter," in *The Sound of Mountain Water* (Garden City, NY: Doubleday, 1969), 146.

12. Marc Reisner, *Cadillac Desert* (New York: Viking Penguin, 1986), 299.

13. Donald Worster, *Rivers of Empire* (New York: Pantheon, 1985), 324.

14. Wallace Stegner, *The Uneasy Chair: A Biography of Bernard DeVoto* (New York: Doubleday, 1974), 297.

15. Bernard DeVoto, "The West against Itself," *Harper's Magazine* (January 1947), 1–13.

16. John Ise, *Our National Park Policy: A Critical History* (Baltimore, MD: Johns Hopkins University Press, 1961), 4.

17. Paul W. Hirt, *A Conspiracy of Optimism: Management of the National Forest Service since World War II* (Lincoln: University of Nebraska Press, 1994), 23.

18. The Clifford memo on conservation is discussed in Allen Yarnell, *Democrats and Progressives: The 1948 Presidential Election as a Test of Postwar Liberalism* (Berkeley: University of California Press, 1974), ch. 3.

19. Brooks, "Lesson in Concrete," 300.

20. Aldo Leopold, *A Sand County Almanac, with Essays on Conservation from Round River* (New York: Oxford University Press, 1949), 239–240.

21. William Vogt, *Road to Survival* (New York: Sloan, 1948), 146–147; Fairfield Osborn, *Our Plundered Planet* (Boston: Little, Brown, 1948), 162.

22. President's Commission on Materials Policy, *Resources for Freedom* (Washington, DC: Government Printing Office, 1952), 1–5.

23. President's Research Committee on Social Trends, *Recent Social Trends* (reprint; Westport, CT: Greenwood, 1970).

24. President's Commission on Materials Policy, *Resources for Freedom*, 75–76.

25. Richardson, *Dams, Parks, and Politics*, 74.

26. Sherman Adams, *Firsthand Report: The Story of the Eisenhower Administration* (New York: Harper, 1961), 78–90.

27. Dwight D. Eisenhower, *Waging Peace, 1956–1961: White House Years* (New York: Doubleday), 321.

28. Ibid., 322.

29. Dwight D. Eisenhower, *Mandate for Change, 1953–1956: The White House Years* (New York: Doubleday, 1963), 353.

30. Richardson, *Dams, Parks, and Politics*, 119.

31. Ibid., 50.

32. Stephen E. Ambrose, *Eisenhower: Soldier and President*, vol. 2 (New York: Simon and Schuster), 201.

33. Bernard DeVoto, *DeVoto's West: History, Conservation, and the Public Good*, ed. Edward K. Muller (Athens, GA: Swallow Press, 2005), 237–253.

34. Nash, *Wilderness and the American Mind*, 216–217.

35. Michael Cohen, *History of the Sierra Club, 1892–1970* (New York: Random House, 1988), 179.

36. James L. Sundquist, *Politics and Policy: The Eisenhower, Kennedy, and Johnson Years* (Washington, DC: Brookings Institute, 1968), 331.

37. Geoffrey Perret, *Eisenhower* (New York: Adams Media, 1999), 516.

38. Elmer T. Peterson, *Big-Dam Foolishness* (New York: Devin-Adair, 1954), 53–55.

39. Conrad Wirth, *Parks, Politics, and the People* (Norman: University of Oklahoma Press, 1980), 234–256.

40. Richardson, *Dams, Parks, and Politics*, 182.

41. *Public Papers of Presidents of the United States* (PPPUS), Dwight D. Eisenhower, "Special Message to Congress," February 23, 1960, 208–209.

42. Leopold, *Sand County Almanac*, 246.

43. Derek Hoff, *The State and the Stork* (Chicago: University of Chicago Press, 2012), 135.

44. PPPUS, John F. Kennedy, Remarks at Warren, Ohio, October 9, 1960.

45. Robert Dallek, *An Unfinished Life: John F. Kennedy, 1917–1963* (Boston: Little, Brown, 2003), 178.

46. James MacGregor Burns, *John Kennedy: A Political Profile* (New York: Harcourt, Brace, 1960), 274–281.

47. Maurice Isserman and Michael Kazin, *America Divided* (New York: Oxford University Press, 2000), 47.

48. Richard Parker, *John Kenneth Galbraith: His Life, His Politics, His Economics* (New York: Farrar, Straus, and Giroux, 2005), 357.

49. Ibid., 658–660.

50. Thomas G. Smith, "John Kennedy, Stewart Udall, and New Frontier Conservation," *Pacific Historical Review* (August 1995): 332–362.

51. Michael O'Brien, *John F. Kennedy: A Biography* (New York: Dunne, 2005), 575.

52. Smith, "John Kennedy, Stewart Udall, and New Frontier Conservation," 339.

53. Ibid., 332–362.

54. PPPUS, John F. Kennedy, "Remarks to the White House Conference on Conservation," May 25, 1962, 441–218.

55. Smith, "John Kennedy, Stewart Udall, and New Frontier Conservation," 345.

56. PPPUS, John F. Kennedy: 1963, vol. 2, 715–738.

57. Richard Reeves, *President Kennedy: A Profile of Power* (New York: Simon and Schuster, 1993), 606–608; Schlesinger, *A Thousand Days*, 979–981.

58. Smith, "John Kennedy, Stewart Udall, and New Frontier Conservation," 339–356. On Kennedy's western tours, see O'Brien, *John F. Kennedy*, 574–575.

59. Stewart Udall, *The Quiet Crisis* (New York: Holt, Rinehart, and Winston, 1963), viii.

60. Stephen Raushenbush, "Conservation in 1952," in *Annals of the American Academy of Political and Social Sciences* (May 1952), 3; Grant McConnell, "The Conservation Movement—Past and Present," *Western Political Quarterly* (September 1954), 463–478.

61. Udall, *Quiet Crisis*, 175–177.

62. Stewart Udall, *Quiet Crisis and the New Generation* (Salt Lake City, UT: Peregrine Smith, 1988), 180.

63. Adam Rome, *The Bulldozer in the Countryside* (New York: Cambridge University Press, 2001), 15–17. For other estimates, see Hal K. Rothman, *The Greening of a Nation* (New York: Harcourt Brace, 1998), ch. 1.

64. Christopher J. Bosso, *Environment, Inc.: From Grassroots to Beltway* (Lawrence: University Press of Kansas, 2005), 20–35.

65. Rachel Carson, *Silent Spring* (Boston: Houghton Mifflin, 1962), 1–8.

66. Albert Gore, "Introduction," in Rachel Carson, *Silent Spring* (Boston: Houghton Mifflin, 1994), xv.

67. Paul Hawken, *Blessed Unrest* (New York: Viking, 2007), 51; Carl Pope, "Trash-

ing Rachel Carson," *Sierra* (September–October 2007), http://vault.sierraclub.org/
sierra/200709/ways_and_means.asp.

CHAPTER 7. LYNDON BAINES JOHNSON, RICHARD NIXON, GERALD FORD,
AND JIMMY CARTER

1. Vaughn Davis Bornet, *The Presidency of Lyndon B. Johnson* (Lawrence: University
Press of Kansas, 1983), 134.

2. Lyndon B. Johnson, *The Vantage Point: Perspectives of the Presidency, 1963–1969*
(New York: Holt, Rinehart, and Winston, 1973), 323. See also G. Calvin MacKenzie
and Robert Weisbrot, *The Liberal Hour: Washington and the Politics of Change in the 1960s*
(London: Penguin, 2008).

3. *Public Papers of Presidents of the United States (PPPUS)*, Lyndon B. Johnson, 1965,
"Special Message to Congress on Conservation," February 5, 156–165.

4. Martin Melosi, "Lyndon Johnson and Environmental Policy," in Robert A. Di-
vine, ed., *The Johnson Years*, vol. 2 (Lawrence: University Press of Kansas, 1987), 117.

5. Sierra Club, "The Wilderness Idea," in David Brower, ed., *Wilderness: America's
Living Heritage* (Proceedings of the Seventh Wilderness Conference, San Francisco,
1961), 97; Douglas Scott, "Howard Zahniser: Architect of Wilderness," *Sierra Club Bulletin* (October 1976), 16–17.

6. PPPUS, Lyndon B. Johnson, 1963–1965, vol. 2, 1083.

7. Ibid., 1084.

8. Melosi, "Lyndon Johnson and Environmental Policy," 113.

9. Bornet, *Presidency of Lyndon B. Johnson*, 142.

10. PPPUS, Lyndon B. Johnson, vol. 3, 155–156.

11. Johnson, *Vantage Point*, 339.

12. Ibid. For Eisenhower's role, see Donald T. Critchlow, *Intended Consequences:
Birth Control, Abortion, and the Federal Government in Modern America* (New York: Oxford
University Press, 1999), 44.

13. Bornet, *Presidency of Lyndon B. Johnson*, 145–146. See also John P. Crevelli, "The
Final Act of the Greatest Conservation President," *Prologue: The Journal of the National
Archives*, VII (Winter 1980), 173–184.

14. Johnson, *Vantage Point*, 336.

15. Joseph A. Califano, Jr., *The Triumph and Tragedy of Lyndon Johnson* (New York: Simon and Schuster, 1991), 330.

16. Hal Rothman, *LBJ's Texas White House:"Our Heart's Home"* (College Station: Texas
A&M University Press, 2001), 258; For Johnson's ranch image, see Ronnie Dugger,
The Politician: Life and Times of Lyndon Baines Johnson (New York: Norton, 1984).

17. Theodore White, *The Making of a President: 1964* (New York: Atheneum, 1965), 36–37.

18. J. Brooks Flippen, *Nixon and the Environment* (Albuquerque: University of New Mexico Press, 2000), 20, 23.

19. Ibid., 17–18; Stephen E. Ambrose, *Nixon: The Education of a Politician, 1913–1962* (New York: Simon and Schuster, 1987), 27.

20. Russell Train, *Politics, Pollution, and Pandas: An Environmental Memoir* (Washington, DC: Island, 2003), ch. 1, 4–5; Flippen, *Nixon and the Environment*, 22–25; PPPUS, Richard M. Nixon, vol. 1, 1.

21. Steven F. Hayward, *The Age of Reagan: The Fall of the Old Liberal Order, 1964–1980* (New York: Three Rivers, 2001), 250.

22. Elizabeth Drew and Arthur M. Schlesinger, Jr., eds., *Richard M. Nixon* (New York: Times Books, 2007), 23.

23. Jeremy Main, "Conservationists at the Barricades," *Fortune* (February 1970): 144–146.

24. PPPUS, Richard M. Nixon, vol. 2, 1–3.

25. Train, *Politics, Pollution, and Pandas*, 77.

26. "Summons to a New Cause," *Time* (February 2, 1970): 11.

27. Conrad Black, *Richard Milhous Nixon: The Invincible Quest* (London: Quercus, 2007), 653.

28. PPPUS, Richard M. Nixon, vol. 2, "Remarks on Transmitting a Special Message to the Congress on Environmental Quality," February 10, 1970, 95–97.

29. Whitaker, *Striking a Balance: Environment and Natural Resources Policy in the Nixon-Ford Years* (Washington, DC: American Enterprise Institute, 1976), 186–187.

30. PPPUS, Richard Nixon, vol. 4, "State of the Union Address," January 22, 1970, 8–16.

31. Dennis Hevesi, "Walter J. Hickel, Former Alaska Governor and Nixon Official, Is Dead at Ninety," *New York Times*, May 9, 2010, 21.

32. John Ehrlichman, *Witness to Power* (New York: Simon and Schuster, 1982), 70.

33. Flippen, *Nixon and the Environment*, 75.

34. Ibid., 8–16.

35. Ibid., 133, 135.

36. Ibid., 156.

37. Commission on Population Growth and the American Future, *Population and the American Future* (Washington, DC: Government Printing Office, 1972), 56, 66.

38. *Sierra Club Bulletin* (September 1972): 30; *Washington Post*, August 3, 1972, 26.

39. Flippen, *Nixon and the Environment*, 190.

40. PPPUS, Richard M. Nixon, "State of the Union Message to the Congress on Natural Resources and the Environment," February 15, 1973.

41. Train, *Politics, Pollution, and Pandas*, xi.

42. John Barkdull, "Nixon and the Marine Environment," *Presidential Studies Quarterly* 28 (Summer 1998): 593; also, Barkdull offers a measured appraisal between Nixon's aides and James Rathlesberger, *Nixon and the Environment: The Politics of Devastation* (New York: Taurus Communications, 1972), written for the League of Conservation Voters.

43. Train, *Politics, Pollution, and Pandas*, 163.

44. Flippen, *Nixon and the Environment*, 231.

45. Douglas Brinkley and Arthur M. Schlesinger, Jr., *Gerald R. Ford* (New York: Times Books, 2007), 7.

46. PPPUS, Gerald R. Ford, vol. 1, "Remarks to the White House Conference on Domestic and Economic Affairs," Portland, Oregon, November 1, 1974, 543–548.

47. PPPUS, Gerald R. Ford, vol. 1, "Message to the Congress Transmitting Annual Report of the Council on Environmental Quality," December 12, 1974, 740–741; Train, *Politics, Pollution, and Pandas*, 200.

48. "Strip Mining," *Congressional Quarterly Almanac* (1975): 185–186.

49. PPPUS, Gerald R. Ford, vol. 1, 36.

50. John R. Greene, *The Presidency of Gerald R. Ford* (Lawrence: University Press of Kansas, 1995), 85.

51. Quoted in Mary H. Cooper, "The Environmental Movement at 25," *Congressional Quarterly Researcher* (March 31, 1995), 418.

52. Andrew Downer Crain, *The Ford Presidency: A History* (Jefferson, NC: McFarland, 2009), 38–39.

53. Richard Reeves, *A Ford, Not a Lincoln* (New York: Harcourt, Brace, 1975), 8–9.

54. Richard Reeves, "I'm Sorry, Mr. President," *American Heritage* (December 1996), 53.

55. James Cannon, *Time and Chance: Gerald R. Ford's Appointment with History* (Ann Arbor: University of Michigan Press, 1998), 205.

56. Jimmy Carter, *An Hour before Daylight: Memories of a Rural Boyhood* (New York: Simon and Schuster, 2001), 15, 97.

57. Jimmy Carter, *An Outdoor Journal: Adventures and Reflections* (New York: Bantam, 1988), 8.

58. Jimmy Carter, *Why Not the Best?* (Nashville, TN: Broadman, 1975), 147.

59. Jeffrey Stine, "Environmental Policy in the Carter Administration," in Gary M.

Fink and Hugh Davis Graham, eds., *The Carter Presidency: Policy Choices in the Post–New Deal Era* (Lawrence: University Press of Kansas, 1998), 181–182.

60. Douglas Brinkley, "Introduction," in Carter, *Why Not the Best?* (Fayetteville: University of Arkansas Press, 1996), xviii.

61. Carter, *Why Not the Best?*, 117, 120–121.

62. P. S. Ward, "Ford and Carter: Contrasting Approaches to Environment," *Journal of the Water Pollution Control Federation* (October 1976): 2238–2242.

63. Betty Glad, *Jimmy Carter* (New York: Norton, 1980), 358.

64. Carter, *Why Not the Best?*, 122, 141; Glad, *Jimmy Carter*, 507.

65. Glad, *Jimmy Carter*, 347.

66. Quoted in Charles O. Jones, *The Trusteeship Presidency: Jimmy Carter and the U.S. Congress* (Baton Rouge: Louisiana State University Press, 1988), 1.

67. Carter, *Why Not the Best?*, 152.

68. Theodore White, *America in Search of Itself: The Making of the Presidents, 1956–1980* (New York: Harper and Row, 1982).

69. Ibid., 203.

70. See Philip Fradkin, *A River No More* (New York: Knopf, 1981).

71. PPPUS, James E. Carter, vol. 1, "Message to Congress re: the Environment," May 23, 1977, 967–1003; see also P. S. Ward, "Carter Environmental Message Stresses Administration, Enforcement," *Journal of the Water Pollution Control Federation* (July 1977): 1572–1575.

72. Jones, *Trusteeship Presidency*, 153–154.

73. PPPUS, James E. Carter, vol. 2, "Address to the Nation Regarding Energy and National Goals," July 15, 1979, 1235–1241; Daniel Horowitz, *Jimmy Carter and the Energy Crisis of the 1970s* (Boston: St. Martin's, 2005), 114–119.

74. White, *America in Search of Itself*, 214.

75. PPPUS, James E. Carter, May 23, 1977, 967–968.

76. Luther Carter, "Carter Places Environment High on Agenda," *Science* (June 3, 1977): 1065.

77. C. Brant Short, *Ronald Reagan and the Public Lands: America's Conservation Debate, 1979–1984* (College Station: Texas A&M University Press, 1989), 89–127; Jeffrey K. Stine, "Environmental Policy during the Carter Administration," in Fink and Graham, eds., *Carter Presidency*, 193.

78. Joseph Davis, "The Grand Plans of Congressman Udall," *Sierra* (May–June 1989): 90.

79. Anthony Downs, "Up and Down with Ecology: The 'Issue-Attention Cycle,'" *Public Interest* 28 (Summer 1972): 38–50.

80. Mary Graham, *The Morning after Earth Day: Practical Environmental Politics* (Washington, DC: Brookings Institute, 1999), 37.

81. Peter Carroll, *It Seemed Like Nothing Happened* (New Brunswick, NJ: Rutgers University Press, 1990), 69.

82. Lou Cannon, *Governor Reagan* (New York: PublicAffairs, 2003), 177.

83. Craig Shirley, *Rendezvous with Destiny: Ronald Reagan and the Campaign That Changed America* (Wilmington, DE: Intercollegiate Studies Institute, 2009), 495; Tim Radford, *The Guardian*, May 13, 2014, http://www.theguardian.com/science/2004/may/13/thisweekssciencequestions3.

84. John F. Stacks, *Watershed: Campaign for the Presidency, 1980* (New York: Times Books, 1981), 218–219.

85. Elizabeth Kolbert, "The Catastrophist," *New Yorker* (June 29, 2009): 39.

CHAPTER **8.** RONALD REAGAN, GEORGE H. W. BUSH, AND BILL CLINTON

1. William E. Leuchtenburg, *In the Shadow of FDR* (Ithaca, NY: Cornell University Press, 1983); see also John F. Stacks, *Watershed: Campaign for the Presidency, 1980* (New York: Times Books, 1981), 218–219.

2. Kiron Skinner et al., eds., *Reagan: In His Own Hand* (New York: Simon and Schuster, 2001); see also Ronald Reagan, *Ronald Reagan's Call for Action* (New York: Warner, 1976); and Kiron Skinner et al., eds., *Reagan's Path to Victory* (New York: Simon and Schuster, 2004).

3. C. Brant Short, *Ronald Reagan and the Public Lands* (College Station: Texas A&M University Press, 1989), 9.

4. Lou Cannon, *Governor Reagan* (New York: PublicAffairs, 2003), 300. See also Cannon, *President Reagan: Role of a Lifetime* (New York: Simon and Schuster, 1991), 526–527.

5. Hugh Davis Graham, "Civil Rights Policy," in W. Eliot Brownlee and Hugh Davis Graham, eds., *The Reagan Presidency: Pragmatic Conservatism and Its Legacies* (Lawrence: University Press of Kansas, 2003), 286.

6. Michael E. Kraft, "A New Environmental Policy Agenda," in Norman J. Vig and Michael E. Kraft, eds., *Environmental Policy in the 1980s: Reform or Reaction* (Washington, DC: Congressional Quarterly Press, 1984), 35.

7. Paul Boyer, ed., *Reagan as President* (Chicago: Ivan R. Dee, 1990), 179. See also Constance Holden, "The Reagan Years: Environmentalists Tremble," *Science* (November 28, 1990), 988.

8. Charles L. Heatherly, *Mandate for Leadership* (Washington, DC: Heritage Foundation, 1981), esp. chs. 8 and 30; Kraft, "New Environmental Policy Agenda," 29–40.

9. Ron Arnold, *At the Eye of the Storm: James Watt and the Environmentalists* (Washington, DC: Regnery Gateway, 1982), 54–55.

10. C. Brant Short, *America's Conservation Debate, 1979–1984* (College Station: Texas A&M University Press, 1989), 89–127.

11. Robert A. Dallek, *Ronald Reagan: The Politics of Symbolism* (Cambridge, MA: Harvard University Press, 1984), 82–85.

12. Short, *America's Conservation Debate*, 59; Dallek, *Ronald Reagan*, 84–85.

13. Michael J. Lacey, ed., *Government and Environmental Politics: Essays on Historical Developments since World War Two* (Washington, DC: Woodrow Wilson Center, 1989), 96–98.

14. See for example Katherine Gilman and Jonathan Lash, eds., *Hitting Home* (Washington, DC: Natural Resources Defense Council, 1982); Friends of the Earth, *Indictment: The Case against the Reagan Environmental Record* (Washington, DC: Friends of the Earth, 1982); Jonathan Lash et al., *A Season of Spoils: The Story of the Reagan Administration's Attack on the Environment* (New York: Pantheon Books, 1984); John H Adams, ed., *An Environmental Agenda for the Future* (Washington, DC: Agenda Press, 1985).

15. Short, *America's Conservation Debate*, 52.

16. *Public Papers of Presidents of the United States* (PPPUS), Ronald W. Reagan, vol. 1, "Inaugural Address," January 20, 1981, 1–5.

17. PPPUS: Ronald W. Reagan, vol. 1, "Question and Answer," August 13, 1981, 711.

18. PPPUS: Ronald W. Reagan, vol. 2, "Interview with Reporters from the *Los Angeles Times*," January 20, 1982, 69–70.

19. PPPUS: Ronald W. Reagan, vol. 2, "Interview with Julius Hunter of KMOX-TV in St. Louis, Missouri," July 22, 1982, 964–965.

20. Arnold, *At the Eye of the Storm*, 53.

21. PPPUS, Ronald W. Reagan, vol. 2, "Address before a Joint Session of the Congress Reporting on the State of the Union," January 26, 1982, 77.

22. Short, *America's Conservation Debate*, 51–59.

23. William E. Pemberton, *Exit with Honor: The Life and Presidency of Ronald Reagan* (Armonk, NY: M. E. Sharpe, 1997), 122–123.

24. Lash, *A Season of Spoils*, 29.

25. Steven Cohen, "Defusing the Toxic Time Bomb," in Norman J. Vig and Michael E. Kraft, eds., *Environmental Policy in the 1980s: Reform or Reaction* (Washington, DC: Congressional Quarterly Press, 1984), 284–288.

26. David Vogel, *Fluctuating Fortunes: The Political Power of Business in America* (New York: BasicBooks, 1989), 266.

27. Russell Train, "The Destruction of EPA," *Washington Post*, February 2, 1982, A15.

28. Harold C. Barnett, *Toxic Debts and the Superfund Dilemma* (Chapel Hill: University of North Carolina Press, 1994), 76–81.

29. PPPUS, Ronald W. Reagan, vol. 3, "Remarks and a Question-and-Answer Session with Reporters on Domestic and Foreign Policy Issues," March 11, 1983, 388–389.

30. PPPUS, Ronald W. Reagan, vol. 3, "Radio Address to the Nation on Environmental and Natural Resources Management," June 11, 1983, 852–853.

31. Michael Kraft and Norman Vig, "Environmental Policy in the Reagan Presidency," *Political Science Quarterly* (Autumn 1984): 424–431.

32. *Congressional Quarterly Almanac: 1981*, 503–507.

33. Charles Heatherly et al., eds., *Mandate for Leadership III* (Washington, DC: Heritage Foundation, 1989), 309; Barnett, *Toxic Debts and the Superfund Dilemma*, 80–81.

34. Edmund Morris, *Dutch: A Memoir of Ronald Reagan* (New York: Random House, 1999), 579; Pemberton, *Exit with Honor*, 18–19; Richard Reeves, *President Reagan* (New York: Simon and Schuster, 2005), 60.

35. Laurence Barrett, *Gambling with History: Ronald Reagan in the White House* (New York: Penguin, 1983), 458.

36. James M. Turner, "The Specter of Environmentalism: Wilderness, Environmental Politics, and the Evolution of the New Right," *Journal of American History* (June 2009): 123.

37. Vogel, *Fluctuating Fortunes*, 260–264; Harold C. Barnett, "Hazardous Waste Cleanup and Reagan Ideology," *Political Science Review* (Autumn 1988): 29.

38. Carl Pope, "The Politics of Plunder," *Sierra* (November–December 1988), 49–55.

39. Steven M. Gillon, *The Democrats' Dilemma: Walter F. Mondale and the Liberal Legacy* (New York: Columbia University Press, 1992), 376–377.

40. Peter Haas, "Banning Chlorofluorocarbons," *International Organization* 46 (Winter 1992): 196–197; Glen Sussman, "The USA and Global Environmental Policy," *International Political Science Review* 25 (October 2004), 349–369.

41. Richard E. Benedict, *Ozone Diplomacy* (Cambridge, MA: Harvard University Press, 1998), 59–67; Steven F. Hayward, "Ronald Reagan and the Environment," *InFocus Quarterly* (Fall 2009), http://www.jewishpolicycenter.org/1409/ronald-reagan-environment; "Ronald Reagan's Environmental Achievements," www.climate conservative.org; Jim DiPeso, "What Would Reagan Do about Global Warming?" April 5, 2010, http://cquestor.blogspot.com/2010/04/what-would-reagan-do-about-global.html.

42. Jessica L. Whittemore, "Reagan and the Montreal Protocol: Environmentalism at Its Unlikely Finest," unpub. diss., University of Southern California, nd.

43. Benedict, *Ozone Diplomacy*, 67.

44. Ibid., 59–60.

45. *PPPUS*, Ronald W. Reagan, vol. 5, "Farewell Address to the Nation," January 11, 1989.

46. John Holusha, "Bush Pledges Aid for Environment," *New York Times*, September 1, 1988, 9; Bill Peterson, "Bush Vows to Fight Pollution, Install Conservation Ethic," *Washington Post*, September 1, 1988, A1; George Hager, *Congressional Quarterly*, January 20, 1990, p 139, https://library.cqpress.com/cqweekly/toc.php?mode=weekly-date&level=3&values=1990%7E01|January#.

47. Jim McGrath, ed., *Heartbeat: George Bush in His Own Words* (New York: Scribner, 2001), 29.

48. Martin Allday, quoted in William Levantrosser and Rosanna Perotti, eds., *A Noble Calling: Character and the George H. W. Bush Presidency* (Westport, CT: Praeger, 2004), 21.

49. Byron W. Daynes and Glen Sussman, eds., *White House Politics and the Environment: Franklin D. Roosevelt to George W. Bush* (College Station: Texas A&M University Press, 2010), 155.

50. Levantrosser and Perotti, *Noble Calling*, 66.

51. *PPPUS*, George H. W. Bush, vol. 1, "Remarks at the Swearing-in Ceremony for William K. Reilly as Administrator of the Environmental Protection Agency," February 8, 1989, 68.

52. "Bush's Bumpy Road to Rio," *U.S. News and World Report*, June 22, 1992, 112.

53. *PPPUS*, George H. W. Bush, "Remarks at the Washington Centennial Celebration in Spokane," September 19, 1989, 935.

54. Katherine Langford, "George Bush's Struggle with the Vision Thing," in Martin J. Medhurst, ed., *The Rhetorical Presidency of George Bush* (College Station: Texas A&M University Press, 2006), 13–15.

55. Herbert Parmet, *George Bush: The Life of a Lone Star Yankee* (New York: Scribner, 1997), 367.

56. Roman Popadiuk, *The Leadership of George Bush* (College Station: Texas A&M University Press, 2009), 49.

57. Albert Gore, *Earth in the Balance* (Boston: Houghton-Mifflin, 2007), 315.

58. David Maraniss, *First in His Class: A Biography of Bill Clinton* (New York: Simon and Schuster, 1995).

59. Ernest Dumas, ed., *The Clintons of Arkansas: An Introduction by Those Who Know Them Best* (Fayetteville: University of Arkansas Press, 1993), 3.

60. Maraniss, *First in His Class*, 454.

61. Ibid., 359, 361, 365–367, 403.

62. William J. Clinton, *My Life* (New York: Knopf, 2004), 216–217.

63. Gore, *Earth in the Balance*, 8–9.

64. David Remnick, "Ozone Man," *New Yorker* (April 24, 2006): 47.

65. William Clinton, "Remarks on the Observance of Earth Day," *Weekly Compilation of Presidential Documents* 30 (April 21, 1994): 868.

66. Ibid., 740–743.

67. Ibid., 868.

68. Gore, *Earth in the Balance*, 9.

69. Daynes and Sussman, *White House Politics*, 101; Paul Wapner, "Clinton's Environmental Legacy," *Tikkun* (March–April 2001), 11–14.

70. Timothy Egan, "Sweeping Reversal of U.S. Land Policy Sought by Clinton," *New York Times*, February 24, 1993.

71. John Cushman, "Why the U.S. Fell Short of Goals for Reducing Greenhouse Gases," *New York Times*, October 20, 1997.

72. Bruce Babbitt, *Cities in the Wilderness* (Washington, DC: Island, 2005), 169.

73. Dennis L. Soden, ed., *The Environmental Presidency* (Albany: State University of New York Press, 1999), 95.

74. Ronald Ketter et al., "The Changing Agenda of the Environment and the Commander-in-Chief," in Dennis L. Soden, ed., *The Environmental Presidency* (Albany: State University of New York Press, 1999), 247–248.

75. James M. Burns and Georgia Sorenson, *Running Alone: Presidential Leaders from JFK to Bush II* (New York: BasicBooks, 2006).

76. Gore, *Earth in the Balance*, 73.

77. Marc Eisner, *Governing the Environment* (Boulder, CO: Rienner, 2007), 62–72, 232–234.

78. Gerald O. Barney, ed., *Global 2000 Report to President of the U.S.* (New York: Pergamon, 1980), 1–3.

79. Otis L. Graham, Jr., *Little-Known Presidential Population Leadership* (Alexandria, VA: Negative Population Growth, 2013), 1–8.

80. See Richard A. Matthew, "The Environment as a National Security Issue," in Otis L. Graham, ed., *Environmental Politics and Policy, 1960s–1990s* (University Park: Pennsylvania State University Press, 2000), 101–122.

81. Elizabeth Drew, *On the Edge: The Clinton Presidency* (New York: Simon and Schuster, 1995).

CHAPTER 9. GEORGE W. BUSH AND BARACK OBAMA

1. George W. Bush, *Decision Points* (New York: Crown, 2010), 5.

2. David Frum, *The Right Man* (New York: Random House, 2003), 66–67.

3. *Public Papers of Presidents of the United States* (PPPUS), George W. Bush, vol. 1, "Address before a Joint Session of the Congress on Administration Goals," February 27, 2001, 1075.

4. Meg Jacobs, "Wreaking Havoc from Within," in Julian Zelizer, ed., *The Presidency of George W. Bush* (Princeton, NJ: Princeton University Press, 2010), 148.

5. "Developing Energy Bill Ignites Power Scramble," *Washington Post*, May 20, 2001, 1.

6. Walter A. Rosenbaum, *Environmental Politics* (Washington, DC: Congressional Quarterly Press, 2008), 332–333.

7. PPPUS, George W. Bush, "Statement on the Observance of Earth Day," April 21, 2001.

8. "T.R? He's No T.R.," *New York Times*, February 11, 2007.

9. "Feeling the Heat," *New York Times*, June 14, 2005, A18.

10. Office of the Press Secretary, "President Bush Discusses Climate Change: 'Yes, It Is Real, Sure Is!," http//www.politico.com, June 11, 2001.

11. Bill McKibben, "The Tipping Point," http://e360.yale.edu/feature/the_tipping_point/2012/, October 29, 2012.

12. Deborah L. Guber and Christopher Bosso, "Past the Tipping Point: Debating the Future of Public Discourse on the Environment," in Norman J. Vig and Michael E. Kraft, eds., *Environmental Policy: The New Directions for the Twenty-First Century*, 7th ed. (Washington, DC: Congressional Quarterly Press), 151–153.

13. Timothy Egan, "Final Days Fire Sale," *New York Times*, December 14, 2008, 12.

14. John D. Graham, *Bush on the Home Front* (Bloomington: Indiana University Press, 2010), 1.

15. Byron Dayne and Glen Sussman, "Comparing the Environmental Policies of Presidents George H. W. Bush and George W. Bush," in Anthony J. Eksterowicz and Glenn P. Hastedt, eds., *The Presidencies of George H. W. Bush and G. W. Bush* (Hauppauge, NY: Nova Science, 2008), 59–63.

16. David Mendell, *Obama: From Promise to Power* (New York: HarperCollins, 2007), 7–9.

17. Dan Balz and Haynes Johnson, *The Battle for America: The Story of an Extraordinary Election* (New York: Penguin, 2009).

18. Barack H. Obama, *The Audacity of Hope* (New York: Crown, 2006), 9.

19. Quoted in Morton Keller, *The Unbearable Heaviness of Governing* (Stanford, CA: Hoover Institution, 2010), 2.

20. Mendell, *Obama*, 9.

21. Balz and Johnson, *Battle for America*, 27.

22. Mendell, *Obama*, 13.

23. Jonathan Alter, *The Promise: President Obama, Year One* (New York: Simon and Schuster, 2010), 17.

24. Charles Blow, "All Atmospherics, No Climate," *New York Times*, April 19, 2008, A31.

25. David Maraniss, *Barack Obama: The Story* (New York: Simon and Schuster, 2012), 168–169.

26. Barack H. Obama, *Dreams from My Father* (New York: Times Books, 1995), 23.

27. Michael Grunwald, *The New New Deal* (New York: Simon and Schuster, 2012), 42.

28. Barbara Kingsolver, "Truth to Power," *New York Times Book Review* (June 1, 2008): 12–13.

29. J. McDaniel, "Science Lessons," *E Magazine* (October 2008): 27.

30. Mark Hertsgaard, *Hot* (Boston: Houghton Mifflin Harcourt, 2011), 270–272.

31. Barack Obama, June 2008.

32. Carl Pope, "Change Is Coming," *Sierra* (January–February 2009): 6; Miranda Schreurs, "Climate Change under Barack Obama," *Environment at the Crossroads* (conference publication), 155.

33. Grunwald, *New New Deal*, 3, 7–9, 11, 13, 447–448.

34. David Remnick, "Going the Distance," *New Yorker* (January 27, 2014): 45.

35. Margaret Kriz, "Financial Crisis Dims Chances for U.S. Climate Legislation," October 6, 2008, www.e360.yale.edu.

36. Nick Paumgarten, "The Death of Kings," *New Yorker* (May 18, 2009): 42.

37. Ryan Lizza, "The Obama Memos," *New Yorker* (January 30, 2012): 51.

38. John Broder, "Obama, Who Vowed Rapid Action on Climate Change, Turns More Cautious," *New York Times*, April 11, 2009, A10.

39. Albert Gore, quoted in *Rolling Stone* (April 2009), http://www.rollingstone.com/politics/news/climate-of-denial-20110622.

40. Darren Samuelsohn, "Obama Wins Nobel Prize," *New York Times*, October 9, 2009.

41. Natural Resources Defense Council, "Welcome Change," January 2010.

42. George Packard, "Obama's Lost Year," *New Yorker* (March 15, 2010).

43. John Broder, "Obama Offers Targets to Cut Greenhouse Gas," *New York Times*, November 26, 2009, A1.

44. Hendrick Hertzberg, "Cooling on Warming," *New Yorker* (February 7, 2011): 21–22; see also John M. Broder, "Cap and Trade Loses Its Standing," *New York Times*, March 26, 2010; Matthew Wald, "EPA Is Pressing Ahead on Greenhouse Rules," *New York Times*, December 24, 2010.

45. Yale Environment 360, "Obama vs. Romney," http://e360.yale.edu/feature /obama_vs_romney_a_stark_contrast_on_the_environment/2572, September 17, 2012.

46. John Broder, "Candidates Agree World Is Warming, but Talk Stops There," *New York Times*, October 26, 2012, A16.

47. National Wildlife Federation, "Where the Presidential Candidates Stand on Conservation," September 19, 2012.

48. S. Lacey, "Thousands Circle White House," http://thinkprogress.org/climate /2011/11/07/363036/white-house-protest-keystone-xl-pipeline-abandon-obama/.

49. Mary Hitt, http://www.huffingtonpost.com, October 31, 2012.

50. Mark Halperin and John Heilemann, *Double Down* (New York: Penguin, 2013), 53–63.

51. Bradford Plumer, "Has the Environment Become a Non-Issue in the 2012 Presidential Race?" www.audubonmagazine.org, October 31, 2012.

52. Bettina Boxall and Neela Banerjee, "Sandy May Fuel Warming Debate," *Los Angeles Times*, November 5, 2012, 1.

53. James Glanz, "Engineers' Warnings in 2009 Detailed Storm Surge," *New York Times*, November 5, 2012, A23; Jim Dwyer, "Reckoning with Realities Never Envisioned by City's Founders," *New York Times*, October 31, 2012, A16.

54. Maureen Dowd, "An Irish Catholic Wake-up," *New York Times*, October 14, 2013.

55. Matt Bai, "Still Waiting for Narrator in Chief," *New York Times Magazine* (November 4, 2012): 16–18.

56. Jackie Calmes, "In Debt Talks, a Revived Obama Is Ready," *New York Times*, November 12, 2012, A19.

57. Thomas Friedman, "The Launching Pad," *New York Times*, July 22, 2012.

58. Richard W. Stevenson, "Obama Offers Liberal Vision," *New York Times*, January 22, 2013, A1.

59. PPPUS, Barack H. Obama, "Address before a Joint Session of Congress on the State of the Union," February 12, 2013.

60. Elizabeth Kolbert, "Paying for It," *New Yorker* (December 10, 2012): 29–30.

61. John Broder, "Report May Ease Path for New Pipeline," *New York Times*, March 3, 2013, A1.

62. http//www.huffingtonpost.com/2012/03/23/obama_and_environmentalists.

63. Shaun Marcott, Jeremy Shaku, Peter Clark, and Alan Mix, "A Reconstruction of Regional and Global Temperature for the Past 11,300 Years," *Science* (March 8, 2013), 1198–1201.

64. John Broder, "Obama's Remarks Offer Hope to Opponents of Oil Pipeline," *New York Times*, June 24, 2013.

65. William Ruckelshaus, Lee M. Thomas, William K. Reilly, and Christine Todd Whitman, "A Republican Case for Climate Action," *New York Times*, August 1, 2013.

66. See http://clinton4.nara.gov/PCSD, cited in http://en.wikipedia.org/wiki /National_Strategy_for_a_Sustainable_America; see also Steven Cohen, "Obama's Second Term and the Sustainability Agenda," http://www.huffingtonpost.com, January 22, 2013.

67. Jody Kantor, "His Epochal Vision of a Place in History," *New York Times*, November 7, 2012, 86.

68. Doyle McManus, "Obama Hits the Road," *Los Angeles Times*, May 8, 2013.

69. Peter Baker, "An Onset of Woes Raises Questions on Obama's Vision," *New York Times*, May 16, 2003, 1.

70. *New York Times*, November 23, 2013, A23.

71. *Wall Street Journal*, November 15, 2013, A1.

72. *New York Times*, September 18, 2013, A13.

73. Bill McKibben, "Obama and Climate Change: The Real Story," *Rolling Stone* (December 17, 2013), http://www.rollingstone.com/politics/news/obama-and-climate-change-the-real-story-20131217.

CHAPTER 10. TRYING AGAIN FOR GREENER PRESIDENTS

1. Christopher Klyza and David Sousa, *American Environmental Policy* (Cambridge: Massachusetts Institute of Technology Press, 2013).

2. See Stanley Renshon, "In Search of Greatness: Obama's Place in History," *Commentary* (July–August, 2014): 46.

3. John Cronin and Robert F. Kennedy, Jr., *The Riverkeepers* (New York: Simon and Schuster, 1999), 97.

SUGGESTED FURTHER READING

CHAPTER 1. THE NEW NATION'S PUBLIC LANDS

Andrews, Richard N. L. *Managing the Environment, Managing Ourselves: A History of American Environmental Policy.* New Haven, CT: Yale University Press, 2006.

Audubon, John James. *Birds of America.* New York: Macmillan, 1942.

Cronon, William. *Changes in the Land: Indians, Colonists, and the Ecology of New England.* New York: Hill and Wang, 1983.

Dana, Samuel T., and Sally Fairfax. *Forest and Range Policy.* New York: McGraw-Hill, 1956.

Duncan, Dayton, and Ken Burns. *The National Parks: America's Best Idea.* New York: Knopf, 2009.

Ekirch, Arthur A., Jr. *Man and Nature in America.* New York: Columbia University Press, 1963.

Fox, Stephen. *The American Conservation Movement: John Muir and His Legacy.* Madison: University of Wisconsin Press, 1981.

Gates, Paul W. *History of Public Land Law Development.* Washington, DC: Government Printing Office, 1968.

Graham, Wade. *American Eden: From Monticello to Central Park to Our Backyards: What Our Gardens Tell Us about Who We Are.* New York: HarperCollins, 2011.

Greeley, William B. *Forests and Men.* Whitefish, MT: Kessinger, 2009.

Hibbard, Benjamin H. *A History of the Public Land Policies.* Madison: University of Wisconsin Press, 1965.

Lewis, Michael, ed. *American Wilderness: A New History.* New York: Oxford University Press, 2007.

Lowenthal, David. *George Perkins Marsh: Versatile Vermonter.* New York: Columbia University Press, 1958.

MacCleery, Douglas W. *American Forests: A History of Resiliency and Recovery.* Washington, DC: US Department of Agriculture, US Forest Service, 1992.

Mackintosh, Barry. *The National Parks: Shaping the System.* Washington, DC: US Department of Agriculture, National Park Service, 2005.

Marsh, George Perkins. *Man and Nature; or Physical Geography as Modified by Human Action.* Cambridge, MA: Harvard University Press, 1864.

McNeill, J. R. *Something New under the Sun: An Environmental History of the 20th Century.* New York: Norton, 2001.

Merk, Frederick. *History of the Westward Movement.* New York: Knopf, 1978.

Nash, Roderick. *Wilderness and the American Mind.* New Haven, CT: Yale University Press, 1967.

Philippon, Daniel J. *Conserving Words: How American Nature Writers Shaped the Environmental Movement.* Athens: University of Georgia Press, 2005.

Reiger, John F. *American Sportsmen and the Origins of Conservation.* Corvallis: Oregon State University Press, 2000.

Riley, Glenda. *Women and Nature: Saving the "Wild" West.* Lincoln: University of Nebraska Press, 1999.

Steen, Harold K. *Origins of the National Forests.* Durham, NC: Forest History Society, 1992.

Steinberg, Ted. *Down to Earth: Nature's Role in American History.* New York: Oxford University Press, 2002.

Turner, James Morton. *The Promise of Wilderness.* Seattle: University of Washington Press, 2012.

Wellock, Thomas. *Preserving the Nation: The Conservation and Environmental Movements, 1870–2000.* Hoboken, NJ: Wiley-Blackwell, 2007.

Worster, Donald. *A River Running West: The Life of John Wesley Powell.* New York: Oxford University Press, 2001.

Wyant, William. *Westward in Eden: Public Lands and the Conservation Movement.* Berkeley: University of California Press, 1982.

CHAPTER 2. BENJAMIN HARRISON, GROVER CLEVELAND, AND WILLIAM MCKINLEY

Graff, Henry. *Grover Cleveland.* New York: Holt, 2002.

Merill, Horace. *Bourbon Leader: Grover Cleveland and the Democratic Party.* Boston: Little, Brown, 1957.

Miller, Char. *Gifford Pinchot and the Making of Modern Environmentalism.* Washington, DC: Island, 2001.

Moore, Anne C. *Benjamin Harrison: Centennial President.* New York: Nova Science, 2009.

Nevins, Allan. *Grover Cleveland: A Study in Courage.* New York: Dodd, Mead, 1934.

Sobel, Robert. *Coolidge: An American Enigma.* Washington, DC: Regnery, 1998.

Socolofsky, Homer, and Allen B. Spetter. *The Presidency of Benjamin Harrison.* Lawrence: University Press of Kansas, 1987.

Welch, Richard E. *The Presidencies of Grover Cleveland.* Lawrence: University Press of Kansas, 1988.

CHAPTER 3. THEODORE ROOSEVELT

Bamberger, Mark J. "The Emerald Thread: An Examination of Environmental Impacts of American Presidents, 1901–1945," Ph.D. diss., Union Institute, 1995.

Brands, H. W. *T.R.: The Last Romantic*. New York: BasicBooks, 1998.

Brinkley, Douglas. *The Wilderness Warrior: Theodore Roosevelt and the Crusade for America.* New York: HarperCollins, 2009.

Collins, Michael L. *That Damned Cowboy: Theodore Roosevelt and the American West, 1883–1898.* New York: Lang, 1989.

Cutright, Paul Russell. *Theodore Roosevelt: The Making of a Conservationist.* Urbana-Champaign: University of Illinois Press, 1985.

Egan, Timothy. *The Big Burn: Teddy Roosevelt and the Fire That Saved America.* Boston: Houghton Mifflin Harcourt, 2009.

Gould, Lewis. *The Presidency of Theodore Roosevelt.* Lawrence: University Press of Kansas, 1991.

Harbaugh, William H. *The Life and Times of Theodore Roosevelt.* New York: Collier, 1967.

Hays, Samuel P. *Conservation and the Gospel of Efficiency: The Progressive Conservation Movement, 1890–1920.* Cambridge, MA: Harvard University Press, 1959.

Morris, Edmund. *The Rise of Theodore Roosevelt.* New York: Coward, McCann, and Geoghegan, 1979.

———. *Theodore Rex.* New York: Random House, 2001.

Morrison, Elting, ed. *The Letters of Theodore Roosevelt.* Cambridge, MA: Harvard University Press, 1951.

Muir, John. *John Muir: Nature Writings: The Story of My Boyhood and Youth; My First Summer in the Sierra; The Mountains of California; Stickeen; Essays.* New York: Library of America, 1997.

Peffer, E. Louise. *The Closing of the Public Domain: Disposal and Reservation Policies, 1900–1950.* Palo Alto, CA: Stanford University Press, 1951.

Reiger, John F. *American Sportsmen and the Origins of Conservation.* Corvallis: Oregon State University Press, 2001.

Pinchot, Gifford. *Breaking New Ground.* New York: Harcourt, Brace, 1947.

———. *The Fight for Conservation.* New York: Doubleday, 1910.

Pisani, Donald J. *Water and American Government: The Reclamation Bureau, National Water Policy, and the West, 1902–1935.* Berkeley: University of California Press, 2002.

Robbins, Roy M. *Our Landed Heritage: The Public Domain, 1776–1936.* Princeton, NJ: Princeton University Press, 1942.

Roosevelt, Theodore. *An Autobiography.* New York: Macmillan, 1913.

Roosevelt, Theodore, and Hermann Hagedorn. *The Works of Theodore Roosevelt.* New York: Scribner, 1926.

Stradling, David. *Smokestacks and Progressives: Environment and Air Quality in America, 1991–1951.* Baltimore, MD: Johns Hopkins University Press, 1999.

Trefethen, James B. *An American Crusade for Wildlife.* New York: Winchester Press, 1975.

Van Hise, Charles. *The Conservation of Natural Resources in the United States.* New York: Macmillan, 1913.

Warren, Louis S. *The Hunter's Game: Poachers and Conservationists in Twentieth-Century America.* New Haven, CT: Yale University Press, 1997.

Worster, Donald. *A Passion for Nature: The Life of John Muir.* New York: Oxford University Press, 2008.

CHAPTER 4. WILLIAM TAFT, WOODROW WILSON, WARREN HARDING, CALVIN COOLIDGE, AND HERBERT HOOVER

Adams, Samuel Hopkins. *Incredible Era: The Life and Times of Warren Gamaliel Harding.* Boston: Houghton Mifflin, 1939.

Allen, Frederick Lewis. *Only Yesterday: An Informal History of the 1920s.* New York: Harper, 1964.

Brands, H. W. *Woodrow Wilson.* New York: Times Books, 2003.

Burner, David H. *Herbert Hoover: A Public Life.* New York: Knopf/Doubleday, 1979.

Burton, David H. *William Howard Taft: In Public Service.* Malabar, FL: Krieger, 1986.

Clements, Kendrick. *Hoover, Conservation, and Consumerism: Engineering the Good Life.* Lawrence: University Press of Kansas, 2000.

———. *The Presidency of Woodrow Wilson.* Lawrence: University Press of Kansas, 1992.

Coletta, Paolo E. *The Presidency of William Howard Taft.* Lawrence: University Press of Kansas, 1973.

———. *William Howard Taft: A Bibliography.* Westport, CT: Greenwood, 1989.

Coolidge, Calvin. *The Autobiography of Calvin Coolidge.* New York: Cosmopolitan, 1929.

Cooper, John Milton, Jr. *Woodrow Wilson: A Biography.* New York: Knopf, 2009.

Cronon, E. David. *The Political Thought of Woodrow Wilson.* Indianapolis, IN: Bobbs-Merrill, 1965.

Dean, John W. *Warren G. Harding.* New York: Times Books, 2004.

Dicks, John D. *Republican Ascendancy, 1921–1933.* New York: Harper, 1960.

Fausold, Martin L., and George T. Mazuman. *The Hoover Presidency: A Reappraisal.* New York: State University of New York Press, 1974.

Ferrell, Robert H. *Presidential Leadership: From Woodrow Wilson to Harry S. Truman.* Columbia: University of Missouri Press, 2006.

Fleser, Arthur F. *A Rhetorical Study of the Speaking of Calvin Coolidge.* New York: Mellen, 1990.

Fuess, Claude M. *Calvin Coolidge: The Man from Vermont.* Boston: Little, Brown, 1940.

Harding, Warren G. *Our Common Country: Mutual Good Will in America.* Indianapolis, IN: Bobbs-Merrill, 1921.

Havemeyer, Loomis, ed. *Conservation of Our Natural Resources Based on Van Hise's "The Conservation of Natural Resources in the United States."* New York: Macmillan, 1930.

Hawley, Ellis W., ed. *Herbert Hoover as Secretary of Commerce: Studies in the New Era Thought and Practice.* Iowa City: Iowa State University Press, 1982.

Hoff, Joan. *Herbert Hoover: Forgotten Progressive.* Boston: Little, Brown, 1975.

Hoover, Herbert. *Public Papers of the President of the United States: Herbert Hoover, 1929–1933.* 4 vols. Washington, DC: Federal Register, 1976.

Irwin, Will. *Herbert Hoover: A Reminiscent Biography.* New York: Century, 1928.

Ise, John. *The United States Oil Policy.* New Haven, CT: Yale University Press, 1926. Reprint. Baltimore, MD: John Hopkins University Press, 1967.

Johnson, Charles C. *Why Coolidge Matters: Leadership Lessons from America's Most Underrated President.* New York: Encounter, 2013.

Kalb, Deborah, Gerhard Peters, and John T. Woolley. *State of the Union: Presidential Rhetoric from Woodrow Wilson to George W. Bush.* Washington, DC: Congressional Quarterly Press, 2006.

King, Judson. *The Conservation Fight: From Theodore Roosevelt to the Tennessee Valley Authority.* Washington, DC: Public Affairs, 1959.

Leuchtenburg, William E. *Herbert Hoover.* New York: Macmillan, 2009.

Link, Arthur S. *Wilson: The New Freedom.* Princeton, NJ: Princeton University Press, 1956.

———. *Wilson: The Road to the White House.* Princeton, NJ: Princeton University Press, 1947.

———. *Wilson: The Struggle for Neutrality.* Princeton, NJ: Princeton University Press, 1960.

McCoy, Donald. *Calvin Coolidge: The Quiet President.* New York: Macmillan, 1967.

Montgomerey, Erick. *Thomas Woodrow Wilson: Family Ties and Southern Perspectives.* Augusta, GA: Historic Augusta, 2006.

Moran, Philip R. *Calvin Coolidge Documents, 1872–1933.* Dobbs Ferry, NY: Oceana, 1970.

Murray, Robert K. *The Harding Era: Warren G. Harding and His Administration.* Minneapolis: University of Minnesota Press, 1969.

Nash, George H. *The Life of Herbert Hoover: The Engineer, 1874–1914.* New York: Norton, 1983.

Olson, Keith. *Biography of a Progressive: Franklin K. Lane, 1864–1921*. Westport, CT: Greenwood, 1979.

Osborn, George. *Woodrow Wilson: The Early Years*. Baton Rouge: Louisiana State University Press, 1968.

Penick, James L. *Progressive Politics and Conservation: The Ballinger-Pinchot Affair*. Chicago: University of Chicago Press, 1968.

Pringle, Henry. *The Life and Times of William Howard Taft*. 2 vols. New York: Farrar and Rinehart, 1939.

Righter, Robert W. *The Battle over Hetch Hetchy: America's Most Controversial Dam and the Birth of Modern Environmentalism*. New York: Oxford University Press, 2006.

Russel, Francis. *The Shadow of Blooming Grove: Warren G. Harding in His Times*. New York: McGraw-Hill, 1968.

Scheuering, Rachel White. *Shapers of the Great Debate on Conservation: A Biographical Dictionary*. Westport, CT: Greenwood, 2004.

Shlaes, Amity. *The Forgotten Man: A New History of the Great Depression*. New York: Harper, 2008.

Silver, Thomas B. *Coolidge and the Historians*. Durham, NC: Carolina Academic Press, 1983.

Sinclair, Andrew. *The Available Man*. New York: Macmillan, 1967.

Smith, Richard Norton. *An Uncommon Man: The Triumph of Herbert Hoover*. New York: Simon and Schuster, 1984.

Swain, Donald C. *Federal Conservation Policy, 1921–1933*. Berkeley: University of California Press, 1963.

Trani, Eugene P., and David L. Wilson. *The Presidency of Warren G. Harding*. Lawrence: University Press of Kansas, 1977.

Vileisis, Ann. *Discovering the Unknown Landscape: A History of America's Wetlands*. Washington, DC: Island, 1997.

Walworth, Arthur. *Woodrow Wilson: American Prophet*. New York: Longman's Green, 1958.

Wert, Hal E. *Hoover, the Fishing President: Portrait of the Private Man and His Life Outdoors*. Mechanicsburg, PA: Stackpole, 2005.

Wilson, Woodrow. *The New Freedom*. New York: Bernhard Tauchnitz, 1913.

CHAPTER 5. FRANKLIN D. ROOSEVELT

Beeman, Randal S., and James A. Pritchard. *A Green and Permanent Land: Ecology and Agriculture in the Twentieth Century*. Lawrence: University Press of Kansas, 2001.

Brant, Irving. *Adventures in Conservation with Franklin D. Roosevelt*. Flagstaff, AZ: Northland, 1989.

Burns, James. *Roosevelt: The Lion and the Fox*. New York: Harcourt, Brace, 1956.

———. *Roosevelt: The Soldier of Freedom*. New York: Harcourt, Brace, 1970.

Campanella, Thomas J. *Republic of Shade: New England and the American Elm*. New Haven, CT: Yale University Press, 2003.

Davis, Kenneth. *FDR: The Beckoning of Destiny, 1882–1928*. New York: Putnam, 1972.

———. *FDR: The New Deal Years, 1933–1937*. New York: Putnam, 1979.

Dunlap, Thomas. *Saving America's Wildlife: Ecology and the American Mind, 1850–1990*. Princeton, NJ: Princeton University Press, 1988.

Egan, Timothy. *The Worst Hard: The Untold Story of Those Who Survived the Great American Dust Bowl*. Boston: Mariner, 2006.

Fox, Stephen. *American Conservation Movement: John Muir and His Legacy*. Madison: University of Wisconsin Press, 1986.

Friedel, Frank. *Franklin D. Roosevelt*. Boston: Little, Brown, 1956.

Graham, Otis L., Jr., and Meghan Robinson Wander. *Franklin D. Roosevelt: His Life and Times—An Encyclopedic View*. Boston: Hall, 1985.

Hurt, Douglas R. *The Dust Bowl: An Agricultural and Social History*. Lanham, MD: Rowman and Littlefield, 1981.

Kennedy, David M. *Freedom from Fear: The American People in Depression and War, 1929–1945*. New York: Oxford University Press, 1999.

Lehman, Tim. *Public Values, Private Lands: Farmland Preservation Policy, 1933–1985*. Chapel Hill: University of North Carolina Press, 1995.

Leopold, Aldo. *A Sand County Almanac, with Essays on Conservation from Round River*. New York: Oxford University Press, 1949.

Leuchtenburg, William E. *Franklin D. Roosevelt and the New Deal*. New York: Harper, 1963.

Lorbiecki, Marybeth. *Aldo Leopold: A Fierce Green Fire*. New York: Oxford University Press, 1999.

Lowitt, Richard. *New Deal and the West*. Bloomington: Indiana University Press, 1984.

Maher, Neil M. *Nature's New Deal: The Civilian Conservation Corps and the Roots of the American Environmental Movement*. New York: Oxford University Press, 2007.

Nash, Gerald D. *World War II and the West: Reshaping the Economy*. Lincoln: University of Nebraska Press, 1990.

Nixon, Edgar B. *Franklin D. Roosevelt and Conservation, 1911–1945*. Washington, DC: US Government Printing Office, 1957.

Phillips, Sarah T. *This Land, This Nation: Conservation, Rural America, and the New Deal.* Cambridge, UK: Cambridge University Press, 2007.

Roosevelt, Franklin D. *Looking Forward.* New York: Day, 1933.

———. *On Our Way.* New York: Day, 1934.

Russell, Edmund. *War and Nature: Fighting Humans and Insects with Chemicals from World War I to Silent Spring.* Cambridge, UK: Cambridge University Press, 2001.

Schlesinger, Arthur M., Jr. *The Crises of the Old Order: The Age of Roosevelt.* Boston: Houghton Mifflin Harcourt, 1956.

Sutter, Paul S. *Driven Wild: How the Fight against Automobiles Launched the Modern Wilderness Movement.* Seattle: University of Washington Press, 2002.

Tanner, Thomas, ed. *Aldo Leopold: The Man and His Legacy.* Des Moines, IA: Soil and Water Conservation Society, 1995.

Tugwell, Rexford Guy. *The Brains Trust.* New York: Viking, 1968.

Watkins, T. H. *Righteous Pilgrim: The Life and Times of Harold L. Ickes, 1874–1952.* New York: Holt, 1990.

Woolner, David B., and Henry L. Henderson. *FDR and the Environment: World of the Roosevelts.* New York: Palgrave Macmillan, 2005.

Worster, Donald. *Dust Bowl: The Southern Plains in the 1930s.* New York: Oxford University Press, 1979.

CHAPTER **6.** HARRY TRUMAN, DWIGHT EISENHOWER, AND JOHN F. KENNEDY

Adams, Sherman. *Firsthand Report: The Story of the Eisenhower Administration.* New York: Harper, 1961.

Alexander, Charles C. *Holding the Line: The Eisenhower Era, 1952–1961 (America since World War II).* Bloomington: Indiana University Press, 1975.

Ambrose, Stephen E. *Eisenhower: Soldier and President.* New York: Simon and Schuster, 1983.

———. *Milton S. Eisenhower: Educational Statesman.* Baltimore, MD: Johns Hopkins University Press, 1983.

Andrews, Richard N. L. *Managing the Environment, Managing Ourselves: A History of American Environmental Policy.* New Haven, CT: Yale University Press, 1999.

Berkman, Richard, and W. Kip Viscusi. *Damming the West.* London: Penguin, 1973.

Branyan, Robert L., and Lawrence Larson. *The Eisenhower Administration, 1953–1961.* New York: Random House, 1971.

Burk, Robert F. *Dwight D. Eisenhower: Hero and Politician.* Boston, MA: Twayne, 1987.

Burns, James MacGregor. *John Kennedy: A Political Profile.* New York: Harcourt, Brace, 1960.

Burns, Richard D., and Joseph M. Siracusa. *Historical Dictionary of the Kennedy-Johnson Era. Historical Dictionaries of US Politics and Political Eras Series.* Lanham, MD: Scarecrow, 2007.

Carson, Rachel. *Silent Spring.* Boston: Houghton Mifflin, 1962.

Dallek, Robert. *An Unfinished Life: John F. Kennedy, 1917–1963.* Boston: Little, Brown, 2003.

Davies, J. Clarence. *The Politics of Pollution.* New York: Pegasus, 1970.

Eisenhower, Dwight D. *Mandate for Change, 1953–1956: The White House Years.* New York: Doubleday, 1963.

———. *Waging Peace, 1956–1961: White House Years.* New York: Doubleday, 1965.

Giglio, James N. *Presidency of John F. Kennedy.* Lawrence: University Press of Kansas, 1991.

Hays, Samuel P. *Beauty, Health, and Permanence: Environmental Politics in the United States, 1955–1985.* Cambridge, UK: Cambridge University Press, 1987.

Hirt, Paul W. *A Conspiracy of Optimism: Management of the National Forests since World War Two.* Lincoln: University of Nebraska Press, 1994.

Kennedy, John F. *Profiles in Courage.* New York: Macmillan, 1955.

Lear, Linda. *Rachel Carson: Witness for Nature.* New York: Holt, 1997.

Lyon, Peter. *Eisenhower: Portrait of the Hero.* Boston: Little, Brown, 1974.

McCoy, Donald R. *The Presidency of Harry S. Truman.* Lawrence: University Press of Kansas, 1984.

McCullough, David. *Truman.* New York: Simon and Schuster, 1993.

Meine, Curt. *Aldo Leopold: His Life and Work.* Madison: University of Wisconsin Press, 1988.

DeVoto, Bernard. *DeVoto's West: History, Conservation, and the Public Good.* Edited by Edward K. Muller. Athens, GA: Swallow Press, 2005.

O'Brien, Michael. *John F. Kennedy: A Biography.* New York: Dunne, 2005.

Osborn, Fairfield. *Our Plundered Planet.* Boston: Little, Brown, 1948.

Pach, Chester J., Jr., and Elmo Richardson. *The Presidency of Dwight D. Eisenhower.* Lawrence: University Press of Kansas, 1991.

Parmet, Herbert S. *JFK: The Presidency of John F. Kennedy.* New York: Doubleday, 1983.

Perret, Geoffrey. *Eisenhower.* New York: Adams Media, 1999.

Reeves, Richard. *President Kennedy: Profile of Power.* New York: Simon and Schuster, 1993.

Richardson, Elmo. *Dams, Parks, and Politics: Resource Development and Preservation in the Truman-Eisenhower Era.* Lexington: University Press of Kentucky, 1973.

Schlesinger, Arthur M., Jr. *A Thousand Days: John F. Kennedy in the White House.* Boston: Houghton Mifflin, 1965.

Sellars, Richard West. *Preserving Nature in the National Parks: A History.* New Haven, CT: Yale University Press, 1997.

Sorensen, Theodore C. *Kennedy.* New York: Harper and Row, 1965.

Sundquist, James L. *Politics and Policy: The Eisenhower, Kennedy, and Johnson Years.* Washington, DC: Brookings Institute, 1968.

Truman, Harry S. *Memoirs.* New York: Doubleday, 1955.

Truman, Harry S., and Robert H. Ferrell. *The Autobiography of Harry S. Truman.* Boulder: University of Colorado Press, 1980.

———. *Off the Record: The Private Papers of Harry S. Truman.* New York: Harper and Row, 1980.

Vogt, William. *Road to Survival.* New York: Sloan, 1948.

Webb, Walter Prescott. *The Great Frontier.* Boston: Houghton Mifflin, 1952.

Wirth, Conrad L. *Parks, Politics, and the People.* Norman: University of Oklahoma Press, 1980.

CHAPTER 7. LYNDON BAINES JOHNSON, RICHARD NIXON, GERALD FORD, AND JIMMY CARTER

Alagona, Peter S. *After the Grizzly: Endangered Species and the Politics of Place in California.* Berkeley: University of California Press, 2013.

Ambrose, Stephen E. *Nixon: The Education of a Politician, 1913–1962.* New York: Simon and Schuster, 1986.

———. *Nixon: The Triumph of a Politician, 1962–1972.* New York: Simon and Schuster, 1989.

Black, Conrad. *Richard Milhous Nixon: The Invincible Quest.* London: Quercus, 2007.

Bornet, Vaughn Davis. *The Presidency of Lyndon B. Johnson.* Lawrence: University Press of Kansas, 1983.

Bourne, Peter G. *Jimmy Carter: A Comprehensive Biography from Plains to Post-Presidency.* New York: Scribner, 1997.

Brinkley, Douglas. *Gerald R. Ford.* New York: Times Books, 2007.

———. *The Unfinished Presidency: Jimmy Carter's Quest for Global Peace.* New York: Viking, 1998.

Califano Jr., Joseph A. *The Triumph and Tragedy of Lyndon Johnson.* New York: Simon and Schuster, 1991.

Callicott, J. Baird, and Michael P. Nelson. *The Great New Wilderness Debate.* Athens: University of Georgia Press, 1998.

Carter, Jimmy. *An Hour before Daylight: Memories of a Rural Boyhood.* New York: Simon and Schuster, 2001.

———. *Keeping the Faith: Memoirs of a President*. Norwalk: Easton, 1982.

———. *An Outdoor Journal: Adventures and Reflections*. New York: Bantam, 1988.

———. *Why Not the Best?* Nashville, TN: Broadman, 1975.

Crain, Andrew Downer. *The Ford Presidency: A History*. Jefferson, NC: McFarland, 2009.

Critchlow, Donald T. *Intended Consequences: Birth Control, Abortion, and the Federal Government in Modern America*. New York: Oxford University Press, 1999.

Dallek, Robert. *Lyndon B. Johnson: Portrait of a President*. New York: Oxford University Press, 2004.

Drew, Elizabeth. *Richard M. Nixon*. New York: Times Books, 2007.

Dugger, Ronnie. *The Politician: The Life and Times of Lyndon Johnson*. New York: Norton, 1984.

Dumbrell, John. *The Carter Presidency: A Re-Evaluation*. Oxford, UK: Manchester University Press, 1995.

Fink, Gary M., and Hugh Davis Graham, eds. *The Carter Presidency: Policy Choices in the Post-New Deal Era*. Lawrence: University Press of Kansas, 2001.

Firestone, Bernard J., and Alexej Ugrinsky. *Gerald R. Ford and the Politics of Post-Watergate America*. Westport, CT: Greenwood, 1992.

Flippen, J. Brooks. *Nixon and the Environment*. Albuquerque: University of New Mexico Press, 2000.

Ford, Betty, and Chris Chase, ed. *The Times of My Life*. New York: HarperCollins, 1978.

Ford, Gerald R. *A Time to Heal: The Autobiography of Gerald R. Ford*. New York: Harper and Row, 1979.

Genovese, Michael A. *The Nixon Presidency: Power and Politics in Turbulent Times*. Westport, CT: Praeger, 1990.

Glad, Betty. *Jimmy Carter*. New York: Norton, 1980.

Gould, Lewis L. *Lady Bird Johnson: Our Environmental First Lady*. Lawrence: University Press of Kansas, 1999.

———. *1968: The Election That Changed America*. Lanham, MD: Ivan R. Dee, 1993.

Graham, Mary. *The Morning after Earth Day: Practical Environmental Politics*. Washington, DC: Brookings Institute, 1999.

Graham, Otis L., Jr. *Toward a Planned Society: From Roosevelt to Nixon*. New York: Oxford University Press, 1976.

Greene, John R. *Gerald R. Ford: A Bibliography*. Westport, CT: Greenwood, 1994.

———. *The Limits of Power: The Nixon and Ford Administrations*. Bloomington: Indiana University Press, 1992.

———. *The Presidency of Gerald R. Ford*. Lawrence: University Press of Kansas, 1994.

Haldeman, H. R., and Stephen E. Ambrose. *The Haldeman Diaries: Inside the Nixon White House.* New York: Putnam, 1994.

Hoff, Joan. *Nixon Reconsidered.* New York: BasicBooks, 1994.

Johnson, Lyndon B. *The Vantage Point: Perspectives of the Presidency, 1963–1969.* New York: Holt, Rinehart, and Winston, 1974.

Jones, Charles O. *The Trusteeship Presidency: Jimmy Carter and the US Congress.* Baton Rouge: Louisiana State University Press, 1988.

Kaufman, Burton I., and Scott Kaufman. *The Presidency of James Earl Carter, Jr.* Lawrence: University Press of Kansas, 2006.

Lacey, Michael J., ed. *Government and Environmental Politics: Essays on Historical Developments since World War Two.* Washington, DC: Woodrow Wilson Center, 1993.

Mackenzie, G. Calvin, and Robert Weisbrot. *The Liberal Hour: Washington and the Politics of Change in the 1960s.* London: Penguin, 2008.

Mattson, Kevin. *"What the Heck Are You Up To, Mr. President?": Jimmy Carter, America's "Malaise," and the Speech That Should Have Changed the Country.* New York: Bloomsbury, 2009.

Nixon, Richard. *In the Arena: A Memoir of Victory, Defeat, and Renewal.* New York: Simon and Schuster, 1990.

———. *The Memoirs of Richard Nixon.* New York: Grosset and Dunlap, 1978.

Parmet, Herbert S. *Richard Nixon and His America.* Old Saybrook, CT: Konecky, 1990.

Pious, Richard M. *Why Presidents Fail: White House Decision Making from Eisenhower to Bush II.* Lanham, MD: Rowman and Littlefield, 2008.

Reeves, Richard. *President Nixon: Alone in the White House.* New York: Simon and Schuster, 2001.

———. *A Ford, Not a Lincoln.* New York: Harcourt, Brace, 1975.

Rathlesberger, James. *Nixon and the Environment: The Politics of Devastation.* New York: Taurus Communications, 1972.

Reichley, James. *Conservatives in an Age of Change: The Nixon and Ford Administrations.* Washington, DC: Brookings Institute, 1981.

Rosenbaum, Herbert D., and Alexej Ugrinsky. *The Presidency and Domestic Policies of Jimmy Carter.* Westport, CT: Praeger, 1993.

Rothman, Hal K. *LBJ's Texas White House: "Our Heart's Home."* College Station: Texas A&M University Press, 2001.

Small, Melvin. *The Presidency of Richard Nixon.* Lawrence: University Press of Kansas, 1999.

Speth, James Gustave. *Red Sky at Morning: America and the Crisis of the Global Environment.* New Haven, CT: Yale University Press, 2004.

Turner, James Morton. *The Promise of Wilderness.* Seattle: University of Washington Press, 2012.

Train, Russell E. *Politics, Pollution, and Pandas: An Environmental Memoir.* Washington, DC: Island, 2003.

US Federal Commissioners. *Population and the American Future: Report of the Commission.* New York: Signet, 1972.

Vogel, David. *Fluctuating Fortunes.* New York: BasicBooks, 1989.

Whitaker, John C. *Striking a Balance: Environment and Natural Resources Policy in the Nixon-Ford Years.* Washington, DC: American Enterprise Institute, 1976.

White, Theodore H. *The Making of a President, 1964.* New York: Atheneum, 1965.

CHAPTER 8. RONALD REAGAN, GEORGE H. W. BUSH, AND BILL CLINTON

Arnold, Ron. *At the Eye of the Storm: James Watt and the Environmentalists.* Washington, DC: Regnery Gateway, 1982.

Bailey, Ronald. *True State of the Planet.* New York: Free Press, 1995.

Barnett, Harold C. *Toxic Debts and the Superfund Dilemma.* Chapel Hill: University of North Carolina Press, 1994.

Benedick, Richard Elliot. *Ozone Diplomacy: New Directions in Safeguarding the Planet.* Cambridge, MA: Harvard University Press, 1998.

Boyer, Paul. *Reagan as President: Contemporary Views of the Man, His Politics, and His Policies.* Lanham, MD: Ivan R. Dee, 1990.

Brownlee, W. Elliot, and Hugh Davis Graham. *The Reagan Presidency: Pragmatic Conservatism and Its Legacies.* Lawrence: University Press of Kansas, 2003.

Bush, George H. W. *Looking Forward: An Autobiography.* New York: Doubleday, 1987.

———. *A World Transformed.* New York: Vintage, 1999.

Cannon, Lou. *Governor Reagan.* New York: Public Affairs, 2003.

———. *President Reagan: The Role of a Lifetime.* New York: Simon and Schuster, 1991.

Clinton, Bill. *My Life.* New York: Knopf, 2004.

Cooper, Phillip J. *By Order of the President: The Use and Abuse of Executive Direct Action.* Lawrence: University Press of Kansas, 2002.

Cramer, Richard Ben. *What It Takes: The Way to the White House.* New York: Vintage, 1992.

Dallek, Robert. *Ronald Reagan: The Politics of Symbolism.* Cambridge, MA: Harvard University Press, 1984.

Daynes, Byron W., and Glen Sussman. *White House Politics and the Environment: Franklin D. Roosevelt to George W. Bush.* College Station: Texas A&M University Press, 2010.

D'Souza, Dinesh. *Ronald Reagan.* New York: Free Press, 1997.

Dugger, Ronnie. *On Reagan: The Man and His Presidency*. New York: McGraw-Hill, 1983.

Dumas, Ernest. *The Clintons of Arkansas: An Introduction by Those Who Know Them Best*. Fayetteville: University of Arkansas Press, 1993.

Gillon, Steven M. *The Democrats' Dilemma*. New York: Columbia University Press, 1992.

Graham, Otis L., Jr., ed. *Environmental Politics and Policy, 1960s–1990s*. University Park: Pennsylvania State University Press, 2000.

Greene, John Robert. *The George H. W. Bush Years*. New York: Facts on File, 2005.

Hayward, Steven F. *The Age of Reagan: The Fall of the Old Liberal Order, 1964–1980*. New York: Three Rivers, 2009.

Heatherly, Charles L. *Mandate for Leadership III*. Lanham, MD: Rowman and Littlefield, 1989.

Kline, Benjamin. *First along the River: A Brief History of the US Environmental Movement*. Lanham, MD: Arcada, 1997.

Koch, Doro Bush. *My Father, My President: A Personal Account of the Life of George H. W. Bush*. New York: Grand Central, 2006.

Lamm, Richard D., and Michael McCarthy. *The Angry West: A Vulnerable Land and Its Future*. Boston: Houghton Mifflin, 1982.

Lash, Jonathan. *A Season of Spoils: The Reagan Administration's Attack on the Environment*. New York: Pantheon, 1984.

Levy, Peter B. *Encyclopedia of the Reagan-Bush Years*. Westport, CT: Greenwood, 1996.

Litfin, Karen T. *Ozone Discourse*. New York: Columbia University Press, 1994.

Lomborg, Bjorn. *The Skeptical Environmentalist: Measuring the Real State of the World*. Cambridge, UK: Cambridge University Press, 2001.

Medhurst, Martin J. *The Rhetorical Presidency of George H. W. Bush*. College Station: Texas A&M University Press, 2006.

Mervin, David. *Ronald Reagan: The American Presidency*. London: Routledge, 1990.

Metz, Allan, ed. *Bill Clinton: A Bibliography*. Westport, CT: Greenwood, 2002.

———. *Ronald Reagan: A Bibliography*. Lanham, MD: Scarecrow, 2008.

Morris, Edmund. *Dutch: A Memoir of Ronald Reagan*. New York: Random House, 1999.

Mumford, Stephen D. *The Life and Death of NSSM 200: How the Destruction of Political Will Doomed a US Population Policy*. Front Royal, VA: Center for Research on Population, 1996.

Palmer, John L., and Isabel V. Sawhill, eds. *The Reagan Record: An Assessment of America's Changing Domestic Priorities*. Pensacola, FL: Ballinger, 1984.

Parmet, Herbert S. *George Bush: The Life of a Lone Star Yankee*. New York: Scribner, 1997.

Pemberton, William E. *Exit with Honor: The Life and Presidency of Ronald Reagan.* Armonk, NY: M. E. Sharpe, 1998.

Peterson, Tarla Rai. *Green Talk in the White House: The Rhetorical Presidency Encounters Ecology.* College Station: Texas A&M University Press, 2004.

Popadiuk, Roman. *The Leadership of George Bush: An Insider's View of the Forty-First President.* College Station: Texas A&M University Press, 2009.

Portney, Paul R. *Natural Resources and the Environment: The Reagan Approach.* Lanham, MD: University Press of America, 1984.

Rabe, Barry G. *Statehouse and Greenhouse: The Emerging Politics of American Climate Change Policy.* Brookings Institute, 2004.

Reagan, Ronald. *An American Life: The Autobiography.* New York: Simon and Schuster, 1990.

———. *Reagan Diaries.* New York: HarperCollins, 2007.

Savage, Charlie. *Takeover: The Return of the Imperial Presidency and the Subversion of American Democracy.* New York: Back Bay, 2008.

Shanley, Robert A. *Presidential Influence and Environmental Policy.* Westport, CT: Praeger, 1992.

Short, C. Brant. *Ronald Reagan and the Public Lands: America's Conservation Debate, 1979–1984.* College Station: Texas A&M University Press, 1989.

Simon, Julian L. *The Ultimate Resource.* Princeton, NJ: Princeton University Press, 1981.

Skinner, Kiron K., Annelise Anderson, and Martin Anderson. *Reagan: A Life in Letters.* New York: Free Press, 2004.

Soden, Dennis L. *The Environmental Presidency.* Albany: State University of New York Press, 1999.

Tarpley, Webster Griffin. *George Bush: The Unauthorized Biography.* Leesburg, VA: Executive Intelligence Review, 1992.

Vig, Norman J., and Michael E. Kraft. *Environmental Policy in the 1980s: Reagan's New Agenda.* Washington, DC: Congressional Quarterly Press, 1984.

———. *Environmental Policy in the 1990s: Reform or Reaction.* Washington, DC: Congressional Quarterly Press, 1996.

Vogel, David. *Fluctuating Fortunes.* New York: BasicBooks, 1989.

Watt, James G., and Doug Wead. *The Courage of a Conservative.* New York: Simon and Schuster, 1985.

Wicker, Tom. *George Herbert Walker Bush.* New York: Viking, 2004.

Wilentz, Sean. *The Age of Reagan: A History, 1974–2008.* New York: HarperCollins, 2008.

CHAPTER 9. GEORGE W. BUSH AND BARACK OBAMA

Daynes, Byron W., and Glen Sussman. *White House Politics and the Environment: Franklin D. Roosevelt to George W. Bush.* College Station: Texas A&M University Press, 2010.

Dernbach, John C. *Agenda for a Sustainable America.* Washington, DC: Environmental Law Institute, 2009.

Frum, David. *The Right Man: The Surprise Presidency of George W. Bush.* New York: Random House, 2003.

Graham, John D. *Bush on the Home Front: Domestic Policy Triumphs and Setbacks.* Bloomington: Indiana University Press, 2010.

Greenstein, Fred I. *The George W. Bush Presidency: An Early Assessment.* Baltimore, MD: Johns Hopkins University Press, 2003.

Hodge, Roger D. *The Mendacity of Hope: Barack Obama and the Betrayal of American Liberalism.* New York: HarperCollins, 2010.

Intergovernmental Panel on Climate Change. *Climate Change 2007: The Physical Science Basis.* Cambridge, UK: Cambridge University Press, 2007.

Maraniss, David. *Barack Obama: The Story.* New York: Atlantic, 2012.

Mendell, David. *Obama: From Promise to Power.* New York: HarperCollins, 2007.

Obama, Barack. *The Audacity of Hope: Thoughts on Reclaiming the American Dream.* New York: Three Rivers, 2006.

———. *Dreams from My Father: A Story of Race and Inheritance.* New York: Kodansha, 1996.

Vig, Norman J. and Michael E. Kraft. *Environmental Policy: The New Directions for the Twenty-First Century.* 8th ed. Washington, DC: Congressional Quarterly Press, 2013.

Zilizer, Julian E. *The Presidency of George W. Bush: A First Historical Assessment.* Princeton, NJ: Princeton University Press, 2010.

CHAPTER 10. TRYING AGAIN FOR GREENER PRESIDENTS

Bailey, Thomas. *Presidential Greatness.* New York: Appleton-Century, 1966.

Burns, James MacGregor. *The Power to Lead: The Crisis of the American Presidency.* New York: Touchstone, 1985.

Califano, Joseph A. *A Presidential Nation.* New York: Norton, 1975.

Dallek, Robert. *Hail to the Chief: The Making and Unmaking of the American Presidents.* New York: Hyperion, 1996.

Ellis, Richard, and Aaron Wildavsky. *Dilemmas of Presidential Leadership: From Washington through Lincoln.* Piscataway, NJ: Transaction, 1989.

Gould, Lewis L. *The Modern American Presidency.* Lawrence: University Press of Kansas, 2003.

Greenstein, Fred I. *Leadership in the Modern Presidency*. Cambridge, MA: Harvard University Press, 1988.

Hodgson, Godfrey. *All Things to All Men: The False Promise of the Modern American Presidency*. New York: Simon and Schuster, 1980.

Landy, Marc, and Sidney M. Milkis. *Presidential Greatness*. Lawrence: University Press of Kansas, 2000.

Light, Paul. *The President's Agenda: Domestic Policy Choice from Kennedy to Clinton*. Baltimore, MD: Johns Hopkins University Press, 1998.

Lowi, Theodore J. *The Personal President: Power Invested, Promise Unfulfilled*. Ithaca, NY: Cornell University Press, 1985.

McDonald, Forrest. *The American Presidency: An Intellectual History*. Lawrence: University Press of Kansas, 1994.

Nelson, Michael, and Russell L. Riley, eds. *The President's Words: Speeches and Speechwriting in the Modern White House*. Lawrence: University Press of Kansas, 2010.

Neustadt, Richard. *Presidential Power and the Modern Presidents*. New York: Free Press, 1990.

Pfiffner, James P. *The Modern Presidency*. Hoboken, NJ: Wiley, 1994.

Relyea, Harold C. *The Executive Office of the President: A Historical, Biographical, and Bibliographical Guide*. Westport, CT: Greenwood, 1997.

Rockman, Bert A. *Leadership Question: Presidency and the American System*. Westport, CT: Praeger, 1984.

Rudalevige, Andrew. *The New Imperial Presidency: Renewing Presidential Power after Watergate*. Ann Arbor: University of Michigan Press, 2006.

Schlesinger, Arthur M., Jr. *The Imperial Presidency*. Boston: Houghton Mifflin, 1973.

Skowronek, Stephen. *Presidential Leadership in Political Time: Reprise and Reappraisal*. Lawrence: University Press of Kansas, 2008.

INDEX

American Forestry Association, 15

Bennett, Hugh Hammond, 130
Blatnik, John, 181
Boone and Crockett Club of New York,
    urges legislation on President
    Harrison, 1
Brower, David, 161, 179, 214
Bureau of Reclamation, 45, 157, 159–162,
    164, 176, 179
Bush, George Herbert Walker (term of
    office 1989–1993)
    background, 304–305
    presidency, 305–309
Bush, George W. (terms of office 2001–
    2009)
    background, 328–330
    presidency, 330–337

Carson, Rachel, author of *Silent Spring*
    (1962), 113, 204, 247, 307, 335,
    342, 363
Carter, James Earl (term of office 1976–
    1980)
    background, 252–254
    presidency, 254–271
Catlin, George
    early advocate of national parks, 10
Cleveland, Grover (terms of office 1885–
    1889, 1893–1897)
    background, 29–30
    presidency, 30–33
Clinton, William Jefferson (terms of office
    1993–2001)
    background, 309–310
    presidency, 310–318, 321–327
conservation movement gets a name,
    devised by Gifford Pinchot and W. J.
    McGee, 51
Cooke, Morris L., "A Permanent Country,"
    151

Coolidge, Calvin (terms of office 1923–
    1928)
    background, 91–92
    presidency, 93–96

dams
    built by both political parties, 45
    controversy over Echo Park, 161–162,
        175, 179–180, 200
    controversy over Glen Canyon, 179–
        180, 295
    controversy over Hetch Hetchy, 53, 55,
        68–71, 77, 84
    roles in conservation, 45–46, 94–95
    Tennessee Valley Authority (TVA), 127
DeVoto, Bernard, 163–164, 171–173, 178,
    183–184, 279
Douglas, Marjory Stoneman, 80, 158, 363
Dust Bowl, 131–132, 135–137, 174, 182

Earth Day (April 22, 1970), 233
Earth Summit in Rio de Janeiro, 306
ecology, origins of, 13
Ehrlich, Anne and Paul, authors of *The
    Population Bomb* (1967), 227
Eisenhower, Dwight D. (terms of office
    1953–1961)
    background, 173–174
    presidency, 175–185
Eisenhower, Milton, President's brother
    and lieutenant, 182
EPA (Environmental Protection Agency),
    234, 243, 336, 366
extinction
    last passenger pigeon "Martha" died
        1914, 9, 83

Ford, Gerald R. (term of office 1974–
    1976)
    background, 245–246
    presidency, 246–252

global warming/climate change, causes
  and effects, 302–303
Gore, Al, 208, 302, 360
Gorsuch, Anne (aka Anne Burford), 287
Grinnell, George Bird, Field and Stream
  editor, 19

Hamilton, Alice, 80
Harding, Warren G. (term of office 1921–
  1923)
  background, 86–87
  presidency, 87–91
Harrison, Benjamin (term of office 1889–
  1893)
  background, 25–26
  presidency, 26–29
Hoover, Herbert (term of office 1929–
  1933)
  background, 96–100
  presidency, 100–106

Ickes, Harold, Secretary of the Interior
  under FDR, 132, 138–139, 141–143,
  177, 191, 196
Izaak Walton League, 60, 99, 104

Johnson, Lyndon B. (terms of office 1963–
  1969)
  background, 209–212
  presidency, 212–221

Kennedy, John F. (term of office 1961–
  1963)
  background, 187–189
  presidency, 190–204
Kyoto Protocol, 317, 326, 332, 334–335

leading nineteenth century nature
  writers
  Henry David Thoreau, 10
  John Burroughs, 12
  John Muir, 12
  Mabel Osgood Wright, 12
  Olive Thorne Miller, 12
  Ralph Waldo Emerson, 10

legislation of note
  Alaska Lands Act, 1980, 270
  Antiquities Act, 41–43, 138, 218, 314,
    316
  Clean Air Act, 215, 235, 288, 292, 305–
    306, 331, 333
  Clean Water Act, 165, 237, 298, 312
  Endangered Species Acts, 215, 228,
    257, 268, 306, 313
  Fish and Wildlife Acts, 175
  Forest Reserve Act (Section 24 of
    General Revision Act, 1891), 25
  Migratory Bird Acts, 65, 83
  NEPA (National Environmental
    Protection Act), 229, 239, 240
  TOSCA (Toxic Substances Control
    Act), 247
  Wilderness Act, 193, 213, 360
Leopold, Aldo, originated concept of "the
  land ethic," 168

Marsh, George Perkins, 168, 342, 363
McKinley, William (term of office 1897–
  1901)
  background, 33
  presidency, 33–34
modern presidency emerges, 56, 361
Montreal Protocol, 300–303
Muskie, Edmund, 165, 203

National Audubon Society, 20–21
National Park Service (NPS), 43, 70, 138,
  177, 326
Nixon, Richard M. (terms of office 1969–
  1974)
  background, 221–222
  presidency, 223–243
Noble, John W., 24

Obama, Barack (terms of office 2009–
  2017)
  background, 337–343
  presidency, 342–357
Olmsted, Frederick Law, 16–17, 69
Osborn, Fairfield, 169, 318